"An interesting, clear, practical, biblical, and remarkably insightful guide to the main doctrinal teachings of the whole Bible!"

Wayne Grudem, Research Professor of Theology and Biblical Studies, Phoenix Seminary

"Mark Driscoll and Gerry Breshears have written a remarkably insightful treatment of central biblical teachings, with a few surprising but welcome choices. *Doctrine* is meaty, well-researched, clearly written, interesting, and refreshing—a rare combination. Those who know that truth matters will relish this book. If you don't know that truth matters, you should read it anyway and enjoy watching your mind and heart change."

Randy Alcorn, author, *If God Is Good* and *Heaven*

"Christianity is ineradicably doctrinal, and, contrary to popular instincts, doctrine unites, as Paul makes clear in Romans 16:17. The question for church leaders, therefore, is how to communicate Christian doctrine in a clear, faithful, and winsome way. It is therefore a pleasure to commend this book, an excellent primer in basic Christian teaching. It will serve as an introduction for new Christians, a refresher for church members, and a good text for Sunday school classes. Highly recommended."

Carl Trueman, Academic Dean and Vice President, Westminster Theological Seminary

"Sadly, many Christians think that doctrine is terminally boring and inherently divisive. Driscoll and Breshears blow that stereotype out of the water as they tackle thirteen core doctrines with uncommon grace and penetrating clarity. This addition to my personal library will undoubtedly become well-worn."

Larry Osborne, author; pastor, North Coast Church, Vista, California

"This valuable resource will help Christians clearly understand and articulate their beliefs while igniting a deeper love and passion for Christ."

Craig Groeschel, Senior Pastor, LifeChurch.tv; author, *It*

"We used the unpublished manuscript of *Doctrine* as a textbook at ChangePoint. In short, the students loved it! They found it easy to read and very practical. Most are looking forward to buying a copy for their personal libraries. Our church has already benefited from Mark and Gerry's latest effort. Buy the book! Use it with your leaders and watch a deeper understanding of doctrine change their lives."

Dan H. Jarrell, Teaching Pastor, ChangePoint Church, Anchorage, Alaska

"God is raising up a new generation of Christ-followers who long to know him and his missional ways in a theologically-robust manner. This latest book by Driscoll and Breshears is certain to play a major role in forming such doctrinally-sound Christians. Besides covering all the major theological topics, they address deep doctrinal issues in a clear and understandable way. And, as in all their books, they help us grasp what difference these doctrines can and should make in our lives and churches."

Gregg R. Allison, Professor of Christian Theology, Southern Baptist Theological Seminary; faculty member, Re:train

"I like *Doctrine* very much. It is a relatively short, clear, and accurate topical summary of biblical teachings, focused on the practical application of doctrine. There is much here to aid readers who have thought in the past that theology was too complicated, uninteresting, or irrelevant. This book is none of those things. It takes off on wings of eagles. It is so important today that believers understand and become committed to all that God's Word says. This book is a wonderful tool to help them do that."

John Frame, Professor of Systematic Theology and Philosophy,
Reformed Theological Seminary

"Mark Driscoll and Gerry Breshears have accomplished the unusual: they have written a book on doctrine that is both interesting and substantive! *Doctrine* is rigorously biblical and theologically faithful. It lays out with clarity the great truths of the faith, showing their essential character and practical import. This is a good gift for the body of Christ. I will be happy to commend to it to the seasoned saint and the new believer."

Daniel L. Akin, President, Southeastern Baptist Theological Seminary

"I offer my unlimited limited endorsement of *Doctrine*. It's limited with respect to acknowledging that not everyone needs to agree with every point of doctrine outlined in the book in order to benefit from the fair-minded treatment that Mark Driscoll and Gerry Breshears give to each of the Christian doctrines examined. In areas where Christians are known to hold differing views, Driscoll and Breshears respectfully outline options before clearly stating their own beliefs. It's unlimited with respect to wholeheartedly embracing the clear ambition of the book. In an age when people, even Christians, place such high personal value on internal experience, we desperately need to look outside ourselves—to the doctrines of the Bible—to truly hear and receive the good news of Jesus Christ."

James H. Gilmore, author, *The Experience Economy* and *Authenticity*

"I listened to the sermon series that preceded this book and was very excited to hear they were putting it all into print. 'Doctrine' should not be a dirty word in the church. Right now the need for Christians to hold fast to biblical truth is greater than ever, and this book is a solid, sleek, no-nonsense resource that is perfect for equipping every believer with the knowledge of essential biblical doctrines."

Dustin Kensrue, singer and guitarist, Thrice

"Whenever a new book comes across my desk I always ask *What am I going to do with this?* The answer is not always immediately clear. But with this book, I knew within the first few pages: I'm going to buy a number of copies, give them to our leaders, and tell them to give the copies to young Christians to read. Breshears and Driscoll have done us all a huge favor in writing *Doctrine*. Foundational truths are explained in clear and accessible terms. This is doctrine taught as doctrine should be taught: biblically, thoroughly, accessibly, clearly, and practically."

Steve Timmis, Director, Porterbrook and Acts 29 Western Europe

"When my friend Mark Driscoll says he has written a book about what Christians *should* believe, I believe him, and here he has. Mark writes like he preaches: clear, direct, and commanding of your attention. This resource is a challenging yet easy-to-understand guide to the major doctrines of Scripture. I commend it to you as a companion to your study of God's Word."

    James MacDonald, Senior Pastor, Harvest Bible Chapel,
    Rolling Meadows, Illinois

"At the beginning of the twentieth century when many sought to redefine the church in terms of emotional experience and loose ecclesiastical unity, Gresham Machen courageously defended biblical orthodoxy, with the following words: 'It is only as Christ is offered to us in the gospel—that is, in the "doctrine" that the world despises—that Christ saves sinful men.' At the beginning of the twenty-first century, against similar adversaries, Driscoll and Breshears brilliantly, comprehensively, and without compromise restate the absolute importance of doctrine, without which there is no Christ and no Christianity."

    Peter Jones, Director, truthXchange; Scholar-in-Residence and
    Adjunct Professor, Westminster Seminary California

"In this helpful and accessible book, Driscoll and Breshears lay out the key doctrines of the Christian faith. *Doctrine* defines the core beliefs that make up biblical Christianity in a readable, understandable, and authentic way. Furthermore, I am encouraged that it consistently points the reader to God's mission to redeem the world through his Son, Jesus Christ."

    Ed Stetzer, President, LifeWay Research

Other Re:Lit Books:

Re:Lit: Vintage Jesus

Vintage Jesus
Vintage Church
Death by Love
Religion Saves

Re:Lit: A Book You'll Actually Read

On Church Leadership
On the New Testament
On the Old Testament
On Who Is God?

DOCTRINE

WHAT CHRISTIANS SHOULD BELIEVE

MARK DRISCOLL & GERRY BRESHEARS

 **CROSSWAY**

WHEATON, ILLINOIS

Hardback ISBN: 978-1-4335-0625-3
PDF ISBN: 978-1-4335-0626-0
Mobipocket ISBN: 978-1-4335-0627-7
ePub ISBN: 978-1-4335-2311-3

Library of Congress Cataloging-in-Publication Data
Driscoll, Mark, 1970–
   Doctrine : what Christians should believe? / Mark Driscoll and
Gerry Breshears.
      p. cm. — (Re:Lit: vintage Jesus)
  Includes index.
   ISBN 978-1-4335-0625-3 (hc) — ISBN 978-1-4335-0626-0 (pbk)
   ISBN 978-1-4335-0627-7 — ISBN 978-1-4335-2311-3 (ebk)
   1. Theology, Doctrinal. 2. Bible—Theology. I. Breshears, Gerry, 1947–
II. Title. III. Series.
BT75.3.D75   2010
230—dc22   2009031861

Crossway is a publishing ministry of Good News Publishers.

RRDC		19	18	17	16	15	14	13	12	11
14	13	12	11	10	9	8	7	6	5	4

CONTENTS

PREFACE

Doctrine seeks to trace the big theological themes of Scripture along the storyline of the Bible. This book is packed with truth without many stories for illustration and entertainment. These omissions are intentional. We believe God's Story is perfect, and we want it to be in focus.

We dedicate *Doctrine* to five men who were giants in the previous generation, men whose character and teaching we appreciate deeply: J. I. Packer, John Stott, Billy Graham, Carl F. H. Henry, and Francis Schaeffer.

Gerry makes a personal dedication to his teacher and mentor, Gordon R. Lewis. Mark makes a personal dedication to Grace (who pointed him to Jesus), his five children, the church planters of Acts 29, and the elders of Mars Hill Church for being incredibly effective ministry partners.

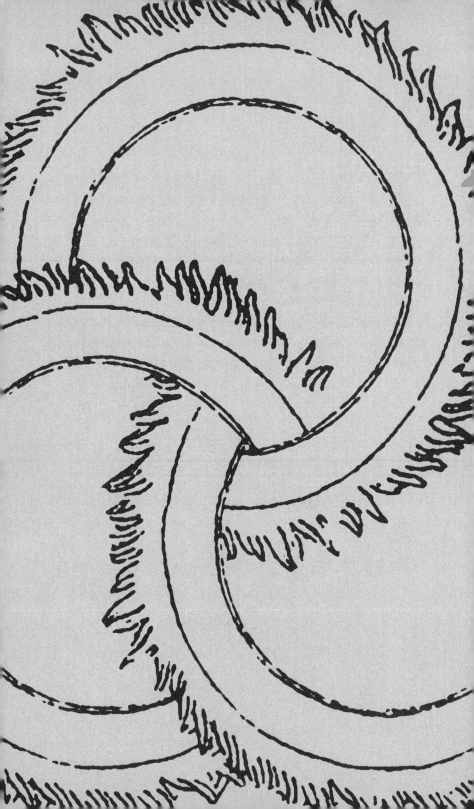

CHAPTER 1

TRINITY: GOD IS

And when Jesus was baptized, immediately he went up from the water, and behold, the heavens were opened to him, and he saw the Spirit of God descending like a dove and coming to rest on him; and behold, a voice from heaven [God the Father] said, "This is my beloved Son, with whom I am well pleased."

MATTHEW 3:16–17

Deep longings pervade the human heart.

We long for selfless, trustworthy, unending love from someone we can trust to be faithful and helpful.

We long for unity within the great diversity of humanity, some means by which we can live in peace and oneness that benefits each of us.

We long for communication—from face-to-face conversations to the proliferation of modern technology created for the purpose of letting us know others and be known by them—and have a seemingly insatiable passion to speak and be spoken to.

We long for community, significant and earnest relationships with others, so that we are part of a people devoted to something larger and greater than our individual lives.

We long for humility, where people pour themselves out unreservedly for the benefit and well-being of others.

11

We long for peace, harmony, and safe altruism for others and ourselves so that abuse, cruelty, misery, and the painful tears they cause could stop.

We long for a selfless common good, a world in which everyone does what is best for all and is not so viciously and exclusively devoted to self-interest and tribal concerns.

Why? Why do we have these persistent deep longings that occasionally compel us to action and often leave us frustrated or disappointed? From where do they emanate, and how can they be satisfied?

Our longings for love, unity in diversity, communication, community, humility, peace, and selflessness are in fact—by design—longings for the Trinitarian God of the Bible and a world that is a reflection of the Trinity. Tragically, human desires corrupted by sin turn in on themselves; rather than finding satisfaction in God, longings become lusts—bottomless pits of selfish desire, never quite satisfied, inevitably leading to despair. Because we are made in the image of the triune God to reflect his glory, we will never stop longing; yet, our sin-stained longings distort that reflection.

The Trinity is the first community and the ideal for all communities. That community alone has not been stained by the selfishness of sin. Therefore, in the diversity of God the Father, Son, and Spirit is perfect unity as one God that communicates truthfully, loves unreservedly, lives connectedly, serves humbly, interacts peaceably, and serves selflessly. In a word, the Trinity is the ideal community in every way. Or, to say it another way, God is a Friend and has Friends.

WHAT IS THE TRINITY?

God is Father, Son, and Holy Spirit. One God. Three persons. While the word *Trinity* does not appear in Scripture, this One-who-is-Three concept very clearly does. The word *Trinity* is used as a shorthand way of explaining a great deal of biblical truth. It was first used by the church father Tertullian (AD 155–220). To say that God exists as a Trinity does not mean that there are three Gods, or that one God merely manifests himself as either Father, Son, or Holy Spirit on various occasions.

The Westminster Confession of Faith (1647) summarizes the doctrine by saying, "In the unity of the Godhead there be three persons, of one substance, power, and eternity: God the Father, God the Son, and God the Holy Ghost."

For our purposes, we will use the following definition: *The Trinity is one God who eternally exists as three distinct persons—Father, Son, and Spirit—who are each fully and equally God in eternal relation with each other.*

To clarify, to say that each member of the Trinity is a "person" does not mean that God the Father or God the Spirit became human beings. Rather, it means that each member of the Trinity thinks, acts, feels, speaks, and relates because they are persons and not impersonal forces. Further, each member of the Trinity is equally God, which means that they share all the divine attributes, such as eternality, omniscience, omnipotence, and omnipresence.

The doctrine of the Trinity brings together three equally essential biblical truths without denying or diminishing any.

First, there is only one true God. The Old Testament contains a number of clear statements that there is only one God.[1] Likewise, the New Testament clearly states that there is only one God.[2] Together, the unending thunderous chorus of Scripture from beginning to end is that there is only one God.

Scripture also clearly teaches that there is no one like God.[3] Scripture teaches that any claim to be like God is a satanic lie.[4] Practically, this means that in addition to there being only one Trinity and no other, there is no other God who is eternally existent and uncreated, all-powerful, all-knowing, or all-present.

The biblical emphasis on the existence of only one true God raises

---

[1]Gen. 1:1; Deut. 4:35, 39; 6:4–5; 32:39; 1 Sam. 2:2; 2 Sam. 7:22; 22:32; 1 Kings 8:59–60; 2 Chron. 15:3; Ps. 86:8–10; Isa. 37:20; 43:10; 44:6–8; 45:5, 14, 21–22; 46:9; Jer. 10:10.

[2]John 5:44; 17:3; Rom. 3:30; 16:27; 1 Cor. 8:4–6; Gal. 3:20; Eph. 4:6; 1 Tim. 1:17; 2:5; 1 Thess. 1:9; James 2:19; Jude 25; 1 John 5:20–21.

[3]Ex. 8:10; 9:14; 15:11; 2 Sam. 7:22; 1 Kings 8:23; 1 Chron. 17:20; Ps. 86:8; Isa. 40:18, 25; 44:7; 46:5, 9; Jer. 10:6–7; Mic. 7:18.

[4]Gen. 3:5; Isa. 14:14; John 8:44.

the question of what is to be made of other "gods" that are worshiped by people in various religions in the days of the Bible and in our present day. The Bible states that these "gods" are very powerful fallen angels who rebelled against God. They hate Jesus and seek worshipers, whom they reward if they serve them well. They perform powerful signs, wonders, and miracles that can deceive people into thinking they are equal with God.[5] Practically, this means that there are incredibly powerful demons—with names such as Baal, Chemosh, Molech, Brahman, Allah, Mother Earth, Mammon (money), and Aphrodite (sex)—that are wrongly worshiped by multitudes as gods.

From the very beginning the people of God have lived with constant pressure to accept other religions and "gods" as equally worthy of worship as the God of the Bible. Too many times people are like Solomon and divide their devotion between God and the "gods."[6] To help embolden us, the Bible presents stirring stories of faithful followers like Shadrach, Meshach, Abednego, and Daniel who would not compromise and who never wavered in their devotion to one God even in the face of great opposition and persecution.[7]

Second, the Father, Son, and Spirit are equally declared throughout Scripture to be God. There are many Scriptures that clearly and emphatically declare the Father to be God.[8] In the history of the Christian church and all the cults and religions that have erred from biblical truth, there has never been any noteworthy false teaching that has denied the deity of God the Father because it is so obviously clear throughout the entirety of Scripture.

Jesus is also repeatedly declared to be God throughout the Scriptures by both others[9] and himself, without apology or correction.[10] It is worth noting that Jesus was ultimately put to death for declaring himself to be

---

[5]Deut. 32:17; Ps. 106:37; 1 Cor. 10:20; Gal. 4:8.
[6]1 Kings 11. This pattern is repeated countless times in Scripture.
[7]Daniel 3; 7.
[8]John 6:27; 17:3; 1 Cor. 8:6; 2 Cor. 1:3; Eph. 1:3; 1 Pet. 1:3.
[9]Matt. 28:9; John 1:1–4, 14; 5:17–18; 8:58; 10:30–38; 12:37–41; cf. Isa. 6:9–11; Acts 20:28; Rom. 1:3–4; 9:5; 1 Cor. 8:4–6; Gal. 4:4; Phil. 2:10–11; Col. 1:16–17; 2:8–9; 1 Tim. 6:15; Titus 2:13; Heb. 1:8; 1 John 5:20; Rev. 1:8, 17–18; 17:14; 19:16; 22:13–16.
[10]Matt. 26:63–65; John 5:17–23; 8:58–59; 10:30–39; 19:7.

God, a declaration that if untrue would have been a violation of the first commandment and a blasphemous sin.[11]

In addition to the Father and Son, the Holy Spirit is clearly called God throughout the Scriptures. In the Old Testament we see he possesses the attributes of God, which reveals his divinity; he is creator,[12] eternal,[13] omnipotent or all-powerful,[14] omniscient or all-knowing,[15] and omnipresent.[16] In the New Testament, he is also clearly declared God.[17]

Third, though one God, the Father, Son, and Spirit are distinct persons. The Father and Son are two persons in frequent salutations of letters in the New Testament,[18] as well as in other Scriptures.[19] Scripture is also clear that Jesus and the Holy Spirit are not the same person.[20] Likewise, the Father is not the Holy Spirit.[21] Jesus was repeatedly clear that he and the Father are distinct persons but one God, saying, "I and the Father are one"[22] and "we are one."[23] Furthermore, the Holy Spirit is not merely an impersonal force but a person who can be grieved,[24] resisted,[25] and insulted.[26] The personhood of the Holy Spirit explains why Jesus speaks of him as a personal "he" and not an impersonal "it."[27]

WHAT IS THE TRINITARIAN GOD OF THE BIBLE LIKE?

Perhaps the best-known statement about the Trinitarian God of the Bible is found in 1 John 4:8, which simply states, "God is love." When plumbed to its depths, this definition of God is unprecedented.

---

[11]Matt. 26:64–66; Mark 14:62–64; John 8:58–59; 10:30–31.
[12]Gen. 1:2; Ps. 104:30.
[13]Heb. 9:14.
[14]Mic. 3:8; see also Acts 1:8; Rom. 15:13, 19.
[15]Isa. 40:13–14; see also 1 Cor. 2:10.
[16]Ps. 139:7.
[17]Acts 5:3–4; see also John 14:16; 2 Cor. 3:16–18.
[18]Rom. 1:7; 1 Cor. 1:3; 2 Cor. 1:2; Gal. 1:3; Eph. 1:2; 6:23; Phil. 1:2; 1 Thess. 1:1; 2 Thess. 1:1–2; 1 Tim. 1:1–2; 2 Tim. 1:2; Titus 1:4; Philem. 3; James 1:1; 2 Pet. 1:2; 2 John 3.
[19]John 3:17; 5:31–32; 8:16–18; 11:41–42; 12:28; 14:31; 17:23–26; Gal. 4:4; 1 John 4:10.
[20]Luke 3:22; John 14:16; 15:26; 16:7; 1 John 2:1.
[21]John 14:15, 15:26; Rom. 8:11, 26–27; 2 Cor. 1:3–4; Gal. 1:1.
[22]John 10:30.
[23]John 17:11.
[24]Eph. 4:30.
[25]Acts 7:51.
[26]Heb. 10:29.
[27]John 14:17, 26; 16:7–14.

Love is spoken of roughly eight hundred times throughout the totality of Scripture. In stating that "God is love," the Bible also reveals that the Trinitarian God of the Bible is simultaneously the definition, example, and source of true love.

In other words, to declare that God is love is to confess that God is Trinitarian. In the very nature of God there is a continuous outpouring of love, communication, and oneness because God is a relational community of love. For example, during his earthly life, Jesus frequently spoke about the deep love between him and God the Father:

- The Father loves the Son and has given all things into his hand.[28]
- The Father loves the Son and shows him all that he himself is doing.[29]
- I do as the Father has commanded me, so that the world may know that I love the Father.[30]

In the Old Testament the most sacred name for God is *Yahweh*. *Yahweh* is a distinctly proper name for the God of the Bible. Because it is sacred, it is never used to refer to any pagan gods; neither is it used in regard to any human. It is reserved solely for the one true God alone. The name Yahweh appears some 6,823 times in the Old Testament, as he is the focus and hero of the Scriptures. The third commandment warns us not to use his name in vain or thoughtlessly.[31] The name of Yahweh is so sacred that Leviticus 24:16 commanded that anyone who used it in a blasphemous manner was to be put to death. The severe consequences associated with misuse of the name Yahweh caused God's people such great reverence that they were exceedingly cautious to write or speak his name. Consequently, when reading the Old Testament Scriptures, Jews did not speak the name Yahweh but replaced it with *'Edonai* ("Lord," often transliterated from the Hebrew as "Adonai"). The ancient Hebrew Bible had only consonants, so the name of God was written as YHWH.

---

[28]John 3:35.
[29]John 5:20.
[30]John 14:31.
[31]Ex. 20:7.

When your translation has the word "Lord," in all capital letters, you know this is the personal name of God, YHWH.

Sometime between AD 600 and AD 900 the rabbis put dots and dashes around the ancient consonants so people would be able to see the vowels. When they came to the divine name YHWH, they added vowels from 'Edonai. This was transliterated as JeHoWaH. There is nothing wrong with the name Jehovah, but we are sure it is not the name God gave Moses and his people.[32]

In light of the unprecedented power, might, and glory of Yahweh, it is also amazing to consider how he chose to reveal himself to his people in Exodus 34:6–7 (this is the most quoted passage in the Bible by the Bible):

> The Lord, the Lord, a God merciful and gracious, slow to anger, and abounding in steadfast love and faithfulness, keeping steadfast love for thousands, forgiving iniquity and transgression and sin, but who will by no means clear the guilty.

This description of the entire Trinity is so packed that we must consider each truth it reveals.

1) Yahweh, the Trinitarian God of the Bible, is a person with the name "Lord." In the Old Testament, God's people were surrounded by the Assyrians, Babylonians, Phoenicians, Philistines, and other nations that each had gods. These false gods ruled over a people and a place but did not rule over all people and all places as the Lord of the Bible does. The same can be said of the New Testament, wherein God's people were also in a world "full of idols,"[33] and even our own day, when spirituality is popular but very few spiritual people know the Lord who rules over all spirits and spiritualities.

2) Yahweh, the Trinitarian God of the Bible, begins by telling Moses and us that he is a person. He has a name. He wants to relate. This is very different from the contemporary spirituality of Oprah, Hollywood Buddhism, and Star Wars, where there is only "the Force" flowing through everything.

---

[32]Ex. 3:14.
[33]Acts 17:16.

3) Yahweh, the Trinitarian God of the Bible, is compassionate to hurting and suffering people. He sees our lives, knows our frailty, and responds with compassion.

4) Yahweh, the Trinitarian God of the Bible, is helpful. Not only does God rule over us and have compassion on us, but God is also at work for us. Our God is a servant who delights in humbly serving the people he has made; he does so not because he has to but because he longs to, as an outworking of his goodness.

5) Yahweh, the Trinitarian God of the Bible, is slow to anger. Unlike the Greek and Roman gods who are irritable and volatile and take out their anger on people unless they are appeased by sacrifices or praise, the God of the Bible has a long wick. Yahweh can be angered but only after being provoked by sinners determined to arouse his anger through ongoing unrepentant sin and rebellion in abuse of his patience.

6) Yahweh, the Trinitarian God of the Bible, is lovingly faithful, shown by the wonderfully powerful Hebrew word *hesed*. It speaks of the constant, passionate, overflowing, relentlessly pursuing, extravagant, limitless, trustworthy, and merciful love of our God. It speaks of his caring provision coming from his strong mercy.

7) Yahweh, the Trinitarian God of the Bible, is dependable and truthful. He never fails and he never lies. As a result, he alone is fully worthy of faith, trust, and devotion, because he alone will always keep his promises.

8) Yahweh, the Trinitarian God of the Bible, is forgiving. God is keenly aware of our sin. Yet, in his loving mercy he is willing and able to forgive repentant sinners.

9) Yahweh, the Trinitarian God of the Bible, is just. In the end, no one who lives in sin and rejects his offer of loving relationship through forgiven sin will have any excuse. God is altogether holy and good, and because he is just, he cannot and will not excuse or overlook sin that is not repented of to him in relationship with him.

This revelation of God takes on extraordinary depth because the Lord gave it in the context of Israel's horrific betrayal and sin when they worshiped the golden calf.[34] Yahweh, the Trinitarian God of the Bible, is a person who is compassionate, helpful, slow to anger, loving, dependable,

---

[34]Exodus 32.

forgiving, and just to ill-deserving sinners. He is the one we see in the God-man, Jesus Christ. John tells us he is full of grace and truth.[35] This is an unmistakable allusion to Exodus 34:6–7. John is saying that Jesus Christ is full of Yahweh. He has come to reveal the Father.

DOES THE TRINITY APPEAR IN THE OLD TESTAMENT?

The opening lines of Scripture reveal God in a most surprising way:

> In the beginning, God created the heavens and the earth. The earth was without form and void, and darkness was over the face of the deep. And the Spirit of God was hovering over the face of the waters.[36]

We see both God the Father *and* the Spirit of God involved in creation.

It gets even more interesting when we look at how ancient Jewish rabbis understood this passage as they did their interpretative translation of the Hebrew Bible into Aramaic, the common language of the people. They did a word study of "beginning" (*re'shit* in Hebrew) and found that it is used in synonymous parallelism with the Hebrew word for "firstborn" (*bekor* in Hebrew) four times in the Old Testament.[37] This would mean that the two words, "beginning" and "firstborn," can have the same meaning. Thus, their translation of the opening words of the Bible includes both words:

> In the beginning, by the firstborn, God created the heavens and the earth. The earth was without form and void, and darkness was over the face of the deep. And the Spirit of God was hovering over the face of the waters.[38]

In this important translation, predating the birth of Jesus Christ by approximately two hundred years, we find *three* divine persons—the Firstborn, God the Father, and the Spirit—at work in creation.

---

[35]John 1:14.
[36]Gen. 1:1–2.
[37]Gen. 49:3; Deut. 21:17; Pss. 78:51; 105:36.
[38]Gen. 1:1–2 in the *Targum Neofiti*.

Paul reflects this pre-Christian Trinitarian understanding when he describes the Son as "the firstborn of all creation. For by him all things were created, in heaven and on earth, visible and invisible, whether thrones or dominions or rulers or authorities—all things were created through him and for him."[39] John also uses this idea as he teaches about Jesus Christ as the Word: "All things were made through him, and without him was not any thing made that was made."[40] It is evident that the people of God understood the fundamental concepts of the Trinity long before Jesus was born.

Just a few verses later in Genesis, God speaks of himself with plural pronouns: "Then God said, 'Let us make man in our image, after our likeness.'"[41] This is very unusual, happening in only three other places in the whole Bible.[42] It makes no sense at all. But when you see the Trinitarian understanding of Genesis 1:1–2, everything falls into place.

We find the three persons referred to in many other passages. One of the most important is: "The Spirit of the Lord GOD is upon me, because the LORD has anointed me to bring good news to the poor."[43] We see the "Spirit," the "me" who is anointed (which is Messiah Jesus), and the "LORD" (God the Father). We read that Jesus began his public ministry by reading this passage and identifying himself as the "me" of Isaiah 61:1, saying, "Today this Scripture has been fulfilled in your hearing."[44]

Here is another example of the Trinity appearing together in one Old Testament passage:

> In all their affliction he [the Father] was afflicted, and the angel of his presence [the Son] saved them; in his love and in his pity he redeemed them; he lifted them up and carried them all the days of old. But they rebelled and grieved his Holy Spirit; therefore he turned to be their enemy, and himself fought against them.[45]

---

[39]Col. 1:15–16.
[40]John 1:3.
[41]Gen. 1:26.
[42]Gen. 3:22; 11:7; Isa. 6:8. Since God refers to himself with singular pronouns thousands of times and in the plural only four times, this cannot be the royal "we." If God were into that, he would do it consistently. This cannot refer to God and the angels either, since angels don't create.
[43]Isa. 61:1.
[44]Luke 4:18–21.
[45]Isa. 63:9–10.

The "angel of the LORD" is another puzzling phenomenon in the Old Testament, but it makes total sense when you realize it is coming from a Trinitarian perspective.[46] In Genesis 16 "the angel of the LORD" finds Hagar and speaks both command and comfort to her. Then in verse 13 Hagar "called the name of the LORD who spoke to her," *El Roi*, which means, "You are a God of seeing." Is this the LORD (Yahweh) or the angel, which means "messenger" or "word," of the LORD? The conundrum is solved when we realize this is the second person of the Trinity, the eternal Son who became incarnate in Jesus. He came down to comfort and bless Hagar at the spring. She recognized that it was God who had appeared to her in love. In the New Testament, when Jesus comes in the flesh, he again comforts and commands a troubled, non-Hebrew woman by a spring.[47] This was the Samaritan woman, and she, too, recognized that God had appeared to her.

Lastly, the Old Testament reveals in advance the divine Son who will come as the Messiah, God coming to save sinners and crush sin on behalf of God the Father:

- The LORD [Father] says to my Lord [Son]: "Sit at my right hand, until I make your enemies your footstool."[48]
- Draw near to me, hear this: from the beginning I have not spoken in secret, from the time it came to be I have been there. And now the Lord GOD [Father] has sent me [Son], and his Spirit.[49]
- I saw in the night visions, and behold, with the clouds of heaven there came one like a son of man [Son], and he came to the Ancient of Days [Father] and was presented before him. And to him was given dominion and glory and a kingdom, that all peoples, nations, and languages should serve him; his dominion is an everlasting dominion, which shall not pass away, and his kingdom one that shall not be destroyed.[50]

---

[46]See Gen. 22:11, 15; Ex. 3:2; Num. 22:22–35; Judg. 6:11–22; 13:3–21; Zech. 3:1–6.
[47]John 4.
[48]Ps. 110:1.
[49]Isa. 48:16.
[50]Dan. 7:13–14. Gen. 19:24; Ps. 45:6–7; Isa. 48:6–7; Hos. 1:6–7; Zech. 3:2; and Mal. 3:1–2 are some of the other Old Testament passages where two beings are distinguished and both are called Lord or God.

From the beginning of the Bible we see the Trinity, as well as other key doctrines, appearing in bud form. As the Scriptures continue to reveal God, what is called *progressive revelation*, the bud opens bit by bit. The Old Testament people of God looked forward to the coming of the Spirit-anointed Son who would reveal the Father more completely. Then they would understand more of this mysterious promise of the one who is God but differs from the Father, who will be anointed by the divine Spirit who is neither Father nor Son, who would fulfill the ancient promise of God to crush the head of the serpent and redeem God's people.

DOES THE TRINITY APPEAR IN THE NEW TESTAMENT?

The New Testament continues and deepens the revelation of God living and active in three fully divine persons. While we get glimpses into the inner, heavenly life of Father, Son, and Spirit (what theologians call the *immanent* or *ontological Trinity*),[51] Scripture focuses on the concrete and historical acts in which the Trinity is revealed as the three persons working together in creation (what theologians call the *economic Trinity*). This is helpful because it allows us to see how God always works in unison and does so in history for his glory and our good.

The New Testament reveals more of the Trinity doing the work of creation, speaking of the role of the Father,[52] Son,[53] and Spirit.[54]

In the Gospels we see the entire Trinity involved in Mary's conception of Jesus. Luke 1:35 says, "The angel answered her, 'The Holy Spirit will come upon you, and the power of the Most High [Father] will overshadow you; therefore the child to be born will be called holy—the Son of God [Jesus].'"[55]

At the baptism of Jesus we witness one of the clearest pictures of the Trinity. Matthew 3:16–17 says, "When Jesus was baptized, immediately he went up from the water, and behold, the heavens were opened to him,

---

[51]John 17 is the clearest example of this.
[52]Acts 17:24; 1 Cor. 8:6.
[53]John 1:2; 1 Cor. 8:6; Col. 1:16.
[54]Matt. 1:18–20; John 3:5; 1 Cor. 6:11; Titus 3:5; see also Gen. 1:2; Pss. 33:6; 104:30; Isa. 40:12–14.
[55]Cf. Matt. 1:20–23.

and he saw the Spirit of God descending like a dove and coming to rest on him; and behold, a voice from heaven said, 'This is my [Father] beloved Son, with whom I am well pleased.'" All three persons of the Trinity are present, and each one is doing something different: the Father is speaking, and the Son is being anointed and empowered by the Holy Spirit to be the Messiah and missionary.

Jesus' Great Commission is also Trinitarian. Matthew 28:19 says, "Go therefore and make disciples of all nations, baptizing them in the name of the Father and of the Son and of the Holy Spirit." Baptism is in one name and three persons, an unmistakably Trinitarian formula. In addition, Acts 1:7–8 says, "He [Jesus] said to them, 'It is not for you to know times or seasons that the Father has fixed by his own authority. But you will receive power when the Holy Spirit has come upon you, and you will be my witnesses in Jerusalem and in all Judea and Samaria, and to the end of the earth.'"

Another example is our salvation, in which the entire Trinity is involved, but with distinct roles, as the following verses indicate:

- In love he [the Father] predestined us for adoption as sons through Jesus Christ, according to the purpose of his will, to the praise of his glorious grace, with which he has blessed us in the Beloved [Jesus]. In him [Jesus] we have redemption through his blood, the forgiveness of our trespasses, according to the riches of his grace. . . . In him [Jesus] you also, when you heard the word of truth, the gospel of your salvation, and believed in him [Jesus], were sealed with the promised Holy Spirit.[56]
- . . . The foreknowledge of God the Father, in the sanctification of the Spirit, for obedience to Jesus Christ and for sprinkling with his blood.[57]
- But when the goodness and loving kindness of God our Savior [Father] appeared, he saved us, not because of works done by us in righteousness, but according to his own mercy, by the washing of regeneration and renewal of the Holy Spirit, whom he poured out on us richly through Jesus Christ our Savior.[58]

---

[56]Eph. 1:4–13.
[57]1 Pet. 1:2.
[58]Titus 3:4–6.

God the Father devised the plan of salvation and predestined our salvation. God the Son came to die on the cross in our place for our sins. God the Holy Spirit takes up residence in Christians to regenerate them and ensure their final salvation. In this, we see the Trinity clearly at work in our salvation.

Furthermore, the entire Trinity is involved in the bestowing of our spiritual gifts: "Now there are varieties of gifts, but the same Spirit; and there are varieties of service, but the same Lord [Jesus]; and there are varieties of activities, but it is the same God [the Father] who empowers them all in everyone."[59]

When New Testament authors sum things up they often use Trinitarian formulas:

- The grace of the Lord Jesus Christ and the love of God [the Father] and the fellowship of the Holy Spirit be with you all.[60]
- There is one body and one Spirit—just as you were called to the one hope that belongs to your call—one Lord [Jesus], one faith, one baptism, one God and Father of all, who is over all and through all and in all.[61]
- Praying in the Holy Spirit, keep yourselves in the love of God, waiting for the mercy of our Lord Jesus Christ that leads to eternal life.[62]

Finally, Jesus himself describes the Trinity: "Believe me that I am in the Father and the Father is in me, or else believe on account of the works themselves. . . . And I will ask the Father, and he will give you another Helper, to be with you forever, even the Spirit."[63]

WHAT IS THE HISTORY OF THE DOCTRINE OF THE TRINITY?

To be a Christian is also to be a member of the universal church. The church includes everyone from every nation, culture, language, and race whose

---

[59]1 Cor. 12:4–6; see also Eph. 4:4–6.
[60]2 Cor. 13:14.
[61]Eph. 4:4–6.
[62]Jude 20–21.
[63]John 14:11, 16–17.

saving faith is in Jesus Christ. Practically, this means that a Christian is part of a tremendous heritage and does not come to the Scriptures apart from community with all of God's people from throughout all of the church's history. Catholic, Orthodox, and Protestant Christians confess together that the God of the Bible is Trinitarian.

The earliest Christians were Jewish believers. As Jews, they believed that there is only one God and that this God is Yahweh, the God of Abraham, Isaac, and Jacob. It is important to note that the early Christians continued to affirm their belief in one God. But they also confessed belief in Father, Son, and Spirit. While the Apostles' Creed was not written by the twelve disciples, it is ancient, dating back to the second century. It begins, "I believe in God the Father," continues with "and in the Lord Jesus Christ," and culminates with "I believe in the Holy Spirit."

Tertullian, who converted to Christianity just before AD 200 and defended Christianity prolifically until he died around AD 220, initiated the use of the Latin words *Trinitas*, *persona*, and *substantia* (*Trinity*, *person*, and *substance* or *essence*) to express the biblical teaching that the Father, Son, and Holy Spirit are one in divine essence but distinguished in relationship as persons within the inner life of God himself.

The three major ecumenical councils are worth noting in order to trace the development of the doctrine of the Trinity. These gatherings of church leaders discussed major theological issues for the purpose of recognizing what the church believed. One reason the councils were called was to respond to heretical teaching. The Council of Nicaea (AD 325) included some three hundred bishops, many of whom bore the scars of persecution, and was convened primarily to resolve the debate over Arianism, the false teaching that Christ was a creature, an angel who was the highest created being, but not God. The Council of Nicaea concluded that the Son was one substance (*homoousios*) with the Father. The Logos, who was incarnate in Jesus of Nazareth, is God himself. He is not *like* God, but *is* fully and eternally God.

With the deity of Christ officially recognized, the Council of

Constantinople (AD 381) extended the discussion to the identification of the Holy Spirit within the Godhead. Constantinople expanded the Nicene Creed, making the creed fully Trinitarian, and officially condemned Arianism. It solidified the orthodox doctrine of the full humanity of Jesus Christ. The Council of Chalcedon (AD 451) focused on the relationship of Christ's humanity to his divinity (known as *hypostatic union*) and issued the formula of Chalcedon, which became the orthodox statement on the person of Christ. *Hypostatic union* means that Jesus is one person with two natures and therefore simultaneously fully God and fully human.

The contributions of the councils to the doctrine of the Trinity can be summarized under four headings:

1) *One Being, Three Persons.* God is one being and has one essence. There is no God but the triune God who exists eternally in three distinct persons: Father, Son, and Holy Spirit. The whole God is in each person, and each person is the whole God. Threeness of person is not just a matter of action or revelation but of eternal being.

2) *Consubstantiality.* One identical divine substance is shared completely by the Father, Son, and Holy Spirit. Any essential characteristic that belongs to one of the three is shared by the others. Each of the three divine persons is eternal, each almighty, none greater or less than another, each God, and yet together being but one God.

3) *Perichoresis.* This concept, also called *circumincession* or *interpenetration*, refers to the loving interrelation, partnership, or mutual dependence of the three persons. Some define this in terms of dance, leading to all sorts of strange speculations. But this is a mistake that comes from their ignorance of Greek. *Dance* looks the same in its transliteration but is spelled differently in Greek. Since all three persons are fully God and the whole God is in each of the three, it follows that the three mutually indwell or contain one another, as Jesus said: "Just as you, Father, are in me, and I in you."[64] This oneness of indwelling is not just in their functioning in this world but even more foundationally in their eternal existence as Trinity.

---

[64]John 17:21.

4) *The Order of the Persons.* There is a clear order of the relations between the three fully divine persons: from the Father through the Son by the Holy Spirit.

As the doctrine of the Trinity developed, theologians struggled to explain the eternal relationships of the Trinity. What differentiates Father from Son from Spirit? Using philosophical methodology, they worked backward from God's economic working in the world to define his eternal relationships. The Bible says the Father sent the Spirit to conceive Jesus in the womb of Mary.[65] Jesus is therefore referred to as the "only begotten [*monogenes*] Son."[66] Theologians extended this begetting in history back into the eternal Trinity and posited that the Son is eternally begotten of or generated by the Father. Similarly, they went from Jesus' historical promise to his disciples, "I will send to you from the Father, the Spirit of truth, who proceeds from the Father,"[67] to posit that the Spirit eternally proceeds from the Father. Thus, the Nicene Creed (325) defined the Son as "begotten of the Father." The First Council of Constantinople (381) added the definition that the Holy Spirit "proceeds from the Father." This formulation was universally accepted by the church at the Council of Chalcedon (451).

Theologians of the Western church often extended the procession phrase to read that the Holy Spirit "proceeds from the Father *and the Son* [*filioque*]." This revision of the Nicene Creed was made at the Third Council of Toledo (589) and was officially endorsed in 1017. This insertion of a single Latin word to an ecumenical creed caused a crisis of authority that eventually led to the split between the Eastern Orthodox churches and the Western Roman church in 1054. The subtle theological points were far less responsible for the split than the ecclesiastical power struggle over the authority of the pope.

The whole attempt to define the eternal relations in the immanent or ontological Trinity seems misguided. First, God has given us no revelation

---

[65]Luke 1:31–35; Matt. 1:20.
[66]John 1:14, 18; 3:16, 18; Acts 13:33; Heb. 1:5; 5:5; 1 John 4:9; 5:1. The KJV uses "begotten."
[67]John 15:26.

of the nature of their eternal relations. We should follow the command of the Bible: "The secret things belong to the LORD our God"[68] and refuse to speculate. Second, the Apostles' Creed defines the Son as "begotten, not made." The point was that something begotten was of the same substance as the one who does the begetting. But the term "begotten" could never be defined with any clarity, so it was of little use. Third, *begotten* unavoidably implies a beginning of the one begotten. That would certainly lend support to the Arian heresy that the Son is a created being and not the Creator God. For these reasons it is best to omit the creedal terms "begotten" and "proceeds" from our definition of Trinity. Our authority is not in creeds but in Scripture.

We stand with the universal Trinitarian definition of the church to confess that God is one God, eternally existing in three persons, Father, Son, and the Holy Spirit. Each of the three shares fully the one divine essence. God is not simply unity, but eternally exists in rich, loving fellowship as the one and only God.

WHY SHOULD WE STUDY THE DOCTRINE OF THE TRINITY?

Many Christians find the doctrine of the Trinity difficult to understand. Sadly, out of laziness or fear, some give up far too quickly and subsequently have little interest in diligently studying to grow in their understanding of God. Further, they commonly defend themselves by saying that if they love God in their heart, they need not concern themselves with deep understanding in their mind. Yet, Jesus himself urges us to love God with both our heart and mind.[69]

While the doctrine of the Trinity is certainly difficult to understand, J. I. Packer reminds believers that it is nonetheless true: "The historic formulation of the Trinity . . . seeks to circumscribe and safeguard this mystery (not explain it; that is beyond us), and it confronts us with perhaps the most difficult thought that the human mind has ever been asked to handle. It is not easy; but it is true."[70]

---

[68]Deut. 29:29.
[69]Matt. 22:37; Mark 12:30; Luke 10:27.
[70]J. I. Packer, "Trinity," *Concise Theology: A Guide to Historic Christian Beliefs* (Carol Stream, IL: Tyndale, 1993), 40.

Indeed, Christians should study the doctrine of the Trinity because God has given the church a great blessing in truthfully revealing something so glorious about himself; namely, he is triune. If he reveals it to us, he must consider it important and valuable for our relationship. He loves us deeply. He wants our relationship to be intimate and deep so he gives us precious insights into who he is. If we treasure our relationship with God, we should also treasure the revelation he gives us about himself so that we can know him as best as we are able.

Practically speaking, studying the doctrine of the Trinity helps believers appreciate their great salvation, which is frequently described in Paul's writings as the work of the triune God.[71] Our salvation is enriched as we understand this triune working. We come into relation with the Father and experience perfect fatherliness as he invests in us. So Paul prays, "May the God of peace himself sanctify you completely."[72] The author of Hebrews prays that the God of peace, the great shepherd of the sheep, will "equip you with everything good that you may do his will, working in us that which is pleasing in his sight."[73] God the Son is the one who loves the church so much that he died to "sanctify her, having cleansed her by the washing of water with the word, so that he might present the church to himself in splendor, without spot or wrinkle or any such thing, that she might be holy and without blemish."[74] God the Spirit is the holy one who makes us holy: "But you were washed, you were sanctified . . . by the Spirit of our God. . . . [You] are being transformed into the same image from one degree of glory to another . . . [by] the Lord who is the Spirit."[75]

As we grow to more deeply understand the saving plan of God the Father, the sacrifice of Jesus Christ, and the sealing of the Holy Spirit, we become more intimately thankful to each member of the Trinity for their work for us, in us, and through us.

---

[71]Rom. 8:3–4, 15–17; 1 Cor. 1:4–7; 2:4–5; 6:11, 19–20; 2 Cor. 1:21–22; Gal. 3:1–5; Eph. 1:17; 2:18, 20–22; Phil. 3:3; Col. 3:16; 1 Thess. 1:4–5; 2 Thess. 2:13. See Gordon D. Fee, *God's Empowering Presence: The Holy Spirit in the Letters of Paul* (Peabody, MA: Hendrickson, 1994), 48n39.

[72]1 Thess. 5:23.

[73]Heb. 13:21.

[74]Eph. 5:26–27.

[75]1 Cor. 6:11; 2 Cor. 3:18.

Sinclair Ferguson keenly points out from John 13–17 that it is before Jesus goes to the cross that he has the most to say to his disciples about the blessed Trinity and about his relationship to the Father and to the Spirit.[76] Christ's final words to his disciples before going to the cross were to explain, although in part, the doctrine of the Trinity. Since the doctrine of the Trinity was so important for Jesus to stress at such a pivotal moment in history, we are right to assume that it is also imperative for us to understand the person and work of Jesus.

We are further blessed when we study the Trinity because we then learn how the cross enables believers to share the unity and love that exist eternally between the Father and the Son,[77] and how the cross, resurrection, and ascension of Christ bring to us the full power and knowledge of the Holy Spirit.[78]

WHAT ARE THE MAJOR DOCTRINAL ERRORS REGARDING THE TRINITY?

Many heresies have arisen throughout the history of the church that deny the basic assertions of the doctrine of the Trinity, which are these:

1) God is three persons.
2) Each person is fully God.
3) There is one God.[79]

The tendency is for either the threeness or the oneness of God to be overly stressed at the expense of the other, resulting in heretical false teaching.

The three main heresies that contradict the doctrine of the Trinity are *modalism* (the persons are ways God expresses himself, as in Oneness theology), *Arianism* (the Son is a creature and not divine, as with Jehovah's

[76]See Sinclair B. Ferguson, *A Heart for God* (Colorado Springs: NavPress, 1985), 18–37.
[77]John 17:11, 22–26.
[78]John 14:16–17, 26; 15:26; 16:13.
[79]Wayne Grudem, *Systematic Theology: An Introduction to Biblical Doctrine* (Grand Rapids, MI: Zondervan, 1994), 231.

Witnesses), and *tritheism* (there are three distinct gods, as in Mormonism and Hinduism).

Modalism

Modalism teaches that God is *successively* Father, Son, and Holy Spirit; he is not *simultaneously* Father, Son, and Holy Spirit. Modalism is a heresy that does not view the Father, Son, and Holy Spirit as three particular persons in relation but merely as three modes or manifestations of the one divine person of God. God revealed himself successively in salvation history, first as Father (creator and lawgiver), then as Son (redeemer), and finally as Spirit (sustainer and giver of grace).

For a modalist, the God of the Old Testament is the Father. In the incarnation, God was manifested in Jesus. Then, after the resurrection and ascension of Christ, God came in the mode of the Holy Spirit. However, the baptism of Jesus and Jesus' prayer in the garden of Gethsemane reveal clearly that the three persons converse with each other simultaneously.

Some Pentecostal denominations adopt a "Jesus only" formula for baptism and thus oneness theology. They affirm both that their God is one and that Jesus is fully God. But they deny that there are three divine persons.

The United Pentecostal Church is the largest Oneness group in America. They officially deny the doctrine of the Trinity, saying:

> In distinction to the doctrine of the Trinity, the UPCI holds to a oneness view of God. It views the Trinitarian concept of God, that of God eternally existing as three distinctive persons, as inadequate and a departure from the consistent and emphatic biblical revelation of God being one. . . . Thus God is manifested as Father in creation and as the Father of the Son, in the Son for our redemption, and as the Holy Spirit in our regeneration.[80]

In other words, the Son of God is the manifestation of the Father in the flesh. The Son is not eternal, nor preexistent. Jesus is the Father and the

---

[80]United Pentecostal Church International, "Oneness of God," http://www.upci.org/about.asp.

Son: Father in his divinity and Son in his humanity. Hence, the Trinity is said to be a misunderstanding of the biblical teaching.

Admittedly, the doctrine of the Trinity is complicated. Therefore, the only way to accurately discern what a professing Christian believes about the Trinity is to talk with people directly and hear what they actually believe. We must not fall into the heritage of fundamentalism and condemn people based on secondhand reports or their associations.

Arianism

Arianism was an early heretical teaching about the identity of Jesus Christ, founded primarily on the teachings of Arius. The central characteristic of Arian thought was that because God is one, Jesus could not have also been truly God. In order to deal with the scriptural testimony to the exalted status of Christ, Arius and his followers proposed that Jesus was the highest created being of God. So although Christ was fully human, he was not fully God. Arius's teaching was condemned as heretical at the Council of Nicaea in AD 325.[81]

Sadly, Arianism is the official teaching of Jehovah's Witnesses, which was founded in 1881 by Charles Taze Russell. This group teaches that there is no biblical basis for the doctrine of the Trinity. They teach that there is one solitary divine being from all eternity. This divine being is Jehovah God, the creator and preserver of the universe and all things. Jehovah's Witnesses essentially believe what Arius taught in the third century; namely, that Christ is not God but rather God's first created creature. Thus, Jesus is the archangel Michael, who is mentioned in the Old Testament. Neither is the Spirit divine but rather more of a cosmic force of Jehovah.

Tritheism

Tritheism teaches that the Trinity consists of three equal, independent, and autonomous beings, each of whom is divine. Tritheism stresses the plural-

---

[81]See Stanley J. Grenz, David Guretzki, and Cherith Fee Nording, "Councils," *Pocket Dictionary of Theological Terms* (Downers Grove, IL: InterVarsity, 1999), 15.

ity of the Godhead. Many human analogies for the Trinity actually convey tritheism instead. Examples include the erroneous analogy that the Trinity is like an egg with the three parts of yolk, white, and shell.

Additionally, Mormonism believes that the Trinity is three separate gods; the Father is an exalted man who became a god, Jesus is the first spirit-child between God the Father and his wife, and the Holy Spirit is another spirit-child of the Father and his wife. They teach that none of the three persons of the Trinity are eternal or almighty God. The Son and the Spirit are not truly equal with the Father since they are his spirit-children. There are many gods of many worlds. These three are just the gods of this world, the gods we relate to.

One theologian has refuted these three main heresies well:

> The doctrine of the Trinity does not on the one hand assert that three persons are united in one person, or that three beings in one being, or that three Gods in one God (tri-theism); nor on the other hand that God merely manifests Himself in three different ways (modalism); but rather that there are three eternal [personal] distinctions in the substance of God.[82]

Alarmingly, every generation has some who fall into the same ruts of error that have surrounded the doctrine of the Trinity throughout the church's history. These people are prone to question if not renounce the doctrine of the Trinity. It is important for each generation of Christians, particularly Christian leaders, to be able to lovingly and winsomely define and defend the doctrine of the Trinity because no less is at stake than the issue of who God is.

WHAT ARE THE PRACTICAL IMPLICATIONS OF THE TRINITY?

Indeed, while that which is hypothetical, theoretical, and philosophical may be interesting to a few people, only that which is practical is of service

---

[82]E. A. Park, quoted in Augustus Hopkins Strong, *Systematic Theology* (Old Tappan, NJ: Revell, 1907), 304.

to all people. Subsequently, we have chosen to close this chapter with some practical implications of the doctrine of the Trinity.

First, Trinitarian life is humble. The doctrine of the Trinity is so complex and wonderfully mysterious that it humbles us. This is because while God can be known truly, he cannot be known fully. This forces us to be humble in our understanding of God and establishes a precedent in our thinking to allow room for mystery, as we indeed see and know in part, as Scripture states.[83]

Second, Trinitarian life is loving. When 1 John 4:7 says, "Love is from God," it is revealing that love emanates from the Trinitarian community of God. Trinitarian love includes love for God, family, friend, neighbor, stranger, and even enemy. This is because even though we were enemies of God, estranged by sin, Jesus came to be our neighbor, loved us as a friend, died for our sins to make us family, and shared with us God's love.

Third, Trinitarian life is worshipful. This means that we worship, including singing, serving, and praying, to the Father, through the Son, by the power of the Spirit.

Fourth, Trinitarian life is relational. John 1:1 says, "In the beginning was the Word [Jesus], and the Word was with God [Father], and the Word was God." In the original Greek, John is saying that God the Father and God the Son were proverbially face-to-face in eternity past. This is the language of friendship, which compels us to live face-to-face with others in companionship and community. This is why Christians practice hospitality to strangers and why they participate in the life of their local church as they live face-to-face with their spouses and children. All of this is to practice for the day when, as Paul says, we too will see God "face to face."[84]

Fifth, Trinitarian life is unified and diverse. Greek Christian theologians are fond of describing the Trinity with the term *perichoresis*. As the three persons of the Trinity are mutually indwelling, or permeating one another, we are deeply connected as part of the body, yet we retain our own identity. We are always persons in community.

---

[83] 1 Cor. 13:12.
[84] Ibid.

Sixth, Trinitarian life is submissive. As we hear Jesus teaching us to pray, "Your will be done,"[85] and himself praying, "Not my will, but yours, be done,"[86] while he sweated drops of blood from anxiety caused by the looming horror of his crucifixion, we learn to submit ourselves to the will of the Father by the Spirit like the Son.

Seventh, Trinitarian life is joyful. Tim Keller explains:

> To glorify something or someone is to praise, enjoy, and delight in them. When something is useful you are attracted to it for what it can bring you or do for you. But if it is beautiful, then you enjoy it simply for what it is. Just being in its presence is its own reward. To glorify someone is also to serve or defer to him or her. Instead of sacrificing their interests to make yourself happy, you sacrifice your interests to make them happy. Why? Your ultimate joy is to see them in joy.[87]

What Keller is rightly saying is that the Trinity is the place of the greatest joy that has ever been or ever will be; each member delights in the others and pours himself out continuously for the good of the others in unparalleled delight. Indeed, another synonym for the Trinity is Happy.

The God of the Bible is in himself eternally relational. Some religions teach that God made people to cure his loneliness; conversely, the fact is that God as a Trinitarian community was never without loving community. Rather, he is a relational God who welcomes us into relationship with himself.

In closing, the Trinity is not a doctrine to be philosophized beyond the teachings of Scripture but rather a humble, loving, worshipful, relational, diverse, submissive, and joyful life to be entered into by the Spirit through the Son to the Father.

---

[85]Matt. 6:10.
[86]Luke 22:42.
[87]Timothy Keller, *The Reason for God: Belief in an Age of Skepticism* (New York: Penguin, 2008), 214.

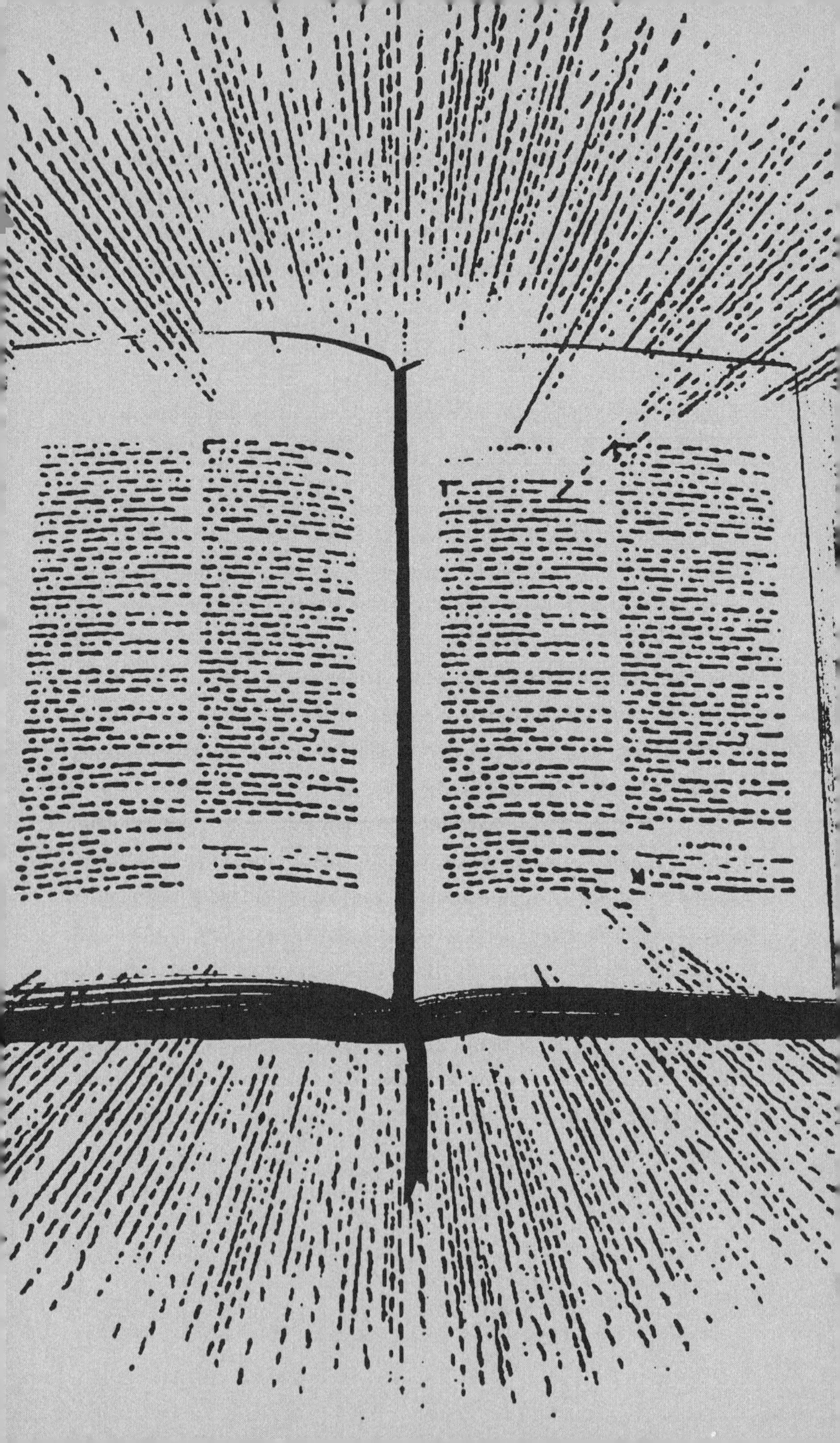

CHAPTER 2

REVELATION: GOD SPEAKS

So also no one comprehends the thoughts of God except the Spirit of God. Now we have received not the spirit of the world, but the Spirit who is from God, that we might understand the things freely given us by God.

1 CORINTHIANS 2:11a–12

As God's image bearers, people have a seemingly insatiable appetite for information and communication. From cell phones to televisions, e-mail, radios, iPods, Web sites, blogs, books, magazines, newspapers, movies, songs, text-messages, face-to-face conversations, and the like, people want to know and be known.

In this deluge of information, the daunting question is, how do we hear the voice of God? Does God speak internally through my spirit? Does God speak externally through a holy man such as a guru or prophet? Does God speak through ancient wisdom or collected tradition? Or, perhaps God does not speak at all because God is not a person but a mute force, distant and disinterested in us? Or perhaps God does not exist at all?

One of the first things we learn about God, in Genesis, is that God reveals himself in words; no less than ten times, the opening chapter of Genesis says, "God said." God speaks. That great truth is affirmed thousands of times in the Bible. It is the foundation of Christian faith. The Creator of the whole universe created humans in his image, thereby enabling them to communicate with him in relationship. Despite sin, God still initiates relationship by making himself known, which is what theologians mean by the doctrine of revelation. The opposite of revelation is speculation, whereby religions, spiritualities, and philosophies seek to discover who God is apart from God's self-revelation.

Revelation is all about getting to know God. Our relationship with God begins as he reveals information about himself. As we receive it and believe it, which is an act of faith, we begin to experience life together with God. Then there is commitment and transformation as faith grows as the result of revelation. This results in the joyous desire to spend time with God's people to learn more about him by witnessing his work in their lives, as well as the desire to share the revelation of who God is and what he has done through Jesus Christ with the world. Revelation culminates in mission in the same way that someone who has fallen deeply in love cannot stop talking about the person they enjoy and introducing him or her to everyone they know.

HOW DOES GOD REVEAL HIMSELF?

General Revelation

God reveals himself to everyone everywhere through general revelation. General revelation includes creation, common grace, and conscience.

Concerning how God reveals himself generally through creation, the psalmist says, "The heavens declare the glory of God, and the sky above proclaims his handiwork. . . . Their voice goes out through all the earth, and their words to the end of the world."[1] Isaiah proclaims, "The whole earth is full of his glory!"[2] Romans 1:19–20 echoes and expands the Old Testament, saying, "For what can be known about God is plain to them, because God has shown it to them. For his invisible attributes, namely, his eternal power and divine nature, have been clearly perceived, ever since the creation of the world, in the things that have been made." Through creation—the heavens and earth, flower and fly, galaxy and quark—God has

---

[1] Ps. 19:1, 4.
[2] Isa. 6:3.

made himself and his power, love, and glory known. People everywhere see his wisdom,[3] majesty,[4] power and divine nature,[5] justice,[6] and goodness.[7]

Among the most awe-inspiring aspects of creation is the human body. Every doctor who studies the body, every mother who births a child, every grandfather who holds a grandchild, and every person who stops for a moment to consider the eyes that God gave them to read these words and the mind he gave them to understand them should be brought to a sense of worshipful wonder. Understanding the love and mindfulness God has bestowed upon humanity, Psalm 8:3–4 says, "When I look at your heavens, the work of your fingers, the moon and the stars, which you have set in place, what is man that you are mindful of him, and the son of man that you care for him?"

God's general revelation also includes common grace. Augustine (AD 354–430) used the term *common grace* because it is for everyone and therefore common to all human beings. Through common grace God reveals his love to all people, though not in a saving way. God's common grace includes the water we drink, food we eat, sun we enjoy, and rain we need, as God is good to the sinner and saint alike.[8]

The effects of God's common grace are innumerable. God's common grace allows even those who despise him to learn and make gains in areas such as science, philosophy, technology, education, and medicine. God's common grace allows societies to flourish, families to exist, cities to rise up, and nations to prosper.[9] Common grace also allows people who are not connected to God through Jesus Christ to live seemingly decent moral lives of compassion and service, though their deeds are not in any way done to God's glory as acts of worship. The result of God's common grace is that life as we experience it is far better than would otherwise be possible if sinners were simply left to themselves. Everyone experiences the grace of

---

[3]Psalm 104.
[4]Ps. 8:1.
[5]Rom. 1:20.
[6]Rom. 2:14–15.
[7]Acts 14:17.
[8]Pss. 65:9; 104:14; Matt. 5:45; Acts 14:17.
[9]E.g., Ex. 31:2–11; 35:30–35.

God to varying degrees, no matter how sinful they are, simply because God is loving and good and is determined to do good in love. Anyone who has laughed, held a baby, enjoyed the warmth of the sun on their face, gone for a swim, or watched a sunset has enjoyed a measure of God's common grace.

Internally, God also reveals himself generally through the conscience he gave us as his image bearers. Almost everyone knows it is wrong to murder your neighbor, lie to your neighbor, and steal your neighbor's wife, because God has written his morality on human hearts.[10] Additionally, God the Holy Spirit convicts the whole world of sin, righteousness, and judgment.[11] Even sinners know to give good gifts to their children because God created us as his image bearers with a conscience that serves as a moral compass.[12] While some people ignore and even break their conscience, the fact that others see their violation of what is right and good serves only to reinforce the truth that through our conscience God has revealed himself as holy and just.

Positively, general revelation means that all people know God in a general way because he has made himself known through creation, common grace, and conscience. As a result, Romans 1 says that those who "suppress" the truth of God made known through general revelation are "without excuse"; subsequently, their damnation is deserved.[13] His goodness and kindness, which are shown to all, are intended to lead people to repentance.[14] Conversely, those who follow the truth of general revelation can enjoy further special revelation about God that can lead to eternal life.[15] Innumerable examples could be given, but some include God bringing missionaries to an unreached people group open to the gospel, God sending dreams and visions of Jesus to Muslims in countries otherwise closed to the gospel, and even sending an angel if necessary to communicate the gospel of Jesus Christ. In short, we trust the goodness and sovereignty of God to deal justly with all people.

---

[10]Rom. 2:14–15.
[11]John 16:8–11.
[12]Matt. 7:11.
[13]Rom. 1:18–32; 2:5–6, 8–9; John 3:19.
[14]Rom. 2:4.
[15]Acts 10:1–7; Rom. 2:7, 10; 10:15–18.

Special Revelation

For anyone to have a saving knowledge of God requires that, in addition to general revelation, they also must receive and believe special revelation. This is because while general revelation is good and true, it is not sufficient for someone to know that God became a man and died on the cross in our place for our sins.

Christians have always believed that God is real, personal, and relational. We believe it is only by God's gracious self-revelation that anyone comes to know him. God has acted and spoken in such a way as to make himself known so that people will be able to enter into a personal relationship with him.

He revealed himself supremely through the incarnation, where the second person of the Trinity humbly entered into human history as the God-man Jesus Christ. During his earthly ministry, Jesus was led and empowered by the third member of the Trinity, God the Holy Spirit. That same Holy Spirit also inspired the writing of the Holy Bible.

God continues to reveal himself today, and the primary way he reveals himself is through the divinely inspired, inerrant, and authoritative Bible. The Bible is uniquely and solely God's completely trustworthy revelation to us today. Scripture is the court of highest authority for Christians and their leaders, by which any alleged revelation from God is to be tested.

WHAT ARE THE SCRIPTURES?

Scripture is God speaking his truth to us in human words. The New Testament writers claim that the Old Testament is sacred Scripture, which literally means "writing."[16] The word *Bible* comes from the Greek word for book. *Holy Bible*, therefore, means "Holy Book." It was written in three languages (Hebrew, Greek, and a bit in Aramaic) over a period of more than fifteen hundred years by more than forty authors (of varying ages and backgrounds) on three continents (Asia, Africa, and Europe).

---

[16]Matt. 21:42; 22:29; 26:54, 56; Luke 24:25–32, 44–45; John 5:39; 10:35; Acts 17:2, 11; 18:28; Rom. 1:2; 4:3; 9:17; 10:11; 11:2; 15:4; 16:26; 1 Cor. 15:3–4; Gal. 3:8, 22; 4:30; 1 Tim. 5:18; 2 Tim. 3:16; James 4:5; 2 Pet. 1:20–21; 3:15–16.

The Bible actually contains sixty-six separate books. Thirty-nine books, approximately three-quarters of the Bible, are in the Old Testament, which is a record of God's speaking and working in history from when he created the universe and our first parents, Adam and Eve, up until about 450 BC. In the period between the two testaments, the people waited for the coming of the Messiah into human history. The twenty-seven books of the New Testament begin with the four Gospels, which record the life, death, burial, resurrection, and return to heaven of Jesus, and then proceed to instruct various Christians and Christian churches about how to think and live in light of who Jesus is and what he has done.

Thus, the Bible is a library of books that are one Book, showing a divine unity and continuity. This point is illustrated by the fact that the New Testament has roughly three hundred explicit Old Testament quotations, as well as upwards of four thousand allusions to the Old Testament. In many ways, the Old Testament is a series of promises that God makes and the New Testament is the record of the fulfillment of those promises and the anticipation of the fulfillment of the remaining promises at Jesus' second coming.

The Bible is the best-selling book of all time. The Old Testament was originally written on papyrus—a form of paper made out of reeds. By the time the New Testament was written, parchments (prepared animal skins) were also used.[17] The pages were put together into scrolls.[18]

Chapters and verses were added to provide addresses (not unlike those on our homes) that help us find particular sections. In 1205, Stephen Langton, a theology professor who became the archbishop of Canterbury, began using Bible chapters. In 1240, Cardinal Hugo of St. Cher published a Latin Bible with the 1,189 chapter divisions that exist today. Robert Stephanus, a Protestant book printer, was condemned as a heretic for printing Bibles. As he fled with his family to Geneva on horseback, he arbitrarily made verse divisions within Langton's chapter divisions. His system was used for the first English Bible (The Geneva New Testament of

---

[17]2 Tim. 4:13.
[18]Ezra 6:2; Ps. 40:7; Luke 4:17, 20.

1557) and became today's system of 31,173 verses. It is important to realize that the Bible's chapters and verses were not applied with any logical or consistent method and, while helpful, they are not authoritative. Because the Bible was not intended to be read in bits and pieces, reading verses out of context can lead to serious misunderstanding. Thus, rightly interpreting particular sections of Scripture requires paying attention both to the immediate context and the overall context of all of Scripture.

HOW IS JESUS THE HERO OF THE BIBLE?

The opening line of Scripture introduces us to its hero, God. Throughout the pages of Scripture this God is revealed. In the closing line of the New Testament Scriptures, we are reminded that the God who is the hero of the true story of Scripture is Jesus Christ. Thus, the written Word of God reveals to us the incarnate ("in human flesh") Word of God, Jesus Christ. Further, without the written Word, we cannot rightly know the incarnate Word. Therefore, defining the central message of the Old Testament is the key to our interpretive process, because without a proper understanding of Scripture we do not have access to truly loving and knowing the real Jesus.

Some people prefer the New Testament to the Old Testament because they wrongly believe that only the New Testament is about Jesus. However, it was Jesus himself who taught that the Old Testament was primarily about him. While arguing with the theologians in his day, Jesus chastised them, saying, "You search the Scriptures [Old Testament] because you think that in them you have eternal life; and it is they that bear witness about me, yet you refuse to come to me that you may have life."[19]

Following his resurrection, Jesus opened the Old Testament to teach others about himself: "Beginning with Moses and all the Prophets, he interpreted to them in all the Scriptures the things concerning himself."[20] Likewise, in speaking to his disciples, Jesus said, "These are my words that I spoke to you while I was still with you, that everything written about me

---

[19]John 5:39–40.
[20]Luke 24:27.

in the Law of Moses and the Prophets and the Psalms must be fulfilled."[21] We then read that he "opened their minds to understand the Scriptures."[22]

Jesus' own words about himself as the central message of the Old Testament are pointedly clear. He said, "Do not think that I have come to abolish the Law or the Prophets; I have not come to abolish them but to fulfill them. For truly, I say to you, until heaven and earth pass away, not an iota, not a dot, will pass from the Law until all is accomplished."[23] Jesus repeated this fact throughout his ministry by saying he "fulfilled" particular Scriptures.[24]

Simply, when Scripture is rightly interpreted, it is ultimately about Jesus as God, our Savior, the object of our faith, forgiver of our sins, and giver of eternal life. Therefore, to correctly interpret Scripture you will need to connect its verses, concepts, and events to Jesus.

The Old Testament predicts the coming of Jesus and in a variety of ways prepares people for his person and work. The New Testament reflects on the life of Jesus, particularly in the four Gospels, and reports the results of Jesus' life and ministry, particularly in the Epistles.

The Old Testament uses various means to reveal Jesus, including promises, appearances, foreshadowing types, and titles. First, the Old Testament teaches about Jesus in the numerous prophetic promises given about him. At the time of its writing, more than one-quarter of Scripture was prophetic in nature, promising future events. No other world religion or cult can present any specific prophecies concerning the coming of their prophets. However, in the Old Testament we see hundreds of fulfilled prophecies extending hundreds and sometimes over a thousand years into the future, showing God's foreknowledge of and sovereignty over the future.

Second, the Old Testament teaches about Jesus through appearances that he makes before his birth, or what are called *Christophanies*. Examples include walking with Abraham,[25] wrestling with Jacob,[26] appearing to

---

[21] Luke 24:44.
[22] Luke 24:45.
[23] Matt. 5:17–18.
[24] E.g., Matt. 26:56; Luke 4:20–21; 22:37.
[25] Genesis 18; cf. John 8:56.
[26] Gen. 32:30.

Moses,[27] joining Daniel's friends in the fiery furnace,[28] and calling Isaiah into ministry.[29] Other examples may include the occasional appearance of "the angel [messenger] of the LORD," who is sometimes identified as God.[30] This angel provided the sacrifice in Isaac's place[31] and spoke and journeyed with Moses.[32]

Third, *types* are Old Testament representative figures, institutions, or events that foreshadow Jesus. Examples include Adam, who foreshadows Jesus as the second Adam; the priesthood, which prefigures Jesus as our high priest; David and other kings, who prefigure Jesus as the King of kings; Moses and the prophets, who prefigure Jesus as our ultimate prophet; animal sacrifices, which prefigure Jesus as the sinless Lamb of God slain for our sins; the temple, which prefigures God's presence dwelling among us in Jesus; shepherds who care for their sheep, which remind us we are as foolish and vulnerable as sheep but that Jesus our shepherd keeps constant watch over us; judges, who foreshadow Jesus as the final judge of all people; and many others, such as Jesus the true bread, the true vine, and true light.

We also see people in the Old Testament who perform various kinds of service that is analogous to the service that Jesus performs perfectly. Unlike the first Adam, Jesus Christ is the Last Adam who passed his test in a garden and in so doing imputed his righteousness to us to overcome the sin imputed to us through the sin of the first Adam. Jesus is the true and better Abel who, although he was innocent, was slain and whose blood cries out. When Abraham left his father and home, he was doing the same thing that Jesus would do when he left heaven. When Isaac carried his own wood and laid down his life to be sacrificed at the hand of his father Abraham, he was showing us what Jesus would later do. Jesus is the greater Jacob who wrestled with God in Gethsemane and, though wounded and limping, walked away from his grave blessed. Jesus is the greater Joseph who serves

---

[27]Ex. 3:2–6; cf. John 8:58.
[28]Dan. 3:24–25.
[29]Isa. 6:1–5; cf. John 12:41.
[30]Judg. 6:11–21; 13:22.
[31]Gen. 16:7–13.
[32]Ex. 3:14; 23:20–21; cf. John 8:56–59.

at the right hand of God the king and extends forgiveness and provision to those of us who have betrayed him and uses his power to save us in loving reconciliation. Jesus is greater than Moses in that he stands as a mediator between God and us, bringing us the new covenant.

Like Job, innocent Jesus suffered and was tormented by the Devil so that God might be glorified, while his dumb friends were no help or encouragement. Jesus is a king greater than David; he has slain our giants of Satan, sin, and death, although in the eyes of the world he was certain to face a crushing defeat at their hands. Jesus is greater than Jonah in that he spent three days in the grave, not just in a fish, to save a multitude even greater than Nineveh. When Boaz redeemed Ruth and brought her and her despised people into community with God's people, he was showing what Jesus would do to redeem his bride, the church, from all the nations of the earth. When Nehemiah rebuilt Jerusalem, he was doing something similar to Jesus, who is building for us a New Jerusalem as our eternal home. When Hosea married an unfaithful whoring wife that he continued to pursue in love, he was showing us the heart of Jesus, who does the same for his unfaithful bride, the church.

We also see various Old Testament events preparing people for the coming of Jesus Christ. For example, in the Exodus account of Passover the people were to place blood over the doorframe with hyssop (a common herb bundled for cleaning) and no one was to leave their home until the morning. Death would not come to any home marked with lamb's blood. Peter says our salvation is given by Jesus Christ and "sprinkling with his blood."[33]

Fourth, there are many titles for God in the Old Testament that refer to Jesus Christ as God. In Daniel 7:13–14 God is called the "son of man," and Jesus adopted that as his favorite title, using it some eighty times in the four Gospels. Jesus is the Suffering Servant that was promised in Isaiah.[34] Jesus is also known by many other Old Testament titles for God, includ-

---

[33]1 Pet. 1:2.
[34]Isa. 42:1–4; 49:1–7; 52:13–53:12; cf. Phil. 2:1–11.

ing first and last,[35] light,[36] rock,[37] husband or bridegroom,[38] shepherd,[39] redeemer,[40] savior,[41] and the Lord of glory.[42]

To properly understand the Old Testament we must connect it to the person and work of Jesus. This should not be done in an allegorizing manner where arbitrary meanings foreign to Scripture are assigned to Old Testament words and images, thereby changing their meaning. Rather, the meaning of the Old Testament includes symbolism and identity that are most fully revealed in Jesus.

Unless Jesus is the central message of the Scriptures, many errors abound. The most common is moralizing. Moralizing is reading the Bible not to learn about Jesus but only to learn principles for how to live life as a good person by following the good examples of some people and avoiding the bad examples of others. That kind of approach to the Scriptures is not Christian, because it treats the Bible like any other book with moral lessons that are utterly disconnected from faith in and salvation from Jesus.

WHO WROTE THE BIBLE?

As part of his teaching ministry, Jesus often taught his students (disciples) about the future. On a few occasions he promised them that one day he would leave them and send the Holy Spirit to perfectly remind them of his life and teachings so that they could write and teach accurately and truthfully to complete the Bible.[43]

The human authors of the Bible include kings, peasants, philosophers, fishermen, poets, statesmen, a doctor, and scholars. The books of the Bible cover history, sermons, letters, songs, and love letters. There are geographi-

---

[35]Isa. 41:4; 44:6; 48:12; cf. Rev. 1:17; 2:8; 22:13.
[36]Ps. 27:1; cf. John 1:9.
[37]Pss. 18:2; 95:1; cf. 1 Cor.10:4; 1 Pet. 2:6–8.
[38]Hos. 2:16; Isa. 62:5; cf. Eph. 5:28–33; Rev. 21:2.
[39]Ps. 23:1; cf. Heb. 13:20.
[40]Hos. 13:14; Ps. 130:7; cf. Titus 2:13; Rev. 5:9.
[41]Isa. 43:3; cf. John 4:42.
[42]Isa. 42:8; cf. 1 Cor. 2:8.
[43]John 14:25–26; 16:12–15.

cal surveys, architectural specifications, travel diaries, population statistics, family trees, inventories, and numerous legal documents.

Unlike any other book, the Bible is a book written by both God and man. But it was not coauthored, as is this book you are reading. It was not God and humans collaborating, or a human writing a draft with God making revisions, or God giving ideas that the human authors put into words. They were not words dictated to humans, as with the Koran. The Bible is not human writings that become divine when the reader discovers spiritual meaning in them, as with the writings of many Eastern religions. It is not one of many books containing the religious insights of ancient sages, as many liberals teach.

People who were providentially prepared by God,[44] and motivated and superintended by the Holy Spirit,[45] spoke and wrote according to their own personalities and circumstances in such a way that their words are the very Word of God.[46] God's supernatural guidance of the writers and their situations enabled them to receive and communicate all God would have us know for his glory and our salvation.

We call this *divine inspiration*. Putting it a bit more technically, the writings themselves have the quality of being God-breathed. It is not the authors or the process that is inspired, but the writings.

The belief that God wrote Scripture in concert with human authors whom he inspired to perfectly record his words is called *verbal* (the very words of the Bible)[47] *plenary* (every part of the Bible)[48] *inspiration* (are God-breathed revelation). Very simply, this means that God the Holy Spirit inspired not just the thoughts of Scripture but also the very details and exact words that were perfectly recorded for us as Scripture.

When we say *verbal*, we believe that the very words are inspired and important, chosen by God, so every word does matter. That's why Jesus can say "not an iota, not a dot" of the Bible can be ignored.[49] We cannot

[44]Jer. 1:5; Gal. 1:15.
[45]1 Cor. 2:13; 2 Tim. 3:16; 2 Pet. 1:20–21.
[46]Mark 12:36; 1 Cor. 14:37.
[47]Matt. 4:4; 1 John 1:1–3.
[48]Matt. 5:17; Rom. 15:4; 2 Tim. 3:16.
[49]Matt. 5:18.

limit the divine inspiration to concepts that God put in the mind of human authors who did their best to put those ideas into words. Rather, his revelation comes to us in those exact words.

When we say *plenary*, we mean there are no parts of the Bible we don't believe, don't like, or won't teach or preach or obey. We cannot be like Thomas Jefferson, who brazenly sat down in the White House with a razor in one hand and a Bible in the other and cut out the portions he rejected, asserting his own authority over the authority of the Lord. And we cannot be like those who are more subtle than Jefferson and simply ignore parts of the Bible as primitive, dismiss them as outdated, or explain them away with human reasoning. Paul shows us the proper attitude toward Scripture:

> All Scripture is breathed out by God and profitable for teaching, for reproof, for correction, and for training in righteousness, that the man of God may be competent, equipped for every good work.[50]

He teaches us that the very words are miraculous revelation. Every part of Scripture is God's word to us, the product of his creative breathing, just as the world,[51] humans,[52] and apostles[53] were. It is profitable, or helpful. It is not helpful like a phone book, but helpful as a person who loves you, cares for you, converses with you, counsels you, comforts you, and confronts you. The Bible is how God speaks to us.

Peter echoes Paul's words:

> We have something more sure, the prophetic word, to which you will do well to pay attention as to a lamp shining in a dark place, until the day dawns and the morning star rises in your hearts, knowing this first of all, that no prophecy of Scripture comes from someone's own interpretation. For no prophecy was ever produced by the will of man, but men spoke from God as they were carried along by the Holy Spirit.[54]

---

[50]2 Tim. 3:16–17.
[51]Ps. 33:6.
[52]Gen. 2:7; Job 33:4.
[53]John 20:22.
[54]2 Pet. 1:19–21.

Peter tells us that the Bible is not just made up like a fairy tale. Rather, the authors were carried along by the Holy Spirit as a boat is carried by a breeze that fills its sails. Because the Scriptures come from God, they speak to things no human could know and do it with perfection. For example, the writers of the Old Testament could not have made up prophesied details such as a virgin birth in the tiny town of Bethlehem.[55] If God had not moved them, they could not have seen the future in such detail. Because God alone is sovereign over and all-knowing of the future, he revealed exactly what would happen.

The biblical authors knew they were writing Holy Scripture. Paul told the Corinthians, "The things I am writing to you are a command of the Lord."[56] He had the courage to give them a commandment from Jesus and then put his own command right alongside it, as having equal authority.[57] Paul quotes the Old Testament as Holy Scripture: "For the Scripture says, 'You shall not muzzle an ox when it treads out the grain,'" and then he quotes Luke right alongside it, saying, "The laborer deserves his wages."[58] Peter also compares the letters of Paul to "other Scriptures."[59]

Taken all together, the Scriptures make incredible truth claims. The Scriptures are:

- given by God's inspiration;[60]
- the very words of God;[61]
- all we need to know God;[62]
- a perfect guide for life;[63]
- pure;[64]
- true;[65]
- trustworthy;[66]

---

[55]Isa. 7:14; Mic. 5:2.
[56]1 Cor. 14:37.
[57]1 Cor. 7:10, 12.
[58]1 Tim. 5:18.
[59]2 Pet. 3:15–16.
[60]2 Tim. 3:16; 2 Pet. 1:19–21.
[61]1 Thess. 2:13.
[62]Luke 16:29, 31.
[63]Prov. 6:23.
[64]Pss. 12:6; 119:140.
[65]Ps. 119:160; John 17:17.
[66]Prov. 30:5–6.

- perfect;[67]
- effective;[68]
- powerful;[69]
- not to be taken from or added to;[70]
- for everyone;[71]
- the standard by which all teaching is to be tested;[72]
- to be obeyed.[73]

Speaking poetically, the Scriptures also claim to be:

- sweet like honey;[74]
- a lamp to guide our life;[75]
- food for our soul;[76]
- a fire that purifies and a hammer that breaks us;[77]
- a sword;[78]
- a seed for salvation planted in us;[79]
- milk that nourishes us.[80]

WHAT IS THE CANON OF SCRIPTURE?

The canon of Scripture is the collection of books that the church has recognized as having divine authority in matters of faith and doctrine. The term comes from the Greek word *kanon* and the Hebrew word *qaneh*, both of which mean "a rule," or "measuring rod." The canon is an authority to which other truth claims are compared and by which they are measured. To speak of canonical writings is to speak of those books that are regarded as having divine authority. They are the books of our Bible.

---

[67]Ps. 19:7.
[68]Isa. 55:11.
[69]Heb. 4:12.
[70]Deut. 4:2; 12:32.
[71]Rom. 16:25–27.
[72]Acts 17:11.
[73]James 1:22.
[74]Ps. 19:10.
[75]Ps. 119:105.
[76]Jer. 15:16.
[77]Jer. 23:29.
[78]Eph. 6:17; Heb. 4:12.
[79]James 1:21.
[80]1 Pet. 2:2.

The thirty-nine books of the Old Testament and twenty-seven books of the New Testament graciously preserved by God in the Bible are the inspired Word of God. The church recognized that these books constitute the complete canon inspired by God and received them as uniquely authoritative because they are God speaking to his people. F. F. Bruce says:

> One thing must be emphatically stated. The New Testament books did not become authoritative for the Church because they were formally included in a canonical list; on the contrary, the Church included them in her canon because she already regarded them as divinely inspired, recognizing their innate worth and generally apostolic authority, direct or indirect. The first ecclesiastical councils to classify the canonical books were both held in North Africa—at Hippo Regius in 393 and at Carthage in 397—but what these councils did was not to impose something new upon the Christian communities but to codify what was already the general practice of those communities.[81]

Time after time Jesus and his apostles quoted from this distinctive body of authoritative writings. They designated them as "the Scripture,"[82] "the Scriptures,"[83] "the holy Scriptures,"[84] "the sacred writings,"[85] and so forth. They often introduced their quotations with "It is written"; that is, it stands firmly written.

We call these authoritative writings the Old Testament. Jewish people call them the *Tanakh*, an acronym formed from the first letters of *Torah* (Law), *Naviim* (Prophets), and *Ketubim* (Writings). We see this idea when Jesus explained to his disciples "everything written about me in the Law of Moses and the Prophets and the Psalms must be fulfilled."[86] It is important to note that the *Tanakh* includes the same material as the Protestant Old Testament, though they arrange the books differently.[87]

---

[81]F. F. Bruce, *The New Testament Documents: Are They Reliable?* (Grand Rapids, MI: Eerdmans, 1981), 22.
[82]John 7:38; Acts 8:32; Rom. 4:3.
[83]Matt. 21:42; John 5:39; Acts 17:11.
[84]Rom. 1:2.
[85]2 Tim. 3:15.
[86]Luke 24:44.
[87]Walter A. Elwell and Barry J. Beitzel, *Baker Encyclopedia of the Bible* (Grand Rapids, MI: Baker, 1988), 301.

Beginning two hundred and fifty years before Christ, Greek-speaking Jews living in Alexandria translated the Old Testament into Greek, calling it the Septuagint. For some unknown reason, they changed the content of several books, added many books, and rearranged the order of the books.

Early Christians followed Jesus and used the same books as found in the Hebrew Bible today. But as the center of Christianity moved away from Jerusalem and Christians read and worshiped more in Greek than Hebrew, there was more openness to the books of the Septuagint. There was a long and complicated debate about the validity and status of these books. Eventually the Roman Catholic Church adopted many of the books of the Septuagint into its Latin version, called the Vulgate. They referred to them as *deuterocanonical*, meaning they were canonized later. As the Reformers attempted to rid the church of many traditional teachings and get back to the Bible, they also rejected the deuterocanonical books, calling them the Apocrypha. They kept the ordering of the Vulgate but returned to the authoritative books of Jesus, the Hebrew-speaking Jews, and early Christianity.

The early church immediately recognized most of the books of the New Testament as canonical. The four Gospels, written to preserve and spread the story of Jesus to the whole church, were received gladly and universally, as were the writings of Paul, including 1 Timothy, 2 Timothy, and Titus (also known as the Pastoral Letters). Acts, 1 John, 1 Peter, and Revelation were also universally recognized. However, Hebrews remained in dispute for several centuries, especially in the West, because of the anonymity of its author. The status of James, 2 Peter, 2 John, 3 John, and Jude fluctuated according to church, age, and individual judgment and are occasionally omitted from canonical lists. Some works of the apostolic fathers, such as the Epistle of Barnabas, the Shepherd of Hermas, and the first and second epistles of Clement are sporadically cited as potentially Scripture but are not usually included in formal canonical lists.

In the fourth century the church moved to settle the issues of the New Testament canon. In the East it was done in the Thirty-Ninth Paschal Letter of Athanasius in AD 367. In the West the canon was fixed at the Council of Carthage in AD 397.

Was the New Testament canon disputed? Not really. Virtually all the books were immediately accepted. Did the church canonize the books? Not at all. Rather, they recognized and confirmed their canonical status. J. I. Packer writes:

> The Church no more gave us the New Testament canon than Sir Isaac Newton gave us the force of gravity. God gave us gravity, by His work of creation, and similarly He gave us the New Testament canon, by inspiring the individual books that make it up.[88]

How did the church know which books ought to be recognized as canonical? What were the criteria for canonicity? They used three primary criteria:

1) *Conformity* to "the rule of faith." Did the book conform to orthodoxy, Christian truth recognized as normative in the churches?
2) *Apostolicity.* Was the writer of the book an apostle or did the writer of the book have immediate contact with the apostles? All but a few New Testament writers were eyewitnesses to the events they recorded.[89] Though not eyewitnesses, Luke received his information from Paul[90] and numerous eyewitnesses,[91] while Mark received his information from Peter, who was an eyewitness.[92] James and Jude were closely associated with the apostles in Jerusalem and were probably Jesus' brothers, which would have also made them eyewitnesses.
3) *Catholicity.* Did the book have widespread and continuous acceptance and usage by churches everywhere?

In considering the great agreement surrounding the canon of Scripture, scholars have said:

---

[88]J. I. Packer, *God Has Spoken: Revelation and the Bible*, 3rd ed. (Grand Rapids, MI: Baker, 2000), 109.
[89]John 19:35; 20:30–31; Acts 1:1–3, 9; 10:39–42; 1 Cor. 15:6–8; 1 Pet. 5:1; 2 Pet. 1:16; 1 John 1:1–3.
[90]2 Tim. 4:11.
[91]Luke 1:1–4.
[92]1 Pet. 5:13.

The fact that substantially the whole church came to recognize the same twenty-seven books as canonical is remarkable when it is remembered that the result was not contrived. All that the several churches throughout the Empire could do was to witness to their own experience with the documents and share whatever knowledge they might have about their origin and character. When consideration is given to the diversity in cultural backgrounds and in orientation to the essentials of the Christian faith within the churches, their common agreement about which books belonged to the New Testament serves to suggest that this final decision did not originate solely at the human level.[93]

WHY WERE SOME BOOKS NOT ACCEPTED AS SCRIPTURE?

In recent years, the so-called lost books of the Bible have enjoyed revived interest. For example, Dan Brown built much of the storyline of his bestselling book, *The Da Vinci Code*, on the premise that the church selected the four canonical Gospels from eighty similar books.[94] The others, it is said, were stamped out by "a Church that had subjugated women, banished the Goddess, burned non-believers, and forbidden the pagan reverence for the sacred feminine."[95]

In fact, however, even by the most generous count there are fewer than thirty "gospels." Only the canonical Gospels date from the first century. The earliest of the others was written more than one hundred years after Jesus lived. Most of them are dated at least two hundred years after Jesus.

Contrary to false accusation, not one of these "lost gospels" was hidden by the church. Furthermore, no "lost" gospels have been discovered. All of the discovered books were referred to in the church fathers' writings because the Fathers knew of their existence but simply did not consider them sacred Scripture. Some older or more complete copies of them have been discovered, most significantly in the Egyptian *Nag Hammadi* site. Peter rightly called these kinds of claims about lost gos-

---

[93]Glenn W. Barker, William L. Lane, and J. Ramsey Michaels, *The New Testament Speaks* (New York: Harper & Row, 1969), 29.
[94]Dan Brown, *The Da Vinci Code* (New York: Anchor Books, 2003), 251.
[95]Ibid., 259.

pels and suppressed teachings about Jesus "cleverly devised myths" with no basis in fact or reality.[96]

There is no reason to be concerned about any lost gospels containing truth that we need about God. Anyone curious about their truthfulness should simply read them. The *Gospel of Philip* supposedly says that Jesus and Mary Magdalene were married. In fact, it says, "And the companion of the [. . .] Mary Magdalene, [. . .] her more than the disciples [. . .] kiss her on her [. . .]. The rest of [. . .]. They said to him, 'Why do you love her more than all of us?'" (The ellipses in brackets indicate where the papyrus is broken and lost.) To say the least, this is extremely slender evidence for Jesus' marriage that some purport, even if this very late, clearly Gnostic gospel was accepted as authentic, which it is not.

The *Gospel of Thomas* is one of the earlier and most widely affirmed of the Gnostic gospels. It is not a gospel in the sense of a narrative that tells the story of Jesus. Rather, it consists of 114 sayings attributed to Jesus, some of which clearly parallel sayings in the canonical Gospels.

But that is where the similarity ends. It was written at least a century after the four biblical Gospels, long after the eyewitnesses to Jesus Christ were dead. It clearly reflects Gnostic theology built on a belief system that despised earthly and material realities and exalted the "higher" spiritual plane. The "god" of Thomas is a second-rate angelic being who rebelliously created this physical world. Humans are presented as spiritual beings ensnared in a wretched physical body. The only attention given to the humanity of Jesus was when trying to excuse it. The canonical Gospels, however, provide a very different picture of Jesus: a man who is fully human, in body and spirit, and who had disciples and friends, both male and female.

To make the differences between the real Gospels in the Bible and the Gnostic *Gospel of Thomas* clear, just read its final adage:

> Simon Peter said to him, "Let Mary leave us, for women are not worthy
> of life." Jesus said, "I myself shall lead her in order to make her male,

---

[96]2 Pet. 1:16.

so that she too may become a living spirit resembling you males. For every woman who will make herself male will enter the kingdom of heaven." (114)

Regarding the wrongly termed "lost gospels," New Testament scholar Craig Blomberg has said:

> In no meaningful sense did these writers, church leaders, or councils "suppress" Gnostic or apocryphal material, since there is no evidence of any canon that ever included them, nor that anyone put them forward for canonization, nor that they were known widely enough to have been serious candidates for inclusion had someone put them forward. Indeed, they would have failed all three of the major criteria used by the early church in selecting which books they were, at times very literally, willing to die for—the criteria of apostolicity (that a book was written by an apostle or a close associate of an apostle), coherence (not contradicting previously accepted Scripture), and catholicity (widespread acceptance as particularly relevant and normative within all major segments of the early Christian community).[97]

To be fair, there are a handful of other ancient books that have some good content. Books such as the Shepherd of Hermas and the *Didache* were appreciated by the early church and are akin to some popular Christian books today that can provide some insight but do not rise to the level of Scripture or fall to the level of heresy. But only a few individual churches and teachers wanted them included in the canon. In simplest terms, they were not accepted because they were not God's Word for his whole church.

From the very earliest days, the church knew which books were God's inspired word for them. They read them, studied them, obeyed them, lived them, and passed them on. We should do the same without adding anything to the Scriptures. Proverbs 30:5–6 commands just this, saying, "Every

[97]Craig L. Blomberg, "Jesus of Nazareth: How Historians Can Know Him and Why It Matters" (Deerfield, IL: Christ on Campus Initiative, 2008), http://tgc-documents.s3.amazonaws.com/cci/Blomberg.pdf, 25–26.

word of God proves true; he is a shield to those who take refuge in him. Do not add to his words, lest he rebuke you and you be found a liar."

DOES SCRIPTURE CONTAIN ERRORS AND/OR CONTRADICTIONS?

We believe that what the Bible teaches is true, so we come to the Bible with what J. I. Packer calls "an advance commitment to receive as truth from God all that Scripture is found on inspection actually to teach."[98] So we believe that all that the Bible teaches is truth from God, whether statements of fact about earth, heaven, humans, or God, or moral commands, or divine promises. This has been the universal affirmation of the church until the time of the Enlightenment, when acceptance in the secular academy led some biblical scholars to base their conclusions on culturally misguided reason rather than on revelation and reality.

The affirmation of the truthfulness of the Bible is inextricably tied to the character of God himself. God is a truthful God who does not lie.[99] Therefore, because God is ultimately the author of Scripture, it is perfect, unlike every other uninspired writing and utterance.

Taken altogether, *inerrancy* is the shorthand way of summarizing all that the Scriptures say about Scripture. *Inerrant* means that the Scriptures are perfect, without any error. The doctrine of inerrancy posits that because God does not lie or speak falsely in any way, and because the Scriptures are God's Word, they are perfect.[100] As a result, the entire Bible is without any error.[101]

The Bible claims to be wholly true and therefore inerrant. We find such explicit statements in passages such as 2 Samuel 7:28, "O Lord GOD, you are God, and your words are true"; Psalm 19:7–10, which uses words such as *perfect, sure, right, pure, true,* and *righteous*; Psalm 119:42–43, 142, 151, 160, 163, which uses the specific word *truth* or *true*; and John 17:17,

[98]J. I. Packer, "Hermeneutics and Biblical Authority," *Themelios* 1.1 (Autumn 1975): 11. Also see http://s3.amazonaws.com/tgc-documents/journal-issues/1.1_Packer.pdf.
[99]Heb. 6:18; Titus 1:2.
[100]2 Sam. 7:28; Titus 1:2; Heb. 6:18.
[101]Num. 23:19; Pss. 12:6; 119:89; Prov. 30:5–6.

"Your word is truth." Second Timothy 3:16 rightly says, "*All* Scripture is breathed out by God."

Unlike the Bible, however, those of us who read and study it are not inerrant in our understanding of it. The Bible itself gives us much cause for humility as we approach the Scriptures because:

- God's thoughts are much loftier than ours;[102]
- God has secrets that he has not revealed to anyone;[103]
- sometimes we see the truth as if through a dirty and fogged window;[104]
- we are prone to resist God's truth because it forces us to repent, and sometimes we are simply hard-hearted;[105]
- we know in part;[106]
- some parts of the Bible are just hard to understand.[107]

Therefore, if it appears that there is a contradiction in Scripture, we should first dig deeply into our Bible to see if what appears to be an error is, in fact, not an error once we have examined it more closely.[108] In the end, it is perfectly reasonable to say that we do not have an answer for every question we may have, though we may as we learn more, or when we get to heaven and get the final word on everything. The kind of humility that a priori assumes that when we do not understand or initially disagree with Scripture that we, and not the Bible, are in error is essential to truly Christian study.

A key point to remember is that self-testimony is valid and strong when that testimony is validated by sufficient evidence. The remarkable accuracy of the Bible in areas where we can check it gives us confidence that it is true in all areas.

A telling example of the Bible's accuracy is in the transliteration of the names of foreign kings in the Old Testament as compared to contem-

---

[102]Isa. 55:9.
[103]Deut. 29:29.
[104]1 Cor. 13:12.
[105]Rom. 1:18–19.
[106]1 Cor. 13:9.
[107]2 Pet. 3:15–16.
[108]*When Critics Ask*, by Norman Geisler and Thomas Howe, is very helpful in doing this (Grand Rapids, MI: Baker, 1992).

porary extra-biblical records, such as monuments and tablets. The Bible is accurate in every detail in the thirty-six instances of comparison, a total of 183 syllables. To see how amazing this is, Manetho's ancient work on the dynasties of the Egyptian kings can be compared to extra-biblical records in 140 instances. He is right forty-nine times, only partially right twenty-eight times, and in the other sixty-three cases not a single syllable is correct! The Bible's accuracy is shown not only in the original work but in its copies as well.[109]

Luke correctly identifies by name, title, job, and time such historical individuals as Annas,[110] Ananias,[111] Herod Agrippa I,[112] Herod Agrippa II,[113] Sergius Paulus,[114] the Egyptian prophet,[115] Felix,[116] and Festus.[117] Political titles were very diverse and difficult to keep straight since every province had its own terms and, worse yet, the terms constantly changed. Yet Luke gets them right: a proconsul in Cypress and Achaia,[118] the undeserved title Praetor in Philippi,[119] the otherwise unknown title of Politarchs in Thessalonica,[120] Asiarchs in Ephesus,[121] and "the chief man" in Malta.[122] The descriptions of local custom and culture are equally accurate. As John Elder states:

> It is not too much to say that it was the rise of the science of archaeology that broke the deadlock between historians and the orthodox Christian. Little by little, one city after another, one civilization after another, one culture after another, whose memories were enshrined only in the Bible, were restored to their proper places in ancient history by the studies of archaeologists. . . . Contemporary records of biblical events have been unearthed and the uniqueness of biblical revelation has been emphasized by contrast and comparison to newly discovered

---

[109]See John Wenham, *Christ and the Bible*, 3rd ed. (Grand Rapids, MI: Baker, 1994), 170–71.
[110]Acts 4:6; 23:2.
[111]Acts 23:2.
[112]Acts 12:1–3, 20, 23.
[113]Acts 25:13–26:32.
[114]Acts 13:7.
[115]Acts 21:38.
[116]Acts 23:23–24:27.
[117]Acts 24:27.
[118]Acts 13:7; 18:12.
[119]Acts 16:12, 20ff., 35ff.
[120]Acts 17:6, 9.
[121]Acts 19:31, 35.
[122]Acts 28:7.

religions of ancient peoples. Nowhere has archaeological discovery refuted the Bible as history.[123]

This affirmation of the truthfulness of the Bible is exactly the attitude of Jesus himself. Frederick C. Grant, who is not any sort of fundamentalist Christian, acknowledges that the New Testament consistently takes "for granted that what is written in Scripture is trustworthy, infallible and inerrant. No New Testament writer would ever dream of questioning a statement contained in the Old Testament."[124]

Those parts of the Old Testament that are most commonly rejected as error are also those sections of Scripture that Jesus clearly taught. This includes creation,[125] the literalness of Genesis 1 and 2,[126] Cain and the murder of Abel,[127] Noah and the flood,[128] Abraham,[129] Sodom and Gomorrah,[130] Lot,[131] Isaac and Jacob,[132] the manna,[133] the wilderness serpent,[134] Moses as lawgiver,[135] the popularity of the false prophets,[136] and Jonah in the belly of a whale.[137]

In matters of controversy, Jesus used the Old Testament as his court of appeals.[138] On many occasions where an Old Testament teaching was questioned, Jesus simply believed the clear teaching of Old Testament Scripture and defended himself by saying, "it is written."[139]

Some of the most common critiques launched at the Old Testament are in regard to authorship, but Jesus actually named the authors of some

[123]John Elder, *Prophets, Idols, and Diggers: Scientific Proof of Bible History* (New York: Bobbs-Merrill, 1960), 16.
[124]Frederick C. Grant, *An Introduction to New Testament Thought* (New York: Abingdon-Cokesbury Press, 1950), 75.
[125]Luke 11:51.
[126]Matt. 19:4–5; Mark 10:6–8.
[127]Matt. 23:35; Luke 11:51.
[128]Matt. 24:37–39; Luke 17:26–27.
[129]John 8:56.
[130]Matt. 10:15; 11:23–24; Luke 10:12; 17:29.
[131]Luke 17:28–32.
[132]Matt. 8:11; Luke 13:28.
[133]John 6:31, 49, 58.
[134]John 3:14.
[135]Matt. 8:4; 19:8; Mark 1:44; 7:10; 10:5; 12:26; Luke 5:14; 20:37; John 5:46; 7:19.
[136]Luke 6:26.
[137]Matt. 12:40.
[138]Matt. 5:17–20; 22:29; 23:23; Mark 12:24.
[139]Matt. 4:4, 6, 10; 11:10; 21:13; 26:24, 31; Mark 1:2; 7:6; 9:12–13; 11:17; 14:21, 27; Luke 2:23; 4:4, 8, 10, 17; 7:27; 10:26; 19:46; 22:37; John 2:17; 6:31, 45; 8:17; 10:34.

Old Testament books. For example, many Old Testament "scholars" boldly claim that Moses did not pen any of the first five books of the Bible, or that two or three authors penned Isaiah, none of whom was actually Isaiah. But Jesus taught that Scripture was authored by Moses,[140] Isaiah,[141] David,[142] and Daniel.[143]

Following Jesus' example, while the New Testament authors often refer to the Old Testament in a rather general way, they also feel confident to appeal to the smallest detail. In Matthew 22:29–33, Jesus' argument rests on the present tense of "to be" in Exodus 3:6. Matthew 22:41–46 refers to the use of "Lord" in Psalm 110:1. In John 10:34, Jesus' argument comes from the Old Testament use of the word "gods."[144] Also, Galatians 3:16 rests on the singularity of the Old Testament word translated "seed" or "offspring."[145]

The standard for true prophecy was complete truthfulness, which is why Elijah was affirmed as a prophet: "Now I know that you are a man of God, and that the word of the LORD in your mouth is truth."[146] Can the standard for the Bible be any less, if it is truly prophetic?

Because Scripture is God speaking to us because he wants us to understand, we also believe Scripture usually speaks accurately in ordinary language. Typically the writers use popular language rather than technical terminology. So they say, "the sun had risen,"[147] or refer to "the four corners of the earth."[148] There are figures of speech like "the trees of the field shall clap their hands."[149] There are also summaries, such as the Sermon on the Mount and Peter's sermon at Pentecost, which we do not have full transcriptions of but rather only a portion of what was preached.[150] Sometimes, the Bible also gives us rounded numbers rather than exact

---

[140]Mark 7:10.
[141]Matt. 13:14; Mark 7:6.
[142]Mark 12:36.
[143]Matt. 24:15.
[144]Ex. 4:16; 7:1; 22:28; Ps. 138:1.
[145]Gen. 12:7; 15:3; 17:19.
[146]1 Kings 17:24.
[147]Gen. 19:23; Mark 16:2.
[148]Isa. 11:12; Rev. 7:1; 20:8.
[149]Isa. 55:12.
[150]Mark 6:44; Acts 4:4.

head counts of, for example, the number of men killed each day during a war.[151] To interpret the Bible accurately we must consider it carefully. Thus we interpret historical accounts, figures of speech, approximations, summaries, and such according to the author's intent, taking care lest our cultural and personal presuppositions distort our interpretation.

This does not mean there are no questions to explore. My (Gerry's) biggest question revolves around the numbers in Numbers. Compared to archaeological estimates, they are too big by a factor of ten. There are several proposals for what is going on, but at this point, we don't know. A few decades ago, I also had questions about Jericho. According to the best archaeological reports, it was uninhabited from about 1600 BC to about 1200 BC. The Bible says the walls came tumbling down about 1440 BC. That would be hard if the city was already destroyed. But as excavations were done in a different part of the ancient site, a thick layer of ash containing grain was discovered. Dating by three different methods showed a burn date of (try to guess before you look!)—1440 BC.[152]

CAN I TRUST THAT MY BIBLE IS GOD'S WORD?

Yes. If you have a good modern translation of the Bible, then you have almost exactly what the ancient authors wrote. It is amazing that people try to argue that we cannot trust the Bible because we do not have the original copies. But it would never occur to them to question the writings of Plato, Sophocles, Homer, or Caesar Augustus, when we have fewer than ten copies of each book, and those copies were made at least one thousand years after the author wrote the original.

Until the middle of the twentieth century, the situation was similar with the Hebrew Old Testament. Our oldest copies dated from about AD 900. We knew the extreme care the rabbis used to copy the sacred text before they destroyed the worn one. But still, the copies we had were historically distant from the original (called the *autographa*). But then in 1947 the Dead

---

[151]Judg. 20:44–47.
[152]For good answers to questions about specific biblical "contradictions," see Gleason L. Archer Jr., *New International Encyclopedia of Bible Difficulties* (Grand Rapids, MI: Zondervan, 2001).

Sea Scrolls were discovered at Qumran. Suddenly we had copies of much of the Old Testament that were more than a thousand years older than our previous oldest copies.

A comparison of the Qumran manuscript of Isaiah with the Masoretic text from AD 900 showed the most minor variations, mostly spelling (like the American *honor* and the British *honour*) or stylistic changes such as adding a conjunction. Checking the pivotal text of Isaiah 53, we find that out of the 166 words in that chapter, only one word is really in question, and it does not at all change the meaning of the passage. The Qumran text added the word "light" after "he shall see" in verse 11. It's a word that was implied but not actually written. Our confidence in the text was confirmed.

In the case of the New Testament, we have 14,000 ancient copies, with fragments written no later than one hundred years after the original books and letters. This is truly amazing because the Bible was copied onto fragile materials like papyrus. The copies weren't stored anywhere that protected them from the elements, but in God's providence they still survived.

As we compare copies of both Old and New Testament we do find variations, but most of the variations in the many handwritten copies involve spelling, word order, or style. We would expect such minor human error no matter how careful the scribes were. Less than 1 percent of all the variations have anything to do with doctrine, and no doctrine is affected by any variation.

Lastly, Jesus himself used copies and translations. He trusted them, so we should too, especially when the science of textual criticism has confirmed that our text is accurate. Because we have so many manuscripts to check, we are virtually certain that the text of over 99 percent of the Bible we have is faithful to the original manuscripts.

CAN SCRIPTURE BE WRITTEN TODAY?

No. The only people who could write Scripture were prophets and apostles—people who were witnesses of God's revelation in Jesus, or authors like Luke who based his Gospel on eyewitness testimony[153] and on the report of the apostles who were eyewitnesses.[154]

Books of the Bible cannot be written today for two primary reasons.

First, the Old Testament ended with the prophet Malachi promising that the next major event in redemptive history would be the coming of John the Baptist, who would prepare the way for Jesus.[155] There were then four hundred years of silence in which no book of the Bible was written until John came, as promised.[156]

Likewise, the New Testament ends with its final book, Revelation, telling us that no other books of the Bible are to be written after it[157] and that we will again have silence until Jesus comes for the second time.[158] Today, we are like God's people in the days between Malachi's promise and Jesus' coming. We are in a season of long silence where we know the future but are awaiting its coming. For this reason we do not need any more information but rather the fulfillment of the promises we have already received.

Second, the Bible tells us that Jesus is God's final word to us[159] and that we should not add anything to the Bible.[160] Furthermore, we have no need for any new book of the Bible because we already have all we need for faith and godliness. If there were some knowledge that we desperately needed, God would certainly not have waited some two thousand years to reveal it while his people sat in the darkness of partial knowledge.

Our way of saying this is that the canon of Scripture is closed. No books, not even a word, will be added to the Bible. John's warning at the end of Revelation applies to the Bible as a whole:

> I warn everyone who hears the words of the prophecy of this book:
> if anyone adds to them, God will add to him the plagues described in

---

[153]Luke 1:1–4.
[154]Acts 1:1–3, 9.
[155]Mal. 3:1; 4:5–6.
[156]Luke 1:11–17.
[157]Rev. 22:18–19.
[158]Rev. 22:20–21.
[159]Heb. 1:1–2.
[160]Deut. 4:2; 12:32; Prov. 30:5–6.

this book, and if anyone takes away from the words of the book of this prophecy, God will take away his share in the tree of life and in the holy city, which are described in this book.[161]

However, this does not mean that God's special revelation has ceased. God still speaks to people and groups, albeit not in apostolic, inspired, canonical revelation. Examples include such things as predictive prophecies, dreams, visions, angelic visits, and the like that Scripture itself speaks of.

In dealing with any alleged extra-biblical revelation, we must follow the biblical cautions. We must be neither gullible nor skeptical. On one hand, we must "not despise prophecies," but on the other, we must "test everything; hold fast what is good."[162] John echoes Paul, saying, "Beloved, do not believe every spirit, but test the spirits to see whether they are from God, for many false prophets have gone out into the world."[163] We must follow the biblical guidelines for testing those who prophesy or allege other forms of extra-biblical revelation:

- Are they loyal to the LORD?[164]
- Is their word consistent with the Bible?[165]
- Is what they describe or predict accurate?[166]
- Is their character Christlike?[167]
- Does their word build up and encourage the church in truth?[168]
- Do the church elders affirm their word?[169]

WHY IS SCRIPTURE AUTHORITATIVE?

Holy Scripture is God speaking. That simple but profound statement is why Christians believe that Scripture is our highest authority by which all

---

[161]Rev. 22:18–19.
[162]1 Thess. 5:20–21.
[163]1 John 4:1.
[164]Deut. 13:1–11; 18:20.
[165]Deut. 13:1–11; 1 Kings 13:15–18.
[166]Deut. 18:22.
[167]Jer. 23:9–40; Mic. 3:5–10.
[168]1 Cor. 14:3.
[169]1 Cor. 14:29.

other lesser authorities are tested. Practically, this means that lesser courts of reason, tradition, and culture are under the highest court of truth, which is divinely inspired Scripture.

By contrast, the Roman Catholic and Eastern Orthodox churches teach that Scripture is a part of the larger pool of revelation that the church uses in its teaching. The authority is not in the Bible itself, but in the teaching office of the church.

Others appeal to the so-called Wesleyan Quadrilateral:

> Wesley believed that the living core of the Christian faith was revealed in Scripture, illumined by tradition, vivified in personal experience, and confirmed by reason. Scripture [however] is primary, revealing the Word of God "so far as it is necessary for our salvation."[170]

In practice, though, the Bible often becomes just one of four major sources of authority to be balanced. Thus, when contemporary critical theories of the Bible start to be taken seriously, the Bible often is judged by other authorities.

The central development of the Protestant Reformation was the return to Scripture as supreme authority. The Reformers coined the slogan *sola Scriptura* (sometimes *prima Scriptura*) to summarize this conviction. Nothing judges Scripture. It judges everything else. As followers of Jesus, we take the same stance he did and receive the Bible alone as infallible, inerrant truth from God with full authority in our lives.

The Bible is a living book of God authoritatively speaking as a perfect Father to children he dearly loves. The Bible tells us how to live godly lives. For example, it commands us to "put away falsehood" and "speak the truth with [our] neighbor," not as arbitrary rules of conduct but as church family members who are "members one of another."[171] It is a story of what is best in a loving family, a family we are invited to be a part of, a family leaving sin and dysfunction and growing to maturity and fulfillment. It is the story

---

[170]United Methodist Church, *The Book of Discipline of the United Methodist Church* (Nashville: Abingdon, 2004), 77.
[171]Eph. 4:25.

of the God of redemption rescuing us from rebellion, brokenness, sin, and death. Its authority is that in these inspired words we find how to connect with the forgiving and transforming power of the death and resurrection of Jesus.

IS THE BIBLE SUFFICIENT OR ALL I NEED FOR LIFE WITH GOD?

The Protestant Reformers' slogan *sola Scriptura* means that Scripture alone is our court of highest authority. This should not be confused with *solo Scriptura*, which is the erroneous belief that truth is to be found only in Scripture and nowhere else. Scripture itself speaks of lesser courts of lower authority that Christians should obey: we should submit to the authority of pastors, government, and parents up to the limits of disobeying the highest authority of Scripture.[172]

The Bible itself models the fact that there is at least some truth outside of the Bible when it occasionally quotes other books, such as the book of Jashar[173] and the Book of the Wars of the LORD.[174] In quoting them, the Bible is not saying that they should be included as sacred Scripture but rather that they do contain some helpful truth. Practically speaking, this means that a mechanic, doctor, or computer programmer does not have to consult Leviticus to turn a brake drum, perform open-heart surgery, or make an addition to a software program.

Regarding the sufficiency of Scripture, the Bible and the Bible alone teaches a complete Christian worldview that includes what we need to know about God, how to come into relation with him, who Jesus is and what he did for our salvation, and what will happen at the end of history.

One example from Scripture is perhaps most clarifying in understanding the sufficiency of Scripture. In Luke 16:19–31 Jesus tells the story of a man who died in unbelief and was suffering in torment. Jesus explains how the man in anguish had a conversation with Abraham across a chasm

---

[172]Heb. 13:17; cf. 1 Tim. 5:17–20; 1 Pet. 2:13–15; cf. Acts 4:19; 5:29; Rom. 13:1, 5; cf. Acts 16:35–40.
[173]Josh. 10:13; 2 Sam. 1:18.
[174]Num. 21:14.

that separated those who had died in faith from those who had died in unbelief in the days prior to Jesus' opening heaven. The man in anguish was concerned for his five brothers who remained alive and in unbelief. Luke 16:29–31 reports:

> Abraham said, "They have Moses and the Prophets; let them hear them." And he said, "No, father Abraham, but if someone goes to them from the dead, they will repent." He said to him, "If they do not hear Moses and the Prophets, neither will they be convinced if someone should rise from the dead."

Jesus was emphatically clear that the Scriptures alone are sufficient for all that is needed to know God and enjoy his salvation. As Abraham said in Jesus' story, the Scriptures are even clearer and more compelling than the testimony of a man returned from death to give a personal report of the consequence for dying in unbelief.

WHY ARE THERE DIFFERENT TRANSLATIONS OF SCRIPTURE?

For centuries the Eastern church had the Bible only in Greek. The Western church had the Bible only in Latin. Since most people were not fluent in these languages, they were unable to read the Bible themselves. One of the great developments of the Protestant Reformation was to return the Bible to the people of the church. The Reformers wanted the people to have the Bible in their own language. Martin Luther and John Wycliffe are just two of the men who risked their lives to translate the Bible into German and English. William Tyndale was charged with heresy and condemned to death because he translated the Bible into English. According to *Foxe's Book of Martyrs*, he "was tied to the stake, strangled by the hangman, and afterwards consumed with fire," simply because he wanted people to be able to read the Bible.[175]

Today many translations of the Bible are available. At least part of the Bible has been translated into at least 2,454 languages, at least one of

---

[175]John Foxe, *Foxe's Book of Martyrs* (Charleston, SC: Forgotten Books, 2007), 234.

the two Testaments exists in at least 1,168 languages, and the full Bible is available in at least 438 languages.[176] During the past four centuries there have been hundreds of English Bible translations, and dozens are actively used today. They fall into three major categories.

1) *Word-for-word translations* (also known as formal equivalence translations) emphasize the patterns of the words and seek "as far as possible to capture the precise wording of the original text and the personal style of each Bible writer. . . . Thus it seeks to be transparent to the original text, letting the reader see as directly as possible the structure and meaning of the original."[177] The result is a striving for the precision of what the Bible says, much like one would expect in other important communications, such as legal documents, marriage vows, or contracts.

Word-for-word translations have advantages for studying because of their closeness to the original, though they sometimes become a bit stilted stylistically because the biblical languages use different patterns of grammar and expression from English. The best contemporary word-for-word translation is the English Standard Version (ESV). The King James Version (KJV) is also a word-for-word translation, and remains the best-selling English translation. It sounds very reverent to many people, but it is difficult for some people to read because it uses old English. Other good word-for-word translations in modern English include the New King James Version (NKJV) and the New American Standard Bible (NASB).

2) *Thought-for-thought translations* (also known as dynamic equivalence or functional equivalence) attempt to convey the full nuance of each passage by interpreting the Scripture's entire meaning and not just the individual words. Such versions seek to find the best modern cultural equivalent that will have the same effect the original message had in its ancient cultures.

My favorite thought-for-thought modern English translation, the New International Version (NIV), is also the most popular. Others

---

[176]United Bible Society, "Statistical Summary of Languages with the Scriptures," 2008, http://www.ubs-translations.org/about_us/#c165.

[177]The Standard Bible Society, "Translation Philosophy," 2009, http://www.esv.org/translation/philosophy.

include the New Living Translation (NLT) and the Contemporary English Version (CEV).

3) *Paraphrased translations* put the emphasis on readability in English. Therefore, they pay even less attention to specific word patterns in an attempt to capture the poetic or narrative essence of a passage. Examples of paraphrased translations include The Message (MESSAGE), The Living Bible (TLB), and The Amplified Bible (AMP).

All faithful translations try to achieve a balance of four elements:

1) Accuracy to the original text as much as possible.
2) Beauty of language.
3) Clarity of meaning.
4) Dignity of style.

While some translations are better than others, it is important to note that translations have various strengths and weaknesses and that the student of Scripture benefits from enjoying multiple translations. Furthermore, rather than fighting over translations, Christians should praise God for every good translation and trust God the Holy Spirit to use them to transform our lives as we enjoy them.

Nonetheless, we would encourage you to use the English Standard Version or another good word-for-word translation as your primary study tool, while also using other translations as secondary resources for your studies. In my opinion, the English Standard Version is the best version for accurate Bible reading, studying, teaching, and preaching. Noted theologian and ESV general editor J. I. Packer reflected, "I find myself suspecting very strongly that my work on the translation of the ESV Bible was the most important thing that I have done for the Kingdom, and that the product of our labors is perhaps the biggest milestone in Bible translation in the past fifty years or more."[178]

Lastly, while Christians should enjoy multiple good translations, they must be careful of corruptions. Corruptions are "translations" of Scripture

---

[178]Crossway, "The ESV Bible Reaches Five-Year Milestone," September 26, 2006, http://www.crossway.org/page/news.2006.09.26.

that clearly seek to undermine the very teaching of Scripture. These translations are very poor and should not be used as credible translations for study. These include the Jehovah's Witness translation called the New World Translation, which was written in large part to eliminate the deity of Jesus Christ. This is in no way a translation but rather a terrible corruption of Scripture deceptively masquerading as God's Word.

HOW CAN WE BEST INTERPRET SCRIPTURE?

As someone whom God saved simply through Bible reading, I cannot overly emphasize the importance of regular Bible reading. The very best way to interpret the Bible is to read it. Many people find the Bible hard to understand because they have never really taken the time to carefully, prayerfully, and frequently read it. Therefore, you will be well served to read it in large portions as a single, unfolding story that reveals God.

The easiest place to start is by reading one of the Gospel biographies about Jesus Christ, as you would any other true story. To start, as you read it, be looking for the message of the story as a whole without getting too sidetracked with the specifics of each verse. You will discover that the Gospel biographies of Jesus' life are a continuation of the entirety of the story of Scripture. So, you will want go back and read Genesis to get the first episode. You'll see how God created a beautiful place for him to live with humans, how we ruined that world through sin, and how God began his rescue mission to save his sin-marred world. From there you can continue reading the rest of the Bible to discover the rest of the story.

As you read the Bible, you will invariably have questions about particular sections. As you seek to understand Scripture you will be doing interpretation. To help you, we recommend a four-step process for interpreting the Bible.[179]

The first question to ask is, what does the Scripture actually say? God wants to speak to you through the Bible. One error is to under-read the text, missing what is there through lack of attention. The opposite error is

---

[179]This process is adapted from Ray Lubeck, *Read the Bible for a Change: A Follower's Guide to Reading and Responding to the Bible* (Carlisle, UK: Authentic Media, 2005).

to over-read the text, putting preconceived opinions, ideas, or perspectives into the text, which is called *eisegesis*. Therefore, the goal is to humbly read the text to hear from God, which is called *exegesis*.

As you read Scripture, you will see that it comes in various literary types. One major type is narrative, texts that communicate by telling a story. This includes books such as Genesis, Samuel, and Matthew. A second is poetry, texts in which language is used for its aesthetic and evocative as well as cognitive qualities. It communicates through structures and patterns to create intellectual, emotional, and spiritual response through meaning, sound, and rhythm. This includes books such as Psalms and Proverbs and sections of books such as Genesis 15 and Romans 11:33–36. A third type is discourse, texts that communicate in a logical sequence of ideas. This includes books such as Romans, Hebrews, and Jude. Occasionally all three types of literature appear in one book. For example, Deuteronomy is mostly discourse, but chapter 32 is poetry and chapter 34 is narrative.

To avoid error, it is vitally important to be aware of the type of literature you are reading and interpreting. As one example, Mormons read poetic imagery such as, "His right hand and his holy arm have worked salvation for him,"[180] and believe that God the Father has a literal body, when the Bible is clear that "God is not man"[181] and that the Father is Spirit without a physical body.[182]

The second question is, what does the Scripture mean? In this step, you should look for what Scripture is teaching, especially in the original context. Much of the Bible was written to specific people in specific historical situations. The task is to discover that meaning and to understand the meaning of each text in its own terms, categories, and thought forms, beginning with the questions and issues the writer deals with, not the questions we bring. You will want to ask, what is the author trying to accomplish? What ideas or values is he trying to communicate? It is often helpful to write out

---

[180]Ps. 98:1.
[181]Num. 23:19.
[182]John 4:23–24.

your observations of the specifics of the text in a journal designated for personal Bible study.

The third question is, what timeless principle truths is this section of Scripture teaching that apply to all of God's people in all times and places? There are many questions to ask to find the timeless universal principle. Is the text *describing* an event or belief, or is it *prescribing* (commanding) a practice, precept, promise, or value? Sometimes the form of a command is time-bound, but the principle extends everywhere. For example, Paul's request to the Ephesians to pray for him is specific,[183] but the principle applies to believers praying for leaders in all times. Other times a culturally specific command can apply in broader terms. For example, when the Bible commands us to greet one another with a holy kiss, this makes sense in some cultures, whereas in others the principle of greeting fellow Christians warmly is most appropriately followed with a handshake or a hug, as to kiss someone would not communicate the same thing as it did in the culture the text was originally written to.[184] Also, sometimes what is described in the Bible is a negative example, because the Bible does record human sin as a warning to us. Practically, this means that just because the Bible records that David committed adultery and murder doesn't mean we should do it.

We do not believe that Christians can only do what the Bible commands. We believe that Christians should do everything the Bible commands, not do anything the Bible forbids, and where the Bible is silent, work from biblical principles, conscience, wisdom, and godly counsel to determine what should and should not be done.

Because the meaning of the Bible is for the whole church, it is essential to read it in community. The wider the community, the more likely we are to get the whole intended truth and nothing but the intended truth. For example, I (Gerry) had always read the story of the Samaritan woman as being someone who was a dreadful sinner whom Jesus graciously forgave.[185] But when I read it with some poor people from Central America,

---

[183]Eph. 6:19.
[184]Rom. 16:16; 1 Cor. 16:20; 2 Cor. 13:12; 1 Thess. 5:26; 1 Pet. 5:14.
[185]John 4.

I realized that it may be about an abused woman who had been thrown out by a succession of sinful husbands. Since women could not live alone in that culture, she was reduced to living with a man to avoid living the life of a prostitute.[186] Reading in community reveals connections each one of us would never see by ourselves. It is important to include in our interpretive community Christians not only from other nations but also from other ages. Faithful brothers and sisters from church history can greatly help us see the Scriptures more clearly, as they do not have some of our cultural assumptions.

The fourth question is, how should I respond to what God has said? Here we are seeking to understand how the Bible's teaching applies to our life individually as Christians and corporately as a church today. The Bible shares content with an intended purpose, expecting that we will respond with belief and in other ways, depending upon what it says. Sometimes we are told to repent of sin, obey God, and live according to God's command. Other times the intent of a passage is to comfort, strengthen, encourage, or build us up, and our response is to be a sense of courage, joy, or hope. In any case, we respond with our whole being, heart, soul, mind, emotions, and actions. This is exactly what James 1:22 exhorts, saying, "But be doers of the word, and not hearers only, deceiving yourselves."

HOW DOES OUR VIEW OF SCRIPTURE AFFECT OUR LIFE?

God speaks to us through the Scriptures as a perfectly loving Father. Subsequently, we listen to what Scripture says, learn what it teaches, and make every effort by the Holy Spirit's empowering grace to repent of our sin, renew our minds, and redeem our lives.

Christians worship God, not the Bible. But the Bible informs us of who God is and how he is to be worshiped and is therefore essential to our worship. As a result, we come to the Bible for transformation, not just for information. As the same Holy Spirit who inspired the Scriptures illuminates our understanding, we deeply enjoy our new life guided by our new

---

[186]Matt. 5:31–32.

wisdom of Scripture and our new power from the Holy Spirit, delighting in our new gift of repentance as part of God's kingdom people together on mission in the world for Jesus.

In summary, we agree with Luther, who affirmed, "When the Scripture speaks, God speaks." Because Scripture is God speaking to us, we memorize, meditate, study, teach, and share his truth. Everything in life and ministry is guided by the truth of Scripture. Everything good is a result of the truth of biblical revelation being used by God the Holy Spirit to change our lives so we look more like Jesus both individually as Christians and corporately as the church.

So remember: every time we read the Bible, we hear God speaking. The Bible is the standard for all doctrine and teaching, faith and practice, life and holiness. We agree with the ancient Bereans, who tested all they learned "with all eagerness, examining the Scriptures daily to see if these things were so."[187]

We passionately want this for all of you. We want the Bible in your hand, the Holy Spirit in your heart, other Christians in your life, and Jesus on your horizon, so that you can live a truly biblical life to God's glory, your joy, and others' good.

---

[187]Acts 17:11.

CHAPTER 3

CREATION: GOD MAKES

In the beginning, God created the heavens and the earth.

GENESIS 1:1

According to the Scriptures, creation is a gift from a loving Creator God. From the bodies we inhabit, the air we breathe, the sun we bask in, the food we eat, the flowers we pick, the water we drink, the ground we walk upon, and the pets we love, to the pleasures we enjoy and destinations we visit on vacation, life is filled with good gifts for us to steward and enjoy.

Christians have always believed in creation. There was little debate over the nature or date of creation until the last couple of centuries. However, science began gaining credibility through the great advances in the so-called Age of Reason (also called The Enlightenment or Modernism) developed in the eighteenth century. Science increasingly became identified with the naturalistic worldview that stood in direct opposition to the theistic worldview. Scientific evidence became a weapon used by opponents of Christianity to attack the biblical worldview. Unfortunately, many Christians began to accommodate themselves to naturalism and rationalism. Classic Christian liberalism began to dominate the church in Europe in the nineteenth century and in America going into the twentieth century. A group of biblical Christian scholars published a series of books called *The Fundamentals* in an attempt to define and defend biblical Christianity against this widespread compromise with liberalism. As the debates developed, controversies about the date and nature of creation arose among biblical Christians. Fundamentalism became defensive and suspicious of compromise, and the controversies often became acrimonious and remain so today.

It is our belief that even this controversy can be yet another gift to us from God, compelling us to more deeply ponder his creative works and thereby grow to more clearly savor his Word, see his grace, and sing his praises. Before turning to the opening pages of Genesis where creation commences, a few prefatory comments are in order.

First, there is no conflict between Christianity and science itself. This is because the Christian worldview, which believes that God created the world with natural "laws" and orderliness, is what undergirds the entire scientific enterprise. For example, inductive reasoning and the scientific method are based on the assumption of the regularity of the laws of nature. This means that scientists assume that water will boil tomorrow under the identical conditions that it does today. Without this kind of regularity, we could not learn from experience, including the experiences of scientific testing. This also helps to explain why in cultures where creation is said to be an illusion or disorderly chaos because it was not created by an orderly God, the sciences have not historically flourished; indeed, the scientific method depends upon the kind of underlying worldview that a creating and providentially ruling God of the Bible provides.

Second, there is total conflict between Christianity and scientific naturalism. Naturalism is the belief that all phenomena can be explained in terms of presently operating natural causes and laws. The only true knowledge is that which comes through observable experiments. When natural science is the arbiter of all truth claims, religion becomes superstition and God is omitted from discussion.

Third, the Bible in general, and the book of Genesis in particular, was not written with the intention of being a scientific textbook. Rather, it is a theological narrative written to reveal the God of creation, which means its emphasis is on God and his relationship with humanity and not on creation. Genesis is far more concerned with the questions of who made creation and why he made creation than exactly when he did. Therefore, as Galileo said, "The Holy Ghost intended to teach us how to go to heaven, not how the heavens go." This explains why the lengthiest treatise of creation in all of Scripture, Genesis 1 and 2, is only a few pages of our Bible. It is as if the story of Scripture opens with the panoramic view of creation, and then the camera quickly focuses in on the creation of our first parents and the history that ensues.

Fourth, one's view of the date of creation should not be the litmus test for Christian faithfulness. Within Christian theology there are open- and closed-handed issues. Biblical authority is a closed-handed issue. Christians receive what the Bible actually teaches as truth from God to be believed and obeyed. Regarding creation, anyone who claims to be a Bible-believing Christian must reject such things as the atheistic evolutionists' claims that there is no God and that creation is not a gift but rather an epic purposeless accident. Nevertheless, Bible-believing Christians, as we will explore in this chapter, can and do disagree over the open-handed issues, such as exactly how God made the heavens and the earth, whether the six days of Genesis 1–2 are literal twenty-four-hour days, and the age of the earth. These sorts of issues must remain in the open hand.

WHAT DOES THE BIBLE SAY ABOUT CREATION?

The first book of the Bible, Genesis, takes its name from its first words, "In the beginning," as *genesis* means "beginning." The book of Genesis in general, Genesis 1 to 3 in particular, records the beginning of creation and human history. Moses penned Genesis in roughly 1400 BC as the first of a five-part book called the *Pentateuch*, meaning "book in five parts." The Genesis account of creation was most likely directly revealed to Moses by the same Holy Spirit who was present in Genesis 1:2, since Moses was not present for the creation event. Genesis is not an exhaustive treatment of early history but rather a theologically selective telling of history that focuses on God and mankind while omitting such things as the creation of angels or the fall of Satan and demons.

The first line of Genesis says, "In the beginning, God created the heavens and the earth."[1] The two subsequent chapters of the Bible are devoted to speaking about creation. Brilliantly, the Bible opens with the one true, eternal God as both the author and subject of history and Scripture. Consequently, everything else in history and Scripture is dependent upon God and is only good when functioning according to his intentions for it from creation.

Only in the last few decades has undeniable evidence forced the natural sciences reluctantly to agree with what Scripture has always taught: the universe had a beginning. It is an amazing testimony to the truth of Scripture. The opening phrase, "In the beginning," speaks of an inauguration of a history, a space and a time when the Lord worked. Implicitly, it anticipates an end, a time when he will bring history to an end and create a new heavens and a new earth.[2]

In Genesis 1:1, the word used for *created* is the Hebrew word *bara*, which means "creation from nothing." The other Hebrew word used in a creative sense in Genesis is *asah*, translated "make" or "made,"[3] which means "to fashion or shape," or "to make something suitable," such as making loincloths out of fig leaves[4] or making the ark.[5] *Bara* emphasizes the initiation of an object, whereas *asah* emphasizes the shaping of an object. Along with statements where God does initial creation (the heavens and the earth[6]), the only other things *bara*'d are the living creatures[7] and human beings.[8] When people create we are doing *asah*, not *bara*. We can take things that God has given us such as seed and land to plant crops and harvest food, but in so doing we

---

[1]Gen. 1:1.
[2]Isa. 65:17; 2 Pet. 3:13; Rev. 21:1.
[3]This very common word is used in the creative sense in Gen. 1:7, 16, 25, 26, 31; 2:2, 3, 4, 18; Pss. 86:9; 95:5; 96:5.
[4]Gen. 3:7.
[5]Gen. 8:6.
[6]Gen. 1:1; 2:3, 4.
[7]Gen. 1:21.
[8]Gen. 1:27; 5:1, 2.

are not creating food from nothing but rather creating it from the gifts given to us by God in creation.

In the creation account we see that God created (*bara*) "the heavens and the earth." This phrase could be more literally translated "the skies and the land," since the heavens are not the place where God lives, but the place where stars move[9] and birds fly.[10] The Hebrew word *eretz*, usually translated "earth," in Genesis 1 does not mean the planet but the land under the water,[11] separated from water,[12] where vegetation grows[13] and animals roam.[14] Elsewhere in Scripture it usually means the Promised Land. The phrase "skies and land" is a Hebraic way of saying "everything"[15] from the skies above to the earth below, like saying from top to bottom or head to toe, including space-time, mass-energy, and the laws that govern them. In other places in Scripture, the phrase includes the sun and moon, which could in turn mean that the sun and moon were created as a part of this first creation.[16]

The skies and the land are "without form and void"[17] before God prepared them for humans. Ancient Greek cosmology said that what originally existed was essentially a formless hunk of mud, which God then formed from chaos into cosmos. This ideology has had great sway in many Christian interpretations of Genesis 1:2, including the first English translation of the Bible overseen by William Tyndale, which translated it as "void and empty," thereby sadly setting in motion a precedent for many future Bible translations and Bible commentators, including Martin Luther.[18]

However, the same language for "without form (*tohu*) and void (*bohu*)" used in Genesis 1:2 is used elsewhere in Scripture in reference to uninhabited land. Examples include Deuteronomy 32:10, which speaks of "a desert land, and in the howling waste (*tohu*) of the wilderness." Isaiah 45:18 says that

---

[9]Gen. 1:14.
[10]Gen. 1:21.
[11]Gen. 1:2.
[12]Gen. 1:10.
[13]Gen. 1:11–12.
[14]Gen. 1:20–24.
[15]Isa. 44:24; 65:17; Jer. 10:10–16; Eph. 3:9; Col. 1:16–17; Rev. 21:1.
[16]Isa. 13:10; Joel 3:15–16.
[17]Gen. 1:2.
[18]See Martin Luther, "Lectures on Genesis Chapters 1–5," in *Luther's Works,* American Edition, 55 vols. ed. Jaroslav Pelikan and Helmut T. Lehmann (Philadelphia: Muehlenberg and Fortress; St. Louis: Concordia, 1955–1986), 1:6.

God "formed the earth and made it (he established it; he did not create [*bara*] it empty [*tohu*], he formed it to be inhabited!)." Perhaps the closest parallel is Jeremiah 4:23, where God prophesied the future state of Judah, a nation doomed to exile by its sin: "I looked on the earth, and behold, it was without form and void; and to the heavens, and they had no light." Here, "without form and void" does not mean chaos, but it means empty of humans; "no light" does not mean there is no sun but that the land is without God's blessing. Similarly, in Genesis 1:2 "without form and void" is the condition of the land before God made it good, filling it with light and life. The best understanding is not that God created primordial chaos and formed earth out of it, but that God created everything out of nothing and that the land existed for some unstated period of time in a desert-like, empty state. The dawn of God's light signals the arrival of his blessing. Then, God took six literal days to prepare the land for human habitation, as recorded in Genesis 1–2. This work is forming (*asah*) already-existing material, not creating (*bara*) from nothing. Historically, this is also the teaching of Augustine.

The creation of heavens and earth in the first verse is a concrete, historical, scientific fact. But the text simply does not tell us when it happened, only that it was sometime before the preparation of the land for humans to dwell with God. "In the beginning" means that there was an inauguration, but not when that moment was. Therefore, Genesis 1:1 leaves open both the possibilities of a young and an old earth.

The creation account goes to great lengths to make it clear that the God who created (*bara*) everything according to the first verse is the same God who prepared (*asah*) the land for humans to dwell with him in the remainder of Genesis 1 and 2. The God of creation is also the God of covenant relation.

WHERE DID CREATION COME FROM?

The opening line of Scripture clearly reveals that creation comes from God.[19] Genesis 1 and 2 further reveal God as a prophet who both made

---

[19] Gen. 1:1.

creation and prepared it for us solely by the power of his word. This is indicated by the repeated phrases, "And God said" and "Let there be" or "Let the . . ."[20] When God spoke, creation obeyed his command, as is repeatedly demonstrated by the phrase "And it was so." After each act of creating, God pronounced the perfect and sinless nature of his creation with the phrase "And God saw that it was good." Therefore, creation came not from preexisting matter but rather out of nothing, by God's word.

The Bible teaches that God made creation *ex nihilo* (Latin for "out of nothing") in Hebrews 11:3, which says, "By faith we understand that the universe was created by the word of God, so that what is seen *was not made out of things that are visible*." This doctrine is important because it negates the possibility of naturalistic evolution and an eternal universe. While God did not make creation from any preexisting matter or the proverbial hunk of mud, creation did come into existence and was prepared for human inhabitation by the powerful word of God.

It is curious that God did not create from nothing on each of the six days of creation. Still, God did speak as both a prophet and poet on each day. Furthermore, there is a set pattern to God's words in Genesis 1. It is as follows:

1) Announcement: "And God said."
2) Commandment: "Let there be."
3) Separation: God separated the day and night, water and land, animals and plants.
4) Report: "And it was so."
5) Evaluation: "And God saw that it was good."

In this pattern we see that God's word is living, active, and powerful, and that it accomplishes what he decrees. Later, God explicitly declares this fact to Isaiah: "So shall my word be that goes out from my mouth; it shall not return to me empty, but it shall accomplish that which I purpose,

---

[20]Gen. 1:3, 6, 9, 11, 14, 20, 24, 26.

and shall succeed in the thing for which I sent it."[21] The rest of Scripture confirms that creation was prepared for us by God's powerful word.[22]

Indeed, Genesis 1 portrays God's word as the most powerful force in all of creation. God's word brings order, makes things good, creates an environment in which life can exist, separates things, comes with unparalleled authority, and accomplishes exactly what God intends. Therefore, we are not to dismiss, disdain, or distort God's word, as it is the source of life.

In summary, God brought creation out of nothing and prepared it for us because he cares for us. Because of this, in Jeremiah 10:16 we read, "Not like these is he who is the portion of Jacob, for *he is the one who formed all things*, and Israel is the tribe of his inheritance; the LORD of hosts is his name." As Francis Schaeffer pointed out about this verse, creation was made and lovingly prepared for us by a loving and personal "he," not an impersonal, unloving "it."

WHAT DOES CREATION REVEAL ABOUT GOD?

Genesis 1:1 reveals that "in the beginning, God created." In the same way that a piece of music reveals something of the composer, and artwork reveals something of the artist, so too creation reveals something of the Creator. In this way, creation is a form of general revelation.[23] Therefore, examining creation reveals fourteen glorious truths about God as Creator.

1) *God is the only God.* The opening line of the Bible does not say, for example, "In the beginning, nothing made everything," or, "In the beginning, Creator and creation were one and the same as they had been throughout eternity," or even, "In the beginning, the gods made the heavens and the earth." No, the opening line of the Bible reveals, "In the beginning, God created." Likewise, Isaiah 45:18 says, "For thus says the LORD, who created the heavens (he is God!), who formed the earth and made it . . . 'I am the LORD, and there is no other.'"

---

[21]Isa. 55:11.
[22]Pss. 33:6, 9; 148:5; 2 Pet. 3:7.
[23]Ps. 19:1–2; Rom. 1:20.

2) *God is Trinitarian.*[24] Genesis 1:26 reveals that the Creator God is the Trinity: "Then God said, 'Let *us* make man in *our* image, after *our* likeness.'" Therefore, when Genesis says that God is the creator, it speaks of the entire Trinity. This fact is confirmed in the rest of Scripture, where it is revealed that the Father created,[25] the Son created,[26] and the Spirit created.[27]

3) *God is eternally uncaused.* This means that God eternally existed before creation, that God is not created, and that creation is not eternal.

4) *God is living.* Life in general and human life in particular does not spring forth from the "it" of unliving matter. Rather, God is living and he makes life and, as we will see in the next chapter, he breathes his life into human beings to give us life.

5) *God is independent.* While the rest of creation is dependent upon God, God himself is uncaused, independent, and without need, lack, want, or dependence upon anyone or anything. Everything apart from God is created by God and dependent upon God so that it simply would not have come into existence or continue to exist without God. This is precisely what Paul preached on Mars Hill: "The God who made the world and everything in it, being Lord of heaven and earth, does not live in temples made by man, nor is he served by human hands, as though he needed anything, since he himself gives to all mankind life and breath and everything."[28] Because God is independent, he alone can truly and purely love; since he does not need us, his interactions with us alone are of pure motive.

6) *God is transcendent.* God is separate from his creation. There is a clear demarcation between Creator and creation that does not exist in pantheism, panentheism, radical environmentalism, Wicca, or the New Spirituality.

7) *God is immanent.* Not only is God transcendent over creation, but contrary to the deists' claim, he is also actively at work in his creation, sustaining and providentially ruling over it.

---

[24]We discussed this topic in further detail in chapter 1.
[25]Ps. 19:1; Acts 17:28; 1 Cor. 8:6.
[26]John 1:1–3, 10; Col. 1:16–17.
[27]Gen. 1:2; Job 26:13.
[28]Acts 17:24–25.

8) *God is personal.* Because God is personal, he made mankind in a personal way and gives to us personality and personhood. God is a personal "he," not an impersonal "it." Apart from a personal God, there is no way to explain human personhood.

9) *God is powerful.* In creation, God's power is seen in that he made everything from nothing by himself and that he rules over creation, even suspending natural laws as he wills to perform miracles.

10) *God is beautiful.* Whereas God could have created air filtration machines, he instead chose to create trees. Whereas God could have chosen to cast creation in black and white, he instead chose to paint from a vast palette of colors. Why? Because God is gloriously beautiful, and creation reflects his beauty with ceaseless displays of breathtaking splendor that cause us to rightly feel in the presence of something sacred so as to create in us wonder and worship.

11) *God is holy.* God is without evil, and creation originally reflected his holy purity until it was marred and stained by human sin. Our holy God moves in his sin-marred creation to make it pure. In re-creation, God will again restore all creation to a holy state, when he lifts the curse and removes its effects forever.

12) *God is a prophet.* It was through speaking that God brought creation into existence by his word. Similarly, God also kindly uses the preaching of his Word to bring forth life.

13) *God is gracious.* We see the grace of God in creation as he blesses his creation, including the man and woman whom he makes in his image and likeness. From the opening pages of Scripture to its final line in Revelation 22:20–21, God speaks words of grace, saying, "'Surely I am coming soon.' Amen. Come, Lord Jesus! The grace of the Lord Jesus be with all. Amen."

14) *God is a sovereign king.* As creator, God is king over all that is made, including Satan, demons, mankind, planets, stars, suns, moons, animals, and so on. All of creation comes from God, is ruled over by God, belongs to God, and will give an account before God. As King of kings,

God our creator is far superior to any false tribal, local, or trade deity worshiped around the world.

In sum, we see that God is not a faceless intelligent designer of the universe, but the living Lord, Yahweh, who alone created everything so we could live in loving relation with him now and forever. From the first words of the Bible, the Lord is distinguished from the gods of the nations. The other gods—demons, really—are created beings that can't create anything.[29] They are imaged by dead idols while God is imaged by living humans he created for loving relationship with him now and forever.

WHAT ARE THE VARIOUS CHRISTIAN VIEWS OF CREATION?

Among Bible-believing Christians there are currently at least six primary interpretations of the creation account in Genesis 1 and 2. Personally, we find the first view to be the most persuasive biblically. But, as Paul says, we now see only in part, and one day in Jesus' presence we will know in full, and we will all be in complete agreement on this and other matters. Until that day, may we worship our Creator together and graciously discuss and debate our differences without unnecessarily dividing over them.

View 1: Historic Creationism

The word used for "beginning" in Genesis 1:1 is *re'shit* in Hebrew, which marks a starting point for what comes afterwards. It does not connote any specific length of time, nor does it necessarily mean that the next thing stated follows immediately. What God created in the first verse existed for an undefined period of time (which could be anywhere from a moment to billions of years) before God began the work of preparing the uninhabitable land for the habitation of mankind. The preparation of the uncultivated land and the creation of Adam and Eve occurred in the six literal twenty-four-hour days of Genesis 1, as echoed in Exodus 20:11. This view leaves

---

[29]Deut. 32:17; 1 Cor. 10:19–21; Col. 1:16.

open the possibility of an old earth, six literal days of creation, and a young humanity on the old earth.[30]

View 2: Young-earth Creationism

In this view, God created the entire universe, including Adam and Eve, in six literal twenty-four-hour days. As it seeks to be faithful to its reading of the biblical text, this view affirms that the entire universe is less than ten thousand years old. It interprets the data of science in terms of inspired Scripture, refusing to compromise God's teaching about the date and divine methods of creation with naturalistic scientific theories. It does have some biblical difficulties, such as the creation of sun and moon on day four while there is evening and morning on the first three days.

View 3: The Gap Theory

In this view, Genesis 1:1 explains a first creation that happened perhaps billions of years ago. Then, a catastrophic event, likely the fall of Satan from heaven, left the earth in the destroyed condition of Genesis 1:2. God responded to this disaster by re-creating the earth again a few thousand years later in six literal days and repopulating the earth as recorded in Genesis 1:3–27. According to this view, the earth is old from the first creation and mankind is young because of the recent creation. The problems with this view include the fact that nothing in the Bible speaks of two creations, one prior to Genesis 1:2 and the other more recently. Also, at the end of the six days of creation, God declared all that he had made "very good," which does not correlate with the claim that the earth had been made "very bad" and destroyed.

View 4: Literary Framework View

In this view, Genesis 1 and 2 are intended to be read as a figurative framework explaining creation in a topical, not sequential, order. The six days of

---

[30]Historic creationism is best articulated by John Sailhamer in *Genesis Unbound: A Provocative New Look at the Creation Account* (Sisters, OR: Multnomah, 1996), esp. pp. 44–45, and *The Pentateuch as Narrative* (Grand Rapids, MI: Zondervan, 1992), 81–100. His insights on the Pentateuch, in general, and Genesis, in particular, are brilliantly perceptive.

creation listed in Genesis 1 are also to be interpreted metaphorically, not as literal twenty-four-hour days. The literary framework view is outlined here:

Forming	**Filling**
Day 1: light and darkness separated	Day 4: sun, moon, stars (lights in heaven)
Day 2: sky and waters separated	Day 5: fish and birds
Day 3: dry land and waters separated; plants and trees	Day 6: animals and man

Admittedly, God speaks of creation creatively by including poetry in the creation account of Genesis 1 and 2. Still, even when the Bible uses figurative and poetic language, it does so to communicate a literal truth, a fact that weakens this view.

View 5: Day-Age View

In this view, God created the universe, including Adam and Eve, in six sequential periods of time that are geologic ages, not literal twenty-four-hour days. The biggest problem with this view is that the order of events in the six days is not the same order as held by old-earth science (for example, the sun appears on day four). Another problem with this view is that the six days of creation seem clearly to be literal days, as we will further explore.

View 6: Theistic Evolution

In this view, God essentially began creation and then pulled back from working directly in creation to work instead through the natural process of evolution. The only exception was God involving himself directly again in the making of the human spirit. For the most part, this view accepts the hypothesis of evolution but seeks to insert God as the creator of matter and overseer of the evolutionary process.

The problems with theistic evolution are many, but we will look at three briefly. First, it inherits all the scientific impossibilities of evolution as a theory of origins. Second, evolution teaches that one species evolves into other species, while Genesis 1 says that each species had offspring "according to its kind,"[31] not another kind, as evolution postulates. The scientific data completely agrees with Genesis on the impossibility of one species evolving into another. Third, the rest of Scripture portrays God as continually involved in the details of creation, including making the grass grow,[32] feeding the birds,[33] and feeding other creatures.[34] Scripture clearly does not paint God as remote or only indirectly involved in creation.

ARE THE SIX DAYS OF CREATION LITERAL TWENTY-FOUR-HOUR DAYS?

While the six Christian views of creation listed above are possible, the question remains, which is probable? To answer that question, we have to deal with the very important issue of whether the six days of creation listed in Genesis 1 are in fact literal twenty-four-hour days. If someone believes that the six days of creation are literal twenty-four-hour days, then they must accept one of the first three views of creation (historic creationism, young-earth creationism, or the gap theory); if they do not believe that the six days of creation are literal twenty-four-hour days, then they can accept one of the last three views of creation (the literary framework view, the day-age view, or theistic evolution).

Those Christians who argue for a metaphorical view of the six days of creation rightly point out that the word used for *day* in Hebrew (*yom*), often refers to an extended period of time that is more than a literal twenty-four-hour day.[35] Nonetheless, if we read the Scriptures, it seems apparent that the six days of creation in Genesis 1 are literal twenty-four-hour days for two reasons.

First, each day is numbered so that there is a succession of days. Further, each day is described as having a morning and evening, which

---

[31]Gen. 1:21, 24, 25.
[32]Ps. 104:14; Matt. 6:30.
[33]Matt. 6:26.
[34]Ps. 104:21, 25–30.
[35]E.g., Ps. 20:1; Prov. 11:4; 21:31; 24:10; 25:13; Eccles. 7:14.

is the common vernacular for a day.[36] These details in Genesis 1 clearly indicate that the days are literal.

Second, in Exodus 20:8–11, God says:

> Remember the Sabbath day, to keep it holy. Six days you shall labor, and do all your work, but the seventh day is a Sabbath to the LORD your God. On it you shall not do any work, you, or your son, or your daughter, your male servant, or your female servant, or your livestock, or the sojourner who is within your gates. For in six days the LORD made heaven and earth, the sea, and all that is in them, and rested on the seventh day. Therefore the LORD blessed the Sabbath day and made it holy.

God says that he made creation in six days and on the seventh day he rested. Additionally, his work and rest are to be the precedent for us; his example explains why God's people in the Old Testament had a seven-day week with a Sabbath day.

We hold to historic creationism, which emphasizes that the first two chapters of Genesis, God's inspired and inerrant Word, tell us that the God who created everything (angels, space-time, mass-energy, sun, moon, and stars, and all species of animals) prepared the land for human habitation in six literal twenty-four-hour days. At the end of those days, he shaped dust and breathed the breath of life into it, creating Adam. From Adam's rib, God created the woman. They were created to be in relationship with each other and with God as living Creator and loving Lord.

Nonetheless, there have been ongoing debates by Jesus-loving, Bible-believing scholars throughout the history of the church regarding whether the days of creation were literal twenty-four-hour days. So long as one's position on this issue does not become the litmus test for Christian orthodoxy, ongoing spirited study and discussion can be helpful to God's people; it can force them to build their unity around what they do agree on, such as the fact that the Trinitarian God of the Bible created the heavens and the

---

[36]Gen. 1:5, 8, 13, 19, 23, 31.

earth and lovingly fashioned them as a gift to us and home for us in which to worship and enjoy him.[37]

HOW OLD IS THE EARTH?

There has been no shortage of attempts to determine and defend a particular age of the earth.

For many Christians, the Bible's teaching seems pretty simple: the earth was created on the first of the six twenty-four-hour days of Genesis, which culminated with the creation of Adam, the first human. Adding up the genealogies in Genesis puts the age of the earth at about six thousand years.

Other Christians, ancient and contemporary, have not seen the creation account in strict historical terms. They focus on God as creator rather than on six literal days and think we should not try to specify the date of the earth.

Still others seek to integrate the general scientific consensus—that the earth is around 4.5 billion years old—into their theology. They adapt their view of the Bible to accommodate science and teach that the earth must be old.

Archbishop James Ussher dated creation precisely to 4004 BC. According to traditional Judaism, the year AD 2010 is actually year 5,770 of creation. The Jewish year of creation is Gregorian year 3761 BC. Both Ussher and Jews used the biblical genealogies (e.g., Genesis 5 and 10) and added up the number of years between Adam, Noah, and Abraham to arrive at their creation dates. That they differ somewhat on their dates indicates the difficulty of achieving high accuracy. Still, the method cannot be merely dismissed if one holds to inspired and inerrant Scripture. Jews, Ussher, and many Christians agree within a couple hundred years because of the precision of the genealogies in Genesis 5 and 11. They differ from the genealogies of Jesus in Matthew 1 and Luke 3, which show line of descent rather than specific lengths of time in each generation. The Genesis

---

[37]E.g., see Westminster Theological Seminary's statement regarding the days of creation: http://www. wts.edu/about/ beliefs/statements/creation.html.

genealogies do not have large gaps. If one follows Scripture, Adam, the first human, was created about six thousand years ago.

However, believing in a recent Adam does not require a young earth. If one sees the days other than six twenty-four-hour days, then the age of the earth is not a biblical teaching. Those who agree with us that the Genesis days are twenty-four-hours long still may not hold that Scripture mandates a young earth. The creation of planet earth may not have been during those six days.

Many believe that Genesis 1:1 is a brief summary of an unspecified period of time—perhaps a minute or billions of years, since the Hebrew word for *beginning*, like its English translation, refers to inauguration rather than to a specific timeframe—that preceded the six literal days of Genesis during which God prepared Eden on the already-created earth as the dwelling place of mankind.

In the end, we believe the date of the earth cannot be a closed-handed issue. It seems to us that those who strongly advocate either young- or old-earth dates are inferring a position from the Bible that the Bible simply does not state unequivocally. It must also be admitted that the age of the earth is not of great concern in the Bible. The great authors of the Bible, including David, Isaiah, and Paul, and Jesus himself, never referred to the age of the earth, even though they asserted God as Creator.

As Augustine rightly said, the Bible is not a scientific textbook seeking to answer the ever-changing inquiries of science but rather a theological textbook seeking to reveal God and the means by which he saves us. What the Bible actually teaches is inerrant truth from God that must be believed, but it does not teach everything we want to know. We must be courageous to receive and teach unashamedly what it does say as closed-handed issues[38] but humble enough to let unclear and unrevealed matters be open-handed issues, avoiding unprofitable controversies.[39]

The question persists as to how we deal with the widespread scientific consensus that the earth is 4.5 billion years old and certainly appears to be

[38]2 Tim. 2:15; 3:16–17; Titus 1:9; Jude 3.
[39]Deut. 29:29; 2 Tim. 2:23; Titus 3:9.

old, even to nonscientists. Many solutions have been offered, including the following:

1) Though the earth appears old to most scientists, it is in fact young, and the scientists are simply mistaken. Admittedly, Christians who hold this view are considered unscientific and even unintelligent by the watching world, but they retort that it is better to believe Scripture than the ever-changing theories of scientists.

2) The earth appears old because it was made mature, like Adam was. If we had seen Adam and Eve just after they were created (remember, they were mature enough to be commanded to be fruitful and rule the earth), and asked them how old they were, we would have been astonished at their answer.

3) The flood in Genesis 6 to 9 covered the earth universally, which compressed the geological layers and rearranged the topography so greatly that the earth appears to be old, especially when we assume geologic processes take long periods of time.

4) The earth is in fact old, and the days mentioned in Genesis 1 and 2 are not literal twenty-four-hour days but rather extended periods of time.

5) The earth may be, or likely is, old. As our examination of Genesis 1:1 revealed, God created the earth during an indefinite period of time before the six days of Genesis. That could in fact have been billions of years ago, which would explain the seemingly old age of the earth. Then, in six literal days God prepared the earth for the creation of mankind and on the sixth day made the first man and woman.

We find this last view quite compelling for five reasons. (1) It maintains a literal six-day interpretation of Genesis 1, which seems to be the point of the chapter. (2) It defines key terms biblically rather than scientifically. The word translated "heavens" is better understood as "skies"; "earth" (planet) as "land" (Promised Land); and "without form and void" (primordial chaos) as "uninhabited." (3) It teaches that the first humans appeared recently. (4) It was the most common view of early Christians, such as Augustine, and did not fall out of favor until the rise of modern science. (5) It correlates with the findings of the scientific world from a biblical worldview. The teachings of the Bible always have priority in our theologizing, but of the possible biblical views, we prefer a view that explains the most data with the fewest difficulties.

While there is great debate about the age of the earth, there is much more agreement between the biblical and scientific data on the age of the first true *Homo sapiens*, that is, true humans who lived in villages and practiced agriculture. Scientists generally date the origin of true *Homo sapiens* to less than ten thousand years ago, even as they date other human-like beings much older. Even those people who are committed to naturalistic evolution and an old earth agree with the biblical data that, while the earth may be old, human life as we know it is relatively young. Their studies are now concluding that there was a first human female ("mitochondrial Eve") and a first human male ("Y-chromosomal Adam"). These two original humans are genetically unconnected to other *Homo* species such as *Homo neanderthalensis* and *Homo erectus*. Therefore, even the most conservative Bible scholars and the most unbelieving naturalistic scientists agree that human life as we know it is, at most, roughly ten thousand years old.

HOW DOES CREATIONISM DIFFER FROM NATURALISM?

Naturalism views creation as merely the product of time, energy, and chance. As Carl Sagan famously said, "The Cosmos is all that is or ever was or ever will be."[40] Or, to say it another way, the ultimate explanation of everything from life to love is to be found in particle physics, string theory, and whatever governs the elements of the material world, as there is nothing beyond the physical world and its atoms.

Likely the most famous proponent of naturalism is Charles Darwin (1809–1892). Darwin was an English naturalist who founded the modern theory of evolution. He published his proposal in the 1859 book *On the Origin of Species by Means of Natural Selection, or the Preservation of Favoured Races in the Struggle for Life*. The lengthy original title is

---

[40]Carl Sagan, *Cosmos* (New York: Random House, 1980), 1.

often shortened to *On the Origin of Species*, both because of its length and racist overtones. While it seems that Darwin never disbelieved in the existence of a God of some kind, his evolutionary theory has been used in an effort to explain the origin of life apart from God. In fact, atheist Richard Dawkins says that "although atheism might have been *logically* tenable before Darwin, Darwin made it possible to be an intellectually fulfilled atheist."[41]

As Christians we are free to accept the seemingly self-evident fact of micro-evolution—that species can and do adapt to their environments. In fact, micro-evolution may be simply yet another evidence of the goodness and mercy of God upon his creation, since it helps a species adapt to its environment so as to help protect it from predators. However, Christians are not free to accept the yet unproven and highly suspect thesis of naturalistic and atheistic macro-evolution—that one species can evolve into another species entirely.

Although it reigned as the dominant paradigm for over one hundred years, Darwin's theory of evolution has recently come under intense criticism by both Christian and non-Christian scientists who have been persuaded by what has come to be known as "intelligent design." Even Antony Flew, the preeminent philosopher of atheism, abandoned his failed theory in 2004.[42] The reasons for the decline of confidence in macro-evolution are many, but the following are some of the most implausible leaps of faith that macro-evolution makes, all of which require at least as much faith as believing in an eternal creator God.

1) Macro-evolution purports that nothing made everything. Sometimes this claim goes by the term *spontaneous generation*. Essentially, no-thing causes every-thing to spring into existence, although this is not considered a miracle because there is no God. Francis Collins, head of the Human Genome Project, says, "I can't imagine how nature, in this case the universe, could have created itself. And the very fact that the universe had a

---

[41]Richard Dawkins, *The Blind Watchmaker* (New York: Norton, 1996), 6, emphasis in original.
[42]Antony Flew, *There Is a God: How the World's Most Notorious Atheist Changed His Mind* (New York: HarperCollins, 2007).

beginning implies that someone was able to begin it. And it seems to me that had to be outside of nature."[43]

Macro-evolution is put in a quandary between the undeniable evidence that the universe had a beginning and the equally undeniable principle that nothing comes from nothing.

Most naturalistic and atheistic scientists give credence to the big bang theory, which states that there was some sort of powerful explosion of sorts that set in motion events that in time led to the formation of the world as we know it; thus, the big bang accounts for the continual expanding of the universe. Stephen Hawking wrote: "Almost everyone now believes that the universe, and time itself, had a beginning at the big bang."[44] While Christians would call this Big God rather than big bang, the point in either case is that the universe is not eternal but had a beginning.

In desperation to avoid the quandary of a universe with a beginning, they speculate that there might be an infinite number of invisible parallel universes stretching back into eternity, without a shred of evidence to support their imagining. How can they criticize Christians for being people of blind faith? We have all the historical evidence for Jesus and his resurrection to support our faith, while they have absolutely nothing for their mythology.

2) Macro-evolution purports that chaos made order. The basic telling of the history of the universe according to atheistic naturalism is that the orderliness of our universe is the result of cataclysmic disorder, chaos, and chance that together resulted in great orderliness. As a general rule, our life experiences confirm to us that great chaos and disorder do not, in and of themselves, lead to harmonious order. On this point, the astronomer Fred Hoyle "claimed that the probability of life arising on earth (by purely natural means, without special divine aid) is less than the probability that a flight-worthy Boeing 747 should be assembled by a hurricane roaring through a junkyard."[45]

---

[43]Steve Paulson, "The Believer," interview with Francis Collins, *Salon.com*, 3, http://salon.com/books/int/2006/08/07/collins/index2.html.

[44]Stephen Hawking and Roger Penrose, *The Nature of Space and Time* (Princeton, NJ: Princeton University Press, 1996), 20.

[45]Quoted in Alvin Plantinga, "The Dawkins Confusion," *Books & Culture* 13 (March/April 2007): 21.

Additionally, Stephen Hawking has said, "The odds against a universe like ours emerging out of something like the big bang are enormous. I think there are clearly religious implications."[46] Furthermore, Hawking admitted, "It would be very difficult to explain why the universe would have begun in just this way except as the act of a God who intended to create beings like us."[47]

The *teleological argument* (*telos* means "purpose" or "design") seeks to convince from the amazing harmony in all of creation that the world has been ordered by an Intelligent Designer who is God. In its simple form, the argument contends that when we see something that is designed, we rightly assume that an intelligent designer created it. Further, the more complicated something is, the more intelligent the designer must have been.

Classic advocates of the teleological argument from design include Christian philosophers Thomas Aquinas (1225–1274) and William Paley (1734–1805). Paley's watchmaker analogy stated that if you came across something as complex as a watch, you would rightly assume that an intelligent designer made it. Likewise, as we walk through the world, we continually encounter things made with far greater complexity than a watch, such as the eye you are using to read these words. Biochemistry professor Michael Behe made similar points in his argument for "irreducible complexity": that certain biological systems, like an eye, are too complex to have evolved from simpler predecessors.[48] They had to come into existence as complete systems. Therefore, we are logically compelled to believe that these things were intelligently designed by God.

In recent decades, the "fine-tuning argument" has also gained prominence as a form of the teleological argument. Proponents note that these basic physical constants must fall within very narrow limits if intelligent life is to develop. For example, our world's constant gravitational force, the rate of universe expansion, the average distance between stars, the nature

---

[46]Quoted in Francis S. Collins, *The Language of God: A Scientist Presents Evidence for Belief* (New York: Free Press, 2006), 75.

[47]Ibid.

[48]See Michael J. Behe, *Darwin's Black Box: The Biochemical Challenge to Evolution* (New York: Free Press, 2006).

of gravity, earth's distance from the sun, earth's rotation period, and even our carbon dioxide levels are so finely tuned for life on our planet that no logical explanation other than God is tenable. Collins says:

> When you look from the perspective of a scientist at the universe, it looks as if it knew we were coming. There are 15 constants—the gravitational constant, various constants about the strong and weak nuclear forces, etc.—that have precise values. If any one of those constants was off by even one part in a million, or in some cases, by one part in a million million, the universe could not have actually come to the point where we see it. Matter would not have been able to coalesce, there would have been no galaxy, stars, planets, or people.[49]

Even our own human bodies support this argument. Further findings in science continually increase our understanding of the wondrous complexity of the human body, including the fact that just one human DNA molecule holds roughly the same amount of information as one volume of an encyclopedia.

3) Macro-evolution purports that impersonal matter made personal humanity. Naturalists have reasoned that in addition to the material world, immaterial things such as emotions and intelligence are simply the result of impersonal, unfeeling, and unintelligent matter. Yet, this entire proposal defies logic. How can matter that does not feel create people who weep? How can matter that does not think create not only the physical organ of the brain but the mental thoughts that accompany it? How can impersonal matter create a person with an identity and personality?

Indeed, the burden of proof is on the naturalist to explain the untenable, whereas the Christian simply states the biblical fact that our personal, passionate, and infinitely brilliant God made us with bits of his glory in our heart, mind, and personality. Furthermore, if our views of justice and morality were nothing more than neurochemistry hardwired into us, then we would lose the right to be morally outraged at such things as genocide,

---

[49]Steve Paulson, "The Believer."

rape, murder, and racism. When we deny the dignity of humanity as created in God's image, we saw off the branch upon which we sit to defend it.

4) Macro-evolution purports that evolution happened over long periods of time without transitional forms in the fossil record. If evolution were true, there would be numerous transitional forms of human life in the fossil record that would, to some degree, reflect the evolutionary chart that many were subjected to growing up in school. Yet, the absence of transitional fossil forms is simply yet another evidence of the fact that macro-evolution did not occur.

5) Macro-evolution purports to be unbiased science. Still, after one hundred years of attempts to replicate macro-evolution, all efforts have been in vain. Further, the atheistic naturalists continue to resist any evidence for the hand of God in the making of the world. This is, as Romans 1:18 states, because they suppress the truth due to hardness of heart against God. As Harvard professor Richard Lewontin said, "We are forced by our *a priori* adherence to material causes to create an apparatus of investigation and a set of concepts that produce material explanations."[50] He continues to insist that this "materialism is absolute, for we cannot allow a divine foot in the door."[51]

In addition, Nobel laureate Steven Weinberg says, "I personally feel that the teaching of modern science is corrosive of religious belief, and I'm all for that!"[52] He goes on to say:

> From my own point of view, I can hope that this long sad story will come to an end at some time in the future and that this progression of priests and ministers and rabbis and ulamas and imams and bonzes and bodhisattvas will come to an end, that we'll see no more of them. I hope that this is something to which science can contribute and if it is, then I think it may be the most important contribution that we can make.[53]

---

[50]Richard Lewontin, "Billions and Billions of Demons," *The New York Review of Books*, January 9, 1997, 150.
[51]Ibid.
[52]"Free People from Superstition," *Freethought Today*, April 2000, http://www.ffrf.org/fttoday/2000/april2000/weinberg.html.
[53]Ibid.

Yet, if all we are is simply the result of time and chance, and our thoughts are no more than the random collision of matter, why should we trust our minds to tell us anything truthful or to be a trustworthy guide in scientific discovery? On this point, the prominent atheistic philosopher Thomas Nagel asks if we can have any "continued confidence in reason as a source of knowledge about the nonapparent character of the world? In itself, I believe an evolutionary story tells against such confidence."[54]

Indeed, there is no conflict between science and Christian faith. However, there is a conflict between Christianity and atheistic naturalism, which refuses to follow the truth wherever it leads expressly because it leads to a belief in God. Because of these reasons, as well as its clear conflict with Scripture, Christians should reject atheistic naturalism and the teachings it offers to explain the universe apart from God as both flawed science and aberrant theology.

Christians should not, however, in any way abandon the sciences; instead, they should pursue them with great vigor and faith to learn more about God through what he has made as an act of worship to him.[55]

Tragically, there has been much misreporting about the historical relationship between Christianity and science. Thus, we want to refute some powerful yet untrue myths that have caused some to wrongly see Christianity as suppressing the truth while science pursues it.[56]

The first myth is that, prior to Christopher Columbus's first voyage, people thought the world was flat. The truth is that, more than eight hundred years before Columbus's voyage, Bede the church historian taught that the earth was round, as did Thomas Aquinas. Furthermore, Sacrobosco's book *De Sphaera*, written around 1231, was the standard manual for elementary

---

[54]Thomas Nagel, *The Last Word* (New York: Oxford University Press, 1997), 135.

[55]Francis Collins is an example of a Christian doing just that. In the same year that atheist Richard Dawkins published *The God Delusion* (Boston: Houghton Mifflin Harcourt, 2006), Collins published *The Language of God*. Collins is an eminent research scientist and head of the Human Genome Project. In his book he speaks about how his study of creation led him down a path following the truth until it led him to his Creator and he converted from atheism to Christianity.

[56]See Rodney Stark, *For the Glory of God: How Monotheism Led to Reformations, Science, Witch-Hunts and the End of Slavery* (Princeton, NJ: Princeton University Press, 2003); Philip Sampson, *Six Modern Myths about Christianity and Western Civilization* (Downers Grove, IL: InterVarsity, 2001); and Vinoth Ramachandra, *Subverting Global Myths* (Downers Grove, IL: IVP Academic, 2008).

astronomy until the Renaissance. That work described a spherical earth some two centuries before Columbus.

The second myth is that when Copernicus wrote that the earth revolved around the sun, his conclusions were a revolutionary, and previously untaught, concept. The truth is that Copernicus was taught the essential fundamentals leading to his model by his Scholastic professors, that is, Christian scholars who developed the model gradually over the previous two centuries.

The third myth is that the "scientific revolution" of the seventeenth century invented science as we know it because Christianity had lost the power to prevent it. The truth is that three hundred years before Newton, a Scholastic cleric named Jean Buridan anticipated Newton's first law of motion, that a body in motion will stay in motion unless otherwise impeded. It was Buridan, not an Enlightenment luminary, who first proposed that the earth turns on its axis. Furthermore, science flourished only in Europe, where the worldview was shaped by Christianity. Many civilizations had alchemy, yet only Christian-influenced Europe developed chemistry. Likewise, astrology was practiced everywhere, but only in Europe did it become astronomy.

In closing, we would commend those whom God has gifted to love God with all their mind and to do so in the sciences to God's glory and their joy, as has always been the case with God's people.

WHAT DIFFERENCE DOES THE DOCTRINE OF CREATION MAKE FOR YOUR LIFE?

The Bible teaches that creation in general and human life in particular were made by God, belong to God, exist for God, are restless apart from God, and will return to God. If you do not believe in the doctrine of creation, you likely believe that you came from no one, you are alive on the earth for nothing, and that when you die you will go nowhere. The renowned atheistic philosopher Bertrand Russell summarizes this worldview:

That Man is the product of causes which had no prevision of the end they were achieving; that his origin, his growth, his hopes and fears, his loves and his beliefs, are but the outcome of accidental collocations of atoms; that no fire, no heroism, no intensity of thought and feeling, can preserve an individual life beyond the grave; that all the labours of the ages, all the devotion, all the inspiration, all the noonday brightness of human genius, are destined to extinction in the vast death of the solar system, and the whole temple of Man's achievement must inevitably be buried beneath the debris of a universe in ruins—all these things, if not quite beyond dispute, are yet so nearly certain, that no philosophy which rejects them can hope to stand. Only within the scaffolding of these truths, only on the firm foundation of the unyielding despair, can the soul's habitation henceforth be safely built.[57]

Indeed, the only logical option apart from the biblical doctrine of creation is "the firm foundation of the unyielding despair." Similarly, when Richard Dawkins was asked if his view of reality made him depressed, he replied, "I don't feel depressed about it. But if somebody does, that's their problem. Maybe the logic is deeply pessimistic, the universe is bleak, cold and empty. But so what?"[58]

As a pastor who has preached the funerals of suicide victims and prays often with teenage women who continually cut themselves and comes from a long family history of depression so severe that it often results in mental insanity and self-medication with alcoholism, I (Mark) could not fathom encouraging people to build their lives on "unyielding despair" because "the universe is bleak, cold, and empty" only to flippantly disregard their pain and tears by saying, "So what?"

Indeed, if no savior is coming to rescue me, and there is no better place to which I can escape at the end of this life, then once the pain of this life gets too much to bear, I should simply hasten the inevitable. And many do. Men prefer to put a gun in their mouth or to their head and go out in violence. Women prefer not to leave the mess of their brain matter for someone

---

[57]Bertrand Russell, "A Free Man's Worship," in *Mysticism and Logic* (Mineola, NY: Dover, 2004), 37.
[58]Quoted in Henry F. Schaefer III, *Science and Christianity: Conflict or Coherence?* (Watkinsville, GA: Apollos Trust, 2003), 82.

to clean up, so they most often choose to take enough pills that they never wake up to feel pain again.

People who do not understand the doctrine of creation and the doctrines that relate to it want to die. Some die a little bit at a time, weeping until they are empty and can no longer muster any tears. Others medicate themselves with prescriptions; antidepressants are now the most sold category of medicine, and depression is the most common diagnosis. Still others self-medicate with sex, food, alcohol, drugs, gambling, entertainment, video games, Internet surfing, and anything else that can serve as a diversion from the "unyielding despair."

What is even sadder than this sadness is the tragic fact that we have not learned from history and show no sign of doing so anytime soon. Anglican bishop N. T. Wright has wisely said:

> There are three basic ways (with variations) in which we can imagine God's space and ours relating to one another. . . . Option One is to slide the two spaces [heaven where God dwells and earth where we dwell] together. . . . Since God, as seen in this option, doesn't hide in a corner of his territory but fills it all with his presence, God is everywhere, and—watch this carefully—everywhere is God. Or, if you like, God is everything, and everything is God.
>
> This option is known as "pantheism." It was popular in the ancient Greek and Roman worlds of the first century. . . . it has become increasingly popular in our own times. . . . The main obligation on human beings then is to get in touch with, and in tune with, the divinity within themselves and within the world around.[59]

Wright goes on to explain that it is difficult for people to believe there is divinity in literally everything, including cancer, bugs, and hurricanes. So, the subtle variation of panentheism has become more popular. Panentheism teaches that God is in everything. Wright explains brilliantly:

---

[59]N. T. Wright, *Simply Christian: Why Christianity Makes Sense* (New York: HarperCollins, 2006), 60–61.

The problem with pantheism, and to a large extent panentheism, is that it can't cope with evil. Within the multigodded paganism out of which pantheism grew, when something went wrong you could blame it on a god or goddess who was out to get you. . . . But when everything (including yourself) shares in, or lives within, divinity, there's no higher court of appeal when something bad happens. Nobody can come and rescue you. The world and "the divine" are what they are, and you better get used to it. The only final answer (given by many Stoics in the first century, and by increasing numbers in today's Western world) is suicide.[60]

Option two, Wright says, is to hold the two spaces of heaven and earth firmly apart with great distance between God and us. This, of course, is the teaching of deism. As Wright says, "Human beings should get used to being alone in the world. The gods will not intervene, either to help or to harm."[61] He goes on to explain that in the ancient world, if you were rich, powerful, healthy, successful, and the like, with a good home to live in, good food to eat, and slaves to tend to your every whim, you were often fine with the idea that you were on your own and that there was no divine help at your disposal. On the other hand, "if, like the great majority of the population, your life was harsh, cruel, and often downright miserable, it was easy to believe that the world where you lived was dark, nasty, and wicked in its very essence, and that your best hope was to escape it . . . by death itself (there we go again)."[62]

Finally, option three, Wright says, is not that heaven and earth are one and the same (pantheism and panentheism) or completely separated (deism), but rather that God in varying ways interlocks his heaven with his creation. We see this throughout the Old Testament: Jacob saw a ladder coming down from heaven; a pillar of cloud by day and a pillar of fire by night led God's people in the wilderness; and the Tent of Meeting traveled with God's people as a portable meeting place between heaven and earth

---

[60]Ibid., 61.
[61]Ibid., 62.
[62]Ibid.

until they had the temple where the ark of the covenant was kept in the Most Holy Place, which is a sort of interlocking place between heaven and earth. Wright goes on to say that for the Christian, "the creation of the world was the free outpouring of God's powerful love. . . . And, having made such a world, he has remained in a close, dynamic, and intimate relationship with it, without in any way being contained within it or having it contained within himself."[63]

Therefore, the doctrine of creation sets the stage for the coming of Jesus Christ. Indeed, God becomes a man who is our creator amidst his creation. He comes to connect heaven and earth through himself as the mediator between the two. As we will see in coming chapters, he comes on a rescue mission to save us from "unyielding despair" by dying for us, placing his own Spirit in us, and promising to return one day to rescue creation so that it is no longer "bleak, cold, and empty." Indeed, just as he took a barren wasteland and prepared it for our first parents, he will again prepare creation for his people, and rather than saying "so what?" to our pain, the Bible promises that he will wipe every tear from our eyes.

---

[63]Ibid., 65.

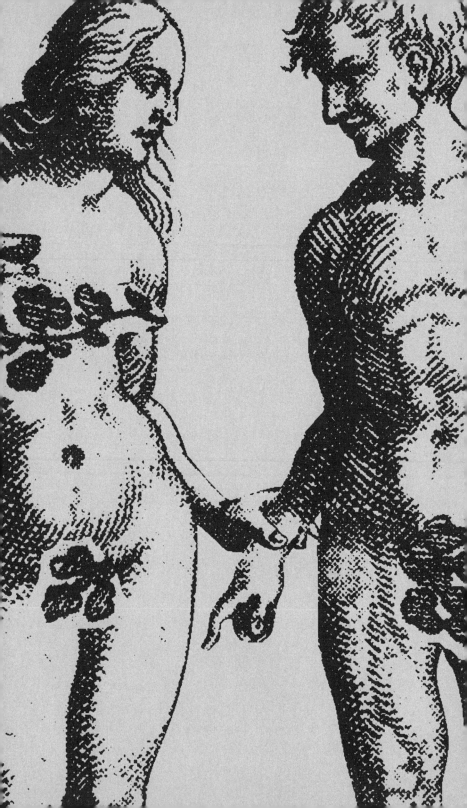

CHAPTER 4

IMAGE: GOD LOVES

Then God said, "Let us make man in our image, after our
likeness. . . ." So God created man in his own image,
in the image of God he created him; male and female he
created them.

GENESIS 1:26–27

What does it mean to be human?

That question has implications for seemingly every discipline, from theology to sociology, history, biology, psychology, and the like. It is this doctrine that answers questions regarding how mankind is different from God the Creator and his creation. It also reveals why we can believe in such things as compassion and equality—truths that an evolutionary worldview simply cannot permit.

By way of preface, it is important to note the historical development of the Western understanding of the human person, which is seen nearly entirely today in terms of an autonomous individual rather than as the member of a community. There was a day in which people did not think of themselves in primarily individual terms. Instead, what it meant to be a person was largely defined by one's relationship to such communities as family, history, parents, ethnicity, nationality, city, religion, and trade. This was consistent with the fact that we know each person of the Trinity not by isolating them but rather by seeing them in relationship with one another at work in our world and for our salvation.

However, everything changed in the days of the church father Augustine. In writing his book *Confessions*, he set in motion a historical trajectory that has forever changed how we answer the question of what it means to be human. Augustine did not look outward to his social network but rather inward to his feelings, convictions, longings, and the like. This elevated the importance of the autonomous individual in understanding the essence of humanity.

Many years later, the Christian philosopher René Descartes built on Augustine's concept of the person as an autonomous individual and defined the essence of what it means to be human in terms of the mind. He synthesized this with his statement, "I think, therefore I am."

Building on Augustine and Descartes, the greatest American theologian ever, Jonathan Edwards, taught that the autonomous reasoning individual can be saved and improved by God's grace to God's glory.

The influential non-Christian philosopher Jean-Jacques Rousseau then taught that the essence of what it means to be human is that the autonomous reasoning individual can be improved by self-acceptance and self-love; thus, we are to look in to self and not out to God for our identity and betterment. According to his teaching, we are not sinners who long for God's acceptance, but rather good people who need to accept ourselves and love ourselves so that we can become better versions of ourselves.

Subsequently, the influential American psychologist William James said that the autonomous reasoning individual can be improved by self-acceptance and self-love aided by psychology. One's hope was then to be found in a trained professional and not ultimately God and his grace. This ideology that human beings are essentially machines that can be worked on by psychology led to the trained professional as a functional savior who makes people's lives better.

Finally, American psychologist Abraham Maslow said that the autonomous reasoning individual is improved by self-acceptance and self-love aided by psychology to self-actualization, which is the defining principle of what it means to be human.

Therefore, the nearly millennium-and-a-half transition from Augustine to the present day has resulted in the commonly held belief that God does not save us for his glory and to make us part of his people, the church, to grow in holiness. Rather, we essentially save ourselves through loving and accepting ourselves and heeding the counsel of psychology. The ultimate goal of this is not that we would glorify God, but rather that we would achieve our potential, experience our greatness, or, in theological terms, live for our own glory as worshipers of ourselves, being all we can be, experiencing all we can experience, and doing all we can do.

In light of this historical transition, the average person, including the average Christian, is far worldlier and less biblical in his understanding of who he is and why he exists than he is aware. He thinks in worldly categories rather than biblical categories because the culture in which he lives is so fundamentally unbiblical in its thinking. Sociologist Christian Smith has said that the true religion of most people in the West today, regardless of what religion they profess to participate in, is *moralistic therapeutic deism*.[1] By *moralistic* he means we are good individuals who can get better, not sinners who need actual salvation. By *therapeutic* he means that it is counseling and therapy, not God or the church, that enable our betterment. By *deism* he means that God is not really involved in our lives; we are essentially on our own with the occasional exceptions of God answering a prayer we send him or sending us a pithy insight to aid our betterment.

Thus, the historical reasons for the current poor, prevailing perspective on personhood are obvious, but we still need to understand what God teaches about who we are as human beings. This is incredibly important, as one rabbi has said: "We become what we think of ourselves. . . . What determines one's being is the image one adopts."[2]

---

[1] See Christian Smith and Melinda Lundquist Denton, *Soul Searching: The Religious and Spiritual Lives of American Teenagers* (New York: Oxford University Press, 2009), 162ff., 166.
[2] Abraham J. Heschel, *Who Is Man?* (Stanford, CA: Stanford University Press, 1965), 7–8.

WHAT DOES THE BIBLE REVEAL ABOUT THE ORIGIN OF HUMAN LIFE?

Ludwig von Feuerbach was a nineteenth-century atheist who curiously declared that God did not make us but rather we made God as a figment of our imagination. Students of his thinking include Karl Marx, who applied this politically, Sigmund Freud, who applied this psychologically, and Friedrich Nietzsche, who applied this philosophically.

Conversely, in Genesis 1 and 2 we see that we did not create God, but rather God created us in his image and likeness. The fountainhead verses on the origin of human life are found in Genesis 1:26–27:

> Then God said, "Let us make man in our image, after our likeness. And let them have dominion over the fish of the sea and over the birds of the heavens and over the livestock and over all the earth and over every creeping thing that creeps on the earth." So God created man in his own image, in the image of God he created him; male and female he created them.

Admittedly, the number of verses in Scripture clearly declaring that God made human beings in his image and likeness (also commonly referred to by the Latin phrase *imago Dei*) are few.[3]

However, it is not enough simply to search the Bible for the phrase "image of God." Sinclair Ferguson writes, "While statistically the phrase is infrequent, the interpretation of man which it enshrines is all-pervasive."[4]

There are twelve vital truths revealed in the biblical revelation that we were made in the image and likeness of God. Taken together, they provide the essence of a biblical anthropology.

1) We were created by the Trinity. Augustine was fond of noting that the plural language of Genesis 1:26, "Let us make man in our image, after our likeness," means we were created by the Trinity. Because of this, we are to understand ourselves not as autonomous individuals but rather as image bearers made for four categories of relationship. Theologically,

---

[3]Gen. 1:26–27; 5:1–3; 9:6; 1 Cor. 11:7; James 3:9.
[4]Sinclair Ferguson, "Image of God," in *New Dictionary of Theology*, ed. Sinclair Ferguson, David Wright, and J. I. Packer (Downers Grove, IL: InterVarsity, 1988), 328.

we are to live in relationship with God. Psychologically, we are to live in relationship with ourselves, knowing who God intends for us to be. Socially, we are to live in relationship with other people, in community. Environmentally, we are to live in relationship with all that God has put under our dominion, including animals.

2) We were created as persons by a personal God. The Scriptures make note of this by explaining how, unlike the rest of creation, which was made solely by God's word, God formed us by his proverbial hands and then breathed life into us.[5]

3) God originally made mankind without sin. Genesis 1:31 calls our first parents "very good" in comparison to the rest of creation, which God simply called "good." Also, Ecclesiastes 7:29 says, "God made man upright." Therefore, all human sin is fully the responsibility of sinners and not of God our creator. In addition, all the effects of sin and the curse were not originally part of the world God created for us in love.

4) God blesses us.[6] In so doing, God reveals to us that he is a good God who does not need to be prompted or compelled to give grace; rather, he delights in doing so and does so without request.

5) Unlike the animals who were made according to their "own kind," we are made in the "image of God." This makes human life distinct from and superior to all other created things. We are altogether unique and bestowed with particular dignity, value, and worth.

6) God gives commands to us because he made us as moral image bearers. We can know right and wrong, and we can respond to God with moral obedience as an act of faith and love.

7) God made us curious adventurers and granted us permission to explore his creation through everything from a telescope to a microscope.[7] Because God made us this way, we have an insatiable curiosity that begins once we are born and continues throughout our life as we seek to experience and learn, travel the world, and explore every nook of creation.

8) God created us to be creative and invited us to make culture.[8] This explains the innate love people have for everything from fashion to film, music, theater, architecture, painting, photography, dance, storytelling, and the like.

---

[5]Gen. 2:7.
[6]Gen. 1:28.
[7]Ibid.
[8]Ibid.

9) God created us to be reproductive and have children.[9] This explains why many people long to be parents and consider children a great blessing.

10) God made us with meaningful work to do.[10] This helps to explain why there is an innate drive in most people to work.

11) God created us as his image bearers, but not because he needed us in any way. He bestowed on us the dignity of being his image bearers solely for our benefit, not his own. The church father Irenaeus explains, "God formed Adam, not as if He stood in need of man, but so that He might have someone upon whom to confer His benefits."[11] Similarly, Lactantius (AD 240–320) said, "It cannot be said that God made the world for His own sake. For He can exist without the world. . . . It is evident, therefore, that the world was constructed for the sake of living beings, since living beings enjoy those things that it consists of."[12]

12) God created us to live *coram Deo*. *Coram Deo* means to live "before the face of God" and was commonly used by John Calvin and others throughout church history to explain the Christian life. Practically speaking, we were created to live all of life in the presence of God, under the authority of God, by the Word of God, to the glory of God. We were created to live all of life before the face of God, knowing that nothing in our life is secular or separated from the sight of God because all of life is sacred. To live otherwise is sacrilege.

After noting that God created our first parents in his image and likeness, we then see that they, unlike the rest of creation, related to God in a unique way. Paul David Tripp sees this as evidence that the image and likeness we bear enables humans to act as revelation receivers, interpreters, and worshipers.[13] Tripp says:

> Immediately after creating Adam and Eve, God *talks* to them. He didn't do this with anything else he created. He simply rested and moved on. . . . Why did God talk to them?

---

[9]Ibid.
[10]Gen. 2:15–17.
[11]Irenaeus, *Haer.* 4.14.1.
[12]Lactantius, *Inst.* 7.4.
[13]See Paul David Tripp, *Instruments in the Redeemer's Hands* (Phillipsburg, NJ: P&R, 2002), 39–45.

God knew that even though Adam and Eve were perfect people living in perfect relationship with him, they could not figure out life on their own. They were created to be dependent. God had to explain who they were and what they were to do with their lives. They did not need this help because they were sinners. They needed help because they were human.

This is the first instance of personal ministry in human history. The Wonderful Counselor comes to human beings and defines their identity and purpose.[14]

As revelation receivers we were given the ability to communicate with God and one another that no other creature was given. We can hear God's Word and live in light of revelation from him. Even in their sinless state our first parents were dependent upon God and needed to hear from God. Thus, in our sinful and fallen state we even more desperately need to hear from God. As revelation receivers we can. This is because, unlike lower creation such as plants and animals, our relationship with God is tethered with words—he speaks to us through Scripture and other forms of revelation, and we speak to him in such things as prayer and song.

As interpreters we are able to make meaning out of the revelation we receive. Simply, we can think, ponder, consider, probe, and learn unlike anything else God has made. For us to correctly understand and apply the revelation we receive, we must do the hard work of loving God with all our mind so that the facts we receive can become not just information, but information that contributes to our transformation.

As worshipers, revelation and interpretation culminate in exaltation. Because they were image bearers, our first parents were created to worship God in thought, word, deed, and motive. All of their life was supposed to be lived in light of who God is, what God does, and what God says. They were supposed to interpret all of this revelation and respond to God in ways that would both bring him glory and them joy as they were doing what he created them to do.

---

[14]Ibid., 40.

WHAT DOES IT MEAN THAT WE ARE GOD'S IMAGE?

Because the defining feature of what it means to be human is that we are God's image bearers, there are few questions regarding our humanity that are more necessary to correctly answer than, what does it mean that we are God's image?

The Bible is clear that men and women, unlike the rest of creation, are made in the image of God.[15] Furthermore, the Bible repeats this truth after sin enters the world, which means that even though sin has stained and marred us, as we will examine more thoroughly in the next chapter, we remain God's image bearers.[16]

The word *image* is often translated "idol." An idol is something that makes the invisible god visible. Admittedly, the Bible renounces idolatry emphatically, repeatedly, and forcefully. Therefore, we want to be clear that we are not endorsing idolatry. Nonetheless, to image the real Trinitarian God of the Bible is to make him visible to the world.

On this point, John Calvin wrote the following comments on Colossians 3:10:

> We are renewed after the image of God. . . . Hence, too, we learn, on the one hand, what is the end of our regeneration, that is, that we may be made like God, and that his glory may shine forth in us; and, on the other hand, what is the image of God, of which mention is made by Moses in Genesis 9:6, the rectitude and integrity of the whole soul, so that man reflects, like a mirror, the wisdom, righteousness, and goodness of God. He speaks somewhat differently in the Epistle to the Ephesians, but the meaning is the same. Paul, at the same time, teaches, that there is nothing more excellent at which the Colossians can aspire, inasmuch as this is our highest perfection and blessedness to bear the image of God.[17]

What Calvin is saying is that to image God is to "mirror" his invisible

---

[15]Gen. 1:26–27.
[16]Gen. 5:1–3; 9:6; James 3:9.
[17]John Calvin, *Commentaries on the Epistles of Paul the Apostle to the Philippians, Colossians, and Thessalonians*, trans. John Pringle (Edinburgh: Calvin Translation Society, 1847; repr., Grand Rapids, MI: Baker, 2003), 211–12.

attributes to the world, somewhat like Moses, who radiated the glory of God after being in God's presence. Therefore, we are not to reflect Adam, the culture, or even ourselves to the world. Rather, God has bestowed upon us the amazing ability and awesome responsibility to be his mirrors on the earth, reflecting his goodness and glory to all for his glory and our joy. All persons are God's image in a basic sense, but Christians image him more than non-Christians and mature Christians do so even more.[18]

Furthermore, image is both personal and communal. By personal, we mean that we as individual worshipers must continually ask whether we are good reflections of our God. By communal, we mean that churches, families, and Christian communities must continually ask whether they are good reflections of God to one another and the world.

This understanding of our created purpose (and subsequently one source of our joy) is radically different from the world's understanding of being true to oneself, or simply reflecting one's sin nature to the world. In fact, this understanding of *imago Dei* is even radically different from many Christian teachings about why we exist. Biblical counselor Edward T. Welch describes how the word *need* is one of the more confusing terms in the English language.[19] Its field of meaning is broad and ambiguous, containing ideas that are completely unrelated but often confused together. He then defines the various popular uses of the term and the history of the concept in the field of psychology before looking at how the idea of "psychological needs" has become grafted into contemporary Christian counseling.[20]

Welch describes how the biblical teaching on the image of God leads us in a different direction by showing that we are not empty cups needing to be filled by God. Rather, we are broken mirrors that need to be put back together by God, beginning with our regeneration and continuing every day in our sanctification, so that we can better and better reflect God. Welch

---

[18]We see this in Rom. 8:29, 2 Cor. 3:18, and Col. 3:10, for example.

[19]Edward T. Welch, "Who Are We? Needs, Longings, and the Image of God in Man," *The Journal of Biblical Counseling* 13, no. 1 (1994): 25–38.

[20]E.g., Larry Crabb, *Understanding People: Why We Long for Relationship* (Grand Rapids, MI: Zondervan, 1987).

says, "Instead of a love cup . . . the image is more accurately that of Moses literally reflecting the glory of God. . . . The center of gravity in the universe is God and His glory-holiness."[21] Welch deconstructs the experience of "feeling empty" and thus deconstructs the erroneous notion that God exists to fill our empty cup of needs; he replaces that view with the biblical idea that we exist to mirror God.

Imaging God practically means that we will mirror both his moral and non-moral likeness. Mirroring God's moral likeness means we will exercise decision-making power, have dominion over lower creation, live in social relationships with others, feel our emotions, love, serve, and communicate. Mirroring God's non-moral likeness means that we use our intellect and reason to think and that we can be creative with the materials God has created; it also includes the fact that we are immortal and will live spiritually even after our physical death.

If we are to reflect God well, we must know who he is. God is not merely an idea or a proposition but instead a living and free person who is completely "other," or holy. Speaking about this entirely other God is difficult. In an effort to explain God according to Scripture, theologians have distinguished between his unshared attributes that belong to him alone (also called *incommunicable attributes*), and God's shared attributes, which he bestows upon us to a lesser degree than he possesses them (also called *communicable attributes*).

Before examining God's attributes as revealed in Scripture, two points are important. First, God's attributes are not merely attributed to him, but they are qualities inseparable from his very being. In every way that God exists, he exists without limit, that is, in perfection. Second, we know God by our experiences through relationship with him: when we recognize his presence all around us, when we recognize his provision in our lives, when we confess our sins and accept his grace to live by faith. In his loving friendship we come to a fuller realization of who he truly is as revealed in Scripture.

---

[21]Welch, "Who Are We?" 33.

Unshared Attributes

Omnipresence: God is everywhere at all times.[22]

Omniscience: God has complete and perfect knowledge of all things, including the past, present, future, and everything actual or potential.[23]

Omnipotence: God is all-powerful and able to do all that he wills.[24]

Immutability: God does not change in his essence, character, purpose, or knowledge but does respond to people and their prayers.[25]

Eternality: God has no beginning or end and is not bound by time, though he is conscious of time and does work in time.[26]

Sovereignty: God is supreme in rule and authority over all things,[27] though he does allow human freedom.[28]

Shared Attributes

Holiness: God is absolutely separate from any evil.[29] We mirror God when we hate sin and love holiness by repenting of our sin and fighting against sin in the world.

Love: God alone is perfectly good and loving, and he alone is the source for all goodness and love.[30] We mirror God when we love God and others, starting with our families, friends, and fellow church members and extending to strangers for hospitality and even enemies for reconciliation.

Truth: God is the source of all truth. He is the embodiment of truth.[31] We mirror God when we believe biblical truth over lies and speak truthfully as an act of worship.

Righteousness: God does not conform to a standard of right and wrong, but right and wrong flow out of his character.[32] We mirror God as we fight oppression, injustice, and evil and pursue justice—particularly for those without power, such as the unborn, sick, poor, marginalized, defenseless, and abused.

---

[22]Deut. 31:6; Ps. 139:7–12; Prov. 15:3; Jer. 23:24; Col. 1:17.

[23]Job 42:2; Pss. 139:1–6; 147:5, Isa. 40:12–14; 46:10; Heb. 4:13.

[24]Job 42:2; Ps. 147:5; Matt. 19:26; Eph. 3:20.

[25]Num. 23:19, Ps. 102:27; Mal. 3:6; Rom. 11:29; Heb. 13:8; James 1:17.

[26]Pss. 90:2; 93:2; 102:12; Eph. 3:21.

[27]2 Sam. 7:28; 1 Chron. 29:10–13; Ps. 103:19; Rom. 8:28.

[28]Gen. 50:21–22.

[29]Ex. 3:5; Lev. 19:2; Pss. 5:4–6; 99:5; Isa. 6:3; 8:13; 57:15; Hab. 1:12–13; 1 Pet. 1:14–19; 1 John 1:5.

[30]Ex. 34:7; Ps. 84:11; John 3:16; Gal. 5:22; Eph. 2:4–7; 1 John 4:8–16.

[31]Num. 23:19; John 14:6; 17:17; 2 Cor. 1:20; Titus 1:2.

[32]Gen. 18:25; Ex. 34:7; Deut. 32:4; Acts 17:31; Rom. 2:11.

Mercy: God does not give some people what they deserve, because he is loving and gracious.[33] We mirror his mercy when we forgive those who sin against us and do good to those who do evil in an effort to bring them to repentance.

Beauty: God is beautiful and his creation reflects his beauty. God made men and women in his image and likeness to also create works of beauty.[34] We mirror God when we create and enjoy beauty in a holy way, such as by stewarding God's beautiful creation (including our own bodies and health), enjoying the arts, and even painting the walls of our home in thanks to God who gives us both color and eyes to see it.

WHAT DOES IT MEAN THAT WE WERE MADE MALE AND FEMALE?

In Genesis 1 God declared what he made "good," except for the man and woman, which he declared to be "very good." The only thing that we are told is not good before sin and the fall is Adam's being alone.[35] Even in a sinless state we were made for human contact, friendship, and love. Even though Adam had God above him and creation beneath him, he lacked an equal with whom to be in community, one who would enable him to function like the Trinity in covenantal partnership as "one."

God's answer to Adam's lack was the creation of Eve as Adam's wife and helper.[36] It is important to note that the word *helper* does not denigrate Eve; in fact, God is also referred to as our helper.[37] The first woman was taken from the side of the man, which beautifully illustrates that she belongs alongside him in partnership, not behind him in denigration (as chauvinism teaches) or in front of him in domination (as feminism teaches). It may also explain why cuddling alongside her man is the favorite pastime of many a bride, as it is for her a sort of homecoming. Though the woman was taken from the man, in the sexual consummation of the marriage the two again become one.

---

[33]Ex. 34:6–7; Matt. 18:23–35; Rom. 12:8; Eph. 2:4–7; Titus 3:5.
[34]Pss. 27:4; 50:2; Eccles. 3:11; Isa. 33:17.
[35]Gen. 2:18.
[36]Gen. 2:19–25.
[37]E.g., Pss. 10:14; 118:6–7; Heb. 13:6.

While God is not engendered, he does reveal himself as Father and comes to us as the God-man Jesus Christ. Nonetheless, he makes both men and women in his image. Practically, this means that though they are in some ways different, the man and woman are equal in dignity, value, and worth by virtue of the fact that they are equally God's image bearers.

Important to note is that God created the covenant of marriage; thus, he alone defines what it is. His definition of one man and one woman, husband and wife for life, as one flesh, eliminates the alternatives such as bestiality, homosexuality, fornication, polygamy, adultery, and the like. At the first wedding God in his sovereignty brought the woman to the man, gave her away as her Father, and officiated the ceremony as their pastor. Upon seeing his bride for the first time, Adam responded to her beauty by singing her a song. The poetic words Adam sang to his bride on their wedding day are the first recorded words of any human being.

Genesis 2:24 then explains how a man can overcome his state of being single that is not good. First, a man should leave his parents' home and be his own man. Second, a man should marry a woman he loves and who loves him and loves the Lord. Third, their marriage should be intimate in every way including sexual consummation, and they should spend the rest of their life becoming "one" as the Trinitarian God is "one."[38] Both Jesus and Paul repeat this process throughout the New Testament as the pattern God intends for marriage and sexuality.[39]

Also important is that in the creation account God establishes an order to the covenant of marriage and organizes the family with the husband as the leader and head. This is evidenced in five ways:

1) God calls the race "man"[40] and "mankind."[41]
2) By naming Eve, as he did the animals, Adam was exercising authority over her.[42]

---

[38]The same Hebrew word for "one" is used for a husband and wife in Gen. 2:24 and for the Trinity in Deut. 6:4.
[39]Matt. 19:5; Mark 10:7–8; Eph. 5:31.
[40]Gen. 1:26.
[41]Gen. 5:2.
[42]Gen. 2:23.

3) Although the woman sinned first, God came calling for the man[43] and held him responsible because he failed to lovingly lead and protect his family from Satan and sin. Sadly, our first father, like many of his cowardly sons, sat idly by and did nothing while his wife was being deceived.[44]

4) It is Adam's sin that is imputed to the human race because he is our head, and that sin can be removed only by Jesus, who is called "the last Adam."[45]

5) Echoing the creation account of our first parents, the Bible repeatedly declares that husbands are to lovingly lead their homes as Christlike heads and wives are to submit to their husbands.[46]

Practically speaking, this biblical teaching (called *complementarianism*) does *not* mean that a husband is in ultimate authority. God is, and other authorities are over the man, such as the state and church governments. Nor does it mean that a wife does not have independent thoughts or seek to influence her husband, or must obey her husband's command to sin, or is less intelligent or competent than her husband. This *does* mean that a husband and wife are equal with complementary roles (like a left and right hand that work together, though one is dominant). It does mean that wives are to submit to their husbands like Jesus does to God the Father, that husbands are to lovingly lead their wives as Jesus does the church, that a woman should only marry a man she respects and trusts enough to follow, and that marriage is supposed to reflect something of the Trinity and the gospel, where Jesus pursues us in love and takes responsibility for us as an example to husbands and fathers.

Tragically, however, sin has caused much pain and misunderstanding surrounding this teaching, culminating in what some have even called the gender wars or the battle of the sexes. God declared to our first parents that there would be conflict between men and women. God told Eve that rather than trusting and submitting to her husband, she and her daughters

---

[43]Gen. 3:8–9.
[44]2 Cor. 11:3; 1 Tim. 2:14.
[45]Rom. 5:12–21; 1 Cor. 15:45.
[46]Gen. 2:18; cf. Gen. 5:2; 1 Cor. 11:2–16; 14:33–34; Eph. 5:21–33; Col. 3:18; 1 Tim. 2:11–15; Titus 2:3–5; 1 Pet. 3:1.

since would want to rule over their husbands, like sin sought to rule over Cain (the same language is used to describe both situations).[47] For Adam and his sons since, it was promised that everything under their dominion would be cursed and would fight against them; providing for their families would be a cursed experience designed by God to humble men and provide insight into how difficult it is for God to be his head when he is disobedient.[48]

WHAT ARE THE ASPECTS OF OUR HUMANITY?

The Scriptures speak of human beings in many ways and terms that, when understood together, give us a thorough picture of the aspects of our humanity.[49]

Aspects of Our Humanity in the Old Testament

The Bible speaks of the soul (*nepesh*). *Nepesh* refers to the person as a creation in relation to God rather than immortal, immaterial substance. The term is occasionally used for God. In the broadest sense, it connotes all biological life. Both humans and animals are called living *nepesh* in Genesis, which simply means, "living creature." It is not that people possess souls but that we are souls.

The Bible speaks of spirit (*ruach*) in reference to God, people, and animals. The basic meaning is "wind" or "breath," especially when speaking of the Holy Spirit. In humans it can mean "mind,"[50] "resolve,"[51] or "will."[52] None of these comes from humans themselves, but from God who breathed life into dust in creation to make us alive.

The Bible speaks of flesh (*basar*), one-third of the time in reference to animals and never to God. It refers to what humans share with animals in contradistinction to God. Most often it means flesh as characteristic of

---

[47]Gen. 3:16; 4:7.
[48]Gen. 3:17–19.
[49]The following material is largely summarized from William Dyrness, *Themes in Old Testament Theology* (Downers Grove, IL: InterVarsity, 1979), 79–96.
[50]Ezek. 11:5.
[51]Jer. 51:11.
[52]Isa. 19:3.

bodily existence.[53] It often stands for the human body as a whole—a concept for which Hebrew has no distinct word.[54] Flesh in the Old Testament has none of the sinful connotations that we find in Paul's usage throughout the New Testament to speak of our proclivity to sin.[55]

The Bible speaks of blood (*dam*). It refers to the physical life of humans and animals.[56] Subsequently, shedding blood is shedding life.[57]

Lastly, the Bible speaks of the heart (*leb*) and almost always in reference to humans. Only rarely does it refer to the anatomical heart. The heart is the focus of the personal life—the reasoning, responding, deciding self. It is the deepest center of the human person, the driving force, and the most fundamental values from which our acts and attitudes come.[58] It is so deep that only God fully knows it.[59] The heart is the source of the deepest wishes and desires[60] and decisions of the will.[61] The heart is the center of the intellectual and rational functions that we usually ascribe to the mind.[62] It appears one hundred times in Proverbs alone, and the distinction between head and heart is totally foreign in the Old Testament.[63] A godly person is a person after God's own heart.[64]

Aspects of Our Humanity in the New Testament

The constellations of words and images in the New Testament that speak of aspects of our humanity are, generally speaking, broken into the categories of the inward and outward person.[65] Our outward existence is visible, physical, and world-oriented, and primarily involves our physical body. Conversely, our inward existence is invisible, spiritual, and God-oriented, and involves our mind, heart, and spirit. Importantly, these are both aspects

---

[53]Job 10:11; Ps. 78:39.
[54]Num. 8:7; Ps. 38:3.
[55]Deut. 5:26; Ps. 56:4; Jer. 17:5, 7.
[56]Ps. 72:13–14; Prov. 1:16, 18.
[57]Gen. 9:4–6.
[58]Prov. 4:23.
[59]1 Sam. 16:7.
[60]Gen. 6:5; Pss. 14:1; 21:2.
[61]Ex. 7:22; Josh. 14:8.
[62]1 Kings 3:9, 12.
[63]Prov. 23:7.
[64]1 Sam. 2:35; 13:14.
[65]Rom. 7:22; 2 Cor. 4:16; Eph. 3:16.

of one person and not independent entities that operate apart from the others. Nonetheless, the New Testament does distinguish, though not divide, these aspects of our humanity.

When the New Testament speaks of the body it is referring to the physical aspect of a person or animal.[66] In this way the body is our outward existence in contrast to our inward existence.[67] Humans are created to be embodied for all eternity.

The soul (*psuche*) for Paul throughout the New Testament is neither the immortal in a person nor only the immaterial part of the person.[68] Instead, the soul in Paul's thinking refers to the whole person created by God with an inner life of motive, thought, feeling, and the like. At times, Paul also speaks of the soul negatively, as that part of our being that is stained and marred by sin, or lived without God in view.[69]

When the Bible speaks of the human spirit (*pneuma*) it describes our inner being as juxtaposed with our outer being[70] and is sometimes equivalent to the soul,[71] flesh,[72] and sometimes contrasted with that which is soulish.[73]

When the New Testament speaks of the heart (*kardia*), as Jesus often does, it is speaking of human beings as emotional with feelings, intellectual with thoughts, volitional with a will, moral with decisions, and religious with worship. It is therefore used to denote that which is central and vital in human nature.

By mind (*nous*), the New Testament speaks of the human person as knowing, thinking, judging, self-determining, and responsible. In many contexts, mind connotes one's outlook on life, or what is called "worldview" today. Fundamentally, it refers to the rational activity of the person and is not exalted as the *summum bonum* of our being but rather a very vital and helpful part of our person.

---

[66]1 Cor. 13:3; 2 Cor. 10:10; Gal. 6:17.
[67]Rom. 12:1; Heb. 13:15–16.
[68]Rom. 2:9; 11:3; 13:1.
[69]1 Cor. 2:14; 15:44.
[70]Rom. 8:10; 1 Cor. 7:34.
[71]Philem. 1:17.
[72]2 Cor. 2:13; 7:5.
[73]1 Cor. 2:14; 15:44.

In speaking of the conscience (*suneidesis*), the New Testament is referring to the capacity of universal moral judgment. The primary role of our
conscience is to give warning when an action violates it. While modern
thinking sees conscience as a reliable standard of morality, the Bible sees
it as a tool to be trusted only when it is enlightened by God.

In summary, while the Bible speaks of aspects of our humanity in various terms, it is not in as neat and tidy a manner as some would prefer. And
in an effort to answer the question on which this section is based, a debate
has ensued over what is called *dichotomy* and *trichotomy*.

Dichotomy teaches that we are basically two parts—that which is
material and physical, and that which is immaterial and spiritual. Christian
dichotomists note that the Bible does distinguish our existence into the two
major groupings of material and immaterial[74] and note that upon death we
are only two parts that are separated until our resurrection.[75] They also note
that "soul" and "spirit" are terms the Bible often uses interchangeably.[76]

Trichotomy agrees with dichotomy, with a notable exception. Unlike
the dichotomist who sees the spirit and soul as usually synonymous terms
in the Bible, trichotomists say that we have a spirit with God-consciousness
and a spiritual capacity through which we relate to God *in addition to* a
soul with affections, desires, reason, emotions, will, and self-conscious-
ness. Those Christians arguing for the trichotomist position do appeal to
Scripture,[77] do see places where a distinction is made between the spirit
and soul,[78] and do see that the Holy Spirit works with the human spirit.[79]

While this may all seem like a tertiary debate, it has profound implications for how we treat and care for people. For example, as pastors we
frequently deal with hurting people and long to help them. But how are
they best helped?

In "Dichotomy or Trichotomy? How the Doctrine of Man Shapes the
Treatment of Depression," Winston Smith notes how most Christian coun-

---

[74]Rom. 8:10; 1 Cor. 7:34.
[75]Eccles. 12:7; Matt. 10:28; Luke 23:46; Acts 7:59; James 2:26.
[76]Gen. 41:8; Ps. 42:6; Eccles. 12:7; Matt. 6:25; 20:28; 27:50; Luke 1:46–47; John 12:27; 13:21.
[77]Luke 1:46–47; Phil. 1:27; 1 Thess. 5:23; Heb. 4:12.
[78]Matt. 20:28; 27:50.
[79]Rom. 8:16.

selors take a threefold view of human nature; they see spirit, soul, and body as three constituents that need to be addressed by spiritual, psychological, and medical means, respectively.[80] However, trichotomy is rooted more in Greek philosophy than biblical exegesis. The Bible emphasizes the fundamental unity of human nature in a "duplex" of inner and outer man, which "provides a more unified view of man . . . more psychologically accurate, and truer to human experience."[81]

It is our conviction that the Bible reveals the aspects of our being according to the dichotomist view. Furthermore, we believe that it is best to minister out of the *personal view*, where we are dealing with a whole person, not merely aspects of someone. The *personal view* emphasizes the unity of a person so that his or her spiritual, physical, emotional, intellectual, volitional, familial, and social existence coalesce to make one person. Therefore, to truly help people, particularly those who are hurting and suffering, we have to minister to the whole person.

Practically, this means that if someone has a chemical or hormonal imbalance that would benefit from medication or needs an operation for cancer, they should not be derided for not having enough faith, as if every issue is solely a spiritual issue. Conversely, sometimes people are depressed and struggling for spiritual, not physical, reasons; in these cases, rather then giving them a pill, we need to help them grow in the gospel and lovingly limp with them as empathetic friends.

Admittedly, the Bible is complicated when it speaks about the aspects of our being. But so are people and so is the help they need. Therefore, while the Bible may not be as clear as some systematicians would prefer, it is as perfectly and gloriously messy as life under the sun is; the Bible is thus eminently more helpful than tidy systems that seek in vain to simplify the complexity of human life. Indeed, to truly help whole people, we must minister to the whole person since true spirituality encompasses all of our being.

---

[80]See Winston Smith, "Dichotomy or Trichotomy? How the Doctrine of Man Shapes the Treatment of Depression," *The Journal of Biblical Counseling* 18, no. 3 (2000): 21–29.
[81]Ibid., 22.

We must minister to people physically by considering their health and diet and exercise, emotionally with love and compassion, intellectually by answering their questions biblically, volitionally by appealing to their will for obedience, familially by dealing with issues related to their family of origin and current family dynamics, as well as socially by dealing with the social network and interpersonal relationships both in and out of the church.

This is all necessary because the aspects of our being are not isolated but instead impinge upon and affect one another because we are whole persons. A woman struggling with serious depression serves as one example. As I spent time with her, it seemed possible that some of her trouble was physical (she had a long family history of clinically diagnosed depression and high rates of suicide), emotional (she was discouraged because loved ones had recently died, leaving her feeling alone), intellectual (she was struggling to understand how God related to her depression and wrongly assumed Christians were always supposed to be happy), volitional (she was not choosing to pray or read Scripture regularly), familial (she was hurting because her spouse had recently committed adultery), and social (she was hurting, as she had recently moved to our city from another state and thus lost close connection with her friends). For her, like most people, there is not one answer that addresses one aspect of her being but rather answers that address all the aspects of her being.

WHAT ARE SOME COMMON CHRISTIAN ERRORS REGARDING THE DOCTRINE OF THE IMAGE OF GOD?

There are, generally speaking, three broad categories of error regarding the doctrine of image that Christians are prone to. The first is not maintaining the rightful place of humanity in God's created order. The second is reductionism that seeks to make one part of our humanity the defining aspect of what it means to be human. The third is defining what it means to be God's image bearers in terms of something we do rather than who we are. We will deal with each category of error in succession.

First, error occurs regarding the doctrine of image when there is a failure to maintain the theological tension that Scripture does. Genesis 1 and 2 (especially 1:26) reveals that mankind was made under God in and over the rest of creation. Generally speaking, nearly every error in anthropology puts us up to be divine like God or pushes us down to be animals like the rest of creation.

The former is common when human depravity is overlooked and/or there is an erroneous belief that we are somehow part of the divine, as is common in pantheism and panentheism, as if we had at least a spark of divinity within us.

The latter is common when humans are seen as little more than highly evolved animals incapable of denying our depraved instincts. This explains why, for example, such things as sexual sin are often tolerated in our culture. In this view, we are little more than animals and thus do not have the ability to live above our base and sinful desires, which is really a simple way of excusing and promoting sin with an evolutionary excuse. Also, those holding to evolutionary thinking, radical environmentalism, and animal rights activism are most prone to place humanity at or near the same level of plants and animals. Examples of this error include the occasional legal efforts to extend human rights to animals such as chimpanzees that are actually being heard in some courts as viable cases.[82]

Only by seeing ourselves between God and the animals can we have both our humility and dignity; there alone are we in the right place that God intended for us at creation. By noting our position under God as created beings, we should remain humble toward and dependent upon God. By noting our position in dominion over the rest of creation, we should embrace our dignity as morally superior to animals and expect more than is common from ourselves and others as God's image bearers. It is vitally important that we know that our place is between God and the rest of creation. In fact, our English word *human* derives its meaning from the same Latin root word as *humility*, which means "knowing your place."

---

[82]E.g., "European Court agrees to hear chimp's plea for human rights," *Evening Standard*, May 21, 2008, http://www.thisislondon.co.uk/news/article-23486466-details/European+Court+agrees+to+hear+chimp's+plea+ for+human+rights/article.do.

Second, numerous errors emerge when it is believed that rather than being God's image bearers, we bear the image of God in some specific part of us. This is called the *substantive view* and has been the predominant position historically. Paul Ramsey writes that in this mode of thought, the *imago Dei* refers to "something *within* the *substantial form* of human nature, some faculty or capacity man possesses" that distinguishes "man from nature and from other animals."[83]

The truth is that it is not just a part of us that bears God's image while the rest of us does not. Instead, we are in totality (mind, body, soul, etc.) the image of God. When a part of us is thought to be the image of God, or at least the defining aspect of what it means to be human, it is lifted up above the rest of our person in various ways.

For some, we are entirely material so that our body alone is the totality of our humanity. Those holding this belief deny any immaterial or spiritual aspect to our being, such as a soul. Atheism and a denial of life after death are common beliefs related to this position.

For others, it is the mind and our ability to reason, communicate, learn, and the like that is the defining aspect of what it means to be human. This kind of belief was perhaps most popular during the era of modernity, which was marked by rationalism.

Perhaps the most popular error for those religiously and spiritually oriented is the belief that the soul alone is the defining aspect of what it means to be human. Even the great Bible teacher John Calvin erred by elevating the immaterial soul as what the Bible means by *imago Dei*. In some Eastern religions (e.g., Sikhism, Bahá", Hinduism) our physical body has little worth, which explains why meditation and yoga are used in an effort to connect with one's soul and disconnect from one's body.

Quite popular since the Romantic period is the belief that the essence of our humanity is to be found in our emotional feelings. In this ideology, to be human is to be most deeply connected to one's feelings and the worst of sins is to not be true to one's emotions. This kind of thinking is promul-

---

[83]Paul Ramsey, *Basic Christian Ethics* (Louisville, KY: Westminster, 1950), 250, emphasis in original.

gated by such things as pop psychology and the prevalent teaching about self-love and self-esteem. The result is that we are defined not as much by God's love for us but rather by our love for ourselves. Some even try in vain to Christianize this thinking by saying that learning to feel love for ourselves allows us in turn to love God, when the Bible says God loves us first.[84] Furthermore, the practical implication of this teaching is that we must be true to our feelings over and above God's commands. This excuses much sin in the name of being true to oneself, which is often simultaneously being untrue to God.

Lastly, as psychologists such as B. F. Skinner have become popular, it is increasingly common for people to define themselves in light of their environment. This teaching says that who we are is in large part the result of our environment so that, generally speaking, we are victims of environmental conditions beyond our control. In popular terms, this explains why people are prone to blame their genes, father, socio-economic background, media, and the culture for who they are and how they act. In some ways, this is little more than a more nuanced and mature version of the blame-shifting that our first parents did when God confronted them about their sin.

The problem with each of these errors is found in Romans 1:25, which defines idolatry as worshiping anything created. By taking an aspect of our being (e.g., body, mind, soul, emotions, environment) and elevating it to be the defining aspect of what it means to be human, we are guilty of worshiping that part of our being instead of seeing ourselves as one whole person who bears God's image.

The third error regarding *imago Dei* occurs when we define our humanity in terms of things we do. This view is often called the *functional view* because it emphasizes a human function, usually the exercise of dominion over creation.[85] The problem with this view is that those who are not able to function as most people do would logically be considered somehow less human than the rest of us. Yet, the unborn, sick, comatose,

---

[84]1 John 4:10.

[85]For another helpful summary of these views see Millard J. Erickson, *Christian Theology* (Grand Rapids, MI: Baker, 1998), 517–36.

elderly, infirm, and the like are as much image bearers of God as those who can do certain things.

In sum, we believe five things regarding the *imago Dei*. (1) Human beings alone are God's image bearers. (2) As God's image bearers, human beings are under God and over lower creation, and great error arises when they are pulled up toward God or pushed down toward animals. (3) Human beings are the image of God, and this fact is not reduced to any aspect of their person or performance. (4) As God's image bearers, human beings have particular dignity, value, and worth. (5) As God's image bearers, humans were made to mirror God as an act of worship, which is only possible as we turn toward God.

WHEN DOES HUMAN LIFE BEGIN?

Because human beings are God's image bearers and bestowed with particular dignity, value, and worth, the question of when life begins is incredibly important. The importance of this question is amplified because of the widespread practice of abortion and the issue of whether it is in fact the taking of a human life and therefore murder.

Scientifically and medically, it is beyond debate that human life begins at conception. From the initial joining of sperm and egg, the tiny baby is alive, distinct from its mother, and living and growing as a human.[86] While the ability to express humanity and personhood change throughout the life cycle, human essence and human personhood are innate to the living being. No matter how tiny or weak, humans deserve support and protection because they are God's image bearers. Princeton professor and former member of the President's Council on Bioethics, Robert P. George, rightly says:

> Human embryos are not . . . some other type of animal organism, like a dog or cat. Neither are they a part of an organism, like a heart,

---

[86]See Douglas Considine, ed., *Van Nostrand's Scientific Encyclopedia*, 5th ed. (New York: Van Nostrand Reinhold, 1976), 943; Keith L. Moore and T. V. N. Persaud, *Before We Are Born: Essentials of Embryology and Birth Defects*, 6th ed. (Philadelphia: W. B. Saunders, 2001), 2; Bruce M. Carlson, *Patten's Foundations of Embryology*, 6th ed. (New York: McGraw-Hill, 1996), 3; Jan Langman, *Medical Embryology*, 3rd ed. (Baltimore: Williams & Wilkins, 1975), 3; Ronan O'Rahilly and Fabiola Müller, *Human Embryology and Teratology*, 2nd ed. (New York: Wiley-Liss, 1996), 8, 29.

a kidney, or a skin cell. Nor again are they a disorganized aggregate, a mere clump of cells awaiting some magical transformation. Rather, a human embryo is a whole living member of the species Homo sapiens in the earliest stage of his or her natural development. Unless severely damaged, or denied or deprived of a suitable environment, a human being in the embryonic stage will, by directing its own integral organic functioning, develop himself or herself to the next more mature developmental stage, i.e., the fetal stage. The embryonic, fetal, child, and adolescent stages are stages in the development of a determinate and enduring entity—a human being—who comes into existence as a single-celled organism (the zygote) and develops, if all goes well, into adulthood many years later.

But does this mean that the human embryo is a human person worthy of full moral respect? Must the early embryo never be used as a mere means for the benefit of others simply because it is a human being? The answer . . . is "Yes."[87]

Furthermore, there are many texts of Scripture that confirm human life does begin at conception and that an unborn baby is an image bearer of God. Psalm 51:5 reveals that we are not only human beings but sinners from conception: "Behold, I was brought forth in iniquity, and in sin did my mother conceive me." God called both Isaiah and Jeremiah for prophetic ministry from their mothers' wombs.[88] Furthermore, Luke 1:15 says that John the Baptizer "will be filled with the Holy Spirit, even from his mother's womb."

Perhaps the most extensive section of Scripture on human life in the womb is Psalm 139:13–16, which says:

[87]Robert P. George and Christopher Tollefsen, *Embryo: A Defense of Human Life* (New York: Doubleday, 2008), 3–4. George is a professor of jurisprudence and director of the James Madison Program in American Ideals and Institutions at Princeton University and a former member of the President's Council on Bioethics. Right-to-life arguments have typically been based explicitly on moral and religious grounds. In *Embryo*, the authors eschew religious arguments and make a purely scientific and philosophical case that the fetus, from the instant of conception, is a human being, with all the moral and political rights inherent in that status. The authors argue that there is no room for a "moral dualism" that regards being a "person" as merely a stage in a human life span. An embryo does not exist in a "prepersonal" stage that does not merit the inviolable rights otherwise ascribed to persons. Instead, the authors argue, the right not to be intentionally killed is inherent in the fact of being a human being, and that status begins at the moment of conception. Moreover, just as none should be excluded from moral and legal protections based on race, sex, religion, or ethnicity, none should be excluded on the basis of age, size, or stage of biological development.
[88]Isa. 49:1b; Jer. 1:5.

For you formed my inward parts;
>
> you knitted me together in my mother's womb.
>
> I praise you, for I am fearfully and wonderfully made.
>
> Wonderful are your works;
>
> my soul knows it very well.
>
> My frame was not hidden from you,
>
> when I was being made in secret,
>
> intricately woven in the depths of the earth.
>
> Your eyes saw my unformed substance;
>
> in your book were written, every one of them,
>
> the days that were formed for me,
>
> when as yet there was none of them.

Christians have always followed the teaching of the Old Testament Jews, that abortion of a preborn child and exposure of a born child are both murderous sins. In the *Didache*, which was an ancient manual for church instruction, we read, "You shall not commit murder. . . . You shall not procure abortion, nor commit infanticide."[89]

Some will argue that there is a difference between a child in a mother's womb and one outside of it, yet the early church saw both as equally living people and the taking of life in either state as equally murderous. Their convictions were based on Scripture, which uses the same word (*brephos*) for Elizabeth's unborn child (John the Baptizer)[90] as that used for the unborn baby Jesus in Mary's womb[91] and also for the children brought to Jesus.[92] Simply, in the divinely inspired pages of Scripture, God reveals to us that a child in the womb and a child singing and dancing around Jesus in worship are equally human beings who bear the image of God, and thankfully Mary did not abort the "tissue" in her womb, because he was God.

Additionally, the Bible assumes that an unborn baby is a human life and assigns the death penalty for anyone who takes an unborn life because it is murder. Exodus 21:22–25 says:

[89]*Didache* 2.2.
[90]Luke 1:41, 44.
[91]Luke 2:12.
[92]Luke 18:15. See Charles H. H. Scobie, *Ways of Our God: An Approach to Biblical Theology* (Grand Rapids, MI: Eerdmans, 2003), 834.

When men strive together and hit a pregnant woman, so that her children come out [*yasa*, a live birth—not *shakal*, the typical term for miscarriage], but there is no harm, the one who hit her shall surely be fined, as the woman's husband shall impose on him, and he shall pay as the judges determine. But if there is harm, then you shall pay life for life, eye for eye, tooth for tooth, hand for hand, foot for foot, burn for burn, wound for wound, stripe for stripe.

Indeed, not to extend legal protections to preborn children because of age, size, or phase of development is a grievous discrimination and injustice akin to racism, sexism, and ageism.

WHO HAS BEST IMAGED GOD?

Jesus alone has imaged God perfectly. Many New Testament Scriptures, and even Jesus himself, declare this:

- Christ, who is the image of God.[93]
- He is the image of the invisible God.[94]
- He is the radiance of the glory of God and the exact imprint of his nature.[95]
- Whoever sees me [Jesus] sees him who sent me.[96]
- Whoever has seen me [Jesus] has seen the Father.[97]

Practically speaking, this means that we are completely incapable of knowing anything about mirroring God until we look to the Trinity, in general, and Jesus Christ during his earthly incarnation, in particular. As Harold Best has written:

Because God is the Continuous Outpourer, we bear his image as continuous outpourers. Being made in the image of God means that we were created to act the way God acts, having been given a nature

---

[93]2 Cor. 4:4.
[94]Col. 1:15.
[95]Heb. 1:3.
[96]John 12:45.
[97]John 14:9.

within which such behavior is natural. The difference between God and humankind, merely and mysteriously, is one of singular finitude and unique and multiplied finitude. Whatever character or attribute God inherently possesses and pours out, we are created finitely to show and to pour out after his manner.[98]

Jesus' mirroring of God the Father and God the Spirit results in his continually and ceaselessly pouring himself out for the glory of God and the good of others. Therefore, to understand what a life of love, grace, mercy, justice, truth, compassion, holiness, righteousness, grief, suffering, poverty, pain, loneliness, and friendship that mirrors God is supposed to look like, we must look to Jesus Christ. Sadly, too often we look at sinful people—cracked mirrors—as our standard for what a truly holy imaging life is. Or we define noble qualities apart from Jesus and then aspire to them rather than imitating him.

HOW CAN WE BEST IMAGE GOD?

To continue with Calvin's metaphor that we have been using throughout this chapter, as sinners (a subject more thoroughly dealt with in the next chapter) we remain God's mirrors, but mirrors that have been thrown to the floor and broken and scattered into numerous shards and bits. Consequently, we reflect the glory and goodness of God infrequently and poorly.

The restoration of the image of God, or proverbial collecting of the pieces and restoration of our mirror, is found only in the renewing power of the gospel. On this point Martin Luther says:

> The Gospel has brought about the restoration of that image. Intellect and will indeed have remained, but both very much impaired. And so the Gospel brings it about that we are formed once more according to that familiar and indeed better image, because we are born again into eternal life or rather into the hope of eternal life by faith, that we

---

[98]Harold M. Best, *Unceasing Worship: Biblical Perspectives on Worship and the Arts* (Downers Grove, IL: InterVarsity, 2003), 23.

may live in God and with God and be one with Him, as Christ says (John 17:21).[99]

This is precisely what Romans 8:29 means when it says, "For those whom he foreknew he also predestined to be conformed to the image of his Son, in order that he might be the firstborn among many brothers." To be conformed to the image of Jesus means God by his grace and through his Spirit by his gospel, bit by bit, causes the mirror of our life to be increasingly like Jesus Christ's so that we image God increasingly well.

The renewal of the image of God in man is a process that God works in believers over the course of their lifelong sanctification by the Spirit. Importantly, this is not merely something passive that God does for us, but something that, by his grace through his Spirit, we have the honor of participating in as an act of mirroring him.[100] Colossians 3:9–10 speaks of the "new self . . . renewed in knowledge after the *image* of its creator." In 2 Corinthians 3:18 Paul says, "We all, with unveiled face, beholding the glory of the Lord, are being transformed into the same *image* from one degree of glory to another. For this comes from the Lord who is the Spirit."

Admittedly, as Christians we do sin, chase folly, and in our worst moments seem to be breaking our mirror while God is repairing it. Regardless, to image God requires ongoing humble repentance and a fiercely devoted steadfastness to change as God commands and with God pick up the pieces of our life shattered through sin.

In this valiant effort we must constantly choose to believe the truth—that this reflecting God alone is a great life. It is not an easy life, or a simple life, or a perfect life. But it is a wonderful life in that it is filled with evidences of God's grace, healing from our past, and hope for our future. Furthermore, because mirroring God is the essence of our true humanity, as we reflect his glory we discover the source of our deepest joy, even when life hurts the most.

Amazingly, upon death this life not only continues but is perfected,

[99]Martin Luther, "Lectures on Genesis Chapters 1–5," 1:64.
[100]Eph. 4:22–24; Col. 3:1–10.

and the mirror of our life, along with all of creation, is fully restored and will reflect the light of the glory of God perfectly, beautifully, magnificently, unceasingly, and unendingly. Paul describes this mirroring we will experience to God's glory and our joy in the resurrected and perfected state: "Just as we have borne the image of the man of dust, we shall also bear the image of the man of heaven."[101] In addition, "our citizenship is in heaven, and from it we await a Savior, the Lord Jesus Christ, who will transform our lowly body to be like his glorious body, by the power that enables him even to subject all things to himself."[102]

WHAT DOES A LIFE THAT IMAGES GOD LOOK LIKE?

Humans worship or "outpour" continuously, as Harold Best writes:

> We were created continuously outpouring—we were created in that condition, at that instant, *imago Dei*. We did not graduate into being in the image of God; we were, by divine fiat, already in the image of God at the instant the Spirit breathed into our dust. Hence we were created continuously outpouring.[103]

Therefore, a life that images God is one in which we are increasingly sanctified by the Holy Spirit to be more and more like Jesus, thereby enabling us to mirror the glory of God in a way that is akin to how Moses radiated the glory of God after meeting with him on Mount Sinai. This worshipful reflecting of the glory of God is done in multiple ways:

1) We image God by connecting with God in an informed and passionate way through repenting of sin, believing in Jesus Christ, and living in an ongoing humble and repentant relationship with God.
2) We image God by submitting to godly authority and ultimately to God's authority. In this way we are reflecting the nature of the Trinity: "For a man ought not to cover his head, since he is the image and glory

---

[101]1 Cor. 15:49.
[102]Phil. 3:20–21.
[103]Best, *Unceasing Worship*, 23.

of God, but woman is the glory of man."[104] This submission to godly authority includes wives submitting to husbands, children submitting to parents, church members submitting to church leaders, players submitting to coaches, employees submitting to employers, citizens submitting to governments, and so on. This submission to authority is ultimately done in submission to Scripture, which is our highest authority as God's Word (this does leave open the rare exception when not submitting to a lesser authority is required because the lesser authority has commanded someone to sin and thus violate the higher authority of Scripture).

3) We image God by serving him in ways that advance his kingdom, including making culture that honors him. This also includes fighting injustice, evil, and oppression by working for justice and mercy. On this point, theologian D. A. Carson says, "As God's image bearers we have peculiar responsibilities toward the rest of the created order—responsibilities of governance and care, as we recognize our oneness with the created order and our distinguishing place within it. [105]

4) We image God by respecting all of human life, particularly the weak, oppressed, sick, elderly, and unborn. Because people bear God's image, we are not only to promote life but also not to commit the sin of murder. As Genesis 9:6 says, "Whoever sheds the blood of man, by man shall his blood be shed, for God made man in his own image." Practically speaking, this means that racism is absolutely inexcusable and that previous attempts in America's history to define blacks as only partly human and also partly animal were nothing short of false teaching that maligns Scripture and mocks God.

5) We image God by refusing to live autonomous lives and by contending for community. This includes fellowship with Christians in our church and other churches, honoring our parents, forgiving our enemies as God in Christ forgave us, and practicing hospitality by welcoming strangers into our homes and lives as God has welcomed us.

6) We image God by suffering well. When the clouds of trial, pain, loss, hardship, hurt, and tears roll in, we must never forget that our Lord Jesus Christ imaged God well even when suffering. When Jesus was hurting the most, as he hung on the cross for our sins, he reflected the mercy and

---

[104]1 Cor. 11:7.
[105]D. A. Carson, *Christ and Culture Revisited* (Grand Rapids, MI: Eerdmans, 2008), 46.

justice of God perfectly. Jesus invites us to not waste the worst moments and seasons of our life but rather consider them treasures to be invested purposefully in glorifying God by imaging the character of Jesus by the power of the Holy Spirit. This is Jesus' point when he says, "If anyone would come after me, let him deny himself and take up his cross and follow me."[106] Thankfully, unlike so many half-true theologies that speak only of the victories of Christian life and how to image God when we are winning, Jesus shows us that if our aim is to image God, then when we win and lose and as we live and die, every moment is a sacred opportunity to be captured for his glory, our joy, and others' good.

---

[106]Mark 8:34.

CHAPTER 5

FALL: GOD JUDGES

God made man upright, but they have sought out many schemes.

ECCLESIASTES 7:29

Something has gone terribly wrong. And everyone knows it.

The Bible reveals that God created this world in a perfect state and upon the creation of the man and woman, God declared his entire creation "very good."[1] This intended state of perfect beauty in all things is described in the Old Testament as "shalom."[2] Even those who do not believe in the Bible persist in longing for a shalom on the earth, because deep down in God's image bearers there is a faint echo of Eden and how things are supposed to be.

Yet, no matter how much money we spend, how many elections we hold, how many organizations we start, how many blogs we write, how many complaints we air, how many tears we cry, or how many wars we wage, boredom, annoyances, miseries, fears, tragedies, suffering, injustice, evil, sickness, pain, and death continue unabated.

Why? The fall.

WHAT IS THE FALL?

Genesis 3 is one of the most important chapters in the entire Bible because it explains the source of and solution for sin and death. In painful brevity,

---

[1]Gen. 1:31.
[2]Isa. 2:2–4; 11:1–9; 32:14–20; 43:1–12; 60:1–22; 65:17–25; Joel 2:24–29; 3:17–18.

with each word dripping horror, we read how the human rebellion against God that began with the first sin is altogether foolish, tragic, and mad. Commenting on the opening pages of Genesis, John Sailhamer says:

> A more studied attempt to treat the problem of evil and temptation cannot be found in all the Scriptures. As a part of his deliberate strategy, the author . . . has left the reader virtually alone with the events of the story. He does not reflect or comment on the events that transpired. We, the readers, are left to ourselves and our sense of the story for an answer to the questions it raises. We must seek our own clues to the story's meaning from the few signs of the author's own shaping of the story.[3]

The scene is the beautiful and perfect garden made by God for our first parents to live in together without sin and its many effects. There, God lovingly and graciously speaks as a father to Adam and Eve, giving them complete freedom to enjoy all of creation, except partaking of the fruit of the tree of the knowledge of good and evil, which was forbidden.

But the entrance of the Serpent marks the beginning of chaos in creation. The Serpent is Satan according to Revelation 12:9 and 20:2. Sailhamer describes the scene:

> The snake speaks only twice, but that is enough to offset the balance of trust and obedience between the man and the woman and their Creator. The centerpiece of the story is the question of the knowledge of the "good." The snake implied by his questions that God was keeping this knowledge *from* the man and the woman (3:5), while the sense of the narratives in the first two chapters has been that God was keeping this knowledge *for* the man and the woman (e.g., 1:4, 10, 12, 18, 21, 25, 31; 2:18). In other words, the snake's statements were a direct challenge to the central theme of the narrative of chapters 1 and 2: God will provide the "good" for human beings if they will only trust him and obey him.[4]

---

[3]John H. Sailhamer, *The Pentateuch as Narrative* (Grand Rapids, MI: Zondervan, 1992), 102.
[4]Ibid., 103–4.

Satan began by tempting Eve to mistrust God's word by changing its meaning, just as he did when likewise tempting Jesus in Matthew 4:1–11. Rather than rebuking Satan, Eve entertained his lies[5] and was subsequently deceived by his crafty arguments.[6] Satan was so bold as to accuse God of being a liar and to tempt the pride of Adam and Eve by declaring that if they disobeyed God they could in effect become his peer and gods themselves. Eve was faced with either trusting her own judgment[7] or God's protective warning that it was deadly.[8] Satan promised that, upon sinning against God, they would become like God. Yet, they were already like God by virtue of the fact he made them in his image and likeness.[9]

Eve believed Satan over God and chose pride over humility by partaking of the tree of the knowledge of good and evil in sin against God. Hers was a sin of commission, whereby she did what God forbade.

Tragically, we further read that while all of this occurred, Adam stood by silently, failing to lead his family in godliness.[10] This was Adam's sin of omission, whereby he failed to do what God created him to do—lovingly lead his family and humbly serve God. Adam then joined his wife's sin of commission, bringing shame, distrust, and separation between Adam and Eve, and between them and God. This included hiding from God and one another and covering themselves, as sinners have done in varying ways ever since.[11]

God then came looking for the man, holding him responsible for the sinful condition of his family as its head.[12] Rather than repenting of his sin, Adam essentially argued with God by blaming Eve for his sin and blaming God for making Eve.[13] Eve, too, failed to repent of her sin and blamed the Serpent for deceiving her.[14]

As a result of the fall, the descent into sin has continued unabated

---

[5]John 8:42–47.
[6]2 Cor. 11:3; 1 Tim. 2:14.
[7]The wording in Gen. 2:9 and 3:6 is identical.
[8]Gen. 2:17.
[9]Gen. 1:26.
[10]Gen. 3:6.
[11]Gen. 3:7–8.
[12]Gen. 3:9.
[13]Gen. 3:12.
[14]Gen. 3:13.

ever since. A respect for authority was replaced by rebellion. A clear conscience was replaced by guilt and shame. Blessing was replaced by physical, spiritual, and eternal punishment. Viewing God as a friend to walk with was replaced by viewing him as an enemy to hide from. Trust was replaced by fear. Love was replaced by indifference and even hatred. Intimacy with God was replaced by separation from God. Freedom to obey God was replaced by enslavement to sin. Honesty was replaced with lying and deceit. Self-sacrifice was replaced by self-centeredness. Peace was replaced by restlessness. Responsibility was replaced by blaming. Authenticity was replaced by hiding.

Theologian D. A. Carson says, "Consumed by our own self-focus, we desire to dominate or manipulate others: here is the beginning of fences, of rape, of greed, of malice, of nurtured bitterness, of war.[15]

Nonetheless, sin and the fall do not have the world, but God does. And he speaks a promise of hope in the coming of Jesus who will respect authority, bring blessing, and be a friend we can walk with, a savior we can trust in, love incarnate, and God come down to be close to us and liberate us from sin's presence and penalty, by calling us to honest repentance to live God-centered lives of peace, responsibility, and authenticity as saved sinners.

WHAT IS SIN?

Sin is so nefarious, complex, and far-reaching that it is difficult to succinctly define. Cornelius Plantinga says:

> The Bible presents sin by way of major concepts, principally lawlessness and faithlessness, expressed in an array of images: sin is the missing of a target, a wandering from the path, a straying from the fold. Sin is a hard heart and a stiff neck. Sin is blindness and deafness. It is both the overstepping of a line and the failure to reach it—both transgression and shortcoming. Sin is a beast crouching at the door. In sin, people attack or evade or neglect their divine calling. These and other images suggest deviance: even when it is familiar, sin is never normal. Sin is

---

[15]D. A. Carson, *Christ and Culture Revisited* (Grand Rapids, MI: Eerdmans, 2008), 46.

disruption of created harmony and then resistance to divine restoration of that harmony. Above all, sin disrupts and resists the vital human relation to God.[16]

D. A. Carson says:

The heart of all this evil is idolatry itself. It is the de-godding of God. It is the creature swinging his puny fist in the face of his Maker and saying, in effect, "If you do not see things my way, I'll make my own gods! I'll *be* my own god!" Small wonder that the sin most frequently said to arouse God's wrath is not murder, say, or pillage, or any other "horizontal" barbarism, but idolatry—that which dethrones God. That is also why, in every sin, it is God who is the most offended party, as David himself well understood: "Against you, only, have I sinned and done what is evil in your sight; so you are right in your verdict and justified when you judge" (Psalm 51:4).[17]

The Bible uses a constellation of images to explain sin as everything from rebellion to folly, self-abuse, madness, treason, death, hatred, spiritual adultery, missing the mark, wandering from the path, idolatry, insanity, irrationality, pride, selfishness, blindness, deafness, a hard heart, a stiff neck, delusion, unreasonableness, and self-worship. To help you understand sin, in general, and your sin, in particular, we will examine eight aspects of sin that the Old Testament teaches us.

1) Sin in the Old Testament is first a relational breach. This is painfully clear in Genesis 2–3 where, because of their sin, our first parents are separated from God and one another; they hide from God and one another, fear God, blame one another, and seek to cover their sin and shame while living their life apart from God.

2) Sin in the Old Testament is a social matter because shalom has been vandalized. This is evidenced by the litany of murder, perversion, drunkenness, the continual evil that precipitated the flood, and human attempts

---

[16]Cornelius Plantinga Jr., *Not the Way It's Supposed to Be: A Breviary of Sin* (Grand Rapids, MI: Eerdmans, 1995), 5.
[17]Carson, *Christ and Culture Revisited*, 46.

at an Edenic-like society without any regard for God that spring forth in Genesis 4–11.

3) Sin in the Old Testament is a covenantal rebellion against God and his authority. This is witnessed perhaps most clearly in Exodus 32 to 34, where following God's liberation of his people, they dishonor, disregard, and disobey him by worshiping idols while God is giving them the Ten Commandments through their leader Moses.

4) Sin in the Old Testament is a legal transgression that results in guilt that necessitates punishment. One clear example is found in Deuteronomy 32, where in worshipful song Moses recollects some of the most treasonous behavior of God's people and the price that had to be paid for justice to be maintained.

5) Sin in the Old Testament results in ritual uncleanness, pollution, and filth, marked by the use of words such as "filth," "defiled," "unclean," and "whore."[18] Importantly, this defilement happens both to sinners and victims; we defile ourselves by our own sin and are defiled by others when they sin against us.

6) Sin in the Old Testament includes emotional pain such as shame and disgrace.[19] This is first seen in Genesis 3, where our first parents sin and then hide in shame and disgrace, whereas prior to their sin they "were not ashamed."[20]

7) Sin in the Old Testament is spoken of in historical terms as an accumulating burden whereby sin is piled up from one generation to the next.[21] In this way, sin only worsens over time as people invent new ways to do evil more effectively.

8) Sin in the Old Testament is spoken of with the finality of death.[22] Sin is deadly, and ends only in death. This is because when we sin and prefer created things to our creator God, we stop ruling over creation and are ruled by it so that in the end we lose and the dust wins.[23]

The New Testament also speaks of sin in many ways, though four words are used most often.

---

[18]Gen. 34:5; Lev. 19:31; 21:14; Num. 5:27; 1 Chron. 5:1; Ps. 106:39; Prov. 30:11–12; Lam. 4:14; Ezek. 14:11.
[19]E.g., Jer. 6:15; Ezek. 36:16.
[20]Gen. 2:25.
[21]E.g., Gen. 15:16; Deut. 9:4–8; 18:24–28.
[22]E.g., Genesis 5; Deuteronomy 30.
[23]Gen. 3:17–19.

1) The most common New Testament word for *sin* is the Greek word *hamartia*, which means wrongdoing, or missing the mark. It is the most general word used for sin and refers to the innumerable ways in which we fall short of what God intends for us and miss his will for our conduct.

2) The New Testament frequently uses the Greek word *paraptoma*, which means "to trespass." This word speaks of crossing a line of God's law, whether intentionally or unintentionally.

3) The New Testament also uses the Greek word *parabasis* to speak of sin as disobedience and transgression. By using this word, the Bible is referring to evil intent, whereby someone defiantly chooses to disobey God and thus sin, knowing full well what they are doing.

4) The New Testament often uses the Greek word *asebeias* to speak of sin in terms of ungodliness and godlessness. This word refers to sinners' active character of rebellion whereby they act as if there were no God and/or as if they were their own God and the highest authority in their life.

In summary, sin includes both omission, where we do not do what we ought, and commission, where we do what we ought not do. Sin includes our thoughts, words, deeds, and motives. Sin includes godlessness, which is ignoring God and living as if there were no God or as if we were God. Sin is invariably idolatry, which is the replacing of God as preeminent with something or someone else—most often oneself.

Sin includes individuals, communities, networks, and the like as individuals labor together for the cause of sin. Sin includes entire ways of thinking and acting, such as racism and pornography. Sometimes a sin is also a crime, such as murder, and sometimes it is not, such as adultery. Sin can be done deliberately or in ignorance. The practice of a particular sin can occur once, regularly, or even frequently.

Sin includes breaking God's laws, breaching just human laws, defying godly authority such as parents or pastors, and violating one's own conscience as well as conviction wrought by God the Holy Spirit. Sin includes perversion, using good things for evil purposes. Sin includes pollution, infecting good things with evil. Lastly, sin is the turning of a good thing (e.g., sex, work, money, comfort) into an ultimate thing so that it is worshiped as a god in place of God and becomes a false god.

Or, to say it as Proverbs 20:9 does, "Who can say, 'I have made my heart pure; I am clean from my sin'?" The answer is no one but Jesus Christ.

Nonetheless, some sinners seek to minimize their sin by comparing their sins to others' so that theirs appear minor and therefore somehow less sinful. Regarding degrees of sin, on one hand, God sees people in the categories of perfection and imperfection[24] and considers any sin a violation of the entirety of his law.[25] Therefore, all sin is grievous. One example is Jesus' teaching that people cannot excuse lust because it is not as bad as adultery.[26] Practically, this means that sinners must not compare themselves or their sin to others but rather to Jesus, and see all of their sin without diminishing any of it.

On the other hand, sins have degrees of severity. Jesus told Pilate the high priest, "He who delivered me over to you has the greater sin."[27] Some sins have greater consequences than others. This is why the Bible speaks of the sin that leads to death,[28] more severe judgment,[29] stricter judgment for teachers,[30] greater punishment,[31] greater consequences for intentional sin than unintentional sin,[32] greater punishment for child abusers,[33] greater punishment for a man who does not feed his family than for an infidel,[34] and twice the judgment for self-righteous religious people than for "sinners."[35] This principle makes practical sense, seeing that, for example, it would be a sin for one man to lust after another man's wife but the damage would be far greater if he actually seduced her and committed

---

[24]Matt. 5:48.
[25]James 2:10.
[26]Matt. 5:27–28. Jesus doesn't say they are equal but that both are sin even though the Law of Moses only forbids adultery. Legalists always look for such things to excuse their sin.
[27]John 19:11.
[28]1 John 5:16–18.
[29]Luke 12:47–48.
[30]James 3:1.
[31]Matt. 11:20–24.
[32]Lev. 4:1–35; 5:15–19; Num. 15:22–30; Ezek. 45:20; Luke 12:48.
[33]Matt. 18:6.
[34]1 Tim. 5:8.
[35]Matt. 10:15; 23:15.

adultery with her. All parents would prefer that their neighbor simply covet their child rather than actually kidnap her.

WHERE DID SIN ORIGINATE?

Regarding evil and sin, Christian doctrine professes four essential truths. First, God is fully and continually all-powerful. Second, God is altogether good and there is no evil in him whatsoever.[36] Third, evil and sin really do exist. Fourth, sinners are fully responsible for their sin.

Various erroneous attempts to deal with evil do away with one of these truths and thus explain away evil or reduce the problem. Perhaps God is not all-powerful, or maybe God is not good, or maybe evil is an illusion. Maybe sin is not our fault but the fault of our parents' failures or our circumstances. In opposition to these errors, the Bible—the most honest book ever written—faces evil in its thorough darkness without blushing or backpedalling and commands us to do the same. Rising up from the pages of Scripture is the greatest evil and sin of all, the murderous and bloody crucifixion of Jesus Christ.

We do need to make a distinction between moral evil and natural evil. Moral evil is the result of choices of a responsible agent, whether intentional or negligent. Natural evil is suffering that occurs without a moral agent involved (hurricanes, floods, earthquakes). Humans make no (or very few) actions causing natural evils.

Defining evil (the essence) and sin (the action) is very important. Among the most helpful thinkers in the history of Christian doctrine on this point is Augustine. Prior to his conversion to Christianity, he was part of a cult called Manichaeism. That cult—like many Eastern religions, pantheism, panentheism, and the New Spirituality (or New Age)—considered God to be both good and evil.

Augustine's prayer in his book *Confessions* describes his own experience whereby God opened his eyes to his personal sin. Augustine prays:

---

[36]Ps. 5:4; Isa. 59:2; 64:7; Zech. 8:17; 1 John 1:5.

But You, Lord, while he was speaking, turned me back towards myself, taking me from behind my own back where I had put myself all the time that I preferred not to see myself. And You set me there before my own face that I might see how vile I was, how twisted and unclean and spotted and ulcerous. I saw myself and was horrified, but there was no way to flee from myself. . . . You were setting me face to face with myself, forcing me upon my own sight, that I might see my iniquity and loathe it. I had known it, but I had pretended not to see it, had deliberately looked the other way and let it go from my mind.[37]

Following his conversion, Augustine rightly said that evil was a flaw, a lack or deficiency in something inherently good. Evil is therefore a privation, or that which deprives a being of some good that is proper to that being. As a parasite, evil is all the more heinous because it destroys that which is beautiful and whole. Examples include blindness, which is not a thing in and of itself but rather a lack of sight, and rot, which is not a thing but rather the corruption of something like metal or wood. For this reason, Zechariah 10:2 uses the four words *nonsense*, *lies*, *false*, and *empty* to explain sin in terms of privation.

Not only is sin a privation, it is also corruption, according to Romans 5:12–21. Adam's sin affects us all in three ways. (1) There is inherited sin from the original sin of Adam that causes the rest of humanity to be born into a sinful state or condition. The corrupted sin nature that we inherit from Adam begins in our mother's womb.[38] This is what John Calvin referred to as "a hereditary depravity and corruption of our nature."[39] (2) There is imputed sin whereby Adam's sin and guilt is attributed, or reckoned, to us and our legal standing before and relationship with God is negated. Additionally, by the grace of God, the sinner's guilt and condemnation is imputed to Jesus Christ, who atones for sin on the cross and enables his righteousness to be imputed to the sinner as a Christian. (3) Adam's sin is imparted to us so that we are conceived in a fallen state and, apart from the

---

[37]Augustine, *Confessions,* 8.7.
[38]Pss. 51:5; 58:3.
[39]John Calvin, *Institutes of the Christian Religion*, 2 vols., ed. John T. McNeill, trans. Ford Lewis Battles (Philadelphia: Westminster, 1960), 2.i.8.

enabling grace of God, are unable to respond to the gospel or remedy our depravity. Simply put, we are each sinners by both nature and choice.[40]

As a result of our sin nature, we are by nature children of wrath,[41] all sinners,[42] and destined to death.[43] Speaking of our sin nature, A. W. Tozer says:

> There is within the human heart a tough fibrous root of fallen life whose nature is to possess, always to possess. It covets "things" with a deep and fierce passion. The pronouns "my" and "mine" look innocent enough in print, but their constant and universal use is significant. They express the real nature of the old Adamic man better than a thousand volumes of theology could do. They are verbal symptoms of our deep disease. The roots of our hearts have grown down into things, and we dare not pull up one rootlet lest we die. Things have become necessary to us, a development never originally intended. God's gifts now take the place of God, and the whole course of nature is upset by the monstrous substitution.[44]

Subsequently, God does not tempt us to sin, but instead the temptation arises from within our own sinful hearts. Jesus' own brother speaks of the source of sin within us:

> Let no one say when he is tempted, "I am being tempted by God," for God cannot be tempted with evil, and he himself tempts no one. But each person is tempted when he is lured and enticed by his own desire. Then desire when it has conceived gives birth to sin, and sin when it is fully grown brings forth death.[45]

Therefore, mere behavioral change is not sufficient to remedy the human condition. Instead, we need a new heart and nature, what the Bible calls regeneration or new birth, followed by ongoing sanctification into

---

[40]Pss. 51:5; 58:3; Isa. 53:6; 64:6; Rom. 3:23; 1 John 1:18.
[41]Eph. 2:3.
[42]Rom. 5:12, 19.
[43]1 Cor. 15:21–22.
[44]A. W. Tozer, *The Pursuit of God* (Radford, VA: Wilder, 2008), 18–19.
[45]James 1:13–15; see also Prov. 27:19; Jer. 17:9; Mark 7:21–23; Luke 6:45.

Christlikeness if there is to be any true victory over sin in our lives. Subsequently, there are only two categories of humanity—those who are under Adam by birth in sin and damnation and those who are under Jesus by new birth in grace and salvation.

WHAT IS TOTAL DEPRAVITY?

Human depravity is an undeniable reality. Even atheists know humans are not as they should be. Psychological pioneer Sigmund Freud views our innermost self as a "hell." In *Civilization and Its Discontents*, Freud writes:

> Men are not gentle, friendly creatures wishing for love, who simply defend themselves if they are attacked, but that a powerful measure of desire for aggression has to be reckoned as part of their instinctual endowment. The result is that their neighbor is to them not only a possible helper or sexual object, but also a temptation to them to gratify their aggressiveness on him, to exploit his capacity for work without recompense, to use him sexually without his consent, to seize his possessions, to humiliate him, to cause him pain, to torture and to kill him. *Homo homini lupus* [man is a wolf]; who has the courage to dispute it in the face of all the evidence in his own life and in history?[46]

Despite the fact we are sinners, the Bible repeatedly states that after the fall we do retain the image of God.[47] Included in this is a vestige of moral sense because of the conscience that God has given us as his image bearers.[48] Because people are made in God's image with a conscience, the Bible does speak of some non-Christians who, while not holy and living to God's glory, do some "good" things. Examples include Abimelech,[49] Balaam,[50] Rahab,[51] Artaxerxes,[52] and the Good Samaritan.[53]

The existence of "good" non-Christians is evidence of God's common

---

[46]Sigmund Freud, *Civilization and Its Discontents*, trans. Joan Riviere (London: Hogarth, 1963), 58.
[47]Gen. 5:1–3; 9:6; 1 Cor. 11:7; James 3:9.
[48]Rom. 2:14–15.
[49]Genesis 20.
[50]Numbers 22–24.
[51]Joshua 2.
[52]Ezra 7; Nehemiah 2.
[53]Luke 10:30–37.

grace. Nonetheless, without saving grace we sinners are unable to do anything that makes us pleasing in God's sight because it is not done in faith as an act of worship out of love for God.

While people are not *utterly depraved* and as evil as they could be, all people are *totally depraved* in that their every motive, word, deed, and thought is affected, stained, and marred by sin. This includes the mind,[54] will,[55] emotions,[56] heart,[57] conscience,[58] and physical body.[59] The totality of a person is pervasively affected by sin, and there is no aspect of their being not negatively impacted by sin.

Describing what can also be called *pervasive depravity*, J. C. Ryle said, "Sin . . . pervades and runs through every part of our moral constitution and every faculty of our minds. The understanding, the affections, the reasoning powers, the will, are all more or less infected."[60] Practically speaking, this means that we cannot fully trust any single aspect of our being (e.g., our mind or our emotions) because each is tainted and marred by sin and therefore not perfect or objective. Subsequently, we need God's Spirit, God's Word, and God's people to help us see truly and live wisely.

WHAT ARE SATAN'S SCHEMES AGAINST US?

Not only did Satan tempt the first Adam in a garden, but he also tempted the Last Adam in a desert. In each of the Synoptic Gospels, Satan appears as the tempter of Jesus Christ.[61] From the opening to the closing pages of Scripture, Satan is presented as an enemy of God and subsequently an enemy of God's people. Throughout Scripture he is named in a variety of ways, including the Devil, the dragon, the Serpent, enemy, tempter, murderer, Father of Lies, adversary, accuser, destroyer, and the Evil One.

Sadly, it is not uncommon for people to make either too much or too

---

[54]Eph. 4:18.
[55]Rom. 6:16–17.
[56]Titus 3:3.
[57]Jer. 17:9.
[58]Titus 1:15.
[59]Rom. 8:10.
[60]John Charles Ryle, *Holiness: Its Nature, Hindrances, Difficulties, and Roots* (Moscow, ID: Charles Nolan, 2002), 4.
[61]Matt. 4:1–11; Mark 1:12–13; Luke 4:1–13.

little of Satan. As C. S. Lewis says, "There are two equal and opposite errors into which our race can fall about the devils. One is to disbelieve in their existence. The other is to believe, and to feel an excessive and unhealthy interest in them."[62]

Foundational to our study of Satan is to recognize that he is in no way equal to God. His knowledge, presence, and power are limited because he is an angelic being created by God for the purpose of glorifying and serving God. However, he became proud in his heart and desired to be worshiped and exalted like God. So he declared war upon God and one-third of the angels joined his army to oppose God.[63] Judged by God for his sin, the Serpent and his servants were then cast down to the earth.[64]

The motivation for all of the Serpent's work is pride and self-glory instead of humility and God-glory.[65] Subsequently, one of his most powerful allies in opposing God's people is their own pride. Some have speculated as to why the Serpent continues in his war against God even though Scripture is clear that he will be ultimately defeated and painfully judged. It may be that the Serpent is indeed so proud that he has deceived himself and now believes that God is a liar who can be beaten.

In his war against God, the Serpent not only has demons but also has people who are allies in his army either by demonic possession, demonic influence, or simply living according to their sin nature and flesh. Such people include false prophets who speak for the Serpent,[66] false apostles who lead ministries for the Serpent,[67] false Christians who divide churches,[68] and false teachers who teach heretical doctrine for the Serpent.[69]

Regarding spiritual warfare as it is experienced on the personal level, 2 Corinthians 2:11 (NIV) says, "Satan might not outwit us. For we are not unaware of his schemes." Therefore, knowing Satan's tactics helps us in anticipating his work and living in victory rather than as victims.

[62]C. S. Lewis, *The Screwtape Letters* (New York: HarperCollins, 2001), *ix*.
[63]Rev. 12:4.
[64]Isa. 14:11–23; Ezek. 28:1–19.
[65]Ezek. 28:2; James 4:6–7.
[66]2 Pet. 2:1.
[67]2 Cor. 11:13.
[68]Gal. 2:4.
[69]2 Pet. 2:1.

Scheme 1: The World

The world is our external enemy that tempts us to sin against God. What is meant by the term *world* in its negative sense? The world is an organized system in opposition and rebellion against God. In 1 John 2:16, the world is defined as corporate flesh working together in three ways. (1) The world is the domain of the desires or lust of the flesh, which is the sinful longings for physical pleasures that tempt us, everything from gluttony to drunkenness, sexual sin, and chemical highs. (2) The world is the place devoted to the desires or lust of the eyes, where the sinful longings for coveted possessions are manifested in everything from advertising and marketing to pornography. (3) The world is where pride in possessions is commended, and haughty selfish ambition is considered a virtue rather than a vice.

In response to the world, the Bible commands a threefold response. (1) We are not to love the world.[70] Because the world is our mission field, rather than our home, and the source of our temptation to sin, we must continually guard ourselves from falling in love with the world and the passions and pleasures it offers, not unlike the forbidden fruit that tempted our first parents. (2) We are not to let the world shape our values.[71] Because the world is where Satan and our sinful desires converge, if we allow the world to shape our value system and define who we are, why we exist, what we believe, and how we behave, then we will be converted to the world rather than seeking the conversion of the world to the kingdom of God. (3) Because Jesus died to the world, we are commanded to live as crucified to the world.[72] This means that we are either alive to the sin of the world and dead to God or dead to the temptation of the world and alive to God. By being dead to the world we can live in true freedom from it and thereby enter into it as a missionary, as Jesus did, seeking to see people saved from the world by the gospel.

Importantly, while the world is a source of sinful temptation, it does not abdicate sinners from their moral responsibility. This is because while

---

[70]1 John 2:15.
[71]Rom. 12:2.
[72]Gal. 6:14.

the world can tempt us, we are still the ones who choose to sin. In his book *Precious Remedies against Satan's Devices*, Puritan Thomas Brooks says that our enemy will use the world to bait our hook with anything that we find desirable.[73] This means that he will gladly give us sex, money, power, pleasure, fame, fortune, and relationships. Satan's goal is for us to take the bait without seeing the hook and once the hook is in our mouth, he reels us in to take us as his captive. Therefore, no matter what our enemy hangs on our proverbial hook as bait, we must always put to death our internal flesh if we hope to avoid sin.

Scheme 2: The Flesh

The flesh is our internal enemy and a seed of corruption that lingers in us until our glorification following death. In brief, the flesh is our fallen internal resistance to obey God and put self-interests above God's interests.[74] Flesh sometimes means a physical body, as when the Word became flesh.[75] But the Bible does not locate our sin in our physicality as ancient and contemporary Gnostics do. The sinful deeds of the flesh come from every part of our person.[76] Paul uses flesh to refer to our innate propensity to sin against God; he says that the flesh is the seat of our sinful passions,[77] the realm of sinners,[78] and the source of our evil desires.[79]

The Bible commands Christians to respond to the flesh in three ways. (1) We are to recognize that we are no longer under the flesh's bondage.[80] Jesus' death for our sin and his resurrection for our salvation give us a new nature and a new power from God the Holy Spirit that enables us to say no to our flesh and yes to God. (2) We are to walk in conscious submission to the Holy Spirit.[81] Because the Holy Spirit is more powerful than our sinful

---

[73]See Thomas Brooks, *Precious Remedies against Satan's Devices* (Philadelphia: Jonathan Pounder, 1810), 16.
[74]Mark 7:21–23; Gal. 5:19–21; Col. 3:5–8; James 1:14–15.
[75]John 1:14.
[76]Gal. 5:19–21.
[77]Rom. 7:18, 25; Gal. 5:16, 19; Eph. 2:3.
[78]Rom. 7:5; 8:8–9.
[79]Col. 3:5.
[80]Romans 6.
[81]Gal. 5:16.

desires, he alone can get us out of unholy sin and into holy worship. (3) We are to put to death, or what the Puritan John Owen called "mortify," sinful desires.[82] The opposite of mortifying sin includes excusing sin, tolerating sin, or merely wounding sin by attempting to manage it. Mortification is Holy Spirit-enabled conviction followed by repentance of sin, faith in God, worship of God, and perseverance in holiness so that sin remains dead and joy remains alive.

Scheme 3: The Devil

Whatever his tactics, the Serpent's ultimate goal for believers is typically a compromised and fruitless life beset by heresy and sin[83] and ultimately death.[84] This demonic opposition is increasingly pronounced for those who serve God most faithfully. As the Puritan William Gurnall was fond of saying, "Where God is on one side, you may be sure to find the devil on the other."[85]

The Bible speaks of Satan's work in what can commonly be understood as the ordinary and extraordinary demonic. Ordinary demonic work entices us to sexual sin,[86] marriage between Christians and non-Christians,[87] false religion with false teaching about a false Jesus,[88] unforgiving bitterness,[89] foolishness and drunkenness,[90] idle gossiping and busybodying,[91] lying,[92] and idolatry.[93] Extraordinary demonic work includes torment,[94] physical injury,[95] counterfeit miracles,[96] accusation,[97] death,[98] and false spirits.[99]

As God promised our first parents following their sin, the defeat of

---

[82]Rom. 8:13–16.
[83]1 Tim. 4:1–2; 1 John 3:7–10.
[84]John 8:44; 1 Pet. 5:8.
[85]William Gurnall, *The Christian in Complete Armour* (London: William Tegg, 1862), 781.
[86]1 Cor. 7:5.
[87]2 Cor. 6:15.
[88]1 Cor. 10:14–22; 1 Tim. 4:1–2; 2 Cor. 11:1–4.
[89]Eph. 4:17–32.
[90]Eph. 5:8–21.
[91]1 Tim. 5:11–15.
[92]John 8:44.
[93]1 John 5:18–21.
[94]Acts 5:16.
[95]Matt. 9:32–33; 12:22–23; Acts 8:4–8.
[96]Acts 8:9–23; 16:16; 2 Thess. 2:9–10.
[97]Rev. 12:10.
[98]Prov. 8:36; John 8:44.
[99]1 John 4:1–6.

Satan and his works is possible only through the death, burial, and resurrection of Jesus Christ in our place for our sins. This is exactly what the Bible teaches. Hebrews 2:14–15 says, "Since therefore the children share in flesh and blood, he himself likewise partook of the same things, that through death he might destroy the one who has the power of death, that is, the devil, and deliver all those who through fear of death were subject to lifelong slavery."

WHAT ARE SOME SINFUL VIEWS OF SIN?

Because sin is a humanity-wide problem, answers for the definition, source, and cause of sin are postulated from seemingly every conceivable ideology. By examining some sinful views of sin, we are able to better understand erroneous views and help explain biblical truth to those holding these positions.

In materialism that believes in no spiritual reality, "sin" is the result of electro-chemical imbalances leading to biological dysfunction. Therefore, the solution to evil and sin is medical and chemical improvement of the human body.

In evolutionism, "sin" is essentially anything that hinders the perceived progress of the human race rather than any offense against a personal God.

In psychologism, "sin" is caused by low self-esteem that results in the repression of one's true feelings. Subsequently, the answer to sinful behavior is not repentance and faith in God for help, but rather love and acceptance of oneself.

In humanism, "sin" is reduced to attitudes or actions that hurt other people. Because humanists also tend to see human beings as essentially good, the answer to evil behavior is better education and social conditioning to help people act out of the goodness of their nature.

In environmentalism, "sin" results from not acting on the truth that the earth is ultimately our mother and living as if all living things—from plants to animals—were of equal value to oneself. People are encouraged to be one with and live in harmony with the rest of creation as the means by which they can overcome sinful actions.

In pantheism and panentheism, "sin" is being out of balance with our immediate environment and living out of harmony with the rest of the earth. So, the answer to evil behavior is for people to meditate and do yoga to connect with the cosmic consciousness and tap into their innate spirituality.

There are also many errors that people who profess to be Christians believe about sin. As a result, their lives, holiness, and happiness sadly suffer.

Some see sin as only breaking the rules of God. Sin does include this, but people who restrict sin to just this sadly fail to see that sin is fundamentally violating the relationship with God. Thus, they tend to reduce their faith to rule keeping rather than to loving relationship with God that underlies, empowers, and enables obedience.

Some wrongly believe that since Jesus died for their sins, they need not fight for holiness and repent when they fail. What they fail to realize is that, because Jesus died for their sins, they are supposed to join him by putting their sins to death.

Some think that unless they confess every sin, they will wind up in hell because not all of their sins would have been forgiven. The truth is that because Jesus died for all of our sins, we can and should repent of all the sins we are aware of while realizing that our imperfection includes an imperfect sensitivity to our sins, causing us to be unaware of all our transgressions.

Some think that as long as they are nice and have a "good heart" God will not be displeased by their sin. But God is concerned both with our inner life and our outer life. Moreover, since our life is simply the outworking of our heart, it is nonsensical to consider someone as having a good heart but bad actions.[100]

Some consider sin and fun synonymous and therefore continue in sin in the name of having fun. However, because sin leads to death, it kills

---

[100]E.g., Prov. 4:23.

everything it touches, particularly joy. Therefore, while a sin may appear to be fun initially, the distance it brings from God, the guilt it causes, and the damage it does to oneself and others are ultimately anything but fun. Sin poses as an attraction before becoming an affliction because it is deceptive and ultimately a lie.

Some wrongly believe that if no one is hurt then their sin does not really matter. But this is untrue on many accounts. Because our sin is against God, it grieves him and distances us from him. Additionally, sin hurts our church, family, friends, and those we are in community with, even if they are unaware of our sin, because our sin affects and changes us negatively. Lastly, our sin also hurts us because we were not made for sin, and to live in sin unrepentantly is to damage oneself. On this point, Plantinga says, "Sin hurts other people and grieves God, but it also corrodes *us*. Sin is a form of self-abuse."[101]

Some wrongly believe that sin is not a problem unless one is caught, so they persist in secret sin. But sin is never secret, because God knows all, the sinner knows, and those who know the sinner often know something is wrong even if they are unaware of the particular sin being committed.

Some think that if a sin is popular, then it is okay because everyone is doing it. Sometimes a culture even labels a vice as a virtue. However, the Bible speaks often about the world in a negative sense; the Bible is saying that the popular majority and their cultures are prone toward sin and therefore are not to replace God and his Word as the standard for holiness and unholiness.[102]

Lastly, some think that sin and mistakes are synonymous, when they are in fact different things. A sin is a moral wrong, and a mistake is a morally neutral imperfection. Those who do not understand this distinction painfully try to live lives of perfectionism and are devastated at mistakes that do not trouble God and therefore should not trouble them. Even more painfully, parents that fail to recognize this distinction commonly disci-

---

[101]Plantinga, *Not the Way It's Supposed to Be*, 124, emphasis in original.
[102]John 1:27; 3:6; 4:5; Rom. 1:18–32; 1 Cor. 1:20–21, 27–28; 11:32; Gal. 3:22; 4:3; Eph. 2:2, 12; Col. 2:8, 20–33; 1 Pet. 2:11; 2 Pet. 1:4; 1 John 2:15, 17; 3:1, 13; 4:1, 5.

pline their children not only for sins but also for mistakes. I once saw a family eating dinner at a restaurant, and a very young child was drinking out of an open cup. Because her motor skills were not yet well developed, she accidentally spilled a bit of her milk. Rather than simply wiping it up since it was a morally neutral mistake, the parents yelled at the child as if she had sinned, though she had not.

HOW DOES GOD'S SOVEREIGNTY RELATE TO SIN?

God is sovereign, powerful, and good. Evil exists and creatures bear moral responsibility for it. In trying to make sense of the undeniable presence of sin, along with the injustice and suffering it causes, many people deny one or more of these essential truths. People postulate that perhaps God is not truly in charge of the world and rendered finite by sin, that God is somehow limited in his ability to effect change in the world, or that perhaps God is both good and evil. Some try to deny the reality of evil, rendering it an illusion or a matter of perception. Others deny responsibility for their own sinfulness, shifting the blame to other people or a bad environment.

In response, philosophers have long sought to find a way to winsomely and persuasively reconcile the character of God with the reality of sin. Gottfried Leibniz first coined the term *theodicy* in 1710 to describe this quest for understanding. Theologian J. I. Packer says that the word *theodicy* comes from the Greek *theos* ("God") and the root *dik-* ("just") and

> seeks to "justify the ways of God to man" . . . showing that God is in the right and is glorious and worthy of praise despite contrary appearances. Theodicy asks how we can believe that God is both good and sovereign in face of the world's evil—bad people; bad deeds, defying God and injuring people; harmful (bad) circumstances, events, experiences and states of mind, which waste, thwart, or destroy value, actual or potential, in and for humankind; in short, all facts, physical and moral, that prompt the feeling, "This ought not to be."[103]

---

[103]J. I. Packer, "Theodicy," in Sinclair B. Ferguson and J. I. Packer, *New Dictionary of Theology* (Downers Grove, IL: InterVarsity, 2000), 679.

Christian philosophers and theologians have explored several approaches to the problem of theodicy. Christian philosopher C. Stephen Evans says:

> Two of the more important theodicies are the "soul-making theodicy," which argues that God allows evil so as to make it possible for humans to develop certain desirable virtues, and the "free will theodicy," which argues that God had to allow for the possibility of evil if he wished to give humans (and angelic beings) free will. Theodicies are often distinguished from defenses, which argue that it is reasonable to believe that God has reasons for allowing evil even if we do not know what those reasons are.[104]

Specific forms of theodicy speculations vary wildly. Some teach a false universalism whereby everyone will be saved in the end. Others say that we will retain our freedom to sin even in our resurrected heavenly state, which leaves open the possibility of sin occurring again in the eternal state. Also, as J. I. Packer describes:

> Some Calvinists envisage God permissively decreeing sin for the purpose of self-display in justly saving some from their sin and justly damning others for and in their sin. But none of this is biblically certain. The safest way in theodicy is to leave God's permission of sin and moral evil as a mystery, and to reason from the good achieved in redemption.[105]

In regard to the coexistence of God and sin, we are wise to remember that a bit of humility is required, because we presently see and know only in part[106] and because God has secrets he has chosen not to reveal to us.[107]

Nonetheless, a study of the Bible repeatedly declares that God is always, perfectly, and solely sovereign, powerful, and good. It is completely clear that God is angry because of sin and evil because creatures,

---

[104]C. Stephen Evans, "Theodicy," in *Pocket Dictionary of Apologetics and Philosophy of Religion* (Downers Grove, IL: InterVarsity, 2002), 114.
[105]Packer, "Theodicy," 679.
[106]1 Cor. 13:12.
[107]Deut. 29:29.

not the Creator, are responsible for it. Sin never destroys his plan, never limits his power to act, and never stops him from doing good in the worst evil. From the appearance of Satan in the garden onward, sin and evil are not dealt with in a systematic fashion but in such a way as to compel us to continued faith in God, trusting in his ultimate providence that one day the presence and power of sin will be no more. To assume that God cannot (making him not sovereign and/or not powerful) or will not (making him not good) is to judge God before he judges evil, rendering the verdict prematurely. Since we are in the middle of history, until God is done with all of his work, we must not judge him but rather trust him until he is finished with sin and history as we know it.

In the meantime, evil is never outside the providential control of God. He is at work to do his good purposes in the context of evil. We see this in the story of Joseph in the final dozen chapters of Genesis. We read of Joseph's betrayal at the hands of his brothers, his unjust suffering, and his eventual rise to power because the Lord was with him, whereby many lives were saved. When he confronted his brothers, the providence of God at work in the life of Joseph crescendos: "As for you, you meant evil against me, but God meant it for good, to bring it about that many people should be kept alive, as they are today."[108]

Many years later, a descendant of Joseph named Jesus Christ suffered similarly. He too was betrayed by his "brothers," suffered the worst injustice in history, and suffered and died in shame on a Roman cross. At that moment, it would have been tempting to ponder if God was not sovereign and had lost, was not good and had sinned against Jesus, or was not powerful enough to stop the injustice. However, three days later Jesus arose from his grave, atoning for the sins of the world, and God was vindicated as fully sovereign, good, and powerful.

God used the freely chosen evil of Judas, Herod, Pilate, Gentiles, and Jews to accomplish his perfect purpose[109] in the same way he used the Chaldeans, a horribly evil nation, to punish the persistent sin of Judah and

---

[108]Gen. 50:20.
[109]Acts 2:23; 4:27–28.

Jerusalem.[110] This does not mean that their evil is his responsibility. They freely desire to kill and destroy. In a cosmic irony, the God of all providence uses evil to judge evil. Even as his hand brings punishment to Israel and death to Jesus, he also brings redemption and resurrection into the context of judgment and death.

A day is coming when we will also rise with and to Jesus. On that day, our faith will be sight and we will see God fully vindicated as we enter the best possible world after passing through this world that prepares us for it. Until that day, our answer to the question of how God's sovereignty relates to sin is ultimately a prayerful, worshipful, humble, and continual meditation on Romans 8:28, which promises, "We know that for those who love God all things work together for good, for those who are called according to his purpose."

WHAT ARE SOME SINFUL RESPONSES TO SIN?

Sinful responses to sin are so numerous that an exhaustible list is impossible. Nonetheless, an examination of ten particular sinful responses to sin can be helpful in aiding us to not respond sinfully but repentantly. These kinds of insights are practically helpful because sinners are often also sinful in how they speak about their sin and respond to their sin, and if we love them we need to be aware of their tactics. Furthermore, we also need to continually examine our own responses to sin in an effort to uncover our sin.

1) There is a propensity to minimize a sin. This is often as simple as comparing one's sin to seemingly greater and more heinous sins so as to get off the hook of guilt.
2) There is the delusional belief that my sin is different from anyone else's because I have good reasons that legitimize my sin. Sometimes this goes so far as to say that because God in his grace used sin for something good, it was a good thing that the sin occurred. This is a horrendous evil because it uses God's grace, which works in spite of our sin, to portray our sin as a virtue and not a vice.

---

[110]Habakkuk 1.

3) There is the common error of rationalizing sin as acceptable because of some extenuating circumstances. People who rationalize their sin commonly wear down their listeners by speaking a great deal about their perspective on their motives and the conditions surrounding their sin in an effort to compel others to sympathize with them and thereby excuse them. Ed Welch says, "Sin is madness or insanity. It is irrational, delusional, unreasonable. It makes absolutely no sense in light of God's love toward us."[111]

4) There is blame shifting, where someone is blamed for the sin of another. This was the tactic of our first parents in the garden, where Eve blamed Satan for her sin, and Adam blamed Eve and blamed God for making her.

5) There is diversion, where we try to avoid our sin by, for example, saying we were just joking, someone misunderstood us, or the person who confronted us about our sin was not as loving as we would have liked and hurt our feelings. Diversionary tactics are subtle and deceptive means by which sinners change the topic from their sin in an effort not to be confronted by their sin or required to repent.

6) There is partial confession, where we tell only a part of our sin. In pride, rather than simply, clearly, truthfully, and thoroughly telling all that we have done, it is common to only confess a portion of it.

7) There is what Paul calls "worldly grief,"[112] where we merely regret the consequences of our sin. We do not repent of our sin and put it to death because we only regret its effects, not the sin itself.

8) There is victimization, where I appear helplessly pitiful and unable to have done otherwise by naming someone (e.g., parent, Satan, past abuser) or something (e.g., genes, culture, personality) as responsible for my sin. The aim of victimization is to get sympathy and empathy rather than a rebuke and is an offense to true victims who have suffered actual sin.

9) There is mere confession, where I name the sin but do not repent of it and put it to death by God's grace. Mere confession is incredibly tricky because people who practice it acknowledge their sin, show remorse, and ask for forgiveness. But they do not change and only repeat their sin, thereby revealing that they were not truly repentant and willing to put their sin to death because Jesus died for it.

---

[111]Edward T. Welch, "The Madness of Anger," *Journal of Biblical Counseling* 24, no. 4 (2006): 26.
[112]2 Cor. 7:10.

10) There is a growing tendency to speak of sin in secular counseling circles as more of a disease than an evil offense. Indeed, like an addiction or disease, sin affects our entire being; it is painful, tragic, and leads to death. Still, there are many ways in which sin is not like a disease; it is something we do rather than something we catch, and something we confess rather than treat.[113] In the end, speaking of sin as a disease is yet another effort to excuse ourselves and shift the blame for our evil actions away from ourselves.

All of this matters because we are supposed to love sinners. In order to love sinners we must take their sin seriously, as God does. If we do not, we rob sinners, including ourselves, of the dignity God bestows on us as his image bearers. Indeed, as Plantinga says, "We ought to pay evildoers, including ourselves, the 'intolerable compliment' of taking them seriously as moral agents, of holding them accountable for their wrongdoing. This is a mark of our respect for their dignity and weight as human beings."[114] We were not made for sin, and to allow sinners to sinfully respond to their sin and not be confronted by it is unloving toward God and unhelpful for them.

HOW DOES GOD RESPOND TO SIN?

As we study the doctrine of the fall, it is incredibly important that we see things, as much as possible, from the vantage point of God so as to identify with him over and above sinners, including ourselves. Human beings are sinners who commit cosmic treason in rebellion against their Creator and King. Theologian R. C. Sproul reminds us:

God voluntarily created us. He gave us the highest privilege of being His image bearers. . . . We are not turtles. We are not fireflies. We are not caterpillars or coyotes. We are people. We are the image bearers of the holy and majestic King of the cosmos.

---

[113]See Edward Welch, "Addictions: New Ways of Seeing, New Ways of Walking Free," *Journal of Biblical Counseling* 19, no. 3 (2001): 19–30.
[114]Plantinga, *Not the Way It's Supposed to Be*, 68.

We have not used the gift of life for the purpose God intended. Life on this planet has become the arena in which we daily carry out the work of cosmic treason. . . . No traitor to any king or nation has even approached the wickedness of our treason before God. . . .

When we sin as the image bearers of God, we are saying to the whole creation, to all of nature under our dominion, to the birds of the air and the beasts of the field: "This is how God is. This is how your Creator behaves. Look in his mirror; look at us, and you will see the character of the Almighty." We say to the world, "God is covetous; God is ruthless; God is bitter; God is a murderer, a thief, a slanderer, an adulterer. God is all of these things that we are doing."[115]

What would you do if you were God and were treated as he has been by sinners, in general, and as by our first parents, in particular? Would your first instinct be to act in grace toward sinners by pursuing them, speaking to them, teaching them, covering them, and promising them that the second member of the Trinity would come as the Last Adam to suffer and die at the hands of sinners for their salvation?[116] The stunning account of Genesis shows a God that no one would ever have invented, because he does what no one ever could have predicted.

In Genesis 3:15 God preached the *protoevangelion* (meaning "first gospel") to our first parents and promised the coming of Jesus, who would be harmed by Satan but would ultimately crush him and bring salvation to sinners.

God then cursed the parties involved as consequence for their sin.[117] The Serpent was cursed for what he had done and was told he would be defeated one day by the "seed" of the woman, who is Jesus, according to Galatians 3:16.

The woman was given increased pain in childbirth, and God notes that she will struggle with the sinful tendency to rule over her husband rather than submit to his leadership as God intended.[118] The greatest pains

---

[115]R. C. Sproul, *The Holiness of God* (Carol Stream, IL: Tyndale, 2000), 115–16.
[116]1 Cor. 15:45.
[117]Gen. 3:14–19.
[118]Gen. 3:16. When the woman's desire for her husband is expressed sinfully, it becomes destructive, just as sin desires to destroy Cain in Genesis 4:7. Conversely, desire for a spouse can be positive, as we see in Song of Solomon 7:10. Similarly, the husband's rule can be sinfully dominating or lovingly protective.

for women henceforth have been in relation to men with whom they are romantically involved and with children.

The man's work that God gave him before he sinned became pain for him because God cursed the ground. This means that as men seek to work their jobs and pay their bills, they will continually be as frustrated with that which is supposed to be under their dominion as God is with the rebellious man who is likewise supposed to be under God's dominion. In this toil, men are continually humbled as they learn how they too are rebellious under God's authority.

God then dealt graciously and kindly with the man and woman even though they had sinned. God came to them, called to them, promised his Messiah, and lovingly clothed Adam and Eve to protect them. God also lovingly banished the couple from the garden and the tree of life so that they would not live forever in a state of sin.

Later in the storyline of the Bible, we learn that Jesus did in fact come to save people from their sins.[119] He did this by becoming the one who succeeded where the first Adam failed.[120] He died in our place for our sins and rose for our salvation. Amazingly, God not only judged sin in righteousness but then bore its penalty himself as an act of love; he offers forgiveness and reconciliation by grace even though he is the offended person against whom we have all sinned. In so doing, he remains perfectly perfect, and we are more wicked than we ever feared yet more loved than we ever hoped.

When we understand our sin biblically, we understand why we are prone to great evil and know why the world is not the way it should be. But by knowing that God made us in his image and likeness, we find the source of our dignity, value, and identity. By knowing of the fall and our state as sinners, we understand depravity as the root problem with our life and world. And by understanding the work of Jesus in our place for our sins, we enjoy the depth of God's love for us, work in us, and eternal future with us as he restores us to the holy state from which we have fallen.

---

[119]Matt. 1:21.
[120]1 Cor. 15:45.

HOW SHOULD WE RESPOND TO SIN?

Like a loving Father, God warned our first parents of the consequences of sin. Nonetheless, they and we have each chosen sin. Because God is holy, he must deal with our sin. Because God is loving, he has chosen to do so in a way that we could be forgiven and restored to right relationship with him. In so doing, God is honoring us by showing that we are made for more than sin and that he expects more from us.

Therefore, the proper response to sin is deep, full, true, broken, earnest, devoted, tearful, prayerful, thorough, and continual humble repentance. Repentance is a glorious gift given to the children of God because of the sacrifice of Jesus Christ, our great and grand dragon slayer. So, it is only fitting to keep the words at the closing of this chapter brief because your time is better spent practicing repentance than reading a tome about it. We leave you with the great gift of repentance and encourage you to use it often, share it liberally, and rejoice in it continually for God's glory, your joy, and others' good.

CHAPTER 6
COVENANT: GOD PURSUES

I will take you to be my people, and I will be your God.

EXODUS 6:7

Who is your enemy? Whose betrayal of you, disregard of you, and injury to you has been the most treasonous? What has your response been?

The sin we have committed against God is far darker, deeper, and more disgusting than any sin that has been committed against us. God created the world as a gifted home for us. God created us and bestowed on us particular dignity as his image bearers. God gave us companionship through the gift of marriage. And God spoke nothing but grace to us and did nothing but bless us.

Our response was sin—damnable, horrible, inexcusable sin.

God's response to our sin was covenant—saving, glorious, loving covenant. This is because God is, by nature of being Trinitarian, covenantal. As the Father, Son, and Spirit are a covenantal community as one God, so too they are graciously covenantal with the elect, despite the fact they are sinful enemies and rebels.

Practically speaking, at the most basic level a covenant is an agreement between two parties.[1] Various covenants are made between people, between people and God, and between God and people. In the Old

---
[1]Gen. 26:28; Dan. 11:6.

Testament, the word *covenant* appears hundreds of times and is used in a variety of ways. Personally, Job made a covenant with his eyes not to look at women lustfully.[2] Relationally, deep brotherly love is spoken of as covenantal,[3] as is marriage.[4] Nationally, the elders of Israel made a covenant with King David.[5] Benefits of covenants can include protection from an enemy,[6] peace,[7] financial blessing,[8] and obtaining a homeland.[9]

When the Bible speaks of God's covenant with his people, it is explaining how our relationship with God is made by his provision and exists by his terms. That God deals with his people in covenant includes all of these glorious truths. Through covenant with God we enjoy a relationship with him that is akin to marriage and includes protection from Satan our enemy, peace with God though we declared war on him through sin, material provision in this life and the life to come, and a coming perfect kingdom as our home where Jesus will forever rule over all as our gracious covenant king.

The word for covenant is *berith* in Hebrew and *diatheke* in Greek. A covenant is "a solemn commitment, guaranteeing promises or obligations undertaken by one or both parties, sealed with an oath."[10] When God enters into a covenantal relationship with humanity, God sovereignly institutes a life-and-death bond.[11] Or, to say it another way, a covenant is a life-and-death relationship with God on his terms.

As a bond, a covenant is a relationship that commits people to one another, God to God's people, and people to God. Oaths, promises, and signs accompany the bond or commitment. This aspect of God's covenants reveals his loving grace and mercy because although people deserve nothing but condemnation, God gives covenantal salvation.

---

[2]Job 31:1.
[3]1 Sam. 18:3.
[4]Prov. 2:16–17; Mal. 2:14.
[5]2 Sam. 5:3.
[6]Gen. 26:28–29; 31:50–52; 1 Kings 15:18–19.
[7]Josh. 9:15–16.
[8]1 Kings 5:6–11.
[9]Gen. 23:14–16.
[10]Paul R. Williamson, *Sealed with an Oath: Covenant in God's Unfolding Purpose*, New Studies in Biblical Theology (Downers Grove, IL: IVP Academic, 2007), 43.
[11]See O. Palmer Robertson, *Christ of the Covenants* (Phillipsburg, NJ: P&R, 1980), 4.

By initiating covenants, God never enters into the relationship casually or informally. Covenant relationship signifies the life-and-death intensity of the bond. This intensity is seen in all three types of covenants, human to human,[12] God to human,[13] and human to God.[14] The establishment of a covenant is called "cutting a covenant." It usually entails the slaughter of an animal. This symbolizes or represents the curse that the covenant maker calls down upon himself or herself if they should violate the commitment that was made. This aspect of God's covenants reveals his perfect holiness and justice.

In a covenant with God there is no bargaining, bartering, or contract negotiations regarding the terms of the covenant. Neither is God's covenant something we must earn by our good works. It is always a gracious provision from the loving Lord to his people. The sovereign Lord of heaven and earth dictates the terms of God's covenants. It is God's covenant in that it is conceived, devised, determined, established, confirmed, and dispensed by God himself, who often says, "I will establish my covenant with you."[15] This aspect of God's covenants reveals his sovereign rule as Lord. God makes five major covenants in the Bible with the following:[16]

1) Noah and his family.[17]
2) Abraham and his descendants.[18]
3) Moses and the Israelites.[19]
4) David and the kingdom of Israel.[20]
5) The new covenant of Jesus and the church.[21]

---

[12]Gen. 21:27, 32; 2 Sam. 3:12, 13.

[13]Abraham: Gen. 15:18; Moses: Ex. 24:8; Deut. 5:2; David: 2 Chron. 21:7; Ps. 89:3; the new covenant: Jer. 31:31; Ezek. 37:26.

[14]2 Kings 11:17; 23:3; 2 Chron. 29:10.

[15]See Gen. 6:18; 9:9, 11, 17; 17:7, 19, 21; Ex. 6:4; Ezek. 16:60, 62; Heb. 8:8.

[16]Some systematic theologies add a sixth covenant with Adam. They appeal to Hosea 6:7, which is the only place the word *covenant* is used in connection with Adam. The debate that surrounds this point on such things as a covenant of works in covenantal theology or a dispensation of innocence in dispensational theology is more than we can address in this one chapter on covenant. Still, since the Genesis account of Adam does not speak of him as being in covenant with God, we have chosen not to include the possibility of the Adamic covenant as part of this chapter, but we do acknowledge that there were Adamic commands.

[17]Gen. 6:18; 9:8–17.

[18]Gen. 12:1–3; 15:18; 17:1–14; 22:16–18.

[19]Ex. 3:4–10; 6:7; 19:5–6; 24:8.

[20]2 Sam. 7:8–19; Ps. 89:3.

[21]Matt. 16:17–19; 26:28; Luke 22:20.

For each of these covenants, it is helpful to highlight five special features:

1) The *covenant mediator* (the person with whom God makes the covenant) and his *covenant role* (whom the mediator represents);
2) The *blessings* promised in the covenant;
3) The *conditions* (or *curses*) of the covenant;
4) The *sign* by which the covenant will be celebrated and remembered;
5) The *form* that God's family takes as a result of the covenant.

The purpose of these covenants was to address the problem of the human race and of the entire created order. Across the Old Testament echo the promises and relationships in the covenants that will redeem God's people and restore God's sin-alienated creation to himself. It is important to note that covenants themselves do not solve the problem, but they do point to Jesus who does.

WHY DOES GOD COVENANT?

As the story develops throughout the Old Testament, covenant love is referred to in various terms, but the main one is *hesed*. In fact, it is not a stretch to say that the word *hesed* in essence summarizes the entire history of God's covenantal relationship with Israel.

Hesed is God's lovingkindness—the consistent, ever-faithful, relentless, constantly pursuing, lavish, extravagant, unrestrained, one-way love of God. It is often translated as covenant love, lovingkindness, mercy, steadfast love, loyal love, devotion, commitment, or reliability. *Hesed* turns up regularly in the Old Testament, particularly in the Psalms. It is typically translated "love" and sometimes as "mercy."[22] However, *hesed* has a much narrower definition than the English term *love* conveys. In the Hebrew Scriptures, *hesed* refers to a sort of love that has been promised and is owed—covenant love—as in Hosea 11:1: "When Israel was a child, I loved him, and out of Egypt I called my son." Covenant love is the love God promised to give to his covenant people, and which they in

---

[22]Ps. 23:6.

turn were to respond in kind, loving God with all their hearts, minds, and strength. *Hesed* does not suggest some kind of generic love of everyone. Rabbi Kamsler suggests that the best English word to use as a translation for *hesed* is *loyalty*, which refers to God's covenant loyalty because of his love for his people.[23] Perhaps *The Jesus Storybook Bible* for children says it best of all: "God loves us with a Never Stopping, Never Giving Up, Unbreaking, Always and Forever Love."[24]

Malachi 1:1–5 is a clear presentation of *hesed*. Malachi opens with the declaration of the word of Yahweh: "I have loved you." The people were not immediately convinced of this declaration; to them, because of their state of spiritual rebellion, it sounded good but was not convincing, because things had not worked out to their satisfaction. "How have you loved us?" they asked.

The prophet's response reminded them of their status as the chosen people of God: "Is not Esau Jacob's brother?" Yahweh says. "Yet I have loved Jacob but Esau I have hated." Malachi was stressing that their existence as the people of God was the clearest evidence of the love of God. God chose the Israelites to be his kingdom of priests in the world. He gave them the Scriptures, the temple, the priests, the prophets, the covenants, and the Messiah. And his love for them was an everlasting love—even though they failed him again and again, he still retained his covenant with them. Not only did God choose Israel ("Jacob"), but he also cared for the Israelites whenever they were in trouble. The simple fact was that God protected Israel down through the ages.

Being God's people is a repeated theme throughout Scripture: "I will live among them and walk among them, and I will be their God and they will be my people."[25] The Christian story begins with creation in harmony, unity, and peace, and it ends with a restored creation. In between these two bookends is the drama of redemption. The covenants are major acts of

---

[23]Rabbi Harold M. Kamsler, "Hesed—Mercy or Loyalty?" The Jewish Bible Quarterly, vol. 27, no. 3 (1999): 184–85.
[24]Sally Lloyd-Jones, *The Jesus Storybook Bible: Every Story Whispers His Name* (Grand Rapids, MI: Zondervan, 2007), 200.
[25]Lev. 26:12; Jer. 32:38; Ezek. 37:27.

this drama. The goal is to see the work and person of Christ in light of the Old Testament and to highlight aspects that we have possibly overlooked. Christ's work is intimately related to and fulfills each of the four covenants (with Noah, Abraham, Moses, and David) that God initiated in the Old Testament. New dimensions are brought to light when Christ's covenant is understood in the context of the previous covenants. Covenants are about God's activity and intention to redeem us, and the covenants tell us about ourselves—our condition, our brokenness, our dignity, our role as images of God, our suffering, and our calling.

Regarding our calling, Christopher J. H. Wright says of God's covenant people (Israel and the church):

> This people also has a mission, derived from the mission of God. Again the word is used to mean that this people exists for a purpose, or more precisely, have been brought into existence for the sake of the purposes of God. But, in their case, especially in the New Testament (though not absent from the Old Testament), the concept of mission as "sending and being sent" is an essential component in that overall orientation towards the goal of God's mission.[26]

Indeed, one way of walking through the story of God in Scripture is to see God sending his Son and his people into the world through covenants as an act of worship in relation to himself and as an act of witness in relation to the nations.

WHAT IS THE NOAHIC COVENANT?

God's calling of Noah to build the ark begins with the lengthy genealogy of Adam's descendants until the birth of Noah.[27] The primary theological point of the genealogy is to show that every descendant of Adam was a sinner who lived and died without exception; it reveals this in a rather monotonous and unspectacular fashion, simply saying "and he died" repeatedly.

---

[26]Christopher J. H. Wright, "Covenant: God's Mission through God's People," in *The God of Covenant*, ed. Alistair I. Wilson and Jamie A. Grant (Nottingham, UK: Inter-Varsity, 2005), 55.
[27]Gen. 5:1–7:1.

Peter, reflecting on God's patience in the days of Noah, sees a correlation with our own day.[28] As decades, centuries, and millennia pass with little change in the world, it is easy for us to lose hope that things will ever be different. Don't you wonder if God will ever change the world in a dramatic way? We may doubt at times, but we can take heart. God did not allow sin to go unpunished in Noah's time; he will not let it go unpunished in the future. He did not fail to rescue his people from judgment in Noah's day; he will not fail to rescue us in the future. Christ certainly will return and bring us into a new heaven and new earth in time, just as he brought the flood. Genesis 6:5–9 breaks from the cycle of mere sin and death:

> The LORD saw that the wickedness of man was great in the earth, and that every intention of the thoughts of his heart was only evil continually. And the LORD was sorry that he had made man on the earth, and it grieved him to his heart. So the LORD said, "I will blot out man whom I have created from the face of the land, man and animals and creeping things and birds of the heavens, for I am sorry that I have made them." But Noah found favor in the eyes of the LORD.
>
> These are the generations of Noah. Noah was a righteous man, blameless in his generation. Noah walked with God.

It is easy to misread this passage and come to the conclusion that Noah was a good guy who earned God's favor through his good works. Tragically, the story of Noah is commonly told like this: "In the days of Noah, all the people were wicked except for Noah, a righteous man who earned God's favor. Therefore God saved him from judgment in the flood." The practical application of this version of the story is that there are good guys and bad guys and that God loves and saves the good guys but kills the bad guys, so we should be good guys so that God will love and save us. However, this false teaching about Noah is antithetical to the rest of Scripture and simply not what Genesis 6:5–9 says.

First, Genesis 6:5–7 depicts the total depravity of everyone on earth with one of the most negative declarations about human sin in all of

---

[28]2 Pet. 3:3–7.

Scripture. We are told that God saw that every person was only evil all the time. God was grieved that he had made mankind because they filled his heart with pain. This statement does include Noah.

Second, Genesis 6:8 does not say that Noah worked hard to merit God's favor. Noah did not begin as a righteous man. Rather he began as a sinner among sinners. His status with God was God's gracious gift, not a result of Noah's religious works. It is beautiful that the word "favor" in this passage is the Hebrew word for *grace*, which appears here for the first time in the Bible and is echoed repeatedly throughout the Bible in the teaching that salvation is by grace through faith alone. Throughout Scripture people are saved through the undeserved working of God. Because everyone was a sinner in Noah's day—just like everyone is a sinner in our day—no one earned God's favor. God's favor is a free gift. So God worked, as he always has, by saving an ill-deserving sinner by grace alone, through faith alone, thereby enabling him to live a righteous life. Genesis 6:9 then explains the effects of God's grace to Noah: "These are the generations of Noah. Noah was a righteous man, blameless in his generation. Noah walked with God."

Indeed, Noah was a blameless and righteous man who, like Enoch, "walked with God,"[29] and like Job, whom God pointed out to Satan as "a blameless and upright man."[30] But Noah was only this sort of man because God saved him by grace and empowered him to live a new life of obedience to God by that same grace.

God began to speak directly to Noah and give him commands to obey. God informed Noah that he planned to end sin by killing all the sinners through an enormous flood as judgment on sinners. God then gave Noah orders to build an ark. The ark measured some 1,400,000 cubic feet, was shaped like a modern-day battleship, and was big enough to house some 522 modern-day railroad boxcars.

Noah obeyed God's commands and built the ark, likely with only the help of his sons. Hebrews 11:7 says that Noah did so in holy fear as a man of faith who believed that God would bring the flood even while others

---

[29]Gen. 5:22, 24.
[30]Job 1:8; 2:3.

continued in sin without repentance. Upon completing the construction of the ark, Noah placed his family on the ark with the animals God had commanded him to bring, and waited for God to fulfill his promise of judgment.

After Noah was saved by God's grace, built the ark according to God's instructions, and loaded his family onboard with the animals as God commanded him, God sent rain.[31] The rain continued for forty days until it covered the land, drowning all the sinners under God's righteous judgment. The only people spared in the flood were Noah and his family because, as Genesis 6:8 states, God gave them grace.

After the flood receded, the land appeared out of the water like in the days of creation for Adam. In many ways, the account of Noah echoes the account of Adam, with a sort of new creation and new humanity and new fall.

After the flood subsided and God dried the ground, Noah and his family exited the ark. Then Noah did a remarkable thing that we must be careful to note and appreciate. In Genesis 8:20 we read, "Then Noah built an altar to the LORD and took some of every clean animal and some of every clean bird and offered burnt offerings on the altar." Recognizing the devastation that God had wrought upon the earth, Noah was convicted of his own sin; he knew that he too should have been killed like everyone else. So he offered a burnt offering for the atonement of his sin.[32] God was so pleased with Noah's offering of atonement that he responded by promising never to flood the earth again; the answer to sin would henceforth be atonement, which foreshadowed the death of Jesus for sin.

God thus entered a covenant with Noah that was intended for all people of the earth.[33] God promised that he would never again send a cataclysmic flood and that the seasons would continue by God's provision. In this covenant, we see that God's answer to human sin would be a covenant of grace, beginning with Noah. The sign of the covenant was the rainbow to remind God's people of his promise to never flood the earth again. Through the covenant, God would restore his intentions to bless people.

---

[31]Gen. 7:1–8:22.
[32]E.g., Lev. 1:4; Job 1:5.
[33]Gen. 9:1–17.

The terms of the covenant for human beings include respect for the sanctity of human life and the freedom to eat animals as, at this point in history, meat was added to the human diet. These commands further build upon the teaching in Genesis 1, that while animal life is to be treated kindly, it is inferior to human life, which alone bears God's image. The effect of the covenant is the renewal of God's intentions in creation by distinguishing between those people, like Noah, in covenant with God from those who are not.

In Genesis 9:18–28, Noah responded to God's kindness by getting drunk and passing out naked in his tent like a hillbilly redneck on vacation. Noah's son Ham then walked into Noah's tent to gaze upon his father's nakedness. The text does not tell us much more than these bare details, but many people have inserted numerous speculations about what happened, including Ham having homosexual attraction to his passed-out father. Whatever happened, one thing is sure: both Noah and his son sinned.

In the story of Noah we have a sort of second fall; God started over with Noah, who sinned like Adam. The point is simply that sin remains the human problem even after the flood. Furthermore, the Noahic covenant reveals that not only is ours a cursed earth but also a covenanted earth. The Noahic covenant is for both humanity and all of creation. In Genesis 9:9–10, God says, "Behold, I establish my covenant with you and your offspring after you, and with every living creature that is with you, the birds, the livestock, and every beast of the earth with you, as many as came out of the ark; it is for every beast of the earth." Therefore, God's plan is to ultimately redeem all his creation along with his covenant people.

This desire is shown in the fact that the flood is in essence a new start for creation and humanity despite the ongoing nature of the fall. Noah and his family are blessed and called to fill the earth and exercise dominion over creation in a manner that echoes God's instructions to Adam and Eve. Additionally, the creation mandate is renewed with a special emphasis on respecting life and exercising creation care as responsible stewards of all that God has made.

We easily forget how much God's covenant with Noah enhances our lives. We grow so accustomed to the order of creation that we act as if it were something automatic, inherent in nature itself. But as scientists learn more about our world, we see more clearly that the universe is not self-sufficient. Nature is fragile, constantly teetering on the edge of disaster. Disruptions in the food chain, water pollution, atmospheric changes, and a host of other modern environmental concerns demonstrate dramatically that the earth needs the constant providential care of the Creator. The food we eat, the air we breathe, the streets we walk, the cars we drive, the books we read, the buildings we erect, the universities we establish—all these good things in life have been possible because God constantly upholds a safe place for humanity to multiply and have dominion. As we reflect on God's blessing in the days of Noah, we should be utterly amazed at its tremendous value.

To summarize the Noahic covenant, the human covenant mediator is Noah, who intercedes for his family and the rest of humanity. The blessings of the covenant include God's saving grace and promise not to flood the earth again, thereby preserving human life so that it could be fruitful and multiply. The conditions of enjoying the covenant include not drinking the blood of animals and the command that God's people are to honor God's image bearers by not committing murder and by upholding the sanctity of all human life. The sign of the covenant internally is faith, as demonstrated by Noah and his family building the ark in the desert for perhaps 120 years while being mocked,[34] and the sign of the covenant externally was the rainbow, which God said was a reminder of his promise not to flood the earth again. The covenant community took the form of an extended family.

WHAT IS THE ABRAHAMIC COVENANT?

God's response to the efforts of Babylon seeking to make its name great was the calling of Abram to be a man with a new name who would become the father of a new nation that God would make great by grace.[35] With the arrival of Abram in Genesis, the book shifts from the theme of God call-

---

[34]Gen. 6:3; 1 Pet. 3:20.
[35]Gen. 11:1–12:9.

ing creation into existence in Genesis 1 to 11, to God calling people into covenant in chapters 12 to 50.

God did not speak from the time of his covenant with Noah until he spoke to Abram to again initiate a covenant relationship.[36] When Abram was called by God to become the father of a new nation, the prototype of a life of faith, and one of the most important men in the Bible, he was simply yet another sinner living among the scattered nations. In this way, Abram was as Noah had been before God likewise called him into covenant. We know very little about Abram before God called him other than his genealogy, his barren wife, and his temporary home in Haran after having been born in Ur of the Chaldeans.[37] Since Nehemiah 9:7 and Acts 7:2–3 seem to indicate that God in fact called Abram in Ur of the Chaldeans, and the key city of the Chaldeans was Babylon, Abram may have even been called out of Babylon as a Babylonian who perhaps even sought to help build that great city that God judged, demonstrating the graciousness of God's grace.[38] It is amazing that Abram was seemingly just another sinner from a godless family when, much like Noah, he too found gracious favor in the eyes of the Lord.[39]

God simply told Abram to leave his homeland and father to journey to a new land that God would show him. God then promised Abram that though his wife was barren, he would be a father. He was promised a great nation blessed by God that would be a blessing to the nations of the earth through one of his offspring or seed. This refers back to the original "seed" promise of Genesis 3:15. The noun is singular, meaning Jesus. It is also collective, referring to Israel, the carrier of promise.[40] Galatians 3:16 connects the promise of Abram's seed with Jesus Christ:

> Now the promises were made to Abraham and to his offspring. It does not say, "And to offsprings," referring to many, but referring to one, "And to your offspring," who is Christ.

---

[36]Gen. 12:1–3.
[37]Gen. 11:27–32.
[38]E.g., Isa. 13:19; 48:14; Jer. 24:5; 25:12; 50:1; Ezek. 1:3; 12:13; 23:15.
[39]Josh. 24:2 tells us that Abraham's father "served other gods."
[40]Gen. 3:15; Matt. 1:1, 17.

In this way, God promised that the nation of Israel would come through Abraham and, like Mary, be the "womb" through which Jesus Christ would be brought forth as the blessing to all nations. This fact is so significant that Galatians 3:8 comments on it, saying, "The Scripture, foreseeing that God would justify the Gentiles by faith, preached the gospel beforehand to Abraham, saying, 'In you shall all the nations be blessed.'"

Abram was also told that his descendants would receive the Promised Land if he made a radical break with his past and left his home in faith. He and his descendants eventually spent four hundred years in Egypt. Genesis ends with Joseph requesting that his bones be taken from Egypt to the Promised Land when God's people would finally enter that place. Exodus also ends with the expectation of one day entering the Promised Land,[41] a longing not realized until after the death of Moses in the opening chapters of the book of Joshua.

In faith Abram believed and obeyed God, doing as God commanded at the age of seventy-five. He took his wife, Sarai, their household, and his nephew Lot, who becomes a troublesome figure later in the story. God again appeared to Abram, who responded by worshiping God in faith by building an altar, something he does throughout the book after encountering God.[42]

The central point of the account of Abram is discovered when contrasting Abram with Babylon in the story that preceded his call, the Tower of Babel. The Babylonians sought to be a great nation and a blessed people, great in name, protected from their enemies, and the centerpiece of world affairs.[43] But they pursued their aims apart from faith and apart from God. So God called one of them, Abram, out into covenant with himself and promised to give to Abram, by his gracious provision, all that the Babylonians had strived for. Therefore, God is showing that our hope cannot rest in the efforts of sinners to save and bless themselves. Rather, our only hope is to be found in entering into covenant relationship with God by faith.

---

[41]Ex. 40:34–38.
[42]Gen. 12:7–8; 13:18; 22:9.
[43]Gen. 11:1–9.

Although God promised Abram a son through his wife and a nation in the Promised Land, Abram essentially gave both away.[44] Thankfully, God did intervene and, through inflicting diseases on Pharaoh and his household and causing Lot to choose land other than the Promised Land, God made good on his promises, in spite of his servant. The central theological point in these accounts seems to be that while God's servants are imperfect, it is his sovereign covenant protection that saves them from themselves and makes his covenant promises become reality.

Genesis opens with God speaking and preparing creation for mankind by the power of his word. Throughout Genesis, God has thus far spoken to Adam, Noah, and Abram. In Genesis 15:1, God again speaks to Abram in a vision. God poetically promised to be Abram's protector and provider. God promised that though Abram was childless and his wife, Sarai, was barren, they would have a son, and that through that son a nation would be born. Genesis 15:6 reports Abram's response to God's word, which is among the most important verses in the Bible, saying, "He believed the LORD, and he counted it to him as righteousness."

Genesis 15:6 tells us that Abraham dared to believe God's unlikely promise of a son in his old age. This is the kind of total trust that receives the promise of God. It becomes a verse that is central to the New Testament doctrine of faith, in general, and Paul's doctrine of justification by faith, in particular.[45] Additionally, Jesus' half-brother James quoted Genesis 15:6 to teach that true faith in God results in good works in life with God.[46]

God's covenant with Abram was confirmed with a sacrifice and the shedding of blood. This act foreshadowed the new covenant of our salvation, which was confirmed with Jesus' sacrifice of his own life on the cross and the shedding of his blood.

God then promised Abram that though his descendants would inherit the Promised Land, it would not be in his lifetime but only after a future four-hundred-year exile in Egypt, recorded in Exodus. God then marked

---

[44]Gen. 12:10–13:18.
[45]Rom. 4:3; Gal. 3:6.
[46]James 2:23–24.

out the boundaries of the Promised Land, the boundaries of which also coincide with the garden of Eden.[47]

Throughout God's dealings with Noah and Abraham, we have witnessed a pattern of God speaking to them, calling them into covenant, establishing them as the head of a new humanity, promising to bless them, and inviting everyone to respond to him in faith. We then see each falter in faith and sin against the Lord despite his patient kindness to them.

In Genesis 16 we see this pattern repeated in yet another mini-fall of sorts. After the establishment of God's covenant in Genesis 15, Abram sought to take matters into his own hands by bearing a son with his Egyptian maidservant and second wife, Hagar. The faithless plot was conceived by Abram's wife, Sarai, who, like her first mother Eve, failed to trust the simple words of God and feared that God had not kept his promise to her.[48] Their actions were likely motivated at least in part by the fact that they had been waiting ten-plus years for God to give them the child he had promised, and Abram was now eighty-six years old and his wife was seventy-six years old and barren.

Following God's covenant with Abram in Genesis 15 and Abram's sexual sin with Hagar in Genesis 16, God institutes circumcision as the sign of the Abrahamic covenant in Genesis 17. The reason why God chose to mark his men on this part of their anatomy is not revealed to us, but it makes sense, since it is generally very important to men—the means by which they conceive children and the cause of some of their most grievous sins.

Circumcision was performed either with a sharp knife or stone. Circumcision began in Genesis 17 with Abram, who was ninety-nine years of age, as a sign of his covenant with God, like the rainbow was the sign of God's covenant with Noah. God spoke to Abram, and Abram responded to God's command in faith, falling down on his face to worship God. God then changed his name from Abram, which means "exalted father," to Abraham, which means "father of a multitude," as the time for God to

---

[47]Gen. 2:10–14.
[48]Gen. 16:2.

fulfill his promise of a son for Abram was very near. God also expanded his covenant with Abraham to include Abraham's descendants.

God then told Abraham that his wife's name would also be changed from Sarai to Sarah, which means "princess." God also promised that through Sarah the princess, kings would come with the ultimate fulfillment being the birth of Jesus Christ, who is the King of kings promised to Sarah's great-grandson Judah.[49]

When God restated his Genesis 15 promise that he would give Abraham a son by Sarah, Abraham laughed at God in distrust that he and Sarah could conceive as God had promised.[50] Rather than giving up on Abraham, God graciously repeated his promise once again, even instructing Abraham to name him Isaac, which means "laughter," since God would get the last laugh.

Abraham immediately obeyed God, as Moses makes clear by writing that he did it "that very day."[51] Abraham was circumcised at the age of ninety-nine along with every member of his household, as God had commanded. He did this because God promised that any male who was not circumcised would be cut off altogether by God. Ever since this occasion, Jews have circumcised their sons on the eighth day, as that was the day chosen for their father Isaac.[52]

Scripture expands the concept of circumcision, the cutting away of the foreskin, to the cutting away of sin from the heart.[53] Abraham's descendants expand from sons by natural birth to include those who are descendants by new birth. Those with hearts circumcised by the Holy Spirit are truly Abraham's descendants, as they, like him, live in covenant relationship with God by faith in Jesus Christ.[54]

Genesis 21 erupts with laughter as Isaac, the promised son whose name means laughter, is born. Sarah jealously demanded Abraham to expel Hagar and Ishmael into the desert to die. But God, always faithful to

---

[49]Gen. 49:10.
[50]Gen. 17:17–18.
[51]Gen. 17:22–27.
[52]Gen. 17:12.
[53]Deut. 10:16; 30:6; Jer. 4:4; Ezek. 44:7–9; Rom. 2:25–29; Col. 2:11.
[54]Romans 4; Gal. 3:6–8.

his promise, heard Abraham's other son and they were spared. The chapter ends with the serene portrait that Abraham's life has finally all come together under God's perfect covenantal blessing. Despite nearly losing his wife twice, Abraham still has Sarah. And despite waiting for twenty-five years, Abraham finally has his son Isaac because God is faithful.

Some time later, when Isaac was likely a young man, Moses tells us that God tested Abraham. Perhaps the point of this test was not for God to see if Abraham had faith, but rather for Abraham to demonstrate the depth of his faith in front of his son Isaac so that he too would learn to walk in faith as his father had.

Echoing God's initial call to Abraham in Genesis 12, God commanded Abraham to "go" and sacrifice his son Isaac as a burnt offering.[55] This would have required that Abraham slaughter his son, dismember him, and burn his body. Obediently, Abraham awoke early the next morning without any noticeable hesitation and set out with his son to do as the Lord commanded. The Bible has no words adequate to describe Abraham's agony.

But just before Abraham killed his son, with the knife in the air above him, the angel of the Lord (likely Jesus) called to Abraham from heaven and commanded him not to harm his son. God then provided a ram to be sacrificed. Abraham, and Moses writing seven hundred years later, recognized that this prefigured God's future messianic provision at the same mountain, Mount Moriah, also known as Mount Zion.[56]

The comparisons between this account and the death of Jesus are many. To help you see them clearly we have listed them:

- Isaac and Jesus were both sons of a promise that was given many years before their birth.
- Isaac and Jesus were both born to women who could not have conceived apart from a miracle.
- Isaac and Jesus were both firstborn sons.
- Isaac and Jesus were both greatly loved by their father/Father.
- Isaac and Jesus went to the top of Mount Moriah/Mount Zion.

---

[55]Gen. 22:1–2.
[56]Gen. 22:2, 14; 2 Chron. 3:1.

- Isaac carried the wood to his own sacrifice, just as Jesus carried his wooden cross to his crucifixion.
- Isaac and Jesus each willingly laid down their lives to their father/ Father.
- Isaac's father and Jesus' Father both felt the agony of killing an innocent son.
- Isaac was brought back from the dead figuratively and Jesus was brought back from the dead literally.

After having walked with God for many years and seeing God provide in very difficult situations, Abraham had apparently learned to trust God no matter what. This fact reveals that those in covenant with God can mature and grow in faith. Abraham's faith in God was so resolute that he believed that even if he killed his son that God, who gave him the son through a miracle, could give him back through yet another miracle.[57] After all, Abraham had also lost his wife on two occasions only to see God bring her back to him, and Abraham believed that God would do the same with Isaac because God is always good for his covenant promises.

To summarize the Abrahamic covenant: the human mediator between God and Abraham's family, the nation of Israel, and the nations of the earth is Abraham. The blessings of the covenant include land, a son, and a nation of people who would bring forth Jesus Christ as the ultimate promised blessing. The condition of enjoying the covenant was obedience to God and "doing righteousness and justice,"[58] as God's people are to be ethical and promote justice on the earth. Like Jesus who would call the church to be a city within the city,[59] God commanded his people in the Abrahamic covenant to live as a nation among the nations for the missional purpose of revealing God to the nations through righteousness and justice. The sign of the covenant internally was faith as Abraham believed God, and the sign externally was circumcision, as visible evidence of internal faith. The covenant community took the form of a family and

---

[57]Heb. 11:17–19.
[58]Gen. 18:19.
[59]Matt. 5:14.

nation that proceeded from that family bringing forth Jesus as the blessing to all nations.

Lastly, the promise of Jesus Christ is that he would come as the seed of Abraham and blessing to all nations of the earth. Revelation 7:9–10 reveals the fulfillment of this aspect of the Abrahamic covenant at the end of time around the throne of Jesus:

> After this I looked, and behold, a great multitude that no one could number, from every nation, from all tribes and peoples and languages, standing before the throne and before the Lamb, clothed in white robes, with palm branches in their hands, and crying out with a loud voice, "Salvation belongs to our God who sits on the throne, and to the Lamb!"

WHAT IS THE MOSAIC COVENANT?

Exodus powerfully demonstrates the faithfulness of God to his covenant promises to Abraham. Out of a barren elderly couple, a nation of perhaps a million was born over the course of four hundred years. It is amazing that the entire exodus event was promised to Abram directly from God himself.[60] As promised, the people of God were enslaved for four hundred and thirty years, then delivered by the judgments of God upon the Egyptians.

In the closing scenes of Genesis, we learn that Abraham's descendant Joseph had been sold into slavery by his jealous older brothers. But God elevated Joseph to a position of power and prominence as the top advisor to Pharaoh, the great ruler of Egypt. Because of Joseph's exemplary service and wisdom from God, the entire nation of Egypt was spared the starvation of a famine, and the Hebrews were given privilege and dignity as slaves in Egypt. The Exodus story opens by noting that, in the years following Joseph's death, a new pharaoh rose to prominence and no longer remembered Joseph's service or the privilege given to his people. He enslaved God's people and treated them cruelly, attempting genocide out of fear of their numbers.[61] The Egyptian empire was the most powerful on earth for an amazing thirteen

---

[60]Gen. 15:13–15.
[61]Ex. 1:1–15:21.

hundred years, twice as long as the famed Greek and Roman empires. But the pharaoh was worshiped as a god and had no regard for the God of Israel.

In Exodus 3 God appears by speaking directly to Moses, promising to deliver his covenant people from slavery. He reveals his tenderness in his powerful protection as he responds to the groaning of his people.[62] In Exodus 3:14, God reveals himself by name, saying, "'I AM WHO I AM.' And he said, 'Say this to the people of Israel, "I AM has sent me to you."'" In Hebrew understanding, a name embodies the entire essence and identity of a person. So, in having a name, God revealed himself as a person and gave sacred access to an understanding and experience of his very person. The divine name Yahweh reveals his eternal self-existence. He is a relational being, unchangingly faithful and dependable, who desires the full trust of his people. As he states his name, he reminds Moses and the people of his promise of help for them in covenant faithfulness.

The Hebrews were so afraid of blaspheming God that they would not utter this sacred name, nor would they write it out in full with the vowels. They rendered it YHWH. There has been some debate as to exactly how the name should be spelled and pronounced, but most scholars now recognize that the most likely rendering is Yahweh. Jesus later takes this same name to designate himself as that person who spoke to Moses in the burning bush, and he was nearly murdered for doing so.[63]

God acted decisively in judgment on Egypt, delivering his people through the ten plagues that culminated in the killing of the firstborn of Egypt. He passed over the houses of Israel because they faithfully obeyed his instructions to paint the doorposts with blood of a slain lamb. They walked across the Red Sea on dry ground and turned to watch the pursuing Egyptians drown as the water returned to its place. In this we clearly see that life and death hinge on whether or not we trust and obey God.

In Exodus 19 we read that God led his people to the foot of Mount Sinai, just as he had promised to Moses in the burning bush.[64] But the peo-

---

[62]Ex. 2:23–25; 3:7–10.
[63]Ex. 3:14; cf. John 8:58.
[64]Ex. 3:12.

ple of God were forbidden from ascending or even touching the mountain and entering into the presence of God because of their sin. Any violation of this command was promised to bring immediate death, as God desired his people to know that they cannot ascend to him, but instead he initiates the relationship and descends to them, as ultimately happened with the incarnation of Jesus Christ. They were told to purify themselves for three days and prepare to receive the message God would give them through his mediators, the prophet Moses and the priest Aaron.

God began by reminding them of his faithfulness and his powerful redemption: "You yourselves have seen what I did to the Egyptians, and how I bore you on eagles' wings and brought you to myself."[65] Based on his grace and provision, he asked them for their faithful response: "Now therefore, if you will indeed obey my voice and keep my covenant . . ." His purpose is that they would "be my treasured possession among all peoples, for all the earth is mine, and you shall be to me a kingdom of priests and a holy nation." If they will respond to his grace they will be a kingdom of priests, having access to God and the joy of mediating him to all people. They will be a holy people set apart to him in all purity and cleanness.

God gave them the Ten Commandments, which were intended to guide their lives as holy people. But instead of responding in faith, their fear drove them away from God,[66] beginning a pattern of moving away rather than drawing near and of disobedience, defilement, and spiritual adultery, culminating in judgment. Christopher J. H. Wright says:

> As the people of YHWH they would have the historical task of bringing the knowledge of God to the nations, and bringing the nations to the means of atonement with God. The task of blessing the nations also put them in the role of priests in the midst of the nations. This dual movement is reflected in the prophetic visions of the law/light/justice and so on of YHWH going out to the nations from Israel/Zion, and the nations coming to YHWH/Israel/Zion. . . . The priesthood of the people of God is thus a missional function.[67]

---

[65]Ex. 19:4–6.
[66]Ex. 20:18–19.
[67]Christopher J. H. Wright, "Covenant: God's Mission through God's People," 65.

To summarize the Mosaic covenant: the human mediator was Moses, who interceded between God and Israel, his covenant people. The blessings of the covenant included redemption from bondage and the freedom to worship God. The conditions of enjoying the covenant centered on obeying all God's laws, synthesized in the Ten Commandments, which are anchored in God alone being worshiped. On this point Wright says:

> The priority of grace is a fundamental theological premise in approaching Old Testament law and ethics. Obedience to the law was based on, and was a response to, God's salvation. Exodus has eighteen chapters of redemption before a single chapter of law. The same is true in relation to Israel's mission among the nations. In whatever way Israel would be or become a blessing to the nations would be on the grounds of what God had done for them, not on the basis of their own superiority in any sense.[68]

The sign of the covenant internally was faith, as Moses and God's people trusted God to deliver them, and the sign of the covenant externally was the celebration of the Passover. Lastly, the covenant community was referred to as a holy nation and a kingdom of priests, and in this way their mission was not to go but to be God's people as an example to and invitation for the nations to worship their God.

The relationship between Moses and Jesus Christ is evidenced in a number of places and ways throughout the Scriptures. In Deuteronomy 18:18, God said to Moses, "I will raise up for them a prophet like you from among their brothers. And I will put my words in his mouth, and he shall speak to them all that I command him." Over a millennium later, in Acts 3:17–22, Peter quotes Deuteronomy 18:18 and applies its fulfillment to Jesus Christ; thus, Jesus' eventual coming was promised to Moses. Hebrews 3:1–6 says that Jesus and Moses were faithful to the Father's leading but that Jesus is worthy of greater honor because he is much greater than even Moses.

---

[68]Ibid., 64.

The gospel of Jesus Christ is clearly and repeatedly foreshadowed throughout the exodus story. It begins with God making a promise to elect a people as his own in the Abrahamic covenant. His people are then taken into slavery and ruled by a godless and cruel lord (foreshadowing Satan and sin). Unable to save themselves, God himself intervenes to redeem them from slavery and deliver them into freedom to worship him alone by his miraculous hand (foreshadowing Jesus' death and resurrection to liberate us from our slavery, including our self-chosen slavery to pharaohs such as drugs, alcohol, sex, and food). After taking his people out of Egypt, God's work with his people continues as he seeks to get Egypt out of his people (foreshadowing sanctification). Resisting God's continual attempt to lead his people as he desires, the people grumble against Moses and long to go back to Egypt (foreshadowing the believer's wrestling with their flesh).

But God's faithfulness persists, and he continues to lead his people by being with them in the pillar and cloud and providing for their needs out of his love, as he leads them on a journey to a land of rest and promise (foreshadowing heaven). God's interaction with his people is clearly that of a living God who speaks, acts, loves, declares his laws, judges sin, delivers, redeems, provides, and is present with them. The central picture of the gospel in Exodus is one of covenantal redemption.

The Law of Moses

The books of Moses (Genesis through Deuteronomy) contain more than six hundred commands. The question of whether new-covenant Christians are under the Law of Moses is incredibly complicated, with everyday implications:[69] May believers eat bacon? May we charge interest on

---

[69]This is an enormously complex issue. For more in-depth study see Thomas R. Schreiner, *Forty Questions on the Law* (Grand Rapids, MI: Kregel, 2010); Thomas R. Schreiner, *The Law and Its Fulfillment: A Pauline Theology of Law* (Grand Rapids, MI: Baker, 1993); Frank Thielman, *Paul and the Law: A Contextual Approach* (Downers Grove, IL: InterVarsity, 1994); Frank Thielman, *The Law and the New Testament: The Question of Continuity* (New York: Crossroad, 1999); Stephen Westerholm, *Israel's Law and the Church's Faith: Paul and His Recent Interpreters* (Grand Rapids, MI: Eerdmans, 1988); and Greg L. Bahnsen, Walter C. Kaiser Jr., Douglas J. Moo, et al., *Five Views on Law and Gospel* (Grand Rapids, MI: Zondervan, 1996).

loaned money? Must we practice Sabbath? Some things are commonly agreed upon.

First, The New Testament declares the law "is holy and righteous and good."[70] Second, the law helps to show us our sin.[71] Third, Jesus perfectly fulfilled all of the law for us.[72] Fourth, justification (being declared righteous before God) is wholly apart from keeping the law.[73] Fifth, those who said believers are required to keep the whole law to be sanctified are wrong.[74] Sixth, the Ten Commandments express fundamentally important principles for the Christian life. Seventh, not every old-covenant law is binding on Christians so that, for example, we do not have to sacrifice animals and can wear clothes made of multiple kinds of fabric.

The difficulty is that we should not dismiss all the old-covenant laws (e.g., stealing and murdering), and we should not retain all the old-covenant laws (e.g., stoning adulterers). One proposed solution is to divide the law into three categories.

1) *Ceremonial laws*, referring to the priesthood, sacrifices, temple, cleanness, and so on, are now fulfilled in Jesus and therefore no longer binding. Nearly all of Hebrews is about this issue for Jews who struggled with the Old Testament laws once they were saved. These laws are no longer binding on us because Jesus is our priest, temple, sacrifice, cleanser, and so on.

2) *Civil laws* are those pertaining to the governing of Israel as a nation ruled by God. Since we are no longer a theocracy, these laws, while insightful, are not directly binding on us. Romans 13:1–6 says we are to obey our pagan government because God will work through it too.

3) *Moral laws* refer to commands that forbid such things as rape, theft, murder, and so on. These laws are still binding on us even though Jesus fulfilled their requirements through his sinless life. Nine of the Ten Commandments are repeated by Jesus, with the only exception

---

[70]Rom. 7:12; 1 Tim. 1:8.
[71]Gal. 3:19–25.
[72]Matt. 5:17–18.
[73]Rom. 3:21, 27–28; 4:1–5; Gal. 2:16; 3:11; 5:4; Phil. 3:9.
[74]Galatians 5.

being the Sabbath, as that is part of the ceremonial law and now Jesus is our rest.

Thus, according to this explanation, ceremonial and civil laws are no longer binding on us, but moral laws are.

Others see the solution in this statement: the whole law is valid until its purpose is accomplished in Christ.[75] Now that Jesus' work is complete, the Law of Moses is abolished and we are now under the law of Christ: love God and neighbor as guided by the Spirit.[76] This seems to be supported by Paul's teaching in Galatians 3:16–4:7 that the law was added to God's promise to Abraham 430 years afterward because of sin. It imprisoned the people of God until Jesus came. Paul summarizes, "So then, the law was our guardian until Christ came, in order that we might be justified by faith. But now that faith has come, we are no longer under a guardian."[77]

WHAT IS THE DAVIDIC COVENANT?

Because God was faithful to his covenant with Noah, sinners continued to live and increase on the earth. Because God was faithful to his covenant with Abraham, his descendants became a nation. And because God was faithful to his covenant with Moses, the nation settled in their Promised Land, which set the stage of history for the establishing of a kingship to rule over the kingdom of Israel. In 2 Samuel 7:8–16, God chooses David to be the next covenant head:

> Thus says the LORD of hosts . . . I will appoint a place for my people Israel and will plant them, so that they may dwell in their own place and be disturbed no more. . . . Moreover, the LORD declares to you that the LORD will make you a house. When your days are fulfilled and you lie down with your fathers, I will raise up your offspring after you, who shall come from your body, and I will establish his kingdom. He shall build a house for my name, and I will establish the throne of his kingdom forever. . . . And your house and your kingdom

---

[75]See Rom. 10:4; Col. 2:17.
[76]Romans 8; 13:8–10; 1 Cor. 9:20–21; Gal. 5:14; James 2:8.
[77]Gal. 3:24–25.

shall be made sure forever before me. Your throne shall be established forever.

David was rightly overwhelmed by the gracious covenant promise that not only would a former shepherd boy be a king, but that from him would come a King whose kingdom would endure forever and be ruled by none other than the Son of God. David's humble response to God's covenantal grace is recorded in 2 Samuel 7:18–19:

> Then King David went in and sat before the LORD and said, "Who am I, O Lord GOD, and what is my house, that you have brought me thus far? And yet this was a small thing in your eyes, O Lord GOD. You have spoken also of your servant's house for a great while to come, and this is instruction for mankind, O Lord GOD!"

The Davidic covenant promise of an eternal kingdom was so treasured by God's people that they worshiped God in faith that he would be faithful to the covenant promises as he had been to Noah, Abraham, and Moses. One example of this is found in Psalm 89:3–4, which declares, "You have said, 'I have made a covenant with my chosen one; I have sworn to David my servant: "I will establish your offspring forever, and build your throne for all generations.""'

Scriptures continue to record how God poured a special measure of his grace on Israel in the days of David to lift his people to greater heights of dignity. He transformed the nation from a loose confederation of tribes into a strong empire. David, as well as many of his sons, accomplished much as they ruled over Israel.

Nevertheless, the Old Testament records a sad end for the house of David. The sin of David's sons caused God to remove the throne from Jerusalem. The nation and its king went into exile in Babylon. The prophets foretold that a descendant of David would restore the nation.

As we see the disarray of Israel's kingdom today, we have to wonder what happened to God's promises. Did God not assure David of an unending dynasty? Whatever came of the kingdom blessings promised to Israel?

The New Testament answers these questions by identifying Jesus as the heir of David's throne. Matthew and Luke composed extensive genealogies to demonstrate that he was the descendant of David.[78] Jesus was born in Bethlehem, the city of David, as God's providence brought pregnant Mary there to register for a governmental census.[79] As David's final heir, Jesus brings incomparable kingdom blessings to God's covenant people. He fulfills all the hopes of honor associated with the royal line in ways that go far beyond what David and his other sons accomplished.

The blessings of Christ's kingdom encompass a vast array of benefits for God's covenant people. To gain a glimpse into what Christ does for us, we will focus on three blessings that came through the line of David during the Old Testament period. Then we will see how Christ brings these gifts to God's people in the New Testament age.

1) David's house was to provide *protection* for Israel against evil. David and his sons had the responsibility of safeguarding the nation. Even when the offensive conquest of the land subsided, the royal house had the responsibility of providing ongoing security. For this reason, the kings of Israel erected walls and maintained armies. Every responsible member of David's house devised ways to protect the people.

2) The royal line of Judah was to ensure *prosperity* for God's people. Within the walls of royal protection, Israel prospered beyond measure. Righteousness prevailed when the king enforced the law. People could live and work without fear of criminals. Economic conditions improved as David's sons did their jobs properly. When kings ruled over the land in righteousness, the people prospered. The house of David not only protected God's people from their enemies, it also brought prosperity to the land.

3) David's house was divinely ordained to ensure the special *presence* of God among the people. David spent his life preparing for the temple, a permanent edifice for the presence of God. Solomon constructed the

---

[78]Matt. 1:2–16; Luke 3:23–37.
[79]Luke 2:4–6.

temple and centered his kingdom on it. The kings of Judah always bore the responsibility of maintaining the proper functioning of the temple. Without the presence of God, all the efforts of royalty were in vain. There could be no protection or prosperity without the presence of God. The prayers, sacrifices, and songs associated with Israel's temple were the sources out of which all kingdom benefits flowed.

The kingdom blessings of protection, prosperity, and divine presence did not cease with the Old Testament. These ancient realities anticipated greater benefits to come in Christ. But we must remember that Jesus bestows these kingdom blessings in two stages. He brought protection, prosperity, and divine presence at his first coming, which we now enjoy, and he will bring them at his second coming, which we are awaiting by faith.

Samuel anointed David as king of Israel,[80] but it was a long time before he began reigning on the throne.[81] In the meantime, David gathered followers who were loyal to him, influencing life in the kingdom ruled by the evil Saul until the day David began his reign on the throne. In a similar way after his resurrection and ascension, Jesus rose to the right hand of the Father as anointed king. From that place, he will one day return to earth as reigning king on the historic throne of David. In the meantime, he is gathering faithful followers who will continue the mission to bring people into the glory of the kingdom. From his exalted position, Jesus bestows kingdom benefits on the people of God.

At this initial stage, Christ's blessings are primarily spiritual in nature. Jesus guaranteed his followers' *protection*: "No one will snatch them out of my hand."[82] As 1 John 4:4b says, "He who is in you is greater than he who is in the world." Neither human nor supernatural forces can rob us of our salvation in Christ. As our king, Jesus protects each one of his covenant people.

Christ also blesses his people with spiritual *prosperity*. Paul said we

---

[80]1 Samuel 16.
[81]2 Samuel 5.
[82]John 10:28b.

have been "blessed . . . in Christ with every spiritual blessing."[83] Jesus said he came "that they may have life and have it abundantly."[84] Christ guarantees spiritual prosperity to the people of his kingdom.

Finally, Christ provides the *presence* of God among his people. When Jesus left for heaven, he removed his physical presence, but he sent the Spirit to comfort his followers with the assurance of God's nearness: "I will not leave you as orphans; I will come to you."[85] For this reason, he could promise his apostles, "I am with you always, to the end of the age."[86]

The kingdom blessings that we enjoy today are grand, but we must remember that they are primarily spiritual. Christ does not promise us protection from all physical evil in this stage of his kingdom. In fact, he warned that his followers would receive persecution and suffering: "If they persecuted me, they will also persecute you."[87] Moreover, Christ's kingship does not guarantee physical prosperity and health today. The trials of poverty and physical illnesses remain with many of us, as the book of 1 Peter continually communicates. Finally, Christ does not give us his physical presence at this time either. He is present in the Spirit, but we long to see him and touch him again. The church now cries out, "Come, Lord Jesus!"[88]

We have the firstfruits of the kingdom, which make us long for the kingdom in its fullness.[89] While Christ guarantees us only spiritual blessings today, his protection, prosperity, and presence will extend even to physical levels when he returns. Within the new creation we will be protected against all forms of evil, physical and spiritual. The enemies of God will be utterly destroyed and we will have nothing to fear:

> Then comes the end, when he delivers the kingdom to God the Father after destroying every rule and every authority and power. For he must

---

[83]Eph. 1:3.
[84]John 10:10.
[85]John 14:18.
[86]Matt. 28:20.
[87]John 15:20b.
[88]Rev. 22:20.
[89]Rom. 8:23; 1 Cor. 15:20–24.

reign until he has put all his enemies under his feet. The last enemy to be destroyed is death.[90]

In the fullness of Christ's kingdom we will receive glorified physical bodies. All illness and grief will be gone: "Death shall be no more, neither shall there be mourning, nor crying, nor pain anymore."[91] Finally, when Christ returns we will no longer yearn to be in his physical presence because he will be among us. We will know Christ's presence both spiritually and physically. As John said, in the New Jerusalem he "saw no temple in the city, for its temple is the Lord God the Almighty and the Lamb."[92]

Thus, Christ fulfills all the hopes of the Davidic covenant. He brings the blessings of God's kingdom to all who serve him faithfully. David and his sons brought outpourings of tremendous benefits for God's people, but those Old Testament blessings fall short of the dignity for which we were designed and the fullness of God's covenantal grace. Christ alone brings full covenantal kingdom blessings.

In summary, the human mediator of the Davidic covenant was King David. The blessings of the Davidic covenant centered on a kingdom and a King who would come through David's family line to rule over all people for all times. The condition by which the Davidic covenant was to be enjoyed was participation in the nation of Israel and the worship of God, who was present in the temple. The internal sign of the covenant was faith in God's promises to establish an everlasting King and kingdom; the external sign was the throne, the symbol of the Davidic covenant and ultimately the seat of Jesus Christ, as is mentioned in fourteen of the twenty-two chapters of Revelation. The covenant community took the form of a kingdom. The promise of Jesus was that he would come from David's line as the King of kings to rule over all creation forever, bringing peace and prosperity with him.

Indeed, the Davidic covenant is fulfilled as the nations come to know Jesus Christ as King of kings through evangelism and church planting. This

---

[90]1 Cor. 15:24–26.
[91]Rev. 21:4.
[92]Rev. 21:22.

explains why the great prayer of Psalm 72 that speaks of Jesus' kingdom includes this echo of the Abrahamic covenant in verse 17: "May his name endure forever, his fame continue as long as the sun! May people be blessed in him, all nations call him blessed!" It is amazing that God's covenant grace is nothing short of a global gift.

WHAT IS THE NEW COVENANT?

Our study of covenants now brings us to the ultimate covenant in all of Scripture, that covenant which is the fulfillment and extension of all prior covenants between God and his people, expanding the benefits to people from the nations of the earth. Jeremiah 31:31–34 promised the new covenant:

> Behold, the days are coming, declares the LORD, when I will make a new covenant with the house of Israel and the house of Judah, not like the covenant that I made with their fathers on the day when I took them by the hand to bring them out of the land of Egypt, my covenant that they broke, though I was their husband, declares the LORD. But this is the covenant that I will make with the house of Israel after those days, declares the LORD: I will put my law within them, and I will write it on their hearts. And I will be their God, and they shall be my people. And no longer shall each one teach his neighbor and each his brother, saying, "Know the LORD," for they shall all know me, from the least of them to the greatest, declares the LORD. For I will forgive their iniquity, and I will remember their sin no more.

Many years after Jeremiah prophesied, as Passover approached, Jesus Christ sat down with his disciples to celebrate the Mosaic covenant by partaking of the Passover meal. For over a millennium God's covenant people had partaken of the Passover by following a strict order with sacred statements of promise interspersed throughout the meal. Keenly aware of the magnitude of the moment, Jesus did not speak the words tradition had dictated. Instead, Matthew 26:26–29 reports:

Now as they were eating, Jesus took bread, and after blessing it broke it and gave it to the disciples, and said, "Take, eat; this is my body." And he took a cup, and when he had given thanks he gave it to them, saying, "Drink of it, all of you, for this is my blood of the covenant, which is poured out for many for the forgiveness of sins. I tell you I will not drink again of this fruit of the vine until that day when I drink it new with you in my Father's kingdom.

The new covenant is God not merely giving us a human mediator but the second member of the Trinity himself coming into human history as the man Jesus Christ. This time, rather than taking life as he did when he flooded the earth in the days of Noah or requiring sacrifices for sin in the Mosaic covenant, he offered himself as the sacrificial substitute for sinners on the cross where he shed his blood in their place.

Commenting on one of the innumerable blessings enjoyed in the new covenant, 2 Corinthians 3:5–6 says, "Not that we are sufficient in ourselves to claim anything as coming from us, but our sufficiency is from God, who has made us competent to be ministers of a new covenant, not of the letter but of the Spirit. For the letter kills, but the Spirit gives life." In the new covenant, God comes to be with each of his people as he did with Noah, Abraham, Moses, and David. He also places the Holy Spirit in them to make them into a temple where worship occurs. The Spirit makes them new creations as the dawning and firstfruits of the finality of the new creation that will dawn with Jesus' second coming. The Spirit's work includes transfiguring us into Jesus' image bearers, as Moses was.

Perhaps the lengthiest treatment of the new covenant and its superiority to all preceding covenants is found in the book of Hebrews. In light of our study of covenants, the most helpful thing would be to simply read Hebrews 8:6–9:28.

In closing, Jesus is a better Noah who brings judgment of sin, salvation by grace to the family of God, and a new world free of sin and its effects. Jesus is a better Abraham, the blessing to the nations of the earth. Jesus is a better Moses as God's prophet who fulfilled the law for us, allows God's wrath to pass over us because of his shed blood, conquered our pharaoh of Satan, redeemed us from sin, and journeys with us toward home despite our sin and grumbling. And Jesus is a better David who is seated on a throne ruling as the King of kings and is coming again to establish his eternal and global kingdom of peace and prosperity.

CHAPTER 7

INCARNATION: GOD COMES

And the Word became flesh and dwelt among us, and we have seen his glory, glory as of the only Son from the Father, full of grace and truth.

JOHN 1:14

Superheroes capture our imagination with their superhuman abilities. Wolverine can rapidly heal from injury. Invisible Woman can become invisible at will. Nitro can reform his own body after it explodes. Superman can fly. The Hulk has superhuman power. Aquaman can breathe underwater. Spiderman can climb walls. Wonder Woman can understand any language. Infinity is all-knowing. The Silver Surfer can manipulate gravity. Doomsday can resurrect from death. Kitty Pryde can pass through solid matter. And the Flash has superhuman speed.

Many children, and more than a few adults, have wondered what it would be like for a human being to have superhuman abilities. Yet Christian theology has something even more amazing because, unlike the superheroes, our Superhero truly lived, and his powers exceed those of comic book lore.

J. I. Packer has described the incarnation as the "supreme mystery" associated with the gospel.[1] The incarnation is more of a miracle than

---

[1] J. I. Packer, *Knowing God* (Downers Grove, IL: InterVarsity, 1973), 45.

the resurrection because in it somehow a holy God and sinful humanity are joined, yet without the presence of sin: "Nothing in fiction is so fantastic as is this truth of the incarnation."[2] In Jesus, God enters the human realm. He walks on water, calms storms, heals the sick, feeds the hungry, raises the dead, and conquers the grave.

WHAT DOES *INCARNATION* MEAN?

Incarnation (from the Latin meaning "becoming flesh") is the word theologians use to explain how the second member of the Trinity entered into human history in flesh as the God-man Jesus Christ. One prominent theological journal explains:

> The English word "incarnation" is based on the Latin Vulgate, *"Et verbum caro factum est."* The noun *caro* is from the root *carn-* ("flesh"). The Incarnation means that the eternal Son of God became "flesh," that is, He assumed an additional nature, namely, a human nature.[3]

The incarnation is expressly stated in John 1:14, which says, "And the Word became flesh and dwelt among us, and we have seen his glory, glory as of the only Son from the Father, full of grace and truth." To better understand the incarnation we must carefully consider the opening chapter of John's Gospel.

The Hebrew people at the end of the first century clung tightly to their proud religious heritage extending from Abraham to Isaac, Jacob, Moses, David, and a host of priests and prophets. At the center of their theology was a devotion to the Word of God. The sacred Scriptures of the Old Testament were penned in their native tongue by their Hebrew brothers with nothing less than the authority of God as his divine voice through appointed men. To the Hebrews, the Word of God was the presence and action of God breaking into human history with unparalleled power and authority. God's Word indicated action, an agent accomplishing the will

---

[2]Ibid., 53.
[3]Dallas Theological Seminary (2004; 2005). Bibliotheca Sacra, vol. 161 (vnp.161.641.75).

of God. Some examples include God bringing things into existence by his word[4] and God's word being sent out to accomplish his purposes.[5] For the Hebrew, God's speech and action were one and the same.

Leon Morris provides insight into the Jewish concept of "the Word" from the Jewish Targums (Old Testament paraphrases), in which Jews substituted "God" for "the Word of God" out of reverence for his name. For example, where the Bible says, "Then Moses brought the people out of the camp to meet God,"[6] the Targum reads, "to meet the Word of God."[7]

The Jewish philosopher and historian Philo taught his understanding of the *logos*. Dualistic and much like early Gnostics, Philo taught that God is spirit and good, but that all matter is evil. Therefore, God could not have created or taken on the material lest he sin. He concluded that both God and matter are eternal and that an intermediary existed that permitted God to interact with the material world. This he called the *logos*.

The Greek people living at the end of the first century also clung tightly to their proud heritage, a philosophical heritage extending from Heraclitus (540–480 BC), to Socrates (470–399 BC), Plato (428–348 BC), Aristotle (384–327 BC), Cicero (106–43 BC), and a host of other philosophers, poets, and playwrights. At the fountainhead of Greek philosophy was Heraclitus, who was known as the "weeping philosopher" and whose image could be found on the coins in Ephesus for several centuries following his death.

For Heraclitus, the creation of the world, the ordering of all life, and the immortality of the human soul were all made possible solely by the word (or *logos*) that was the invisible and intelligent force behind all that we see in this world. Also, it was the word through which all things were interrelated and brought into harmony, such as life and death, good and evil, darkness and light, and the gods and people. He went so far as to say that truth could be known and wisdom, the great aim of Greek existence,

---

[4]Gen. 1:3, 6, 9, 11, 14, 20, 24; Ps. 33:6.
[5]Isa. 55:11.
[6]Ex. 19:17.
[7]See Leon Morris, *The Gospel According to John*, rev. ed., The New International Commentary on the New Testament (Grand Rapids, MI: Eerdmans, 2000), 105–6.

found not by a knowledge of many things but instead by a deep and clear awareness of one thing—the word, or *logos*.

Jesus Christ was born of a virgin as the one true God who became a man, living at a time and place in which the Hebrew and Greek worlds collided. John sought to be a faithful missionary and to remain loyal to the Hebrew heritage and the Old Testament Scriptures, priests, and prophets, and Jesus himself, while still seeking to further the fruitful work of the gospel into the larger world dominated by Greek philosophy and language.

In this context, John wrote his biography of Jesus in the Greek language, and he began with the concept of "the word," a common ground in the presuppositions of both Hebrew theology and Greek philosophy. *Logos* is from the Greek meaning "word," or "reason." As we have seen, it was used by the ancient Greeks to convey the idea that the world was governed by a universal intelligence. However, John used *logos* differently from other writers, that is, to refer to the second person of the Trinity, Jesus Christ.

John begins with a declaration that both Hebrews and Greeks would have agreed with, that before the creation of the world and time, the Word existed eternally. He then scandalizes both groups by stating that Jesus is the Word and was with the one and only God and, in fact, was himself God and was face-to-face with God the Father from eternity.[8] This thundering declaration would have been stunning to both Jews and Greeks who had vigorously argued that a man could never become a god, though they may never have considered that God had become a man, as John's eyewitness testimony revealed.

John then explains that the Word is not merely the invisible force of the Greeks or the agent of God's action for the Hebrews, but a person through whom all things were created,[9] and a person in whom is life and light for men.[10] This light that exposes sin and reveals God has come into the darkness of this sinful, cursed, and dying world. The darkness opposed his light but was unable to understand or overcome him.[11]

---

[8]John 1:1–2.
[9]John 1:3; cf. Col. 1:16.
[10]John 1:4.
[11]John 1:5; cf. 1 John 1:5–10; 2:8–11.

It is important to note that John was fully monotheistic in his understanding of God. He would have understood the magnitude of what he was saying, and, as a result, he very clearly outlined his position. John was acutely aware of and intentional in his revolutionary teaching regarding five aspects of this Logos.

1) The Logos is eternal.[12] According to Ron Rhodes, "'In the beginning' (Gk. *en archei*) refers to a point in eternity past beyond which it is impossible for us to go. Moreover, the verb *was* ('in the beginning was the Word') is an imperfect tense in the Greek, indicating continued existence."[13]

2) The Logos has always been with God, face-to-face with the Father as an equal in relationship.[14]

3) The Logos is a person distinct from yet equal to God.[15] The Greek preposition *pros* (translated "with" in 1 John 1:1 and 1:2) implies two distinct persons. Therefore, while the Father and the Logos are not the same, they do belong together as one.

4) The Logos is the creator[16] and therefore eternal, self-existent, and all-powerful.

5) The Logos became flesh.[17] In refutation to the Gnostics and dualistic teachings of Philo, John clearly taught that matter is not inherently evil and that God does involve himself with the material. It is also noteworthy that Jesus came to dwell among his people in a way that is similar to the tabernacle that God had the Israelites build as his sanctuary so that he might dwell in their midst.[18] Implicitly, we are told that the Logos that was present in the sanctuary became physically present in the space-and-time world. As George Eldon Ladd observes, the Logos became flesh to reveal to humans five things: life,[19] light,[20] grace,[21] truth,[22] glory,[23] and even God himself.[24]

---

[12]John 1:1–2.
[13]Ron Rhodes, *The Counterfeit Christ of the New Age Movement* (Grand Rapids, MI: Baker, 1990), 215.
[14]John 1:1–2.
[15]John 1:1–2.
[16]John 1:3.
[17]John 1:14.
[18]Ex. 25:8.
[19]John 1:4.
[20]John 1:4–5.
[21]John 1:14.
[22]Ibid.
[23]Ibid.
[24]John 1:18; George Eldon Ladd, *A Theology of the New Testament*, rev. ed. (Grand Rapids, MI: Eerdmans, 1993), 278.

How John uses the word *Logos* elsewhere in his writings is also insightful. First John 1:1 indicates that John and others heard, saw, and touched the Logos, "which was from the beginning." Again, this is a clear reference to Jesus Christ. Revelation 19:12–13 also pictures Christ as the conquering warrior, the Logos of God.

In summary, the Logos is one of the strongest arguments for the deity of Jesus as the personal, eternally existing creator of the universe, distinct from yet equal with God the Father, who became incarnate (or came in the flesh) to demonstrate his glory in grace and truth to reveal life and light to men.

HOW DID PEOPLE KNOW GOD WAS COMING?

Because God is sovereign over the future, he alone is capable of giving prophetic insight into the future. In great mercy he did this for his people in the Old Testament. He detailed for them who was coming to save them, how he would come, where he would come, when he would come, and why he would come, so that they would anticipate the incarnation and salvation of Jesus Christ.

Around 4000 BC, after Adam and Eve sinned, God prophesied to them that the Messiah (Jesus) would be born of a woman; he makes no reference to a father, which intimates the virgin birth. This prophecy was given by God himself and was the first time the gospel was preached: "I will put enmity between you [the Serpent] and the woman, and between your offspring and her offspring; he shall bruise your head, and you shall bruise his heel."[25]

Around 700 BC Isaiah prophesied exactly how Jesus would come into human history: "Therefore the Lord himself will give you a sign. Behold, the virgin shall conceive and bear a son, and shall call his name Immanuel."[26] The promise that Jesus' mother would be a virgin who conceived by a miracle did, in fact, come true.[27] Jesus' mother, Mary, was in fact a godly young woman and chaste virgin who conceived by the miraculous power of God the Holy Spirit.

---

[25]Gen. 3:15.
[26]Isa. 7:14.
[27]E.g., Matt. 1:18–23.

Furthermore, Jesus, a name that means "he saves his people from their sins," came as "Immanuel," which means, "God is with us." God became a man at the incarnation of Jesus. Matthew 1:22–23 reveals that Isaiah's prophecy came true: "All this took place to fulfill what the Lord had spoken by the prophet: 'Behold, the virgin shall conceive and bear a son, and they shall call his name Immanuel' (which means, God with us)."

Some contend that the prophecy in Isaiah does not refer to a virgin. They argue that the Hebrew word *almah* (which is used in Isaiah 7:14) typically means "young woman," not "virgin," whereas the Hebrew word *bethulah* typically means "virgin." However, there are many reasons why the verse should be read as referring to a virgin. Even if the word does mean "young woman," that does not mean that she was not a virgin. In that day, young women were virgins, making the terms synonymous for most young Hebrew women. Those unmarried women who were not virgins were subject to possible death under the law. If there was any question about her virginity, a woman was subject to physical inspection, which we see in Deuteronomy 22:14–22.

Additionally, the word *almah* is used elsewhere in the Old Testament to refer specifically to a young virgin woman. One clear example is Rebekah, who is described as "very attractive in appearance, a maiden [*bethulah*] whom no man had ever known."[28] Further in the chapter we read that Rebekah was a "virgin [*almah*]."[29] While the two words are virtually synonymous, apparently *bethulah* required a bit more clarification that the woman was a virgin whereas *almah* did not. Furthermore, two centuries before Jesus was born, we find that the Jews understood exactly what *almah* means: the Septuagint, the Jewish translation of the Hebrew Bible into Greek, translates *almah* as *parthenos*, which unambiguously means "virgin." Lastly, in the New Testament, Isaiah 7:14 is clearly interpreted as a prophetic promise about the birth of Jesus to Mary, who was both a young woman and a virgin.

Concerning Jesus' birthplace, in roughly 700 BC Micah prophesied

---

[28]Gen. 24:16.
[29]Gen. 24:43.

that Jesus would be born in the town of Bethlehem, saying, "But you, O
Bethlehem Ephrathah, who are too little to be among the clans of Judah,
from you shall come forth for me one who is to be ruler in Israel, whose
coming forth is from of old, from ancient days."[30] D. A. Carson says that
this verse reveals that the incarnation of Jesus was the entrance of the
eternal God: "The Hebrew behind *from ancient* means from 'the remotest
times,' 'from time immemorial' . . . when used with reference to some historical event; when it is used of God, who existed before creation, 'everlasting' is an appropriate translation (*e.g.* Ps. 90:2)."[31]

This prophecy was fulfilled in Luke 2:1–7. Caesar Augustus had called
for a census to be taken, which required that every family register in their
hometown. Jesus' adoptive father, Joseph, was thus required to return to
Bethlehem because he was a descendant of the family line of David. In
God's providence, this census was required right when Mary was pregnant;
she journeyed with her husband from their home in Nazareth to Bethlehem
so that Jesus was born in Bethlehem in fulfillment of Micah's prophecy.

As to the timing of Jesus' incarnation, in 400 BC Malachi prophesied,
"Behold, I send my messenger, and he will prepare the way before me.
And the Lord whom you seek will suddenly come to his temple; and the
messenger of the covenant in whom you delight, behold, he is coming, says
the LORD of hosts."[32] The messenger of whom Malachi spoke was John
the Baptizer, who prepared the way for Jesus' incarnation to bring the new
covenant, and the Lord he speaks of is the Lord Jesus Christ. It is important
that we are told that Jesus would come to "his temple." Since the temple
was destroyed in AD 70 and has not existed since, this places the incarnation of Jesus Christ prior to AD 70. Practically, this means that our Jewish
friends who are still awaiting the coming of their Messiah missed him; they
wait in vain because he has already come to his temple and brought the new
covenant of salvation.[33]

---

[30]Mic. 5:2.
[31]D. A. Carson, *New Bible Commentary: 21st Century Edition*, electronic ed. (Downers Grove, IL:
InterVarsity, 1994), Mic. 5:1.
[32]Mal. 3:1.
[33]Luke 2:25–27.

Lastly, Isaiah prophesies in 700 BC about why Jesus would become incarnate—he is God's arm of salvation reaching down to save sinners.[34] Isaiah also says that Jesus would come from humble circumstances and suffer great sorrow and grief by men in order to deal with the human sin problem through his death, burial in a rich man's tomb, and resurrection.[35]

The purpose of Jesus' incarnation was fulfilled when, just as promised, he suffered and died in the place of sinners though he himself was sinless, was buried in a rich man's tomb, and rose from death to make righteous the unrighteous.[36]

Besides these explicit prophecies predicting Jesus' incarnation, on many occasions the Old Testament speaks of God anthropomorphically, or in human terms. Old Testament scholar Roy Zuck says:

> Deuteronomy refers to God's hand (2:15; 3:24; 4:34; 7:19; 11:2; 26:8; 33:11; 34:12) and arm (4:34; 5:15; 7:19; 11:2; 26:8) as expressions of His power. His eyes (11:12; 12:28; 13:18; 32:10) represent His omniscience and constant attention, while His face (5:4; 31:18; 33:20; 34:10) and mouth suggest His communication of His glory and word. In fact the "mouth" of Yahweh is a metonymy for His word as propositional revelation (1:26, 43; 8:3; 9:23; 17:6, 10–11; 19:15; 21:17; 34:4).
>
> In startlingly human terms Yahweh is said to write (10:4), to walk (23:14), and to ride (33:26).[37]

Jacob Neusner is the most respected scholar of Judaism, and his book *The Incarnation of God* examines the notion of divine incarnation as it emerges in rabbinic literature.[38] Neusner is so aware of the force of the anthropomorphisms in Hebrew Scripture that he actually calls them incarnational.[39] He defines *incarnational* as "the representation of God in the flesh, as corporeal, consubstantial in emotion and virtue with human

---

[34]Isa. 53:1–12.

[35]Isa. 52:13–53:12.

[36]Matt. 27:38, 57–60; Luke 23–24; Acts 2:25–32.

[37]Roy B. Zuck, ed. *A Biblical Theology of the Old Testament* (Chicago: Moody, 1991), 66.

[38]Jacob Neusner, *The Incarnation of God: The Character of Divinity in Formative Judaism* (Binghamton, NY: Global Academic, 2001).

[39]See ibid.,12, 17.

beings, and sharing in the modes and means of action carried out by mortals."[40] Neusner goes on to say:

> God's physical traits and attributes are represented as identical to those of a human being. That is why the character of the divinity may accurately be represented as incarnational: God in the flesh, God represented as a person consubstantial in indicative physical traits with the human being.[41]

He argues that some earlier rabbis held to a doctrine of incarnation; he is fully aware of the theological connections this has for Christianity, despite the fact that he is Jewish, because he sees that the biblical evidence of the Old Testament leads to the incarnation.

In summary, people knew of Jesus' incarnation in advance because God prophetically revealed to them who would come, where he would come, when he would come, and why he would come.

HOW DID GOD COME INTO HUMAN HISTORY?

Before we examine how the incarnation occurred, we will note some important truths about this doctrine, for the sake of precision.

First, the incarnation is not an idea borrowed from pagan mythology. In mythology there are stories such as Zeus begetting Hercules, and Apollo begetting Ion and Pythagoras. As a result, some have speculated that Christians stole the virgin birth story from such myths. This speculation must be rejected on three grounds. (1) Some such myths came after the prophecy of Isaiah 7:14 and therefore could not have been the origination of the story. (2) The myths speak of gods having sex with women, which is not what the virgin birth account entails. (3) The myths do not involve actual human beings like Mary and Jesus but rather fictional characters similar to our modern-day superheroes in the comics.

Second, the Mormon teaching that God the Father had physical, flesh-

---

[40]Ibid., 12.
[41]Ibid., 166.

and-bone sexual relations with Mary, thereby enabling her to conceive Jesus, is horrendously incorrect.

Third, the incarnation does not teach that a man became God. From the time the Serpent told our parents, "You will be like God,"[42] there has been an ongoing demonic false teaching that we can be gods (e.g., Mormonism) or part of God (e.g., pantheism, panentheism, and New Ageism). Simply, the incarnation teaches the exact opposite, namely that God became a man.

Fourth, the second member of the Trinity did not come into existence at the incarnation of Jesus Christ. Rather, the eternal Son of God became the God-man Jesus Christ. Theologian Martyn Lloyd-Jones says it this way:

> The doctrine of the incarnation at once tells us that that is not what happened. A person, I repeat, did not come into being there. This person was the eternal Person, the second Person in the Trinity. When a husband and a wife come together and a child is born a new person, a new personality, comes into being. That did not happen in the incarnation.[43]

Fifth, while it is true in one sense that God did become a man, we must be careful to note that the second divine person in the Trinity became a man and that the entire Trinity did not incarnate as a human being. Lloyd-Jones explains:

> But to me it seems always to be wise not to say that God became man. That is a loose statement which we had better not use. We often do say that, but believing as we do in the Persons of the Trinity, what we should say is that the second Person in the Trinity was made flesh and appeared as man. If we merely say, 'God became man', then we may be saying something that is quite wrong, and if people believe something wrong as the result of our statement, we cannot really blame them. We must be particular and we must be specific and we should always be careful what we say. . . .

---

[42]Gen. 3:5.
[43]D. Martyn Lloyd-Jones, *God the Father, God the Son* (Wheaton, IL: Crossway, 1996), 264.

Jesus Christ has not been changed into a man; it is this eternal Person who has come in the flesh. That is the right way to put it.[44]

Therefore, by incarnation we mean that the eternal second person of the Trinity entered into history as the man Jesus Christ.

The incarnation of Jesus Christ is recorded in detail in the first two chapters of both Matthew's and Luke's Gospels. There we read that the angel Gabriel was sent as a messenger from God to the town of Nazareth to a young virgin named Mary who was betrothed to a man named Joseph. The angel announced:

"Do not be afraid, Mary, for you have found favor with God. And behold, you will conceive in your womb and bear a son, and you shall call his name Jesus. He will be great and will be called the Son of the Most High. And the Lord God will give to him the throne of his father David, and he will reign over the house of Jacob forever, and of his kingdom there will be no end."

And Mary said to the angel, "How will this be, since I am a virgin?"

And the angel answered her, "The Holy Spirit will come upon you, and the power of the Most High will overshadow you; therefore the child to be born will be called holy—the Son of God. . . . For nothing will be impossible with God." And Mary said, "Behold, I am the servant of the Lord; let it be to me according to your word." And the angel departed from her.[45]

Further, the Bible reveals the birth of Jesus as the pattern for our new birth—both are miracles of God the Holy Spirit to be received by faith. Belief in Jesus' incarnation is an essential truth that Christians have always held. One scholar says, "Apart from the Ebionites . . . and a few Gnostic sects, no body of Christians in early times is known to have existed who did not accept as part of their faith the birth of Jesus from the Virgin Mary."[46] Another writes, "Everything that we know of the dogmatics of the

---

[44]Ibid., 256–57.

[45]Luke 1:30–38.

[46]James Orr, *The Virgin Birth of Christ* (New York: Scribner's, 1907), 138.

early part of the second century agrees with the belief that at that period the virginity of Mary was a part of the formulated Christian belief."[47] Furthermore, the church father Ignatius, who was trained by the disciple John, testified to this fact, speaking of the "virginity of Mary."[48] Lastly, J. Gresham Machen summarized the evidence for that fact, saying, "There is good ground, we think, to hold that the reason why the Christian Church came to believe in the birth of Jesus without a human father was simply that He was a matter of fact so born."[49]

WAS JESUS FULLY GOD?

Jesus is nearly universally recognized as a great moral example, insightful teacher, defender of the poor and marginalized, humble servant to the needy, and unprecedented champion of overturning injustice with nonviolence. However, the divinity of Jesus Christ is most frequently and heatedly debated. Simply stated, the question as to whether Jesus Christ is fully God is the issue that divides Christianity from all other religions and spiritualities. For example, the Jehovah's Witnesses Watchtower Society says, "Jesus never claimed to be God."[50] Bahá'"s say that Jesus was a manifestation of God and a prophet but inferior to Muhammad and Bahá'ulláh. Buddhism teaches that Jesus was not God but rather an enlightened man like the Buddha. Christian Science founder Mary Baker Eddy flatly states, "Jesus Christ is not God." Conversely, we believe that there are numerous incontrovertible reasons to believe that Jesus Christ was and is fully God.

God the Father said Jesus was God. The Bible is clear that the Father declares the Son to be God. In Hebrews 1:8 the Father speaks of the Son as God, saying, "But of the Son he says, 'Your throne, O God, is forever and ever.'" When Jesus is brought forth out of the water at his baptism, God the Father says, "This is my beloved Son, with whom I am well pleased."[51]

---

[47]*The Apology of Aristides*, trans. and ed. Rendel Harris (London: Cambridge University Press, 1893), 25.

[48]William A. Jurgens, *Faith of the Early Fathers* (Collegeville, MN: Liturgical Press, 1998), ß42.

[49]J. Gresham Machen, *The Virgin Birth of Christ* (New York: Harper & Brothers, 1930), 269.

[50]"Is God Always Superior to Jesus?" *Should You Believe in the Trinity?* Watch Tower Bible and Tract Society of Pennsylvania, Watchtower Society online ed., http://www.watchtower.org/e/ti/index.htm?article=article_06.htm.

[51]Matt. 3:17.

At Jesus' transfiguration, "a voice from the cloud said, 'This is my beloved Son, with whom I am well pleased; listen to him.'"[52] Indeed, there can be no greater testimony to the deity of Jesus Christ than that of God the Father.

Demons said Jesus was God. Even demons called Jesus "the Holy One of God"[53] and "the Son of God."[54] Mark 1:34 says that Jesus "would not permit the demons to speak, because they knew him." Again, Luke 4:41 says Jesus "would not allow them [the demons] to speak, because they knew that he was the Christ."

Jesus said he was God. Jesus' claim to be God is without precedent or peer, as no founder of any major world religion has ever said he was God. Yet, Jesus clearly, repeatedly, and emphatically said he was God in a variety of ways. If this claim were untrue, he would have been guilty of violating the first commandment and as a blasphemer would have deserved death. This is why the people who disbelieved his claim kept seeking to put him to death. The eventual murder of Jesus for claiming to be God is recorded in Matthew 26:63–65, which says:

> But Jesus remained silent. And the high priest said to him, "I adjure you by the living God, tell us if you are the Christ, the Son of God." Jesus said to him, "You have said so. But I tell you, from now on you will see the Son of Man seated at the right hand of Power and coming on the clouds of heaven." Then the high priest tore his robes and said, "He has uttered blasphemy. What further witnesses do we need? You have now heard his blasphemy."

By declaring that he came down from heaven, Jesus revealed that he was eternally God in heaven before his incarnation on the earth.[55] By saying he was the only way to heaven, Jesus claimed to be both God and savior.[56] Jesus refused to be considered merely a good moral instructor and instead claimed to be "God alone."[57]

---

[52]Matt. 17:5.
[53]Mark 1:24; Luke 4:33–34.
[54]Luke 4:40–41.
[55]John 6:38, 41–46.
[56]John 14:6.
[57]Mark 10:17–18.

Those who heard Jesus say these kinds of things wanted to kill Jesus because he was "making himself equal with God."[58] On this point, Billy Graham says, "Jesus was not just another great religious teacher, nor was he only another in a long line of individuals seeking after spiritual truth. He was, instead, truth itself. He was God incarnate."[59]

Jesus' claims to be God were clearly heard and understood by his enemies, and Jesus never recanted.[60] John 8:58–59 reports that Jesus said, "'Truly, truly, I say to you, before Abraham was, I am.' So they picked up stones to throw at him, but Jesus hid himself and went out of the temple." In John 10:30–33 Jesus also said:

> "I and the Father are one." The Jews picked up stones again to stone him. Jesus answered them, "I have shown you many good works from the Father; for which of them are you going to stone me?" The Jews answered him, "It is not for a good work that we are going to stone you but for blasphemy, because you, being a man, make yourself God."

On this point, New York's Judge Gaynor once said of Jesus' trial at the end of his earthly life, "It is plain from each of the gospel narratives, that the alleged crime for which Jesus was tried and convicted was blasphemy."[61]

The Bible plainly says Jesus is God. Without question, the New Testament often refers to Jesus Christ as God, and a few examples will illustrate this truth clearly. Matthew refers to Jesus as "'Immanuel' (which means, God with us)."[62] Thomas calls Jesus, "My Lord and my God!"[63] Romans 9:5 speaks of "the Christ who is God over all, blessed forever. Amen." Titus 2:13 refers to "our great God and Savior Jesus Christ" and Titus 3:4 calls Jesus, "God our Savior." First John 5:20 says that Jesus Christ "is the true God." Lastly, 2 Peter 3:18 speaks of "our Lord and Savior Jesus Christ."

---

[58]John 5:18.

[59]Billy Graham, "God's Hand on My Life," *Newsweek*, March 29, 1999, 65.

[60]Mark 14:61–64.

[61]Quoted in Charles Edmund Deland, *The Mis-Trials of Jesus* (Boston, MA: Richard G. Badger, 1914), 118–19.

[62]Matt. 1:23.

[63]John 20:28.

Jesus is given the names of God. When picking a title for himself, Jesus was apparently most fond of "Son of Man."[64] He spoke of himself by this term roughly eighty times between all four Gospels. He applied the title from the prophet Daniel, who penned it some six hundred years before Jesus' birth.[65] In Daniel's vision, the Son of Man comes to the Ancient of Days, the Lord himself. But he comes from the clouds, from heaven, not from the earth. This indicates that he isn't a human. He is given messianic dominion and authority, something no angel can obtain and is reserved for God. The Old Testament sees this divine person sitting alongside the Lord as an equal. This second person of the Trinity was promised to receive the messianic mission to redeem the world, to defeat every enemy and liberate people. As God, he is exalted over all peoples, nations, cultures, and religions to be worshiped as the eternal King. Jesus is the one who claimed he would be the Son of Man coming with the clouds as God.

Many other names for God are also attributed to Jesus Christ. Jesus claimed to be the "Son of God" on many occasions.[66] In so doing he was claiming to be equal to and of the same substance as God the Father. Those who heard him use this title rightly understood that it was a divine title: "This was why the Jews were seeking all the more to kill him, because not only was he breaking the Sabbath, but he was even calling God his own Father, making himself equal with God."[67]

The New Testament refers to Jesus Christ as "Lord" several hundred times.[68] That term is the equivalent of the Old Testament term "Jehovah," which is one of the highest titles the Bible ascribes to God. Thus, this title is ascribed to Jesus Christ as God and Lord.

In Revelation 22:13 Jesus says, "I am the Alpha and the Omega, the first and the last, the beginning and the end." With these titles he is obviously referring to himself as eternal God. Bible commentator Grant Osborne says:

---

[64]Matt. 24:30; 26:64; Mark 13:26; 14:62–64; Luke 21:27; 22:69; Acts 1:9–11; 1 Thess. 4:17; Rev. 1:7; 14:14.
[65]Dan. 7:13. Also see Psalm 110.
[66]E.g., John 5:17–29.
[67]John 5:18.
[68]E.g., Rom. 10:9, 13; 1 Cor. 2:8; Heb. 1:10.

The titles refer to the sovereignty of God and Christ over history. They control the beginning of creation and its end, and therefore they control every aspect of history in between. Since this is the only passage to contain all three titles, it has the greatest emphasis of them all on the all-embracing power of Christ over human history.[69]

Jesus possessed the attributes of God. In 1 Timothy 1:17, Jesus is "King" and "the only God" who has the divine attributes of eternality, immortality, and invisibility. According to other Scriptures, the other divine attributes Jesus possessed during his life on the earth include omnipresence,[70] omnipotence,[71] immutability,[72] omniscience[73] (including predicting the future[74]), eternality,[75] creator,[76] sustainer of all creation,[77] savior,[78] sovereignty,[79] and deity as the only God.[80] Taken together, the fact that while on the earth Jesus possessed the divine attributes that belong to God alone is compelling evidence that Jesus is God.

Jesus did the works of God. The nearly forty miracles that Jesus performed throughout the New Testament reveal his divinity because they demonstrate his divine authority over creation as the Creator.[81] For example, when Jesus gave sight to the blind man, the people would have been reminded of Psalm 146:8: "The LORD opens the eyes of the blind." The fact of Jesus' miracles is so well established that even his enemies conceded it.[82]

Opponents of Jesus outside of Scripture also testify to his miracles. The Jewish Talmud charged that Jesus "practiced magic."[83] Celsus, a strong opponent of Christianity, later repeated that claim.[84] The noted

---

[69]Grant R. Osborne, *Revelation*, Baker Exegetical Commentary on the New Testament (Grand Rapids, MI: Baker Academic, 2002), 789.

[70]Ps. 139:7–12; Matt. 28:20.

[71]Matt. 28:18.

[72]Heb. 13:8; James 1:17.

[73]Matt. 11:27; John 2:25; 4:18; 16:30.

[74]Matt. 16:21; 17:22; 20:18–19; 26:1–2.

[75]John 1:1; 17:5; Col. 1:17; Phil. 2:6; Heb. 1:11–12.

[76]Isa. 37:16; 44:24; John 1:3; Col. 1:16; Heb. 1:2.

[77]Col. 1:17; Heb. 1:3.

[78]Joel 2:32; Rom. 10:9–13.

[79]1 Cor. 15:27.

[80]Isa. 45:21b–23; Phil. 2:10–11.

[81]John 20:30–31.

[82]Matt. 12:24; 27:42; John 11:47.

[83]*Sanh.* 43a.

[84]Origen, *Contra Cels.* 1.38.

Jewish historian Josephus also reported that Jesus was "a doer of wonderful works."[85] In John 10:36–39 Jesus speaks of these works:

> "Do you say of him whom the Father consecrated and sent into the world, 'You are blaspheming,' because I said, 'I am the Son of God'? If I am not doing the works of my Father, then do not believe me; but if I do them, even though you do not believe me, believe the works, that you may know and understand that the Father is in me and I am in the Father." Again they sought to arrest him, but he escaped from their hands.

Jesus' claim to deity includes declaring himself to be without any sin in thought, word, deed, or motive and therefore morally perfect. In John 8:46 Jesus openly invites his enemies to recall any sin he ever committed saying, "Which one of you convicts me of sin?" Those who testify to the sinlessness of Jesus are those who knew him most intimately, such as his friends Peter[86] and John,[87] his half-brother James,[88] and even his former enemy Paul.[89] Additionally, even Judas who betrayed Jesus admitted that Jesus was without sin,[90] along with the ruler Pilate, who oversaw the murder of Jesus,[91] the soldier who participated in the murder of Jesus,[92] and the guilty sinner who was crucified at Jesus' side.[93]

Furthermore, not only was Jesus God and without sin, but he also forgave sin.[94] The Bible is clear that our sin is ultimately committed against God[95] and that God alone can forgive sin.[96] Thus, Luke 5:20–21 reveals Jesus doing the work of God:

---

[85]Flavius Josephus, "Jewish Antiquities," in *The New Complete Works of Josephus*, trans. William Whiston (Grand Rapids, MI: Kregel, 1999), 18.63.
[86]Acts 3:14; 1 Pet. 1:19; 2:22; 3:18.
[87]John said that anyone who claims to be without sin is a liar (1 John 1:8) and that Jesus was without sin (1 John 3:5).
[88]James 5:6.
[89]2 Cor. 5:21.
[90]Matt. 27:3–4.
[91]Luke 23:22.
[92]Luke 23:47.
[93]Luke 23:41.
[94]E.g., Luke 7:48.
[95]Ps. 51:4.
[96]Ps. 130:4; Isa. 43:25; Jer. 31:34.

And when he [Jesus] saw their faith, he said, "Man, your sins are forgiven you." And the scribes and the Pharisees began to question, saying, "Who is this who speaks blasphemies? Who can forgive sins but God alone?"

Lastly, Jesus also claimed the power to raise the dead,[97] judge our eternal destiny,[98] and grant eternal life.[99]

People worshiped Jesus as God. The Bible is emphatically clear that only God is to be worshiped.[100] To worship anyone other than God is both idolatry and blasphemy—two sins that the Bible abhors from beginning to end with the strongest condemnations. Therefore, the fact that Jesus accepted worship as God is one of the strongest arguments that Jesus Christ was and is fully God.

Jesus repeatedly invited people to pray to him as God.[101] As a result of his teaching, both men like Stephen[102] and women like the Canaanite[103] did pray to Jesus as God.

Jesus also said that he is to be worshiped along with the Father: "All may honor the Son, just as they honor the Father. Whoever does not honor the Son does not honor the Father who sent him."[104] Upon his triumphal entry into Jerusalem when children worshiped him, Jesus quoted Psalm 8:2 in reference to himself as God to be worshiped:

When the chief priests and the scribes saw the wonderful things that he did, and the children crying out in the temple, "Hosanna to the Son of David!" they were indignant, and they said to him, "Do you hear what these are saying?" And Jesus said to them, "Yes; have you never read, 'Out of the mouth of infants and nursing babies you have prepared praise'?"[105]

---

[97]John 6:39–44.
[98]John 5:22–23.
[99]John 10:28.
[100]Deut. 6:13; 10:20; Matt. 4:10; Acts 10:25–26.
[101]John 14:13–14; 15:7.
[102]Acts 7:59–60.
[103]Matt. 15:25.
[104]John 5:23.
[105]Matt. 21:15–16.

Commenting on this event, Craig Blomberg says:

> Jesus' response, again using the introductory rebuke "Have you never read?" tacitly applauds their acclamation in light of Ps 8:2 (LXX [Septuagint] 8:3, which is quoted verbatim). There the children are praising Yahweh, so Jesus again accepts worship that is reserved for God alone.[106]

Also, after being healed by Jesus, a man worshiped Jesus, and Jesus accepted his worship.[107] Lastly, Philippians 2:10–11 envisions a day in which everyone bends their knee in subjection to Jesus and lifts their voice in worship of Jesus as Lord.

Taken together, all of this evidence reveals that Jesus was and is God. Or, as Colossians 2:9 says perfectly, "in him the whole fullness of deity dwells bodily."

WAS JESUS FULLY HUMAN?

The Bible affirms the humanity of Jesus Christ in a variety of ways. Jesus had a human name—Jesus (meaning "Yahweh saves") Christ (meaning "anointed one")—and a human genealogy.[108] He was born of a woman,[109] had brothers and sisters,[110] and was racially Jewish.[111] Jesus grew physically, spiritually, mentally, and socially,[112] learned,[113] experienced fatigue,[114] slept,[115] grew hungry[116] and thirsty,[117] worked as a carpenter,[118] had male and female friends he loved,[119] gave encouraging compliments,[120] loved

---

[106]Craig L. Blomberg, *Matthew*, The New American Commentary (Nashville: Broadman, 1992), 315–16.
[107]John 9:38.
[108]Matt. 1:1–17; Luke 3:23–38.
[109]Matt. 1:18–25; Luke 2:7; Gal. 4:4.
[110]Matt. 13:55.
[111]John 4:9.
[112]Luke 2:42, 52; 3:23.
[113]Matt. 4:12; Mark 11:13–14; Luke 2:40, 52.
[114]Matt. 8:24; Mark 4:38; Luke 8:23–24; John 4:7.
[115]Mark 4:36–41.
[116]Matt. 4:2; Mark 11:12; Luke 4:2.
[117]John 4:7; 19:18.
[118]Mark 6:3.
[119]John 11:3–5.
[120]Mark 12:41–44.

children,[121] celebrated holidays,[122] went to parties,[123] loved his mom,[124] prayed,[125] worshiped,[126] and obeyed God the Father.[127]

Furthermore, not only did Jesus have a physical body,[128] but he also suffered and died "in the flesh."[129] In addition to his body, Jesus also had a human spirit.[130] Jesus was emotional as well, for the Bible notes that Jesus experienced grief,[131] had compassion,[132] was stressed,[133] was astonished,[134] was happy[135] and told jokes,[136] and even wept.[137]

Taken together, these are clearly the ways we speak of human beings and reveal that Jesus was, as Jesus and other Scriptures state, a man.[138] The importance of this fact is found in 1 John 4:2–3:

> By this you know the Spirit of God: every spirit that confesses that Jesus Christ has come in the flesh is from God, and every spirit that does not confess Jesus is not from God. This is the spirit of the antichrist, which you heard was coming and now is in the world already.

The belief in the full humanity of Jesus Christ was the dominant position of the early Christian church. Athanasius expressed the church's opinion well:

> Peter writes in his letter, "Christ therefore suffered *in the flesh* for our sakes" [1 Pet. 4:1]. So when it is said that he hungered and thirsted and toiled and was ignorant and slept and cried out and made requests and fled and was born and turned away from the cup—in general, did all

---

[121]Matt. 19:13–15.
[122]Luke 2:41.
[123]Matt. 11:19.
[124]John 19:26–27.
[125]Matt. 14:23; Mark 1:35; 14:32–42; John 17.
[126]Luke 4:16.
[127]John 5:30; 6:38; 8:28–29, 54; 10:17–18.
[128]Rom. 8:3; Phil. 2:7–8; Heb. 2:14; 1 John 4:2–3.
[129]Rom. 8:3; Eph. 2:15–16; Col. 1:21–22; Heb. 2:14; 10:19–20; 1 Pet. 2:24.
[130]John 12:27; 13:21; 19:30.
[131]Matt. 23:37; Luke 19:41.
[132]Matt. 9:36; Mark 1:41; Luke 7:13.
[133]John 13:21.
[134]Mark 6:6; Luke 7:9.
[135]Luke 10:21–24; John 15:11; 17:13; Heb. 12:2, 22.
[136]Matt. 7:6; 23:24; Mark 4:21.
[137]John 11:34–35.
[138]John 8:40; Acts 17:31; 1 Tim. 2:5.

the things which belonged to the flesh—let . . . all things of this sort be asserted as "for our sakes in the flesh," for this is precisely the reason the apostle himself said, "Christ therefore suffered" not in the Godhead but "for our sakes in the flesh," in order that the passions might be recognized to be natural properties not of the Logos but of the flesh.[139]

HOW COULD GOD BECOME A MAN?

In AD 451, the Council of Chalcedon met to wrestle with the confusion that surrounded the divinity and humanity of Jesus. They issued the Chalcedonian Creed, which cleared up many heresies that wrongly defined the humanity and divinity of Jesus. In sum, the creed declared that Jesus Christ is one person with two natures (human and divine) who is both fully God and fully man.

Theologically, the term for the union of both natures in Jesus Christ is *hypostatic union*, which is taken from the Greek word *hypostasis* for "person." Summarizing the hypostatic union, three facts are noted: (1) Christ has two distinct natures: humanity and deity; (2) there is no mixture or intermingling of the two natures; (3) although he has two natures, Christ is one person. The Chalcedonian summary of the incarnation is the position held by all of Christendom, including Orthodox, Catholic, and Protestant Christians.

In keeping with the biblical position of Chalcedon, we must retain both the full divinity and full humanity of Jesus Christ. To accomplish this, we must conclude that when Jesus became a man, he did not change his identity as God but rather changed his role. According to the church father Augustine, "Christ added to himself which he was not, he did not lose what he was."[140]

Jesus, who was fully equal with God in every way, who was the very form of God, did not see that as something to keep in his grip, but emptied himself of that equal status and role to take the status and role of humanity.

---

[139] Athanasius, "Orations Against the Arians," bk. 3, in Richard A. Norris, trans. and ed., *The Christological Controversy* (Philadelphia: Fortress, 1980), 92–93, emphasis in original.

[140] Quoted in G. C. Berkouwer, *The Person of Christ*, trans. John Vriend (Grand Rapids, MI: Eerdmans, 1954), 94.

He who was and is God took the likeness of humanity. God became the "image of God" for the sake of our salvation.[141]

Theologians capture this laying aside of the divine equality, the divine lifestyle, with the phrase *he laid aside the independent exercise of his divine attributes.* What this means is that he did not continually exhibit the so-called incommunicable attributes such as his immortality, omniscience, or omnipresence, except at the leading of the Holy Spirit.

The key Scripture describing that God came as the man Jesus Christ because of humility and a willingness to be our suffering servant is Philippians 2:5–11, which says:

> Have this mind among yourselves, which is yours in Christ Jesus, who, though he was in the form of God, did not count equality with God a thing to be grasped, but made himself nothing, taking the form of a servant, being born in the likeness of men. And being found in human form, he humbled himself by becoming obedient to the point of death, even death on a cross. Therefore God has highly exalted him and bestowed on him the name that is above every name, so that at the name of Jesus every knee should bow, in heaven and on earth and under the earth, and every tongue confess that Jesus Christ is Lord, to the glory of God the Father.

This amazing section of Scripture reveals to us that the second member of the Trinity came into human history as the man Jesus Christ. In doing so, Jesus exemplified perfect and unparalleled humility. In his incarnation, the Creator entered his creation to reveal God to us, identify with us, and live and die for us as our humble servant.

By saying that Jesus "made himself nothing," Paul means that Jesus set aside his rights as God and the rightful continual use of his divine attributes, with the occasional exception such as forgiving sin. Though Jesus remained God, he chose instead to live by the power of the Holy Spirit. This does not mean that Jesus in any way ceased to be fully God, but rather that he chose not to continually avail himself of his divine rights

---

[141]Gen. 1:27; 2 Cor. 4:4.

and attributes while on the earth. Thus, he lived as we must live—by the enabling power of God the Holy Spirit. We want to be clear: Jesus remained fully man and fully God during his incarnation, and he maintained all of his divine attributes and did avail himself of them upon occasion, such as to forgive human sin, which God alone can do.[142] Nonetheless, Jesus' life was lived as fully human in that he lived it by the power of the Holy Spirit.[143] Regarding the relationship between Jesus and the Holy Spirit, Martyn Lloyd-Jones says:

> What, then, does all this mean? It means that there was no change in His deity, but that He took human nature to Himself, and chose to live in this world as a man. He humbled Himself in that way. He deliberately put limits upon Himself. Now we cannot go further. We do not know how He did it. We cannot understand it, in a sense. But we believe this: in order that He might live this life as a man, while He was here on earth, He did not exercise certain qualities of His Godhead. That was why . . . He needed to be given the gift of the Holy Spirit without measure.[144]

Sadly, all of the major creeds compiled during the early church ignore the life of Jesus between his birth and death. The Apostles' Creed, Nicene Creed, and Athanasian Creed all declare that Jesus was born to the Virgin Mary and then skip forward to his suffering under the rule of Pilate without speaking a word about the years in between; they overlook the example of Jesus' life, in general, and his exemplary relationship with God the Holy Spirit, in particular.

Despite its absence in the church creeds, Abraham Kuyper writes of the importance of the relationship between Jesus and the Holy Spirit:

> This ought to be carefully noticed, especially since the Church has never sufficiently confessed the influence of the Holy Spirit exerted upon the work of Christ. The general impression is that the work of the

---

[142]Mark 2:1–7.

[143]For a more thorough study of this and other issues regarding the Holy Spirit, *He Who Gives Life: The Doctrine of the Holy Spirit* by Graham A. Cole (Wheaton, IL: Crossway, 2007) is a helpful resource.

[144]Lloyd-Jones, *God the Father, God the Son*, 286–87.

Holy Spirit begins when the work of the Mediator on earth is finished, as tho [*sic*] until that time the Holy Spirit celebrated His divine day of rest. Yet the Scripture teaches us again and again that Christ performed His mediatorial work controlled and impelled by the Holy Spirit.[145]

The empowerment of Jesus by God the Holy Spirit is repeatedly stressed in the Gospel of Luke. There we find that Jesus was conceived by the Holy Spirit and given the title "Christ," which means anointed by the Holy Spirit.[146] Jesus' aunt Elizabeth was "filled with the Holy Spirit" when greeting Jesus' pregnant mother Mary, and his uncle Zechariah went on to prophesy that their son John was appointed by God to prepare the way for Jesus.[147] An angel revealed to Mary that she would give birth to Jesus because "the Holy Spirit will come upon you."[148]

Once born, Jesus was dedicated to the Lord in the temple according to the demands of the law by Simeon; "the Holy Spirit was upon [Simeon]" and the Holy Spirit had revealed to him that he would not die until seeing Jesus Christ.[149] Simeon was "in the Spirit" when he prophesied about Jesus' ministry to Jews and Gentiles.[150]

John prophesied that one day Jesus would baptize people with the Holy Spirit.[151] The Holy Spirit descended upon Jesus at his own baptism.[152] It is curious that while the Gospels give scant information about Jesus' childhood, all four include the account of Jesus' baptism. Matthew adds the interesting statement that the Spirit rested on Jesus, as if to suggest that the remainder of his life and ministry on the earth would be done under the anointing and power of the Holy Spirit.[153]

In the remainder of Luke's Gospel, we discover that Jesus was "full of the Holy Spirit," "led by the Spirit,"[154] and came "in the power of the

---

[145]Abraham Kuyper, *The Work of the Holy Spirit*, trans. Henri de Vries (Grand Rapids, MI: Eerdmans, 1975), 97.
[146]Luke 1–2.
[147]Luke 1:41–43, 67, 76.
[148]Luke 1:35–37.
[149]Luke 2:25–27.
[150]Luke 2:27–34.
[151]John 1:14; Phil. 2:5–6; Col. 2:9; 1 John 4:2.
[152]E.g., Matt. 4:1–10; Heb. 4:14–16.
[153]Matt. 3:16.
[154]Luke 4:1–2.

Spirit."[155] After reading Isaiah 61:1–2, which begins, "The Spirit of the Lord GOD is upon me," Jesus declared, "Today this Scripture has been fulfilled in your hearing."[156] Luke continues by revealing that Jesus also "rejoiced in the Holy Spirit."[157]

Gerald Hawthorne, who has written one of the most compelling books on the subject of Jesus' relationship with the Holy Spirit, says, "[Jesus] is the supreme example for them of what is possible in a human life because of his total dependence upon the Spirit of God."[158]

WHAT ARE SOME PROMINENT FALSE TEACHINGS ABOUT THE DOCTRINE OF THE INCARNATION?

Regarding the full divinity and humanity of Jesus Christ, theologian J. I. Packer has said:

> The really staggering Christian claim is that Jesus of Nazareth was God made man—that the second person of the Godhead became the "second man" (1 Cor. 15:47), determining human destiny, the second representative head of the race, and that He took humanity without loss of deity, so that Jesus of Nazareth was as truly and fully divine as He was human. Here are two mysteries for the price of one—the plurality of persons within the unity of God, and the union of Godhead and manhood in the person of Jesus.[159]

There are two general ways in which various thinking has erred regarding the humanity and divinity of Jesus. The first is to deny the full divinity of Jesus in favor of his humanity; the second is to deny the full humanity of Jesus in favor of his divinity.

The denial of the full divinity of Jesus has been done by heretics such as the Ebionites, dynamic monarchianists, Socinians, Servetusites, Nestorians,

---

[155]Luke 4:14.
[156]Luke 4:14–21.
[157]Luke 10:21.
[158]Gerald F. Hawthorne, *The Presence and the Power: The Significance of the Spirit in the Life and Ministry of Jesus* (Dallas: Word, 1991), 234.
[159]Packer, *Knowing God*, 46.

modalists, monarchianists, Sabellianists, Unitarians, Social Gospel proponents, "death of God" theologians, liberal "Christians," Arians, Jehovah's
Witnesses, Mormons, functionalists, Adoptionists, Kenotics, Apollinarians,
and more recently by the popular book and film *The Da Vinci Code*.

The denial of the full humanity of Jesus has been done by heretics such
as Marcionites, Docetists, Gnostics, modal monarchianists, Apollinarian
Paulicians, monophysitists, New Agers, and Eutychians. Perhaps the
people who most commonly prefer Jesus' divinity over his humanity in
our present age are Protestant Christian fundamentalists. They are so
committed to preserving the divinity of Jesus that they tend to portray his
humanity as essentially overwhelmed by his divinity so that he was largely
not tempted to sin, if indeed tempted at all.

In addition, the Bultmannian school (after Rudolf Bultmann) has
separated the "Christ of faith" from the "Jesus of history." Subsequently,
Jesus is more like an ancient Greek god. Some evangelical Christians make
a similar error by removing Jesus' life and teachings from history in the
world and relegating him to the subjective realm of religious experience
so that Jesus becomes little more than a figurative object for devotion and
experience only in our heart.

Lastly, it is falsely believed that the Christian concept of incarnation
is commonly held across many ideologies, if not even borrowed from
them. Humanist mystic Aldous Huxley famously asserted that "the doctrine that God can be incarnated in human form is found in most of the
principal historic expositions of the Perennial Philosophy."[160] In response,
Geoffrey Parrinder has shown that Huxley's claim is grossly overstated.[161]
Nonetheless, it is true that there is a long history of religious beliefs claiming that a god or goddess came to the earth in physical form. These are
considered in the broadest sense to be incarnational teachings, although
none of them is the same as Christian incarnation.[162]

---

[160]Aldous Huxley, *The Perennial Philosophy: An Interpretation of the Great Mystics, East and West* (New York: HarperCollins, 2004), 49.

[161]Geoffrey Parrinder, *Avatar and Incarnation: The Divine in Human Form in the World's Religions* (Oxford: Oneworld, 1997), 13.

[162]See Winfried Corduan, "Jesus: The Avatar I Never Knew," *Christian Apologetics Journal* 4, no. 2 (2005): 29–44.

In many idolatrous religions, a deity is said to be present in or physically manifested as an object, which then comes to eventually be worshiped as the deity itself. Some idolatrous religions (e.g., Sikhism, Bahá", Hinduism) refer to incarnations as *avatars*, which literally means "descent." Christian apologist Timothy C. Tennent notes three ways in which such avatars are different from what Christians believe about the incarnation of Jesus Christ.[163] (1) Avatars are repeated endlessly throughout each cycle of history, whereas the incarnation is a unique, singular act in history. Jesus will not return for another incarnated life cycle or be replaced by another person housing his spirit. (2) An avatar comes forth because of accumulated karma and is therefore not a free act of God, like the determination of the Father to send Jesus into history before time began.[164] (3) An avatar is a mixture and blending of the divine and human, whereas Jesus is not a blending of a god and a man but rather God becoming man.

Therefore, because Jesus is the only God and his incarnation alone is altogether unique, it is a grievous error in any way to portray his earthly life as similar to avatars and the like that are postulated by other religions.

HOW IS JESUS' INCARNATION A SOURCE OF GREAT COMFORT?

There are two categories of reason why Jesus' incarnation is a source of great comfort. The first is that in the incarnation Jesus is like us. The second is that in the incarnation Jesus is unlike us.

How Jesus Is Like Us

As the man Jesus Christ, the second member of the Trinity has lovingly and humbly identified with the frailty of our humanity by enduring temptation, distress, weakness, pain, and sorrow. He did so by coming as our priest.

In the Old Testament, the priest would humbly stand between God and people as a mediator of sorts. He would bring the hopes, dreams, fears, and sins of the people before God as their advocate and intercessor. He would

---

[163]See Timothy C. Tennent, *Christianity at the Religious Roundtable* (Grand Rapids, MI: Baker, 2002), 59–60.
[164]Eph. 1:3–12.

hear their confession of sin and pray for them. Furthermore, offering sacrifices was central to his role, to show that sin was very real and deserved death, while asking God for gracious forgiveness. Then he would speak God's blessing on the people. All the functions of the priest are ultimately fulfilled in Jesus.

The book of the Bible that deals most thoroughly with the priestly role of Jesus is Hebrews. In Hebrews, we are told that Jesus is our "high priest."[165] As our priest, Jesus has offered a sacrifice to pay the penalty for our sin. Not only is Jesus a priest superior to the Old Testament priests, but his sacrifice is also superior to theirs—he gave his own life and shed his own blood for our sin.[166]

Hebrews reveals that Jesus' ministry as our priest did not end with his return to heaven. Rather, Jesus is alive today and ministers to us as our high priest who intercedes for us before God the Father.[167] Practically, this means that Jesus actually knows us, loves us, pays attention to our lives, and cares for us. At this very moment, Jesus is bringing Christians' hurts, suffering, needs, and sins to the Father in a prayerful and loving way as our priest.

Jesus' priestly intercession makes both our prayer and worship possible. We pray and worship the Father through Jesus our priest by the indwelling power of God the Holy Spirit, who has made our bodies the new temples in which he lives on the earth.

When we understand Jesus as our priest, we are able to know that he loves us affectionately, tenderly, and personally. Furthermore, Jesus' desire for us is nothing but good, and his ministry results in nothing less than life-changing intimacy with God the Father. Jesus makes new life and obedience possible by his loving, compassionate, and patient service to us as a faithful priest.

In his role as priest, Jesus is different from all other man-made religions and their false portraits of God. Virtually every religion sees God in

---

[165]Heb. 3:1; 4:14.
[166]Heb. 9:26.
[167]Heb. 7:25.

a harsh way. Jesus is the only God who gets off his throne to humbly serve us and give us grace and mercy.

Perhaps the most insightful text of Scripture on the importance of the priestly ministry of Jesus is Hebrews 4:15–16, which says:

> For we do not have a high priest who is unable to sympathize with our weaknesses, but one who in every respect has been tempted as we are, yet without sin. Let us then with confidence draw near to the throne of grace, that we may receive mercy and find grace to help in time of need.

Thus, Jesus is sympathetic to our temptations, weakness, suffering, sickness, disappointment, pain, confusion, loneliness, betrayal, brokenness, mourning, and sadness. Jesus does not refrain from entering our sick, fallen, and crooked world. Instead, he humbly came into this world to feel what we feel and face what we face while remaining sinless. Subsequently, Jesus can both sympathize with and deliver us. Practically, this means that in our time of need, we can run to Jesus our sympathetic priest who lives to serve us and give us grace and mercy for anything that life brings.

How Jesus Is Unlike Us

In addition to being fully God, a primary way in which Jesus is unlike us is that he alone is without sin.[168] While the Bible is clear that Jesus never sinned, the question of whether he had a sin nature as we do has been a point of historical division between various Christian traditions.

The Eastern church says yes. They focus on Romans 8:3 (that the Father sent his own Son "in the likeness of sinful flesh and for sin") and Hebrews 4:15 (which says he was one "who in every respect has been tempted as we are"). They then argue that this could not be if Jesus did not have any of the sinful thoughts or desires like the ones we wrestle with all the time. It is then argued that although Jesus had a sin nature, he overcame it and showed us the perfect obedience that we can follow to live holy lives.

The Western church says no. They focus on Hebrews 7:26–27: We

---

[168] 2 Cor. 5:21; Heb. 9:14; 1 Pet. 2:22, 1 John 3:5.

"have such a high priest, holy, innocent, unstained, separated from sinners, and exalted above the heavens. He has no need, like those high priests, to offer sacrifices daily, first for his own sins." It is argued that if Jesus had a sin nature, he could not fit this description. Furthermore, if he had sinful character, then he would be a sinner.

We are inclined to agree with the Western church and see the "likeness of sinful flesh" in Romans as a point of similarity rather than a point of character whereby Jesus had a sin nature. Subsequently, as the "last Adam"[169] Jesus was like the first Adam prior to the fall—without a sin nature—and therefore had a completely free will to choose obedience out of love for God the Father.

Because Jesus is like us in that he was tempted, yet unlike us in that he never did sin, he can help us when we are tempted and show us how to escape sinful situations. Hebrews 2:17–18 says:

> Therefore he had to be made like his brothers in every respect, so that he might become a merciful and faithful high priest in the service of God, to make propitiation for the sins of the people. For because he himself has suffered when tempted, he is able to help those who are being tempted.

In conclusion, Jesus alone can mediate between God and us because he alone is fully God and fully man and thereby able to perfectly represent both God and man. Regarding the vital importance of both Jesus' humanity and divinity, theologian Jonathan Edwards says:

> First, I would consider Christ's taking upon him our nature to put himself in a capacity to purchase redemption for us. This was absolutely necessary, for though Christ, as God, was infinitely sufficient for the work, yet to his being in an immediate capacity for it, it was needful that he should not only be God, but man. If Christ had remained only in the divine nature, he could not have purchased our salvation; not from any imperfection of the divine nature, but by reason of its absolute and

---

[169]1 Cor. 15:45.

infinite perfection; for Christ, merely as God, was not capable either of obedience or suffering.[170]

In other words, to redeem man Christ first had to become a man. This is precisely what the Bible teaches: "For there is one God, and there is one mediator between God and men, the man Christ Jesus."[171] This verse reveals the threefold reasoning as to why Jesus' incarnation is of such great comfort. (1) There is one God for all peoples, times, and places. (2) There is one mediator between sinful humanity and the one sinless God. This mediator remedies the sin problem that divides people and God so that there can be salvation and reconciliation. (3) Christ Jesus alone can mediate between God and man because he alone is the God-man.

WHAT DIFFERENCE DOES THE DOCTRINE OF THE INCARNATION MAKE IN OUR LIFE?

In most religions the holiest men are those who are most separated from culture and sinners. They live as monks and the like in remote areas, away from average people. Conversely, Jesus Christ came into the mess of human history and spent time in community with believers and unbelievers alike. Subsequently, religious people who separated themselves from sinners and cultures were prone to denounce Jesus for the kind of company he kept.[172]

Jesus' incarnation is our missional model. Roughly forty times in John's Gospel Jesus declares that the Father sent him. Indeed, the incarnation is the sending of the second member of the Trinity into human history as a missionary. This is what Jesus meant when he taught that Christians would be sent as missionaries like him into cultures by the power of the Holy Spirit: "'As the Father has sent me, even so I am sending you.' And when he had said this, he breathed on them and said to them, 'Receive the Holy Spirit.'"[173]

[170]Jonathan Edwards, *History of Redemption* (Oxford: Oxford University Press, 1793), 312.
[171]1 Tim. 2:5.
[172]Matt. 11:19.
[173]John 20:21–22.

From the missional life of Jesus we learn five great missional truths for our own life. First, an incarnational missional life is contextual and crosses cultural barriers. Just as Jesus left heaven to enter into culture on the earth, Jesus' people are to do the same and not merely remain in community with people of their own gender, race, income level, nationality, and the like. Despite being contextual, a missional life does not condone or partake in the sinful worldly aspects of a culture, just as Jesus never sinned. Nonetheless, Jesus dressed, spoke, and ate according to Jewish culture, participated in their holidays, and observed their customs, so Jesus' people are also to live as missionaries in whatever culture God has sent them. Thus, in a very real sense, every Christian is a missionary whether they minister across the street or across the globe.

Second, an incarnational missional life is evangelistic. Just as Jesus did not merely come only to do good works for the needy but primarily to save lost people, Jesus' people are likewise to pursue lost people for evangelistic friendships.[174]

Third, an incarnational missional life is humble. Just as Jesus willingly left his state in glory to live a humble life and work a humble job, a missional life is one not lived solely for personal glory and upward mobility but rather values the gospel above all else. Subsequently, an incarnational approach to life often means that we make less money and live simpler lives than we could because we value gospel ministry above what worldly standards measure as success.

Fourth, an incarnational missional life is one devoted to the church. Jesus came to found, build, and head the church—his metaphorical body to continue his evangelistic plan for the world; therefore, Jesus' people are to give themselves to the church. This includes service and generosity as Jesus demonstrated[175] so that not only can local churches grow, but more churches can be planted, more people reached, and more nations impacted by the gospel of Jesus Christ.

Fifth, an incarnational missional life is global. While Jesus mainly

---

[174]Luke 19:10.
[175]2 Corinthians 8–9.

confined his ministry to Israel, he did minister to a Samaritan woman who then evangelized to her people, and the deaf man of Decapolis.[176] Additionally, the announcement of Jesus' birth by both the angels and Simeon was to be good news for all nations.[177] This is because Jesus came to take away the sins of the world[178] and establish the church as a mission center for the nations[179] from which he would send out believers to be the salt and light of the nations.[180] Jesus also prophesied that most of his worshipers would be from nations other than Israel[181] because his love is for the entire world.[182]

Indeed, the world is our mission field, and Jesus is our model incarnational missionary who went before us and now goes with us as we continue in his work by his Spirit as his church for his glory to our joy.[183]

---

[176]Matt. 15:21–28; 8:5–13; Mark 5:1–20; 7:31–37; John 4:1–42.
[177]Luke 2:10, 32.
[178]John 1:29.
[179]Mark 11:17.
[180]Matt. 5:13–14.
[181]Matt. 21:43; Luke 13:28–29.
[182]John 1:9, 29; 3:16–17, 19; 4:42; 6:33; 12:47; 16:8; 17:21.
[183]Matt. 26:18–20.

CHAPTER 8

CROSS: GOD DIES

God shows his love for us in that while we were still sinners,
Christ died for us.

ROMANS 5:8

The Bible gives few details about crucifixion. This is likely because the original audience had witnessed them. However, since few people in the modern era have personally witnessed a crucifixion, it is important for us to examine it in detail so as to fully appreciate the suffering of Jesus Christ.

Imagine a long wooden stake being run through a person's midsection, and that stake then being driven into the ground, with the impaled person left to die slowly over the course of many days. It is believed that this kind of barbarous torture may in fact be the earliest form of crucifixion, occurring as early as the ninth century BC.[1]

In the sixth century BC the Persians commonly practiced crucifixion, especially King Darius I, who crucified three thousand Babylonians in 518 BC. In 332 BC Alexander the Great crucified two thousand people whom he conquered in Tyre. The transition from impalement to crucifixion occurred under Alexander, as he was a master of terror and dread. In 71 BC the former gladiator Spartacus and 120,000 prisoners fell in battle to the Romans,

---

[1]Much of the following historical overview of crucifixion is from A&E Television and The History Channel's two-hour special called *Crucifixion* (March 23, 2008).

which resulted in six thousand men being crucified along the shoulder of the highway for 120 miles.

The Romans perfected crucifixion; they reserved it as the most painful mode of execution for the most despised people, such as slaves, the poor, and Roman citizens guilty of the worst high treason. The crucifixion methods varied with the sadism of the soldiers. They tried to outdo one another and experimented with various forms of torture. They grew learned in ways to prolong the pain and agony.

The Romans are believed to be the first to crucify on an actual cross. The *Tau* was a capital *T* cross and the *Latin* was a lowercase *t* cross. Both had the *stipe* (the vertical post) and *patibulum* (the crossbar). The *stipe* was probably permanent while each man carried his own *patibulum*.

As a young boy, Jesus may have viewed crucifixions in Judea, because there was a Jewish uprising against the Romans that resulted in a mass crucifixion of about two thousand Jews in AD 4 at the time of the death of Herod.

The pain of crucifixion is so horrendous that a word was invented to explain it—*excruciating*—which literally means "from the cross." The victim was affixed to the cross with either ropes or nails. The pain of crucifixion is due in part to the fact that it is a prolonged and agonizing death by asphyxiation. Crucified people could hang on the cross for anywhere from three to four hours or for as long as nine days, passing in and out of consciousness as their lungs struggled to breathe while laboring under the weight of their body.

In an effort to end the torment, it was not uncommon for those being crucified to slump on the cross to empty their lungs of air and thereby hasten their death. Further, there are debated archaeological reports that suggest sometimes seats were placed underneath the buttocks of those being crucified to prevent slumping, thereby ensuring a lengthy and most painful death.

None of this was done in dignified privacy, but rather in open, public places. It would be like nailing a bloodied, naked man above the front entrance to your local mall. Crowds would gather around the victims to mock them as they sweated in the sun, bled, and became incontinent from the pain.

Once dead, some victims were not given a decent burial but rather left on the cross for vultures to pick apart from above while dogs chewed on the bones that fell to the ground, even occasionally taking a hand or foot home as a chew toy, according to ancient reports.[2] Whatever remained of the victim would eventually be thrown in the garbage and taken to the dump unless the family buried it. Furthermore, the wooden crosses and nails were considered more valuable than the bodies of the deceased, and those resources were kept and reused.

As a general rule, it was men who were crucified. Occasionally a man was crucified at eye level so that passersby could look him directly in the eye as he died and cuss him out and spit on him in mockery. In the rare event of a woman's crucifixion, she was made to face the cross. Not even such a barbarous culture was willing to watch the face of a woman in such excruciating agony.

The ancient Jewish historian Josephus called crucifixion "the most wretched of deaths."[3] The ancient Roman philosopher Cicero asked that decent Roman citizens not even speak of the cross because it was too disgraceful a subject for the ears of decent people.[4] The Jews also considered crucifixion the most horrific mode of death, as Deuteronomy 21:22–23 says: "If a man has committed a crime punishable by death and he is put to death, and you hang him on a tree, his body shall not remain all night on the tree, but you shall bury him the same day, for a hanged man is cursed by God."

The Roman emperor Nero was so cruel to Christians that he had some of them crucified. Their number included Peter, who, it is said, was crucified upside down at his own request because he did not feel worthy of dying exactly as Jesus did. Roman crucifixion continued until Emperor Constantine reportedly saw the vision of a cross and the next day won a

---

[2]Suetonius, *The Lives of the Caesars*, Vesp. 5.4.
[3]Josephus, *J.W.* 7.203.
[4]Cicero, *Pro Rabirio Perduellionis Reo* 5.16.

historic battle and overtook the Western Roman Empire. Following his victory, Christianity was no longer outlawed but instead became a state-sponsored religion. Historians have debated whether he experienced a true conversion or simply practiced political expediency. Either way, he abolished crucifixion around AD 300.

In light of all this, perhaps most peculiar is the fact that the symbol for Jesus, which has become the most famous symbol in all of history, is the cross. The church father Tertullian (155–230 AD) tells us of the early practice of believers' making the sign of the cross over their bodies with their hand and adorning their necks and homes with crosses to celebrate the brutal death of Jesus. In so doing, the early Christians turned a symbol of terror and intimidation into a symbol of salvation and hope.

HOW CAN JESUS' CRUCIFIXION BE GOOD NEWS?

Among the scandals of the cross is the fact that Christians have called it their *gospel*, or good news, and celebrate it every year on Good Friday. To understand the good news of Jesus' death we must first examine how he died. Then we can examine why he died.

In the days leading up to his death, Jesus was a young man in his early thirties. He was in good health due to his job as a carpenter and his constant walking of many miles as an itinerant minister. Jesus began speaking openly of his impending death, including at the Passover meal he ate with his friends as the Last Supper. There, he broke with fifteen centuries of protocol. In so doing, he showed that the Passover meal, which God's people had been eating annually, found its ultimate fulfillment in him. The Passover memorialized the night in Egypt when in faith God's people covered the doorposts of their home with blood so that death would not come to the firstborn son in their home but would rather pass them over.[5] Jesus, the firstborn Son of God, likewise had come to die and cover us with his blood so that God's just wrath would literally pass over us sinners as the essence of the new covenant.[6]

---

[5]Exodus 6–12.
[6]Luke 22:19–21.

During the Last Supper, Satan entered one of Jesus' disciples, Judas, who had been stealing money from Jesus' ministry fund for some time and had agreed to hand him over to the authorities to be crucified. After Judas left the meal to lead the soldiers to Jesus, Jesus went to the garden of Gethsemane, where he spent a sleepless night in the agony of prayer. Meanwhile, his disciples failed to intercede for him in prayer and instead kept falling asleep. At this point, Jesus was fully aware of his impending crucifixion and was so distressed that, as the Bible records, he sweat drops of blood, a physical condition that doctors report is rare because it requires an elevated level of stress that few people ever experience.

After an exhausting, sleepless night of distress, Judas arrived with the soldiers and betrayed Jesus with a kiss. Jesus was then arrested. He was forced to walk through a series of false trials where contradicting false witnesses were brought forward to offer false testimony. Despite the absence of any evidence supporting the false charges, Jesus was sentenced to be murdered. He was eventually blindfolded as a mob of cowardly men beat him mercilessly. He was then stripped in great shame, and the Bible simply says that they had him scourged.

Scourging itself was such a painful event that many people died from it without even making it to their cross. Jesus' hands would have been chained above his head to expose his back and legs to an executioner's whip called a cat-o'-nine tails or a *flagrum*. Two men, one on each side, took turns whipping the victim. The whip was a series of long leather straps. At the end of some of the straps were heavy balls of metal intended to tenderize the body of a victim, like a chef tenderizes a steak by beating it. Some of the straps had hooks made of glass, metal, or bone that would have sunk deeply into the shoulders, back, buttocks, and legs of the victim. Once the hooks had lodged into the tenderized flesh, the executioner would rip the skin, muscle, tendons, and even bones off the victim. The victim's skin and muscles would hang off the body like ribbons as the hooks dissected the skin to the nerve layers. The damage could go so deep that even the lungs were bruised, which made breathing difficult. Some doctors have compared the damage of flogging to the results of a shotgun blast.[7] The victim would bleed profusely and would often go into shock, due to severe blood loss and insufficient blood flow near and through the heart.

Jesus' bare back and shoulders, though bloodied and traumatized, were then forced to carry his roughly hewn wooden cross to his place of crucifixion. If Jesus carried the entire cross, it would have weighed a few hundred pounds, and many think it is more likely he carried just the crossbar (*patibulum*), which would have been about one hundred pounds.

Despite his young age and good health, Jesus was so physically devastated from his sleepless night, miles of walking, severe beating, and scourging that he collapsed under the weight of the cross, unable to carry it alone. Doctors have said that the trauma from the heavy crossbar crushing his chest into the ground could have caused a bruised heart, similar to the chest trauma caused by a car accident without a seatbelt where the driver is violently thrown against the steering wheel.[8] Understandably unable to continue carrying his cross on the roughly one-mile journey to his execution, a man named Simon of Cyrene was appointed to carry Jesus' cross. Upon arriving at his place of crucifixion, they pulled Jesus' beard out—an act of ultimate disrespect in ancient cultures—spat on him, and mocked him in front of his family and friends.

Jesus the carpenter, who had driven many nails into wood with his own hands, then had five- to seven-inch rough metal spikes driven into the most sensitive nerve centers on the human body, through his hands and feet. Jesus was nailed to his wooden cross. His body would have twitched involuntarily, writhing in agony.

In further mockery, a sign was posted above Jesus that said, "Jesus of Nazareth, the King of the Jews."[9] A painting later discovered from a second-century Roman graffito further shows the disrespect of Jesus at his crucifixion. The painting depicts the head of a jackass being crucified,

---

[7]*Crucifixion*, A&E Television and The History Channel.
[8]Ibid.
[9]John 19:19.

with a man standing alongside it with his arms raised. The caption reads, "Alexamenos worships his god."

At this point during a crucifixion, the victims labored to breath as their bodies went into shock. Naked and embarrassed, the victims would often use their remaining strength to seek revenge on the crowd of mockers who had gathered to jeer them. They would curse at their tormentors while urinating and spitting on them. Some victims would become so overwhelmed with pain that they would become incontinent and a pool of sweat, blood, urine, and feces would gather at the base of their cross.

Jesus' crucifixion was a hideously grotesque scene. Hundreds of years in advance, the prophet Isaiah saw it this way:

> He was despised and rejected by men; a man of sorrows, and acquainted with grief; and as one from whom men hide their faces he was despised, and we esteemed him not. Surely he has borne our griefs and carried our sorrows; yet we esteemed him stricken, smitten by God, and afflicted.[10]

Crucifixion usually kills by asphyxiation in addition to other factors—the heart is deeply stressed, the body is traumatized, the muscles are devastated, and the blood loss is severe. Doctors have thought that Jesus likely had a chest contusion and possibly a bruised heart from falling with the cross on top of him, which caused an aneurysm.[11] Subsequently, Jesus' heart would have been unable to pump enough blood and his lungs would have filled up with carbon monoxide. Jesus not only lived through all of this, but he even spoke lucidly and clearly with enough volume to be heard by those present. Likely sensing he was having a heart attack, Jesus used his final moments to declare his victory over sin. In an effort to silence Jesus, the soldiers took a sponge soaked in vinegar—possibly used in the public restroom as the ancient version of both toilet paper and disinfectant—and put it on a stick and tried to shove it in his mouth.[12]

---

[10]Isa. 53:3–4.
[11]*Crucifixion*, A&E Television and The History Channel.
[12]Matt. 27:48; Mark 15:36; John 19:29.

At last, with this foul taste on his lips, Jesus said in a loud voice of triumph, "It is finished."[13] At this moment, the atonement for sin was made and the holiness, righteousness, justice, and wrath of God were satisfied in the crucifixion of Jesus Christ.

Jesus then said, "Father, into your hands I commit my spirit!"[14] Jesus reserved his final breath from the cross to shout his triumphant victory to the world by confirming that he had been restored to God the Father after atoning for human sin.

The Bible then simply records that Jesus breathed his last and died.

Jesus hung on the cross for at least six hours—from the third hour to the ninth hour, when the darkness ended.[15] How long thereafter that he breathed his last and died is not clear in Scripture. What is more clear is the fact that if a victim remained alive on the cross for too long so that it interfered with another event like a major holiday, it was customary to break the victim's legs, disabling him from pushing himself up on his cross to fill his lungs with air and thereby prolong his life. However, in accordance with the promise of Scripture, Jesus died quickly enough that his legs were not broken.[16]

Furthermore, to ensure Jesus was dead, a professional executioner ran a spear through his side, which punctured his heart sac, and water and blood flowed from his side. This is further evidence that Jesus died of a heart attack; the sac around the heart filled with water until the pressure caused Jesus' heart to stop beating. Thus, Jesus possibly died with both a literal and metaphorical broken heart.

For many years, the most sacred place on earth had been the temple, where the presence of God dwelled behind a thick curtain. Only one person each year, the high priest, was allowed to pass by that curtain and enter the presence of God on one day, the Day of Atonement. At the death of Jesus, however, the temple curtain was torn from top to bottom, signifying that God had opened his presence to the world through the cross of Jesus.

[13]John 19:30.
[14]Luke 23:46.
[15]Mark 15:25, 33.
[16]Ps. 34:20; John 19:36.

The most succinct summary of the gospel in Scripture provides insight into this theological meaning: "that Christ died *for* our sins in accordance with the Scriptures, that he was buried, that he was raised on the third day in accordance with the Scriptures."[17] In this packed section of Scripture, Paul appoints the death, burial, and resurrection of Jesus as the most important event in all of history and the verification of the truthfulness of all Scripture. He then explains why this is good news with the simple word "for," showing that Jesus died "for our sins." The word "for" can mean either "for the benefit of" or "because of." Jesus did not die "for the benefit of" our sins. He did not help them at all! Rather, he died "because of" our sins. So it was *our* sins but *his* death. From the beginning of sacred Scripture[18] to the end,[19] the penalty for sin is death. Therefore, if we sin, we should die. But it is Jesus, the sinless one, who dies in our place "for our sins." The good news of the gospel is that Jesus died to take to himself the penalty for our sin. In theological terms, this means that Jesus' death was substitutionary, or vicarious, and in our place solely for our benefit and without benefit for himself. Therefore, we find the cross of Jesus to be the crux of good news because it was there that Jesus atoned for our sin according to the promises of Scripture.

Jesus' work for us on the cross is called *atonement* (at-one-ment); Jesus our God became a man to restore a relationship between God and humanity. The concept of Jesus' dying in our place to pay our penalty for our sins has been expressed in theological shorthand as *penal substitution*. Scripture repeatedly and clearly declares that Jesus died as our substitute paying our penalty "for" our sins.[20]

One theologian has called the cross the great jewel of the Christian faith, and like every great jewel it has many precious facets that are each worthy of examining for their brilliance and beauty.[21]

Therefore, you will be well served to see each side of this jewel shining

[17]1 Cor. 15:3b–4.
[18]Gen. 2:17.
[19]Rev. 21:8.
[20]Isa. 53:5, 12; Rom. 4:25; 5:8; Gal. 3:13; 1 Pet. 3:18; 1 John 2:2.
[21]To learn more about each facet of the cross, see our book *Death by Love: Letters from the Cross* (Wheaton, IL: Crossway, 2008).

together for the glory of God in complementary, not contradictory, fashion. Most poor teaching about the cross results from someone denying, ignoring, or overemphasizing one of these facets at the expense of the others, often due to an overreaction to someone else's overreaction.

Many of these facets were foreshadowed in the Old Testament, specifically by the annual celebration of the Day of Atonement (Yom Kippur) according to the regulations of the book of Leviticus. The Day of Atonement was the most important day of the year and was often referred to simply as "the day." It was intended to deal with the sin problem between humanity and God. Of the many prophetic elements on this special day, one stands out. On that day, two healthy goats without defect were chosen; they were therefore fit to represent sinless perfection.

The first goat was a propitiating sin offering. The high priest slaughtered this innocent goat, which acted as a substitute for the sinners who rightly deserved a violently bloody death for their many sins. He then sprinkled some of its blood on the mercy seat on top of the Ark of the Covenant inside the Most Holy Place. The goat was no longer innocent when it took the guilt of sin; it was a sin offering for the people.[22] Subsequently, its blood represented life given as payment for sin. The dwelling place of God was thus cleansed of the defilement that resulted from all of the transgressions and sins of the people of Israel, and God's just and holy wrath was satisfied.

Then the high priest, acting as the representative and mediator between the sinful people and their holy God, would take the second goat and lay his hands on the animal while confessing the sins of the people. This goat, called the scapegoat, would then be sent away to run free into the wilderness away from the sinners, symbolically expiating our sins by taking them away.

These great images of the priest, slaughter, and scapegoat are all given by God to help us more fully comprehend Jesus' work for us on the cross, which we will now examine in depth.

---

[22]Lev. 16:15.

New-covenant Sacrifice

One scholar says that blood is mentioned some 362 times in the Old Testament and some ninety-two times in the New Testament and even more often than the cross or death of Jesus; thus, it is the most common means by which the Scriptures refer to the death of Jesus.

Throughout Scripture, blood is inextricably connected with sin for two primary reasons. First, shed blood reminds us that sin results in death. Second, God is sickened by sin, which causes death, a connection first made in Genesis 2:17 and repeated throughout the Bible. So when God sees blood, it points to the sickening reality of sin and death. Leviticus 17:11 says it this way: "For the life of the flesh is in the blood, and I have given it for you on the altar to make atonement for your souls, for it is the blood that makes atonement by the life." Blood is sacred, epitomizing the life of the sacrificial victim given as substitute for the sinner's death. Practically every sacrifice included the sprinkling or smearing of blood on an altar, thus teaching that atonement involves the substitution of life for life.

The Old Testament often used the theme of blood to prepare people for the coming of Jesus to die for our sins. In fact, it was God who shed the first blood in human history in response to sin. In Genesis 3 when our first parents, Adam and Eve, committed the original human sin, it was God who slaughtered an animal to make clothes to cover their nakedness. From then on blood sacrifices were the standard way to worship God.[23]

One of the bloodiest books of the Bible is Exodus. The people were given two choices. (1) They could repent of sin and place their faith in God, demonstrated by slaughtering an animal and covering the doorposts of their home in blood. If this was done, then God promised to pass over (hence the related feast of Passover) their house and not kill the firstborn son in the home but rather accept the substitution of the life of the sacrificial animal. (2) They could fail to repent of their sin and not place their faith in God and see death come to their home. On that night in Egypt, much blood was shed and death

---

[23]Gen. 8:20; 12:7–8; 13:4, 8; Job 1:5; 42:7–9.

came to every home as either the blood of a substitute animal was shed for the sinners, or the firstborn son in each home was put to death by God.

One of the major functions of the Old Testament temple was the slaughtering of animals, as seen by the stream of blood that often flowed out of the temple. Blood is in fact a major aspect of Old Testament religion. There were some eleven different sacrifices that fit into one of four groupings (burnt, peace, sin, or guilt) and sacrifices were made both in the morning and evening, all of which involved blood.

Despite all of this bloodshed, the Old Testament sacrificial system was never meant to be something sufficient in itself. When Israel misunderstood the purpose of the sacrifices, putting their faith in the sacrifices themselves, there were major problems. The first problem was that the bloodshed of a substituted animal did not forgive human sin.[24] The second problem was that it enabled hypocrisy; people could undergo external rituals such as offering a sacrifice without having truly repented of sin and trusted in God internally.[25] The third problem was that it was only preparatory and therefore incomplete until the coming of Jesus, who made the better new covenant possible.[26]

This theme of blood, like every theme of Scripture, finds its fulfillment in the coming of Jesus Christ into human history. Early in Jesus' life, his cousin John saw Jesus coming and declared, "Behold, the Lamb of God, who takes away the sin of the world!"[27] This, of course, would be accomplished when Jesus was slaughtered on the cross where his blood flowed freely.

The results of Jesus' shed blood are staggering. Hebrews 9:22 says, "Indeed, under the law almost everything is purified with blood, and without the shedding of blood there is no forgiveness of sins." Also 1 Peter 1:18–19 says, "You were ransomed from the futile ways inherited from your forefathers, not with perishable things such as silver or gold, but with the precious blood of Christ, like that of a lamb without blemish or spot."

---

[24]Ps. 51:16; Mic. 6:6–8; Heb. 10:4.
[25]1 Sam. 15:22; Prov. 15:8; Hos. 6:6.
[26]Heb. 7:22; 8:5–7, 13.
[27]John 1:29.

In the Bible the word *covenant* appears more than three hundred times and is therefore essential to our rightly understanding how God relates to us. Both the Old and New Testaments speak of the new covenant.[28] The Bible tells us that a new epoch in human history has arrived with the coming of God into human history as the man Jesus Christ. In the new covenant, all of the prophecies, promises, foreshadowing, and longing of the old covenant are fulfilled. In the new covenant it is Jesus Christ who serves as our covenant head.[29] Jesus went to the cross to shed his blood in our place for our sins so that we can have a new covenant relationship with him.

Today, in the new covenant, we no longer need a priest because we have Jesus, who is our Great High Priest.[30] We no longer need to offer blood sacrifices because Jesus is our sacrifice for sin.[31] We no longer need to visit the temple to be near to God because Jesus is our temple.[32] We no longer need to celebrate the Passover because Jesus is our passover.[33] Finally, we no longer need to live in habitual sin because through Jesus we have been made holy and have been given new life.[34]

Propitiation

The Bible is filled with examples of God getting angry at sinners and of his anger as hostile, burning, and furious.[35] Because God is holy, good, and just, he not only feels angry about sin but also deals with it in ways that are holy, good, and just. Because God is perfect, his anger is perfect and as such is aroused slowly,[36] sometimes turned away,[37] often delayed,[38] and frequently held back.[39]

God's anger is not limited to the Old Testament. Even Jesus got angry,

---

[28]E.g., Jer. 31:31–34; Matt. 26:28; Luke 22:20; Rom. 11:27; 1 Cor. 11:25; 2 Cor. 3:6; Heb. 7:22; 8:8–13; 9:15; 12:24.
[29]Eph. 1:10, 22; 4:15; 5:23; Col. 1:18; 2:10, 19.
[30]Heb. 2:17; 4:14–15.
[31]John 1:29.
[32]Rev. 21:22.
[33]1 Cor. 5:7.
[34]Heb. 9:26; 10:10.
[35]Lev. 26:27–30; Num. 11:1; Deut. 29:24.
[36]Ex. 34:6–8.
[37]Deut. 13:17.
[38]Isa. 48:9.
[39]Ps. 78:38.

furious, and enraged.[40] Also, Revelation 19 reveals Jesus coming again as a warrior riding on a white horse to slaughter evildoers until their blood runs through the streets like a river.

Furthermore, God feels angry because God hates sin.[41] Sadly, it is commonly said among Christians that "God hates the sin but loves the sinner." This comes not from divinely inspired Scripture but instead from the Hindu Gandhi who coined the phrase "Love the sinner but hate the sin" in his 1929 autobiography.

The Bible clearly says that God both loves and hates some sinners.[42] People commonly protest that God cannot hate anyone because he is love. But the Bible speaks of God's anger, wrath, and fury more than his love, grace, and mercy. Furthermore, it is precisely because God is love that he must hate evil and all who do evil; it is an assault on who and what he loves.

Additionally, God's anger at sin and hatred of sinners causes him to pour out his wrath on unrepentant sinners. This doctrine is not as popular among professing Christians in our day as it was in past times, but the fact remains that in the Old Testament alone nearly twenty words are used for God's wrath, which is spoken of roughly six hundred times. The wrath of God also appears roughly twenty-five times in the New Testament.[43] Not only does God the Father pour out wrath upon unrepentant sinners, but so does Jesus Christ.[44]

God's wrath is both active and passive. When people think of God's wrath, they generally think of God's active wrath, where people are swiftly punished for their sin with something like a lightning bolt from heaven. God can and does enact his active wrath upon occasion.[45] Still, he seems to also frequently work through his subtler passive wrath. Passive wrath occurs when God simply hands us over to our evil desires and allows us to do whatever we want.[46]

---

[40]Mark 3:5.
[41]Prov. 6:16–19; Zech. 8:17.
[42]Ps. 5:5; 11:4–5; Hos. 9:15; Rom. 9:13 cf. Mal. 1:2–3.
[43]John 3:36; Eph. 5:6; Col. 3:6; 1 Thess. 1:9–10.
[44]Rev. 6:16–17.
[45]Genesis 38; 1 Cor. 11:28–29.
[46]Rom. 1:18, 24, 26.

The truth is that everyone but the sinless Jesus merits the active wrath of God. None of us deserves love, grace, or mercy from God. Demons and sinful people who fail to repent will have God's wrath burning against them forever.[47] The place of God's unending active wrath is hell.

However, God's active wrath is diverted from some people because of the mercy of God. This is made possible because on the cross Jesus substituted himself in our place for our sins and took God's wrath for us. Two sections of Scripture in particular speak to this matter pointedly:

1) Since, therefore, we have now been justified by his blood, much more shall we be *saved by him [Jesus] from the wrath of God.*[48]
2) You turned to God from idols to serve the living and true God, and to wait for his Son from heaven, whom he raised from the dead, *Jesus who delivers us from the wrath to come.*[49]

Scripture also has a single word to designate how Jesus diverts the active wrath of our rightfully angry God from us so that we are loved and not hated. That word is *propitiation*, which summarizes more than six hundred related words and events that explain it. The American Heritage Dictionary defines *propitiation* as something that appeases or conciliates an offended power, especially a sacrificial offering to a god. *Propitiate* is the only English word that carries the idea of pacifying wrath by taking care of the penalty for the offense that caused the wrath.

Many Christians are not familiar with this word, though, because various Bible translations use different words in an effort to capture its meaning. For example, the New International and New Revised translations use "sacrifice of atonement," and the New Living Translation uses "sacrifice for sin" in such places as Romans 3:23–25, Hebrews 2:17, 1 John 2:2, and 1 John 4:10 where the original word was "propitiate."

Worse still are the Revised Standard Version and The New English Bible, which use "expiation" instead of "propitiation." These latter two

---

[47]Deut. 32:21–22; John 3:36; Eph. 5:6; 2 Pet. 2:4; Rev. 14:9–11.
[48]Rom. 5:9.
[49]1 Thess. 1:9–10.

translations change the entire meaning of the verse, because propitiation deals with the penalty for sin whereas expiation deals with the cleansing from sin. The English Standard Version has thankfully retained the original word "propitiation" from the Greek text of the New Testament. There are four primary occurrences of the word *propitiation* in the New Testament:

1) For all have sinned and fall short of the glory of God, and are justified by his grace as a gift, through the redemption that is in Christ Jesus, whom God put forward as a propitiation by his blood, to be received by faith. This was to show God's righteousness.[50]
2) Therefore he [Jesus] had to be made like his brothers in every respect, so that he might become a merciful and faithful high priest in the service of God, to make propitiation for the sins of the people.[51]
3) He is the propitiation for our sins, and not for ours only but also for the sins of the whole world.[52]
4) In this is love, not that we have loved God but that he loved us and sent his Son to be the propitiation for our sins.[53]

At the cross, justice and mercy kiss; Jesus substituted himself for sinners and suffered and died in their place to forgive them, love them, and embrace them, not in spite of their sins, but because their sins were propitiated and diverted from them to Jesus. Jesus did this not by demanding our blood but rather by giving his own.

Justification

God deserves justice. Because of our sinful condition and ensuing sinful actions, though, our impending day in God's proverbial courtroom seems utterly hopeless for anything other than a guilty verdict and a sentence to eternity in the torments of hell. In light of our obvious guilt, if God were to declare us anything but guilty, he would cease to be a just and good God. God himself says that he "will not acquit the wicked."[54]

---

[50]Rom. 3:23–25.
[51]Heb. 2:17.
[52]1 John 2:2.
[53]1 John 4:10.
[54]Ex. 23:7.

Guilty sinners would likely prefer that God simply overlook their offenses against him. To do so, however, would by definition render God unjust, unholy, and unrighteous, which is impossible because he is always just, holy, and righteous.

Clearly, God does not owe us anything. If we were to spend forever in the torments of hell as guilty and condemned sinners, we would have simply gotten what we deserved. Pondering this same point, Job asks, "But how can a man be in the right before God?"[55]

Thankfully, God is merciful, gracious, slow to anger, loving, faithful, and willing to forgive.[56] Thus, the dilemma is this: how could God justify us and remain just?

The answer is the doctrine of justification: guilty sinners can be declared righteous before God by grace alone through faith alone because of the person and work of Jesus Christ alone. Justification is mentioned more than two hundred times in various ways throughout the New Testament alone.

The penalty of sin is death. God warned Adam in the garden that "in the day that you eat of it you shall surely die."[57] Paul confirms this: "they know God's decree that those who practice such things deserve to die."[58] The amazing truth is that God himself, the second person of the Trinity, paid our debt of death in our place.

Additionally, not only did Jesus take all our sins (past, present, and future) on the cross, but he also gave to us his perfect righteousness as a faultless and sinless person.[59] This is why Paul says that Jesus alone is our righteousness.[60] Therefore, justification through the work of Jesus Christ in our place for our sins on the cross is only possible by grace from Jesus Christ alone, through faith in Jesus Christ alone, because of Jesus Christ alone.

There is absolutely nothing we can do to contribute to our justification. When Jesus said, "It is finished" on the cross, he was declaring that

---

[55]Job 9:2.
[56]Ex. 34:6–7.
[57]Gen. 2:17.
[58]Rom. 1:32.
[59]2 Cor. 5:21.
[60]1 Cor. 1:30.

all that needed to be done for our justification was completed in him. For this reason, Titus 3:7 speaks of "being justified by his *grace*." Furthermore, Romans 5:16–17 says:

> The *free gift* is not like the result of that one man's [Adam's] sin. For the judgment following one trespass brought condemnation, but the *free gift* following many trespasses brought justification. For if, because of one man's trespass, death reigned through that one man, much more will those who receive the abundance of *grace* and the *free gift* of righteousness reign in life through the one man Jesus Christ.

To be justified means to trust only in the person and work of Jesus and no one and nothing else as the object of our faith, righteousness, and justification before God.[61]

Gift Righteousness

Because we were created for righteousness, people continue to yearn for righteousness. However, we sinfully pursue it through self-righteousness.[62] Self-righteousness exists in both irreligious and religious forms.

Irreligious self-righteousness includes the attempts to justify one's decency through everything from social causes to political involvement and being a good steward of the planet. Religious self-righteousness is the pursuit of personal righteousness through our own attempts to live by God's laws in addition to our own rules.

Regarding such vain attempts at self-righteousness, Jesus said, "Unless your righteousness exceeds that of the scribes and Pharisees, you will never enter the kingdom of heaven."[63] No one has been more religiously devoted than the Pharisees who, for example, actually tithed out of their spice rack in an effort to be certain that they gave God a tenth of literally all they had. Still, our attempts at self-righteousness are simply repugnant to God.[64]

---

[61] Acts 13:38; Rom. 4:3–5; 5:1.
[62] Rom. 10:3.
[63] Matt. 5:20.
[64] Isa. 64:6.

On the cross what Martin Luther liked to call the "great exchange" occurred. Jesus took our sin and gave us his righteousness. Second Corinthians 5:21 says, "For our sake he [God] made him [Jesus] to be sin who knew no sin, so that in him we might become the righteousness of God." Unlike the self-righteousness of religion, gift righteousness is passive; it is not something we do, but rather something that Jesus does and we receive as a gift by personal faith in him alone.

The gifted righteousness of Jesus is imparted to us at the time of faith, simultaneous with our justification. Not only does God give us family status, but he also gives us new power and a new heart through the indwelling Holy Spirit. This is what theologians call *regeneration*. Therefore, we not only have a new status by virtue of being justified, but we also have a new heart from which new desires for holiness flow and a new power through God the Holy Spirit to live like, for, and with Jesus.

Finally, in saying that righteousness comes from Jesus alone and by virtue of none of our good works, we are not advocating a kind of lawless Christianity where we are permitted to live in unrepentant and ongoing sin, unconcerned about whether we are living righteously. Rather, we are saying that only by understanding the righteousness of Jesus Christ in us can we live holy lives out of his righteousness as our new status as Christians.

Ransom

God made us to love, honor, and obey him in thought, word, and deed. Every time we fail to do that perfectly, we accrue a debt to God. Every person has sinned against God, and hell is the eternal prison for spiritual debtors who have stolen from God by living sinful lives.

First, we need a mediator to stand between us and God to establish our total debt and come up with a resolution that God the Father, to whom we are indebted, will find acceptable. The Bible repeatedly speaks of Jesus as our only mediator: "For there is one God, and there is one mediator between God and men, the man Christ Jesus."[65] Our spiritual debt is to

---

[65] 1 Tim. 2:5; see also Heb. 9:15; 12:24.

God, and there is only one possible mediator between God and us to work out the dangerous mess we are in.

Second, we need a redeemer willing to intercede for us and pay our debt to God the Father. A redeemer is a person who pays the debt of someone else. Paul speaks of "our great God and Savior Jesus Christ, who gave himself for us to redeem us from all lawlessness and to purify for himself a people for his own possession who are zealous for good works."[66] He also says that "Christ redeemed us from the curse of the law by becoming a curse for us—for it is written, 'Cursed is everyone who is hanged on a tree [Deut. 21:23].'"[67] Because our sins are against God, only God can forgive our debt of sin. Jesus is God who paid our debt on the cross in order to forgive our sin.[68]

Third, we need a ransom, which is a repayment sufficient enough to erase our debt to God the Father. The problem, though, is that our sins are against a completely holy and perfect God and therefore require a perfect payment. Since all human beings are sinful, we cannot be a ransom for another. There is no way that any other sinful human can ever repay God for our spiritual debt. Psalm 49:7–8 says it this way: "Truly no man can ransom another, or give to God the price of his life, for the ransom of their life is costly and can never suffice." Referring to himself in Mark 10:45, Jesus said, "For even the Son of Man came not to be served but to serve, and to give his life as a ransom for many." Paul also speaks of "the man Christ Jesus, who gave himself as a ransom."[69]

HOW DOES GOD REDEEM US THROUGH THE CROSS?

Redemption

To use a very biblical word, sinners are slaves. Second Peter 2:19b explains it this way: "For whatever overcomes a person, to that he is enslaved." Like

---

[66]Titus 2:13–14.
[67]Gal. 3:13.
[68]Matt. 26:63–65; Mark 2:5; John 6:41–58; 8:46, 58–59; 10:30–33; 11:25; 14:6, 8–9; 16:28.
[69]1 Tim. 2:5–6.

a prisoner locked in a cell who cannot escape, so sinners too are locked in a prison of sin and cannot get free. This includes self-selected slavery, such as addictions and sin patterns that are habitual.

In the book of Exodus, God's people were enslaved to a king named Pharaoh who ruled over the most powerful nation on the earth, Egypt. He was worshiped as a god and brutally mistreated the people whom he enslaved. God raised up a man named Moses to speak on his behalf to the pharaoh, demanding that the slaves be set free in order to live new lives in worship to the real God. God graciously, but authoritatively, called him to righteousness. Pharaoh became hardhearted under God's provocation, just as God said he would, and he refused to release the people from their brutal slavery. As a result, God sent a succession of plagues as judgments and warnings upon the pharaoh, kindly giving him many opportunities to repent and do what God demanded.

The pharaoh repeatedly refused to repent of his ways and release the people, so God sent a terrible series of judgments upon the entire nation. The wrath of God was eventually poured out on the firstborn son of every household, each killed in one night. As we have noted, the only households spared from death to their firstborn son were those families who, in faith, took a young, healthy lamb without blemish or defect and slaughtered it as a substitute and then took its blood and covered the doorposts around the entry to their home with it. As a result, the wrath of God passed over them and was diverted because of the lamb.

Like the people in Moses' day, we sinners are completely unable to free ourselves from slavery. As slaves we need to be redeemed from our slavery. *Redemption* is synonymous with being liberated, freed, or rescued from bondage and slavery to a person or thing. The word and its derivatives (e.g., *redeemer, redeem*) appear roughly 150 times in the English Bible, with only roughly twenty occurrences in the New Testament.

Sadly, it has been commonly taught by some Christian theologians since the early days of the church (e.g., Origen) that the concept of redemption was adopted from the pagan slave market where a price was paid to free a slave. This led to wild speculation that Jesus died to pay off Satan, which is preposterous because Jesus owes Satan nothing.

The prototype for redemption is not the pagan slave market but rather the exodus. There, God liberated his people but in no way paid off the satanic pharaoh. God simply crushed him. Exodus 6:6 is one of many Bible verses that present the exodus as the prototype of redemption: "Say therefore to the people of Israel, 'I am the LORD, and I will bring you out from under the burdens of the Egyptians, and I will deliver you from slavery to them, and I will redeem you with an outstretched arm and with great acts of judgment.'"[70]

The theme of God the Redeemer echoes throughout the Old Testament.[71] Even before Jesus' birth it was prophesied that he was God coming into human history to redeem sinners from slavery.[72] At the birth of Jesus, it was prophesied that he is God the Redeemer.[73] Paul often spoke of Jesus as our redeemer: "Jesus Christ . . . gave himself for us to redeem us" and "Redemption . . . is in Christ Jesus."[74] Many more examples of Jesus' being offered as the redeemer of slaves are scattered throughout the New Testament.[75]

When Jesus was crucified and his blood was shed, he suffered and died in our place for our sins so that we could be redeemed.[76] Jesus has redeemed us from and to many things. Jesus has redeemed us from the curse of the law,[77] Satan and demons,[78] our sinful flesh,[79] and sin.[80] Furthermore, Jesus has redeemed us to eternal life with God,[81] the return of Jesus,[82] and a glorified resurrection body.[83]

---

[70]See also Ex. 15:1–18; Deut. 7:8; 15:15; 2 Sam. 7:23; 1 Chron. 17:21; Isa. 51:10; Mic. 6:4.
[71]Ps. 78:35; Isa. 44:24; 47:4; 48:17; 63:16; Jer. 50:34; Hos. 7:13; 13:14.
[72]Luke 1:68; 2:38.
[73]Ibid.
[74]Rom. 3:24; Titus 2:13–14; see also 1 Cor. 1:30; Gal. 3:13–14; 4:4–5; Eph. 1:7.
[75]1 Cor. 1:30; Gal. 3:13–14; 4:4–5; Eph. 1:7.
[76]1 Pet. 1:18–19.
[77]Gal. 3:13.
[78]Col. 1:13–14.
[79]Rom. 6:6–12.
[80]Gal. 6:14–15.
[81]Ps. 49:15.
[82]Job 19:25.
[83]Rom. 8:23.

FOR WHOM DID JESUS CHRIST DIE?

Unlimited Limited Atonement

The question, for whom did Jesus Christ die? has generated some of the most heated and varied answers in church history. To help you understand the different answers to this question, we offer Chart 8.1.

CHART 8.1

	Heresy of "Christian" Universalism	Heresy of Contemporary Pelagianism	Unlimited Atonement	Limited Atonement	Unlimited Limited Atonement
View of Sin	We are born sinful but guilty for our sins, not Adam's.	We are born sinless like Adam but follow his bad example.	We are born sinful but guilty for our sins, not Adam's.	We are born sinners guilty in Adam.	We are born sinners guilty in Adam.
Who Jesus Died For	Jesus took all the sin and pain of the world onto himself.	Jesus lived and died only as an example for sinners.	Jesus died to provide payment for the sin of all people.	Jesus died to achieve full atonement for the elect.	Jesus died to provide payment for all, but only in a saving way for the elect.
How Atonement Is Applied	God's powerful love in Jesus will overcome all sin.	Anyone can follow the example of Jesus by living a good life.	God will apply the payment to those who believe in Christ.	God designed the atonement precisely for the elect.	While God desires the salvation of all, he applies the payment to the elect, those whom he chose for salvation.
Heaven & Hell	Everyone will be saved and will go to heaven. There is no eternal hell.	Those who live a Christlike life will be saved and go to heaven. Those who reject goodness will go to hell.	All who accept the gift go to heaven. Everyone else gets to follow their free will and choose to go to hell.	God does not need to save anyone from hell, but chooses to save some.	God does not need to save anyone from hell, but chooses to save some.

The first two answers (universalism and Pelagianism) are unbiblical and therefore unacceptable. Universalism erroneously contradicts the clear teachings of Scripture on human sinfulness and hell.[84] Pelagius denied human sinfulness and taught that people begin their life morally good (like Adam), and through the decision of their own will can live a holy life that would obligate God to take them to heaven upon death. Pelagius was condemned as a heretic at the Council of Carthage in AD 418.

We are left with three options for Christians regarding the question of who Jesus died for. All three positions are within the bounds of evangelical orthodoxy.

First, some Christians believe that Jesus died for the sins of all people. This position is commonly referred to as Arminianism (after James Arminius), Wesleyanism (after John Wesley), or unlimited atonement. Arminians appeal to those Scriptures that speak of Jesus dying for all people,[85] the whole world,[86] everyone,[87] and not wanting anyone to perish.[88] Arminians then teach that to be saved, one must make the decision to accept Jesus' atoning death and become a follower of Jesus. Furthermore, it is said that anyone can make that choice either by inherent free will (Arminians) or by God's universal enabling, so-called prevenient, or first, grace (Wesleyans). Subsequently, election is understood as God choosing those he foreknew would choose him, and since people choose to be saved they can also lose their salvation.

Second, some Christians believe that Jesus died only for the sins of the elect. Election means that before the foundation of the world, God chose certain individuals to be recipients of eternal life solely on the basis of his gracious purpose apart from any human merit or action. He calls them effectually, doing whatever is necessary to bring them to repentance and faith.[89] This position is commonly referred to as five-point Calvinism (after John Calvin), Reformed theology, or limited atonement, which is

---

[84]E.g., Dan. 12:2; Matt. 5:29–30; 10:28; 18:9; 23:23; 25:46.
[85]2 Cor. 5:14–15; 1 Tim. 2:1–6; 4:10; Titus 2:11.
[86]John 1:29; 3:16–17; 1 John 2:2; 4:14; Rev. 5:9.
[87]Isa. 53:6; Heb. 2:9.
[88]1 Tim. 2:4; 2 Pet. 3:9.
[89]Isa. 55:11; John 6:44; Rom. 8:30; 11:29; 1 Cor. 1:23–29; 2 Tim. 1:9.

also sometimes called particular redemption. These Calvinists commonly appeal to those Scriptures that speak of Jesus' dying only for some people but not all people,[90] his sheep,[91] his church,[92] the elect,[93] his people,[94] his friends,[95] and all Christians.[96] They disagree with unlimited atonement, pointing out that if Jesus died for everyone, then everyone would be saved, which is the heresy of universalism. They also teach that people are so sinful that they cannot choose God, and so God regenerates people before their conversion and ensures they will be preserved until the end because salvation cannot be lost.

One vital point of debate is the intent of Jesus when he died on the cross. Did Jesus intend to provide payment for all sins of all people, opening the doorway to salvation for all? That would be unlimited atonement, or what the Wesleyans and the Arminians believe. Do we accept it at face value when Paul said that Christ Jesus "gave himself as a ransom for all" in 1 Timothy 2:6? Or did Jesus die to complete the purchase of our pardon on the cross? That is limited atonement, or what five-point Calvinists believe. Do we accept it at face value when Jesus said, "It is finished" in John 19:30?

At first glance, unlimited and limited atonement appear to be in opposition. But that dilemma is resolved by noting two things. First, the two categories are not mutually exclusive; since Jesus died for the sins of everyone, this means that he also died for the sins of the elect. Second, Jesus' death for all people does not accomplish the same thing as his death for the elect. This point is complicated, but is in fact taught in Scripture. For example, 1 Timothy 4:10 makes a distinction between Jesus' dying as the savior of all people in a general way and the Christian elect in a particular way, saying, "For to this end we toil and strive, because we have our hope set on the living God, who is the Savior of all people, especially

---

[90]Matt. 1:21; 20:28; 26:28; Rom. 5:12–19.
[91]John 10:11, 15, 26–27.
[92]Acts 20:28; Eph. 5:25.
[93]Rom. 8:32–35.
[94]Matt. 1:21.
[95]John 15:3.
[96]2 Cor. 5:15; Titus 2:14.

of those who believe." Additionally, 2 Peter 2:1 speaks of people for whom Jesus died as not being saved from heresy and damnation by Jesus: "False prophets also arose among the people, just as there will be false teachers among you, who will secretly bring in destructive heresies, even denying the Master who bought them, bringing upon themselves swift destruction."

Simply, by dying for everyone, Jesus purchased everyone as his possession, and he then applies his forgiveness to the elect—those in Christ—by grace, and applies his wrath to the non-elect—those who reject Christ. Objectively, Jesus' death was sufficient to save anyone, and, subjectively, only efficient to save those who repent of their sin and trust in him. This position is called unlimited limited atonement, or modified Calvinism, and arguably is the position that John Calvin himself held as a very able Bible teacher.[97]

Christ died for the purpose of securing the sure and certain salvation of his own, his elect. This is the intentionality the five-point Calvinists rightly stress. Christ died for all people. This is the universality the Arminians rightly stress. If the five-point Calvinist is right and no payment has been made for the non-elect, then how can God genuinely love the world and desire the salvation of all people? There is a genuine open door for salvation for anyone who believes in Jesus, and this makes the rejection of Jesus completely inexcusable. Jesus' death reconciles "all things" to God.[98] God will overcome all rebellion through Jesus' blood. In this sense, all those in hell will stand reconciled to God but not in a saving way, as the universalists falsely teach. In hell unrepentant and unforgiven sinners are no longer rebels, and their sinful disregard for God has been crushed and ended.[99]

HOW DOES GOD TRIUMPH THROUGH THE CROSS?

Christus Victor

Scripture clearly says that there is a very real war between Jesus and the angels and Satan and the demons; sinners have been taken as captives in

---

[97]E.g., see his commentaries on Romans 5, Galatians 5, Colossians 1, and Hebrews.
[98]Col. 1:18–20.
[99]On this point, a friend named Bruce Ware has been very helpful to both Gerry and me as we studied this doctrine together.

war.[100] Jesus himself confirmed this fact at the beginning of his earthly ministry when he said he had come to set captives free.[101] Jesus said this because there is no way that Satan would release us from his captivity and no way that we could liberate ourselves. Therefore, Jesus came as our triumphant warrior and liberator.

The first promise of Jesus as our victor over Satan came to our first parents. In Genesis 3:15, God preached the first good news (or gospel) of Jesus to our sinful first mother, Eve. God promised that Jesus would be born of a woman and would grow to be a man who would battle with Satan and stomp his head, defeat him, and liberate people from their captivity to Satan, sin, death, and hell.

Leading up to the cross, Satan entered one of Jesus' own disciples, Judas Iscariot, and conspired with him to betray Jesus and hand him over to be crucified. Through the cross, Satan and his demons thought that they had finally defeated Jesus. However, crucifying Jesus was the biggest mistake the Devil ever made. Had he understood what was happening, he would never have killed Jesus.[102]

An essential portion of Scripture on the victory of Jesus over Satan, sin, and death is Colossians 2:13–15:

> You, who were dead in your trespasses and the uncircumcision of your flesh, God made alive together with him, having forgiven us all our trespasses, by canceling the record of debt that stood against us with its legal demands. This he set aside, nailing it to the cross. He disarmed the rulers and authorities and put them to open shame, by triumphing over them in him.

Thus, the authority of the Devil and his demons has already ended. Matthew 28:18 makes it very clear that Jesus has *all* authority now, which means that Satan has no authority over Christians. As a result, we can now live in accordance with Colossians 1:10–14 and "walk in a manner worthy

---

[100]Col. 1:13; 2 Tim. 2:25–26.
[101]Luke 4:18.
[102]1 Cor. 2:6–9.

of the Lord, fully pleasing to him, bearing fruit in every good work and increasing in the knowledge of God. . . . He has delivered us from the domain of darkness and transferred us to the kingdom of his beloved Son, in whom we have redemption, the forgiveness of sins." The Bible uses the word *grace* to explain the victory Jesus achieved for us on the cross because there is no logical reason that God would love us and die in our place to liberate us from captivity to Satan, sin, and death, other than his wonderful nature.

Expiation

The typical gospel presentation is that we are all sinners and that if we confess our sins to Jesus he will forgive our sins through his sinless life, substitutionary death, and bodily resurrection. This is clearly true according to Scripture. However, this gospel only addresses the sins that you have committed (as a sinner) and neglects to deal with the sins that have been committed against you (as a victim).

Throughout the Bible, some dozen words are used frequently to speak of sin in terms of staining our soul, defiling us, and causing us to be filthy or unclean.[103] The effect of sin, particularly sins committed against us, is that we feel dirty. The Bible mentions a number of causes for our defilement, such as any sin at all, as well as involvement with false religions and/or the occult,[104] violence,[105] and sexual sin.[106]

Thus, souls are stained and defiled by the filth of sins that people commit and that are committed against them. In Scripture, places,[107] objects (such as the marriage bed),[108] and people are defiled by sin. Subsequently, the Old Testament and the Gospels are filled with people who were ritually unclean and not to be touched or associated with. The commandments for ceremonial washings and such foreshadow the cleansing power of the death of Jesus.

---

[103]E.g., Ps. 106:39; Prov. 30:11–12; Mark 7:20.
[104]Lev. 19:31; Ezek. 14:11.
[105]E.g., Lam. 4:14.
[106]Gen. 34:5; Lev. 21:14; Num. 5:27; 1 Chron. 5:1.
[107]Lev. 18:24–30; Num. 35:34.
[108]Heb. 13:4.

The predictable result of defilement is shame, including the fear of being found out and known, and our deep, dark secret getting revealed. This pattern was firmly established with our first parents, who covered themselves in shame and hid from God and one another after they sinned. Shame exists where there is sin, and so feeling ashamed, particularly when we sin, is natural and healthy. Therefore, shame is not bad, but unless the underlying sin that causes the shame is properly dealt with through the gospel, then the shame will remain, with devastating implications.

Jesus forgave our sins at the cross and cleanses us from all sins that we have committed and that have been committed against us. Through the cross, Jesus Christ has taken our sin away forever, as was foreshadowed by the scapegoat on the Day of Atonement. This goat was sent away to run free into the wilderness, symbolically taking the people's sins with it. Theologically, we call this the doctrine of *expiation*, whereby our sin is expiated or taken away so that we are made clean through Jesus, who is our scapegoat.

The Bible uses words such as *atonement*, *cleansing*, and *purifying fountain* that washes away our defilement and shame to explain that our identity must be marked only by what Jesus Christ has done for us and no longer by what has been done by or to us. The Bible clearly teaches that dirty sinners can be cleansed.

> For on this day shall atonement be made for you to cleanse you. You shall be clean before the LORD from all your sins.[109]
>
> I will cleanse them from all the guilt of their sin against me, and I will forgive all the guilt of their sin and rebellion against me.[110]
>
> On that day there shall be a fountain opened . . . to cleanse them from sin and uncleanness.[111]

Jesus not only went to the cross to die for our sin, but also to scorn our shame. As Hebrews 12:1–3 says, "Let us run with endurance the race that is

---

[109]Lev. 16:30.
[110]Jer. 33:8.
[111]Zech. 13:1.

set before us, looking to Jesus, the founder and perfecter of our faith, who for the joy that was set before him endured the cross, despising the *shame*, and is seated at the right hand of the throne of God."

As a result, we can walk in the light with others who love us in authentic community. On this point, 1 John 1:7–9 says:

If we walk in the light, as he is in the light, we have fellowship with one another, and the blood of Jesus his Son cleanses us from all sin. If we say we have no sin, we deceive ourselves, and the truth is not in us. If we confess our sins, he is faithful and just to forgive us our sins and to cleanse us from all unrighteousness.

Jesus does "cleanse us from all unrighteousness." This means that because of Jesus' cross we can be cleansed and made pure. The beauty of this truth of the expiating or cleansing work of Jesus is poetically shown in symbolic acts throughout Scripture, including ceremonial washings,[112] baptism,[113] and the wearing of white in eternity as a continual reminder of the expiating work of Jesus.[114]

HOW DOES GOD INSPIRE US THROUGH THE CROSS?

Christus Exemplar

Jesus died for our sins, thereby enabling us to experience new life. Jesus lived as our example showing us what it means to live a truly holy human life.

Throughout Jesus' life he repeatedly stated that the purpose of his life on earth was to glorify God the Father, or to make the Father's character visible. Jesus' glorifying God the Father included dying on the cross.[115] Practically, this means that there is joy not only in our comfort and success, but also in our suffering and hardship, just as there was for Jesus.[116]

---

[112]Ex. 19:10.
[113]Acts 22:16.
[114]Rev. 19:7–8.
[115]John 12:23, 27–28; 13:30–32; 17:1.
[116]Heb. 12:1–6.

At the cross of Jesus, we learn that to be like Jesus means that we pick up our cross and follow him as he commanded.[117] Practically, this means that we glorify God by allowing hardship, pain, and loss to make us more and more like Jesus and give us a more credible witness for Jesus. As Christians we should neither run to suffering as the early Christian ascetics did, nor run from it as some modern Christians do. Instead, we receive suffering when it comes as an opportunity for God to do something good in us and through us. We rejoice not in the pain but rather in what it can accomplish for the gospel so that something as costly as suffering is not wasted but used for God's glory, our joy, and others' good.

In order to suffer well—that is, in a way that is purposeful for the progress of the gospel both in and through us—we must continually remember Jesus' cross. Peter says:

> What credit is it if, when you sin and are beaten for it, you endure? But if when you do good and suffer for it you endure, this is a gracious thing in the sight of God. For to this you have been called, because Christ also suffered for you, leaving you an example, so that you might follow in his steps. He committed no sin, neither was deceit found in his mouth. When he was reviled, he did not revile in return; when he suffered, he did not threaten, but continued entrusting himself to him who judges justly. He himself bore our sins in his body on the tree, that we might die to sin and live to righteousness. By his wounds you have been healed.[118]

WHAT DOES THE DOCTRINE OF THE CROSS REVEAL ABOUT GOD'S LOVE?

On the cross, Jesus revealed to us the love of God. The following verses state how the love of God is most clearly revealed at the cross of Jesus:

> For God so loved the world, that he gave his only Son, that whoever believes in him should not perish but have eternal life.[119]

---

[117]Matt. 16:24.
[118]1 Pet. 2:20–24.
[119]John 3:16.

Greater love has no one than this, that someone lays down his life for his friends.[120]

But God shows his love for us in that while we were still sinners, Christ died for us.[121]

In this the love of God was made manifest among us, that God sent his only Son into the world, so that we might live through him. In this is love, not that we have loved God but that he loved us and sent his Son to be the propitiation for our sins.[122]

At the cross we see that the love of God is not merely sentimental but also efficacious. When people speak of love, they usually mean an emotional love that feels affectionate but may not do anything to help the beloved. Thankfully, God does not merely feel loving toward us; his love actually compels him to act on our behalf so that we can be changed by his love.

God has lovingly worked out a way for our friendship with him to be reconciled. Through the cross, Jesus took away our sin so that we could be reconciled to God.[123] Thankfully, God not only graciously takes away our sin, but mercifully extends himself to us, knowing that we desperately need him.[124]

The cross is something done by you. You murdered God incarnate.

The cross is something done for you. God loves you and died to forgive you.

---

[120]John 15:13.
[121]Rom. 5:8.
[122]1 John 4:9–10.
[123]Isa. 59:2; Hos. 5:6.
[124]1 Tim. 1:15–16; Titus 3:4–5.

CHAPTER 9

RESURRECTION: GOD SAVES

Jesus said . . . "I am the resurrection and the life.
Whoever believes in me, though he die,
yet shall he live, and everyone who lives and believes
in me shall never die."

JOHN 11:25–26

If Jesus is dead, then Christianity is dead. If Jesus is alive, then Christianity is alive. Paul himself declared as much in 1 Corinthians 15:17: "If Christ has not been raised, your faith is futile and you are still in your sins."

Apart from the resurrection of Jesus Christ, there is no savior, no salvation, no forgiveness of sin, and no hope of resurrected eternal life. Apart from the resurrection, Jesus is reduced to yet another good but dead man and therefore is of no considerable help to us in this life or at its end. Plainly stated, without the resurrection of Jesus, the few billion people today who worship Jesus as God are gullible; their hope for a resurrection life after this life is the hope of silly fools who trust in a dead man to give them life. Subsequently, the doctrine of Jesus' resurrection is, without question, profoundly significant and worthy of the most careful consideration and examination.

WHAT IS RESURRECTION?

Defining what resurrection does and does not mean is incredibly important. Resurrection does not mean revivification. *Revivification* occurs when someone who dies comes back to life only to die again; revivification happens throughout Scripture.[1] Unlike revivification, *resurrection* teaches that someone dies and returns to physical life forever, or what the Bible calls eternal life,[2] patterned after Jesus' death and resurrection.[3]

Resurrection does not mean there is a second chance for salvation after death, as both reincarnation and purgatory wrongly purport. *Reincarnation* is the belief that the human soul individually migrates from one body to another through a succession of lives in pursuit of complete purification where the soul is finally joined to the ultimate reality of the divine. *Purgatory* wrongly teaches that following death there is an extended period of potential maturation and purification that allows someone to then enjoy heaven as an unbeliever. Hebrews 9:27 refutes both errors: "It is appointed for man to die once, and after that comes judgment."

Resurrection does not mean that everyone, believers and unbelievers alike, avoid hellish punishment in the end. Universalism wrongly teaches that everyone is eventually saved and goes to heaven. Annihilationism wrongly teaches that at some point following death unbelievers simply cease to exist rather than going to an eternal hell. Instead, Daniel 12:2 declares that both believers and unbelievers will rise, and some will go to everlasting heaven and others to everlasting hell, which refutes both errors: "Many of those who sleep in the dust of the earth shall awake, some to everlasting life, and some to shame and everlasting contempt."

Resurrection does not mean what is called "soul sleep," where both the body and the spirit lie at rest until the resurrection, as is taught by some Seventh-Day Adventists. When the New Testament speaks of

---

[1] E.g., 2 Kings 4:18–37; Matt. 9:18–26; 27:52–53; Mark 5:22–43; Luke 8:40–56; John 11:1–44; Acts 9:36–42; 20:9–12.
[2] E.g., John 5:24.
[3] 1 Corinthians 15.

believers as "asleep," it does so as a metaphor to distinguish the death of believers from the death of unbelievers. The *Dictionary of Biblical Imagery* says:

> The Bible also uses sleep as a metaphor for the death of the righteous. "Christ has indeed been raised from the dead, the firstfruits of those who have fallen asleep" (1 Cor 15:20). In Christ, death is nothing more than a nap from which the righteous will awaken to endless day.[4]

This is why Paul speaks of his death as gain, because it means his soul goes to be with Jesus: "For to me to live is Christ, and to die is gain."[5]

Neither does resurrection simply mean life after death. This is because life after death does not initially include the physical body; rather, the body lies in the ground while the spiritual soul goes to be with God. Paul speaks of believers being "away from the body and at home with the Lord."[6]

The Bible teaches that we are both a material body and an immaterial soul. Upon death these two parts are separated. Our body goes into the ground, and as believers our soul goes to be with God. For unbelievers, their soul goes to a place called by such names in the Bible as a "prison"[7] and "Hades."[8] That place is a place of just suffering for unbelievers until they stand before Jesus and are sentenced to the conscious eternal torments of hell.[9]

Resurrection refers to the eventual reuniting of our body and soul. In his impressive seven-hundred-page tome *The Resurrection of the Son of God*, notable New Testament scholar N. T. Wright provides a most helpful definition of resurrection, which he repeats throughout the book as one of his main points. Wright proposes that in the first century, *resurrection* did

---

4"Sleep," in Leland Ryken, Jim Wilhoit, et al., *Dictionary of Biblical Imagery* (Downers Grove, IL: InterVarsity, 2000), 799.
5Phil. 1:21.
62 Cor. 5:8.
71 Pet. 3:19.
8Luke 16:19–31.
9Rev. 20:13–14.

not mean "life after death" in the sense of "the life that follows immediately after bodily death."[10] According to Wright:

> Here there is no difference between pagans, Jews and Christians. They all understood the Greek word *anastasis* and its cognates, and the other related terms we shall meet, to mean . . . new life after a period of being dead. Pagans denied this possibility; some Jews affirmed it as a long-term future hope; virtually all Christians claimed that it had happened to Jesus and would happen to them in the future.[11]

In other words, *resurrection* was a way of "speaking of a new life *after* 'life after death' in the popular sense, a fresh living embodiment *following* a period of death-as-a-state." [12]

According to Wright, the meaning of resurrection as "life after 'life after death'" cannot be overemphasized. This is due in large part to the fact that much modern writing continues to use "resurrection" as a synonym for "life after death." In contrast, belief in "resurrection" for the ancients meant belief in what Wright calls a "two-step story":[13]

> Resurrection itself would be preceded . . . by an interim period of death-as-a-state. Where we find a single-step story—death-as-event being followed at once by a final state, for instance of disembodied bliss—the texts are not talking about resurrection. Resurrection involves a definite *content* (some sort of re-embodiment) and a definite *narrative shape* (a two-step story, not a single-step one). This meaning is constant throughout the ancient world.[14]

Wright reiterates what resurrection is and what it is not:

> "Resurrection" denoted a new embodied life which would *follow* whatever "life after death" there might be. "Resurrection" was, by

---

[10]See N. T. Wright, *The Resurrection of the Son of God* (Minneapolis: Fortress Press, 2003), 30–31.
[11]Ibid., 31.
[12]Ibid.
[13]Ibid.
[14]Ibid.

definition, not the existence into which someone might (or might not) go immediately upon death; it was not a disembodied "heavenly" life; it was a further stage, out beyond all that. It was not a redescription or redefinition of death. It was death's reversal.[15]

WHAT WERE ANCIENT NON-CHRISTIAN VIEWS OF THE AFTERLIFE?

It is commonly purported by some that the entire idea of a bodily resurrection was in fact not a novel idea but one borrowed from other ancient philosophies and spiritualities. Wright has done a painstakingly exhaustive and revolutionary study of ancient beliefs regarding resurrection that is incredibly helpful. Most books on the resurrection of Jesus begin by studying the Gospel narratives and then work outwardly from this vantage point to an analysis of the appropriate pagan and Jewish sources found in antiquity. Wright takes the exact opposite approach. He begins with a study on resurrection (or, better, the lack thereof) in ancient paganism and then narrows the scope of his investigation tighter and tighter, concluding with a study of the resurrection as recorded by the writers of the canonical Gospels. Wright concludes, "In so far as the ancient non-Jewish world had a Bible, its Old Testament was Homer. And in so far as Homer has anything to say about resurrection, he is quite blunt: it doesn't happen."[16]

The idea of resurrection is denied in ancient paganism from Homer all the way to the Athenian dramatist Aeschylus, who wrote, "Once a man has died, and the dust has soaked up his blood, there is no resurrection."[17] Wright provides a helpful summary: "Christianity was born into a world where its central claim was known to be false. Many believed that the dead were non-existent; outside Judaism, nobody believed in resurrection."[18]

One of the most influential writers in antiquity was Plato. Wright summarizes Plato's views on the soul and body as follows:

---

[15]Ibid., 83.
[16]Ibid., 32.
[17]Aeschylus, *Eumenides* 647–48, quoted in Wright, *Resurrection*, 32.
[18]Wright, *Resurrection*, 35.

> The soul is the non-material aspect of a human being, and is the aspect that really matters. Bodily life is full of delusion and danger; the soul is to be cultivated in the present both for its own sake and because its future happiness will depend upon such cultivation. The soul, being immortal, existed before the body, and will continue to exist after the body is gone.[19]

This dualistic view promoted a tendency to see the body as a prison of the soul that made death something to be desired. According to Wright, "in Greek philosophy, care for and cure of the soul became a central preoccupation."[20] Furthermore, "neither in Plato nor in the major alternatives just mentioned [e.g., Aristotle] do we find any suggestion that resurrection, the return to bodily life of the dead person, was either desirable or possible."[21]

This view is also evident in the writings of Cicero:

> Cicero is quite clear, and completely in the mainstream of greco-roman thought: the body is a prison-house. A necessary one for the moment; but nobody in their right mind, having got rid of it, would want it or something like it back again. At no point in the spectrum of options about life after death did the ancient pagan world envisage that the denials of Homer, Aeschylus and the rest would be overthrown. Resurrection was not an option. Those who followed Plato or Cicero did not want a body again; those who followed Homer knew they would not get one.[22]

After surveying several other ancient pagan writers and philosophers, Wright concludes: "Nobody in the pagan world of Jesus' day and thereafter actually claimed that somebody had been truly dead and had then come to be truly, and bodily, alive once more." [23]

Death, in ancient paganism, was a one-way street. According to Wright:

---

[19]Ibid., 49.
[20]Ibid., 53.
[21]Ibid.
[22]Ibid., 60.
[23]Ibid., 76.

The road to the underworld ran only one way. Throughout the ancient world, from its 'bible' of Homer and Plato, through its practices (funerals, memorial feasts), its stories (plays, novels, legends), its symbols (graves, amulets, grave-goods) and its grand theories, we can trace a good deal of variety about the road to Hades, and about what one might find upon arrival. As with all one-way streets, there is bound to be someone who attempts to drive in the opposite direction. One hears of a Protesilaus, an Alcestis or a Nero *redivivus*, once or twice in a thousand years. But the road was well policed. Would-be traffic violators (Sisyphus, Eurydice and the like) were turned back or punished. And even they occurred in what everybody knew to be myth.[24]

Wright notes:

We cannot stress too strongly that from Homer onwards the language of 'resurrection' was not used to denote 'life after death' in general, or any of the phenomena supposed to occur within such a life. The great majority of the ancients believed in life after death; many of them developed . . . complex and fascinating beliefs about it and practices in relation to it; but, other than within Judaism and Christianity, they did not believe in resurrection.[25]

Furthermore, not even Judaism believed in the resurrection of an individual from death in the middle of history. Rather, their understanding was that their entire nation alone would rise from death together at the end of history. William Lane Craig's lengthy studies of the resurrection of Jesus Christ culminated in the publishing of two scholarly books on the issue.[26] Craig asserts:

Jewish belief always concerned a resurrection at the end of the world, not a resurrection in the middle of history. . . . The resurrection to glory

---

[24]Ibid., 81–82.

[25]Ibid., 82–83.

[26]Craig spent two years as a fellow of the Humboldt Foundation studying the resurrection of Jesus Christ at the University of Munich. See William Lane Craig, *The Historical Argument for the Resurrection of Jesus During the Deist Controversy* (Lewiston, ID: Edwin Mellen, 1985), and *Assessing the New Testament Evidence for the Historicity of the Resurrection of Jesus* (Lewiston, ID: Edwin Mellen, 1989).

and immortality did not occur until after God had terminated world history. This traditional Jewish conception was the prepossession of Jesus' own disciples (Mark 9:9–13; John 11:24). The notion of a genuine resurrection occurring prior to God's bringing about the world's end would have been foreign to them. . . . *Jewish belief always concerned a general resurrection of the people, not the resurrection of an isolated individual.*[27]

Finally, noted historian and professor Edwin Yamauchi has spoken to this matter with great clarity based upon his lifetime of scholarly research.[28] Yamauchi has said that there is no possibility that the idea of a resurrection was borrowed because there is no definitive evidence for the teaching of a deity resurrection in any of the mystery religions prior to the second century.[29] In fact, it seems that other religions and spiritualities stole the idea of a resurrection from Christians! For example, the resurrection of Adonis is not spoken of until the second to fourth centuries.[30] Attis, the consort of Cybele, is not referred to as a resurrected god until after AD 150.[31]

Some have postulated that the *taurobolium* ritual of Attis and Mithra, the Persian god, is the source of the biblical doctrine of the resurrection. In this ritual, the initiate was put in a pit, and a bull was slaughtered on a grating over him, drenching him with blood. However, the earliest this ritual is mentioned is AD 160, and the belief that it led to rebirth is not mentioned until the fourth century. In fact, Princeton scholar Bruce Metzger has argued that the *taurobolium* was said to have the power to confer eternal life only after it encountered Christianity.[32]

The myths of pagans are admittedly fictitious events centered on the

[27]William Lane Craig, "Did Jesus Rise from the Dead?" in *Jesus Under Fire: Modern Scholarship Reinvents the Historical Jesus*, ed. Michael J. Wilkins and J. P. Moreland (Grand Rapids, MI: Zondervan, 1996), 160, emphases in original.

[28]Yamauchi has immersed himself in no less than twenty-two languages and is an expert in ancient history, including Old Testament history and biblical archaeology, with an emphasis on the interrelationship between ancient near Eastern cultures and the Bible. He is widely regarded as an expert in ancient history, early church history, and Gnosticism. He has published over eighty articles in more than three dozen scholarly journals and has been awarded eight fellowships. His writing includes contributing chapters to multiple books as well as books on Greece, Babylon, Persia, and ancient Africa.

[29]Edwin Yamauchi, "Easter: Myth, Hallucination, or History?" *Christianity Today*, March 15, 1974 and March 29, 1974, 4–7, 12–16.

[30]Ibid.

[31]Ibid.

[32]See Lee Strobel, *The Case for the Real Jesus* (Grand Rapids, MI: Zondervan, 2007), 174–75; and Bruce

annual death and rebirth of vegetation and harvest cycles. Conversely, the resurrection of Jesus Christ is put forth as a historical fact in a place, at a time, with eyewitnesses and numerable lines of compelling evidence. Furthermore, not only is the theory that Christianity borrowed the concept of resurrection untrue, but it also completely ignores the historical facts of the empty tomb and post-resurrection appearances of Jesus Christ.

WHAT IS THE BIBLICAL EVIDENCE FOR JESUS' RESURRECTION?

The biblical evidence for Jesus' resurrection is compelling and can be briefly summarized in ten points. Each of these points is consistent, and together they reveal that the Bible is emphatically and repeatedly clear on the fact of Jesus' resurrection.

1) Jesus' resurrection was prophesied in advance. Roughly seven hundred years before the birth of Jesus, the prophet Isaiah promised that Jesus would be born into humble circumstances to live a simple life, die a brutal death, and then rise to take away our sin.[33]

2) Jesus predicted his resurrection. On numerous occasions Jesus plainly promised that he would die and rise three days later.[34]

3) Jesus died. Before Jesus died, he underwent a sleepless night of trials and beatings that left him exhausted. He was then scourged—a punishment so horrendous that many men died from it before even making it to their crucifixion. Jesus was crucified, and a professional executioner declared him dead. To ensure Jesus was dead, a spear was thrust through his side and a mixture of blood and water poured out of his side because the spear burst his heart sac.[35] Jesus' dead body was wrapped in upwards of one hundred pounds of linens and spices, which, even if he was able to somehow survive the beatings, floggings, crucifixion, and a pierced heart, would have killed him by asphyxiation. Even if through all of this Jesus somehow survived (which would in itself be a miracle), he could not have

---

M. Metzger, *Historical and Literary Studies: Pagan, Jewish, and Christian* (Grand Rapids, Eerdmans, 1968), 11.
[33]Isa. 53:8–12.
[34]Matt. 12:38–40; Mark 8:31; 9:31; 10:33–34; John 2:18–22.
[35]John 19:34–35.

endured three days without food, water, or medical attention in a cold tomb carved out of rock. In summary, Jesus died.

4) Jesus was buried in a tomb that was easy to find. Some seven hundred years before Jesus was even born, God promised through Isaiah that Jesus would be assigned a grave "with a rich man in his death."[36] This was incredibly unlikely, because Jesus was a very poor man who could not have afforded an expensive burial plot. Following Jesus' death, though, a wealthy and well-known man named Joseph of Arimathea gifted his expensive tomb for the burial of Jesus.[37] As a result, the place of Jesus' burial was easy to confirm. Joseph who owned the tomb, governmental leaders and their soldiers who were assigned to guard the tomb, and the disciples and women who visited the tomb and found it empty all knew exactly where Jesus' dead body was laid to rest. Had Jesus truly not risen from death, it would have been very easy to prove it by opening the tomb and presenting Jesus' dead body as evidence.

5) Jesus appeared physically, not just spiritually, alive three days after his death. Following Jesus' resurrection, many people touched his physical body: his disciples clung to his feet,[38] Mary clung to him,[39] and Thomas the doubter put his hand into the open spear hole in Jesus' side.[40] Jesus also appeared to his disciples after his resurrection, but they were uncertain if he had truly physically risen from death. Still, Jesus was emphatic about his bodily resurrection and went out of his way to prove it:

> As they were talking about these things, Jesus himself stood among them, and said to them, "Peace to you!" But they were startled and frightened and thought they saw a spirit. And he said to them, "Why are you troubled, and why do doubts arise in your hearts? See my hands and my feet, that it is I myself. Touch me, and see. For a spirit does not have flesh and bones as you see that I have." And when he had said this, he showed them his hands and his feet. And while they still disbelieved for joy and were marveling, he said to them, "Have you anything here to eat?" They gave him a piece of broiled fish, and he took it and ate before them.[41]

---

[36]Isa. 53:9.
[37]Matt. 27:57–60.
[38]Matt. 28:9.
[39]John 20:17.
[40]John 20:20–28.
[41]Luke 24:36–43.

Furthermore, Jesus appeared physically alive over the course of forty days[42] to crowds as large as five hundred people at a time.[43] It is also significant to note that no credible historical evidence from that period exists to validate any alternative explanation for Jesus' resurrection other than his literal bodily resurrection.[44]

6) Jesus' resurrected body was the same as his pre-resurrection body. His disciples recognized him as the same person who had been crucified,[45] and Mary Magdalene recognized him by the sound of his voice.[46] While Jesus' resurrection body was the same, it was transformed. This explains why Jesus was not always immediately recognized after his resurrection,[47] and seemed to appear and reappear mysteriously.[48] As James Orr noted, "[In] the narratives . . . it is implied that there was something strange—something unfamiliar or mysterious—in His aspect, which prevented His immediate recognition . . . which held them in awe."[49] Paul explains this phenomenon in the lengthiest treatment of the nature of a resurrection body in all of Scripture (1 Corinthians 15): "It is sown a natural body; it is raised a spiritual body. If there is a natural body, there is also a spiritual body."[50] This "spiritual body" refers to a resurrected body that has been perfected to its glorious state by the power of the Holy Spirit.

7) Jesus' resurrection was recorded as Scripture shortly after it occurred. Mark's Gospel account of the days leading up to Jesus' crucifixion mentions the high priest without naming him.[51] It can logically be inferred that Mark did not mention the high priest by name because he expected his readers to know who he was speaking of. Since Caiaphas was high priest from AD 18–37, the latest possible date for the tradition is AD 37.[52] This date is so close to the death of Jesus that there would not have

---

[42]Acts 1:3.
[43]1 Cor. 15:6.
[44]See Craig, "Did Jesus Rise from the Dead?"
[45]Luke 24:31; cf. John 21:7, 12.
[46]John 20:16.
[47]John 20:14, 15; 21:12.
[48]John 20:19; Luke 24:31, 36.
[49]James Orr, *The Resurrection of Jesus* (London: Hodder & Stoughton, 1908), 198.
[50]1 Cor. 15:44.
[51]Mark 14:53, 54, 60, 61, 63.
[52]J. P. Moreland, *Scaling the Secular City* (Grand Rapids, MI: Baker, 1987), 172.

been sufficient time for a "legend" of his resurrection to have developed. This proves that the biblical record of Jesus' resurrection was penned while the eyewitnesses were still alive to verify the facts. Thus, his resurrection is not a mythical legend that developed long after the time of Jesus. In fact, John Rodgers, former dean of Trinity Episcopal School for Ministry, says, "This is the sort of data that historians of antiquity drool over."[53]

8) Jesus' resurrection was celebrated in the earliest church creeds. In 1 Corinthians 15:3–4, Paul says, "Christ died for our sins in accordance with the Scriptures, that he was buried, that he was raised on the third day in accordance with the Scriptures." This statement is widely accepted as the earliest church creed, which began circulating as early as AD 30–36, shortly after Jesus' resurrection. Considering the early age of this creed, there was not sufficient time between the crucifixion and the creed for any legend about Jesus' resurrection to accrue. In addition, the witnesses mentioned were still alive and available to be questioned about the facts surrounding the resurrection. The early date of this creed also proves that the church did not corrupt the truth about Jesus with fables and folklores. Rather, the early church simply clung to the plain and incontrovertible facts of Jesus' death, burial, and resurrection.

9) Jesus' resurrection convinced his family to worship him as God. James, Jesus' half-brother, was originally opposed to the claims of deity by his brother.[54] A transformation occurred in James, though, after he saw his brother resurrected from death.[55] James went on to pastor the church in Jerusalem and authored the New Testament epistle bearing his name.[56] He was also actively involved in shaping the early church, which suffered and died to proclaim to everyone that Jesus is the one true God.[57] Also, Jesus' mother Mary was part of the early church that prayed to and worshiped her son as God,[58] as was Jesus' other brother Jude, who wrote a book of the

---

[53]Quoted in Richard N. Ostling, "Who Was Jesus?" *Time*, August 15, 1988, 41.
[54]John 7:5.
[55]1 Cor. 15:7.
[56]James 1:1.
[57]Acts 12:17; 15:12–21; 21:18; Gal. 2:9.
[58]Acts 1:14.

New Testament bearing his name.[59] While it is not impossible to imagine Jesus convincing some people that he was God if he were not, it is impossible to conceive of Jesus convincing his own mother and brothers to suffer persecution in this life and risk the torments of hell in eternal life for worshiping him as the one true God unless he truly was.

10) Jesus' resurrection was confirmed by his most bitter enemies, such as Paul. Paul was a devout Jewish Pharisee who routinely persecuted and killed Christians.[60] After an encounter with the risen Christ, Paul was converted and became the most dynamic defender and expander of the church.[61] Had Jesus not truly risen from death, it is absurd to assume that Paul would ever have worshiped him as God, particularly when Paul rightly believed that worshiping a false God would send one into the eternal flames of hell. Simply, Paul hated Jesus and would never have changed his religious practice unless Jesus had risen from death to prove him wrong. Furthermore, Paul insisted that Jesus had risen in almost all of his letters that are saved for us in the New Testament.

WHAT IS THE CIRCUMSTANTIAL EVIDENCE FOR JESUS' RESURRECTION?

Effects have causes. Jesus' resurrection is no exception, as is evident by eight effects caused by it. Together, they are compelling circumstantial evidence for Jesus' resurrection. Further, for those wanting to deny Jesus' resurrection, the burden of proof remains on them to account for these multiple effects with a reasonable cause. Craig explains, "Anyone who denies this explanation is rationally obligated to produce a more plausible cause of Jesus' resurrection and to explain how it happened."[62] He goes on to assert, "The conclusion that God raised Him up is virtually inescapable. Only a sterile, academic skepticism resists this inevitable inference."[63]

---

[59] Acts 1:14; Jude 1.
[60] Phil. 3:4–6; Acts 7:54–60.
[61] Acts 9.
[62] William Lane Craig, *The Son Rises: The Historical Evidence for the Resurrection of Jesus* (Eugene, OR: Wipf & Stock, 2001), 134.
[63] Ibid.

1) Jesus' disciples were transformed. Prior to the resurrection, his disciples were timid and fearful, even hiding when Jesus appeared to them.[64] Following the resurrection, however, they were all transformed into bold witnesses to what they had seen and heard, even to the point of dying in shame and poverty for their convictions, including Peter.

Regarding the apostles' eyewitness testimony to Jesus' resurrection, Simon Greenleaf, professor of law at Harvard University and a world-renowned scholar on the rules of legal evidence, said that it was "impossible that they could have persisted in affirming the truths they have narrated, had not Jesus actually risen from the dead, and had they not known this fact as certainly as they knew any other fact."[65]

2) Jesus' disciples remained loyal to Jesus as their victorious Messiah. Modern-day "messiahs" include, for example, politicians who propose to save and deliver us from a terrible fate such as terrorism, poverty, or unreasonable taxation. Supporters flock around their messiah in hopes that he will deliver on his promise to make their dreams come true. However, when a messiah fails to deliver as promised, his followers either abandon both the cause and the messiah, or they retain the cause and abandon the messiah to instead pursue another messiah. Either way, a failed messiah is a forgotten messiah.

However, Jesus' disciples did not abandon their cause of forgiven sin and life with God or their devotion to Jesus as their victorious Messiah. Furthermore, their devotion to both their cause and Messiah grew in numbers and passionate devotion. They endured widespread persecution and even martyrdom, which would have been unthinkable had Jesus merely died and failed to rise as he promised he would. On this point, the historian Kenneth Scott Latourette has said:

> It was the conviction of the resurrection of Jesus which lifted his followers out of the despair into which his death had cast them and which led to the perpetuation of the movement begun by him. But for their

---

[64]John 20:19.
[65]Simon Greenleaf, *The Testimony of the Evangelists: The Gospels Examined by the Rules of Evidence Administered in Courts of Justice* (Grand Rapids, MI: Kregel, 1995), 32.

profound belief that the crucified had risen from the dead and that they had seen him and talked with him, the death of Jesus and even Jesus himself would probably have been all but forgotten.[66]

3) The disciples had exemplary character. To claim that the disciples preached obvious lies and deluded people into dying for the world's greatest farce, one would have to first find credible evidence to challenge the character of the disciples. Also, these men were devout Jews who knew that if they worshiped a false god and encouraged others to do the same, they would be sentenced by God to the fires of eternal hell for violating the first two commandments. Lastly, does not such egregious lying conflict with the character of men and women who gave their lives to feeding the poor, caring for widows and orphans, and helping the hurting and needy?

4) Worship changed. The early church stopped worshiping on Saturday, as Jews had for thousands of years, and suddenly began worshiping on Sunday in memory of Jesus' Sunday resurrection.[67] The Sabbath was so sacred to the Jews that they would not have ceased to obey one of the Ten Commandments unless Jesus had resurrected in fulfillment of their Old Testament Scriptures. Yet, by the end of the first century, Sunday was called "the Lord's Day."[68]

Not only did the day of worship change after the resurrection of Jesus, but so did the object of worship. Considering that one of the Ten Commandments also forbids the worship of false gods, it is impossible to conceive of devout Jews simply worshiping Jesus as the one true God without the proof of Jesus' resurrection.

According to even non-Christian historians, multitudes began worshiping Jesus as the one true God after his resurrection. For example, Lucian of Samosata was a non-Christian Assyrian-Roman satirist who, around AD 170, wrote:

---

[66]Kenneth Scott Latourette, *A History of the Expansion of Christianity*, 7 vols., *The First Five Centuries* (New York: Harper, 1937), 1:59.
[67]Acts 20:7; 1 Cor. 16:1–2.
[68]Rev. 1:10.

The Christians, you know, worship a man to this day—the distinguished personage who introduced their novel rites, and was crucified on that account. . . . You see, these misguided creatures start with the general conviction that they are immortal for all time, which explains their contempt of death and voluntary self-devotion which are so common among them; and then it was impressed on them by their original lawgiver that they are all brothers, from the moment that they are converted, and deny the gods of Greece, and worship the crucified sage, and live after his laws. [69]

Additionally, the early church rejected the observances of the law because they saw it as having been fulfilled in Jesus; thus, the law was no longer binding upon them in the same way as it had been for over a thousand years. This was a cataclysmic shift in belief that was only considered possible because a new epoch had been ushered in by the resurrection of Jesus.

Lastly, God's people welcomed the sacraments of Communion and baptism into their worship of Jesus as God. In Communion the early Christians remembered Jesus' death in their place for their sins. In baptism they remembered Jesus' resurrection in their place for their salvation and anticipated their personal future resurrection.

5) Women discovered the empty tomb. The women who discovered the tomb were mentioned by name, were well known in the early church, and could have easily been questioned to confirm their findings if they were untrue.[70] Moreover, since the testimony of women was not respected in that culture, it would have been more likely for men to report discovering the empty tomb if the account was fictitious and an attempt were being made to concoct a credible lie about Jesus' resurrection. Therefore, the fact that women are said to have been the first to arrive at Jesus' empty tomb is confirmation that the account of Scripture is factual, not contrived.

---

[69]Lucian, "The Death of Peregrine," in *The Works of Lucian of Samosata*, trans. H. W. Fowler and F. G. Fowler, vol. 4 (Oxford: Clarendon, 1949), 11–13. Also see Pliny, *Letters*, trans. William Melmoth, vol. 2 (Cambridge: Harvard University Press, 1935), 10.96.
[70]Mark 15:40, 47; 16:1.

6) The entirety of early church preaching was centered on the historical fact of Jesus' resurrection. If the empty tomb were not a widely accepted fact, the disciples would have reasoned with the skeptics of their day to defend the central issue of their faith. Instead, we see the debate occurring not about whether the tomb was empty, but why it was empty.[71] Also, nowhere in the preaching of the early church was the empty tomb explicitly defended, for the simple reason that it was widely known as an agreed-upon fact. Furthermore, a reading of the book of Acts shows that on virtually every occasion that preaching and teaching occurred, the resurrection of Jesus from death was the central truth being communicated because it had changed human history and could not be ignored. Jesus' resurrection appears in twelve of the twenty-eight chapters in Acts, which records the history of the early church.

7) Jesus' tomb was not enshrined. Craig says, "It was customary in Judaism for the tomb of a prophet or holy man to be preserved or venerated as a shrine. This was so because the bones of the prophet lay in the tomb and imparted to the site its religious values. If the remains were not there, then the grave would lose its significance as a shrine."[72]

Of the four major world religions based upon a founder as opposed to a system of ideas, only Christianity claims that the tomb of its founder is empty. Judaism looks back to Abraham, who died almost four thousand years ago, and still cares for his grave as a holy site at Hebron. Thousands visit Buddha's tomb in India every year. Islam founder Mohammed died on June 8, 632, and his tomb in Medina is visited by millions of people every year.

Additionally, Yamauchi has discovered evidence that the tombs of at least fifty prophets or other religious figures were enshrined as places of worship and veneration in Palestine around the same time as Jesus' death.[73] Yet, according to James D. G. Dunn, there is "absolutely no trace" of any

---

[71]Murray J. Harris, *Raised Immortal: Resurrection and Immortality in the New Testament* (Grand Rapids, MI: Eerdmans, 1985), 40.
[72]Craig, "Did Jesus Rise from the Dead?" 152.
[73]Yamauchi, "Easter: Myth, Hallucination, or History?" 4–7.

veneration at Jesus' tomb. [74] The obvious reason for this lack of veneration is that Jesus was not buried but instead resurrected.

8) Christianity exploded on the earth and a few billion people today claim to be Christians. On the same day, in the same place, and in the same way, two other men died, one on Jesus' left and one on his right. Despite the similarities, we do not know the names of these men, and billions of people do not worship them as God. Why? Because they remained dead and Jesus alone rose from death and ascended into heaven, leaving the Christian church in his wake. On this point, C. F. D. Moule of Cambridge University says, "The birth and rapid rise of the Christian Church . . . *remain an unsolved enigma for any historian who refuses to take seriously the only explanation offered by the Church itself.*"[75]

WHAT IS THE HISTORICAL EVIDENCE FOR JESUS' RESURRECTION?

Because Jesus' death is a historical fact, the corroborating evidence of non-Christian sources in addition to the Bible helps to confirm the resurrection of Jesus Christ. The following testimony of Romans, Greeks, and Jews is helpful because these men are simply telling the facts without any religious devotion to them.

Josephus (AD 37–100)

Josephus was a Jewish historian born just a few years after Jesus died. His most celebrated passage, called the "Testimonium Flavianum," says:

> Now there was about this time Jesus, a wise man, if it be lawful to call him a man; for he was a doer of wonderful works, a teacher of such men as receive the truth with pleasure. He drew over to him both many of the Jews and many of the Gentiles. He was [the] Christ. And when Pilate, at

---

[74]James D. G. Dunn, *The Christ and the Spirit* (Grand Rapids, MI: Eerdmans, 1998), 67–68.
[75]C. F. D. Moule, *The Phenomenon of the New Testament* (London: SCM Press, 1967), 13, emphasis in original.

the suggestion of the principal men among us, had condemned him to the cross, those that loved him at the first did not forsake him; for *he appeared to them alive again the third day*, as the divine prophets had foretold these and ten thousand other wonderful things concerning him. And the tribe of Christians, so named from him, are not extinct at this day.[76]

Suetonius (AD 70–160)

Suetonius was a Roman historian and annalist of the Imperial House. In his biography of Nero (Nero ruled AD 54–68), Suetonius mentions the persecution of Christians by indirectly referring to the resurrection: "Punishment was inflicted on the Christians, a class of men given to *a new and mischievous superstition* [the resurrection]."[77]

Pliny the Younger (AD 61 or 62–113)

Pliny the Younger wrote a letter to the emperor Trajan around AD 111 describing early Christian worship gatherings that met early on Sunday mornings in memory of Jesus' resurrection day:

> I have never been present at an examination of Christians. Consequently, I do not know the nature of the extent of the punishments usually meted out to them, nor the grounds for starting an investigation and how far it should be pressed. . . . They also declared that the sum total of their guilt or error amounted to no more than this: they had met regularly *before dawn on a fixed day* [Sunday in remembrance of Jesus' resurrection] to chant verses alternately amongst themselves in honor of Christ as if to a god.[78]

The Jewish Explanation

The earliest attempt to provide an alternative explanation for the resurrection of Jesus did not deny that the tomb was empty.[79] Instead, Jewish

---

[76]Flavius Josephus, "Jewish Antiquities," in *The New Complete Works of Josephus*, trans. William Whiston (Grand Rapids, MI: Kregel, 1999), 18.63–64, emphasis added.
[77]Suetonius, *Vita Nero* 16.11–13.
[78]Pliny the Younger, *Letters* 10.96.1–7.
[79]Matt. 28:13–15.

opponents claimed that the body had been stolen, thus admitting the fact of the empty tomb. But this explanation is untenable for the following reasons. (1) The tomb was closed with an enormous rock and sealed by the government, and there is no explanation for how the rock was moved while being guarded by armed Roman soldiers. (2) If the body had been stolen, a large ransom could have been offered to the thieves, and they could have been coerced to produce the body. Or if it had been taken by the disciples, then the torture and death they suffered should have been sufficient to return the body. (3) Even if the body was stolen, how are we to account for the fact that Jesus appeared to multiple crowds of people, proving that he was alive? In conclusion, the theft of the body is unlikely and still fails to account for it returning back to life.

Summarily, the historical testimony of those who were not Christians stands in agreement with Scripture that Jesus died and rose because those are the historical facts.

WHAT ARE THE PRIMARY ANCIENT OBJECTIONS TO JESUS' RESURRECTION?

Jesus did not die on the cross but merely swooned. Some have argued that Jesus did not in fact die on the cross but rather swooned or basically passed out and therefore appeared dead. This is also what the Muslim Koran teaches as fact. Regarding this claim, theologian John Stott has asked if we are to believe

that after the rigours and pains of trial, mockery, flogging and crucifix-ion he could survive thirty-six hours in a stone sepulchre with neither warmth nor food nor medical care? That he could then rally sufficiently to perform the superhuman feat of shifting the boulder which secured the mouth of the tomb, and this without disturbing the Roman guard? That then, weak and sickly and hungry, he could appear to the disciples in such a way as to give them the impression that he had vanquished death? That he could go on to claim that he had died and risen, could send them into all the world and promise to be with them unto the end of time? That he could live somewhere in hiding for forty days, making occasional surprise appearances, and then finally disappear without explanations? Such credulity is more incredible than Thomas' unbelief.[80]

Also, as we've noted, crucifixion is essentially death by asphyxiation, because the prisoner grows too tired to lift himself up and fill his lungs with air. This explains why the Romans would often break a prisoner's legs, thus preventing him from continuing to fill his lungs with air. Since the professional executioners did not break Jesus' legs, these professional executioners must have been convinced of his death. The only way Jesus could have deceived the executioners would have been to stop breathing, which in itself would have killed him.

Lastly, John 19:34–35 tells us that the Roman soldier thrust a spear into Jesus' heart to confirm his death. The water that poured out was probably from the sac surrounding his heart, and the blood most likely came from the right side of his heart. Even if he had been alive, this would have killed him.[81]

Jesus did not rise and his body was stolen. The original explanation given for the empty tomb by those Jews who did not choose to worship Jesus as God was that the tomb was indeed empty, but not because of a resurrection but because of a theft of Jesus' dead body.[82] For this to be true, a number of impossibilities would have had to occur. (1) Despite the fact that it would have cost them their lives, all the guards positioned at the tomb would have had to fall asleep at the same time. (2) Each of the guards would have had to not only fall asleep but also remain asleep and not be awakened by the breaking of the Roman seal on the tomb, the rolling away of the enormous stone which blocked the entrance, or the carrying off of the dead body. (3) Even if Jesus' body was stolen, there is no way to account for its returning to vibrant and triumphant life.

The issue of motive is also a key factor in refuting this hypothesis. What benefit would there be for the disciples to risk their lives to steal a corpse and die for a lie as a result? What motive would there be for the

---

[80]John R. W. Stott, *Basic Christianity* (Grand Rapids, MI: InterVarsity, 1971), 49.
[81]C. Truman Davis, "The Crucifixion of Jesus: The Passion of Christ from a Medical Point of View," *Arizona Medicine* (March 1965): 183–87.
[82]Matt. 28:11–15.

Jews, Romans, or anyone else to steal the body? And, if the body were truly stolen, could not a bounty have been offered and someone enticed to provide the body in exchange for a handsome cash reward?

A twin brother, or a look-alike, died in Jesus' place. It has been suggested by some Muslim scholars along with various other people that Jesus was not the one crucified but rather a brother or other man who looked like him. However, there is not a shred of evidence to prove that someone who looked like Jesus existed at that time. Additionally, Jesus' mother was present at his crucifixion, and the likelihood of fooling his mother is minimal. Also, the physical wounds he suffered during the crucifixion were visible on Jesus' resurrection body and carefully inspected by the disciple Thomas, who was very doubtful that Jesus had risen until he touched scars from the crucifixion evident on Jesus' body.[83] In addition, the tomb was empty and the burial cloths were left behind.

Jesus' followers hallucinated his resurrection. Some people have suggested that the disciples did not actually see Jesus risen from death but rather hallucinated, or projected, their desires for his resurrection into a hallucination. One example is John Dominic Crossan, cochairman of the Jesus Seminar. He told *Time* magazine that after the crucifixion, Jesus' corpse was probably laid in a shallow grave, barely covered with dirt, and eaten by wild dogs. The subsequent story of Jesus' resurrection, he says, was merely the result of "wishful thinking."[84]

Similarly, fellow Jesus Seminar member John Shelby Spong, an Episcopal bishop, denies the resurrection and believes Jesus' body was thrown in a common grave along with other crucifixion victims. Subsequently, he says the "Easter moment" happened to Peter, not to Jesus. Peter saw Jesus alive in "the heart of God" and began to open the eyes of the other disciples to this reality.[85] Spong writes, "That was the dawn of Easter in human history. It would be fair to say that in that moment *Simon felt resurrected.*"[86]

---

[83]John 20:24–28.
[84]Richard N. Ostling, "Jesus Christ, Plain and Simple," *Time*, January 10, 1994, 32–33.
[85]John Shelby Spong, *Resurrection: Myth or Reality?* (New York: HarperCollins, 1994), 143.
[86]Ibid., 255, emphasis added.

This thesis is unbelievable for five reasons. (1) A hallucination is a private, not public, experience. Yet Paul clearly states that Jesus appeared to more than five hundred people at one time.[87] (2) Jesus appeared in a variety of times at a variety of locations, whereas hallucinations are generally restricted to individual times and places. (3) Certain types of people tend to be more prone to hallucination than others. Yet Jesus appeared to a great variety of personalities, including his brothers and mother. (4) After forty days Jesus' appearances suddenly stopped for everyone simultaneously. Hallucinations tend to continue over longer periods of time and do not stop abruptly. (5) A hallucination is a projection of a thought that preexists in the mind. However, the Jews had a conception of resurrection that applied to the raising of all people at the end of history,[88] not the raising of any particular individual in the middle of history.[89] Therefore, it is inconceivable that the witnesses to the resurrection could have hallucinated Jesus' resurrection.

In considering the objections to the resurrection of Jesus Christ, C. S. Lewis's charge of "chronological snobbery" begins to make sense.[90] Each of the objections is predicated upon the assumption that people in Jesus' day were less intelligent and more gullible than we are today. However, it can be argued persuasively that in their world with fewer hospitals, medicines, and hospices to care for dying people, they were more personally aware of the finality of death than we moderns are. Additionally, as we have already surveyed, they did not even believe in resurrection, and because of the influence of Greek dualism upon them, which considered the body an unwanted husk to be discarded so the soul could truly live, the entire idea of resurrection was undesirable. Taken together, it is apparent that such chronological snobbery reveals more about the character of those moderns who appeal to it than those ancients who are dismissed by it.

---

[87] 1 Cor. 15:1–6.
[88] E.g., Dan. 12:2.
[89] See Craig, "Did Jesus Rise from the Dead?" 159–60.
[90] C. S. Lewis, *Surprised by Joy: The Shape of My Early Life* (Orlando: Harcourt Brace, 1955), 201.

WHAT HAS THE RESURRECTION ACCOMPLISHED FOR CHRISTIANS?

Jesus' resurrection reveals him as our messiah king. In the Davidic covenant,[91] God the Father promised that his Son, Jesus Christ, would be raised up from David's lineage to rule over an everlasting kingdom. Paul reveals that this was fulfilled at the resurrection of Jesus: "Concerning his Son, who was descended from David according to the flesh and was declared to be the Son of God in power according to the Spirit of holiness by his resurrection from the dead, Jesus Christ our Lord."[92] Now that the risen Christ has been installed as our messiah king, we can rest assured that one day Jesus will return to establish his throne on the earth and rule over his kingdom, which extends to all of creation.

Furthermore, following Jesus' resurrection, an angel declared, "He is not here, for he has risen, as he said."[93] Therefore, the resurrection is proof that Jesus' teaching was and is truth that we can trust. Practically, Jesus' resurrection gives us confidence in his other promises that we are waiting to see fulfilled, such as his returning one day to judge sinners[94] and reward saints.[95]

The Bible often speaks of our being united with Christ by his resurrection,[96] being raised with Christ,[97] and enjoying the same powerful Holy Spirit that raised Christ.[98] In so doing, the Bible is stressing the innumerable blessings and benefits conferred on believers because of Jesus' resurrection.

Paul stresses the fact that through Jesus' death and resurrection we have forgiveness of sins.[99] Because of Jesus, those with faith in him can live with the great joy of knowing that all their sins—past, present, and future—have been forgiven once and for all by Jesus Christ. Furthermore, as the power of Jesus' resurrection works itself out in our sanctification, we grow in holiness, learning to live in victory over sin, until one day upon our own resurrection

---

[91] 2 Sam. 7:7–16.
[92] Rom. 1:3–4.
[93] Matt. 28:6.
[94] John 3:16, 18, 36; 5:25–29.
[95] John 14:3.
[96] Rom. 6:5.
[97] Col. 2:12; 3:1.
[98] 1 Cor. 6:14; 2 Cor. 5:15.
[99] 1 Cor. 15:3–58.

we will live forever, free from the presence, power, and practice of all sin. Elsewhere, Jesus' resurrection is spoken of as the source of our justification, thereby enabling us, though sinners, to be declared righteous in the sight of God. Paul explicitly states that Jesus was "raised for our justification."[100]

Regarding our future, Jesus' resurrection is the precedent and pattern of our own: "Christ has been raised from the dead, the firstfruits of those who have fallen asleep."[101] As his body was resurrected in complete health, so too will we rise and never experience pain, injury, or death ever again. This is because through the resurrection, Jesus has put death to death.

Additionally, Wright makes the insightful observation that "the message of the resurrection is that this present world matters."[102] Because Jesus rose from death physically, we learn that God through Christ intends to reclaim and restore all that he made in creation and saw corrupted through the fall. Our eternity will be spent in a world much like the one enjoyed by our first parents in Eden, because the earth has been reclaimed and restored by God through Jesus' resurrection.

The full effects of Jesus' resurrection will be seen one day, following Jesus' return. The time between Jesus' resurrection and our resurrection is a lengthy season of love, grace, and mercy as news of the gospel goes forth, inviting sinners to repent of sin and enjoy the present and future salvation of Jesus Christ. Paul preached just this fact and the urgent need for sinners to repent: "The times of ignorance God overlooked, but now he commands all people everywhere to repent, because he has fixed a day on which he will judge the world in righteousness by a man whom he has appointed; and of this he has given assurance to all by raising him from the dead."[103]

In closing, no one can remain neutral regarding Jesus' resurrection. The claim is too staggering, the event is too earthshaking, the implications are too significant, and the matter is too serious. We must each either receive or reject it as truth for us, and to remain indifferent or undecided is to reject it.

---

[100]Rom. 4:25.
[101]1 Cor. 15:20.
[102]N. T. Wright, *For All God's Worth: True Worship and the Calling of the Church* (Grand Rapids, MI: Eerdmans, 1997), 65.
[103]Acts 17:30–31.

CHAPTER 10

CHURCH: GOD SENDS

Christ loved the church and gave himself up for her.

EPHESIANS 5:25

The story of the Christian church is stunning: a handful of Jesus' followers have become, two millennia later, a global phenomenon of a few billion people.

During his life, Jesus promised his small band of disciples, "I will build my church."[1] Following his resurrection, Jesus commanded the church to "make disciples of all nations, baptizing them in the name of the Father and of the Son and of the Holy Spirit, teaching them to observe all that I have commanded you."[2]

Just prior to his ascension back into heaven, Jesus promised the first Christians, "You will receive power when the Holy Spirit has come upon you, and you will be my witnesses in Jerusalem and in all Judea and Samaria, and to the end of the earth."[3] This was a seemingly grand promise for one hundred and twenty people. But when that power came at Pentecost, three thousand people "who received his word were baptized, and . . . were added" to the church, "and they devoted themselves to the apostles' teaching and the fellowship, to the breaking of bread and the

---

[1] Matt. 16:18.
[2] Matt. 28:19–20.
[3] Acts 1:8.

prayers."[4] These first church members were awed by the miraculous power of God and shared their possessions with anyone who had need. They had favor with all the people of Jerusalem and more and more people joined them.[5]

What an amazing experience these people had as the church began! People all around Jerusalem saw the power of God at work and wanted to share in his grace. Furthermore, the first believers loved God and each other as demonstrated by their humble service and generous sharing. This is what church should be.

Tragically, in our day, the common perception of the church is vastly different. David Kinnaman conducted extensive research on how young Americans, people from their late teens to early thirties, believers and unbelievers, perceive the church.[6] The results were quite different from Acts 2. They view the church as anti-homosexual (91%), judgmental (87%), hypocritical (85%), old-fashioned (78%), too involved in politics (75%), out of touch with reality (72%), insensitive to others (70%), and boring (68%).[7] They see the church as male-dominated and negative, with a strong political agenda.

It is curious that if you ask these same people what they think of Jesus, many will say they respect him.[8] They are quite interested in spirituality. But they see the church as very unlike Jesus. To them, the church is quite irrelevant because spirituality is a very personal thing that does not require leaders, buildings, or programs.

What happened? Where is the dynamic church of Acts 2? Honestly, part of it is bad press. Sometimes the media only reports the most scandal-ous church activities, while faithful Christians and churches are not well known. Still, a bigger issue is that some churches have become ingrown. They have exchanged mission for institution and have wandered from Jesus' commands for his people. The answer is a simple, humble, and

---

[4]Acts 2:41–42.
[5]Acts 2:43–47.
[6]See David Kinnaman and Gabe Lyons, *UnChristian: What a New Generation Really Thinks about Christianity . . . and Why It Matters* (Grand Rapids, MI: Baker, 2007).
[7]Ibid., 34.
[8]See Dan Kimball, *They Like Jesus but Not the Church* (Grand Rapids, MI: Zondervan, 2007).

continual return to Scripture to rekindle the love of God the Father, life of God the Son, and leading of God the Spirit in order that we be the church for the sake of the world to the glory of God.

WHAT IS THE CHURCH?

There are innumerable erroneous definitions and assumptions about what the church is. The church is not a holy building in which spiritual meetings take place. The church is not a Eucharistic society through which God dispenses grace by means of the sacraments and a duly authorized and empowered hierarchy of bishops and priests operating in unbroken succession from the apostles. The church is not the moral police force of a society seeking mere behavioral change through legislation. The church is not a weekly meeting where people gather to do spiritual things.

Thankfully, what the church is can be found in Scripture. The book of Acts is the historical account of the early church. There, we see the New Testament church birthed through the preaching of Peter's sermon at the holiday of Pentecost. Summarizing the church as described in Acts 2:42–47, we get a biblical definition of church as God meant it to be:

> The local church is a community of regenerated believers who confess Jesus Christ as Lord. In obedience to Scripture they organize under qualified leadership, gather regularly for preaching and worship, observe the biblical sacraments of baptism and Communion, are unified by the Spirit, are disciplined for holiness, and scatter to fulfill the Great Commandment and the Great Commission as missionaries to the world for God's glory and their joy.[9]

WHAT ARE THE CHARACTERISTICS OF THE CHURCH?

When speaking of the church, it is helpful to distinguish between the universal and the local church. The universal church is all God's people in all times and places. Someone becomes a member of the universal church by

---

[9]We develop this definition further in the second chapter of *Vintage Church: Timeless Truths and Timely Methods* (Wheaton, IL: Crossway, 2009), 35–61.

virtue of being a Christian. Local churches are smaller gatherings of the universal church where Christians assemble as God's people. In fact, the word for *church* in the Greek New Testament (*ekklēsia*) means "gathering," "meeting," or "assembly."

Throughout the centuries, church leaders have characterized the church according to four marks. The church is (1) *one*, unified by the confession and shared life of Christ through the Spirit. The church is (2) *holy* by its Christlike character, not just by what it doesn't do through religiously obeying rules, but by actually living out new life modeled after Jesus by the Holy Spirit's power. The church is (3) *catholic* (universal); the church and its gospel have no limits in time or space because Jesus is Lord of all people, not just a people. The church is (4) *apostolic* as it lives under apostolic authority, following the faith and life of the apostles given to us in the Bible. In addition to these marks, the Reformers added the marks of (5) pure preaching of the Word, (6) right administration of the sacraments, and (7) discipline.

While good, we believe that even these seven marks are not quite sufficient to capture the thoroughness of the biblical definition of the church. They omit both the Great Commandment to love God and neighbor and the Great Commission to take the gospel to the whole world. If we follow the definition of church summarized from Acts 2, we can identify eight key characteristics of the local church. Understanding them will provide standards for planning and evaluating every church.

1) The church is made up of regenerated believers.[10] The Spirit dwells in them and has given them new hearts. The church is a fellowship of true disciples who are devoted to the apostles' teaching and the fellowship, to the breaking of bread and the prayers,[11] and to attending meetings together and fellowshiping in their homes with glad and generous hearts.[12]

There are unbelievers and outsiders who participate in the activity of

---

[10]Acts 2:36–41.
[11]Acts 2:42.
[12]Acts 2:46.

the church and have an important place in the extended community.[13] Likewise, children are welcomed into the church to be loved and served so that they would become Christians with saving faith and later become church members. But the church itself, the body of Christ, is made up of confessing believers who are justified by faith and made new by the Spirit. It is a community manifesting the supernatural life of the triune God.

2) The church is organized under qualified and competent leadership. The senior human leaders are men called elders (pastors). In Acts 2 we see them exercising their unique role of teaching the whole church.[14] They led the congregation in wise decision making about a potentially divisive problem.[15] They sent Peter and John to Samaria to confirm the authenticity of the evangelistic outbreak there.[16] We also see the appointment of elders in Acts 14:23. In the next chapter they practice their leadership in a doctrinal dispute with the party of the Pharisees in Jerusalem. The Bible also describes the leadership of deacons, or ministry teams led by both men and women.[17]

3) The church regularly gathers to hear God's Word rightly preached and to respond in worship. The church is under the apostolic authority of Scripture. In Acts people eagerly devoted themselves to the teaching of the apostles,[18] not because they had to but because their regenerated hearts wanted to. They had received the Spirit, seen remarkable miracles, and witnessed an evangelistic event that was history altering. But they refused a simple experience-based Christianity. As disciples, they were keenly aware of their need to continually increase in their understanding of Scripture, and so they studied not just for information but also for transformation in all of their life. Therefore, the church studies Scripture to show submission to the apostolic authority of the Word of God.

Importantly, not only is the church to gather to hear the preaching of Scripture, but it also is to respond to God's truth and grace with worship.

---

[13] 1 Cor. 14:22–25.
[14] Acts 2:42.
[15] Acts 6:1–6.
[16] Acts 8:14.
[17] Acts 6:1–6; Phil. 1:1; 1 Tim. 3:1–13.
[18] Acts 2:42.

In the earliest days of the New Testament church, we witness a worshiping community where believers praised God and had favor with all people.[19] Worship is a response to the revelation of the Lord for who he is, what he has done, and what he will do. It consists of (1) adoration and proclamation of the greatness of the Lord and his mighty works;[20] (2) action, which is serving him by living out his character in gracious service to others in obedience to the commands of Scripture; and (3) participation in the divine life and mission.[21] It is both *proskuneo*, to fall down and kiss Jesus' feet in an expression of one's allegiance to and adoration for God,[22] and *latreia* or *leitourgeo*, which is ministering, or doing work and service in the world in the name of Jesus.[23]

4) The church is where the biblical sacraments of baptism and Communion are performed regularly as visible symbols of the gospel in the life of the church.

5) The church is unified by the confession and shared life of Christ through the Holy Spirit. The unified life of the Trinity itself is manifested among God's people who live in loving unity together as the church. This unity comes in several concrete aspects.

- *Theological unity.* The leaders and members of the church must agree on what they will and will not fight over. Every church must clarify what it considers to be primary, closed-handed doctrines. We would urge as primary for every church doctrines such as the Trinity as the only God and object of worship, the Scriptures as God's perfect Word, Jesus as fully God and man born of a virgin to live without sin before dying for our sins and physically rising for our salvation, and salvation by grace alone through faith alone in Christ alone. There are also secondary, open-handed doctrines, such as musical style, mode of Communion, schooling options for children, or belief in the rapture, which permit a range of beliefs providing they fall within the limits of biblical truth and are held with a humble and teachable spirit.

---

[19]Acts 2:47.
[20]Acts 2:11.
[21]John 17:21; 1 John 4:12–15.
[22]Matt. 2:11; 4:9; 8:2; 28:9; Rev. 19:10.
[23]Rom. 1:9; 12:1; Rev. 7:15.

- *Relational unity* does not necessarily mean that everyone likes one another, but it does mean that people love one another and demonstrate it by being cordial, respectful, friendly, and kind in their interpersonal interactions.
- *Philosophical unity* characterizes ministry methods and style. These are house rules or ministry philosophy about how the church does things, and they are in many ways the cause of a particular and primary cultural style in a church.
- *Missional unity* concerns the objective of the church. Ultimately, the goal of everyone in the church must be to biblically glorify God in all they say and do, with the hope of seeing the nations meet God and also live to glorify him.
- *Organizational unity* is based on how things are done in the church, such as job descriptions, performance reviews, and financial policies, so that the church can be a unified good steward of the resources God has entrusted to its oversight.

6) The church is disciplined for holiness. The heart of discipline is discipleship. Leaders use Scripture to teach, correct, train, and equip Christians to be a holy people who continually grow in Christlikeness. When believers sin, they are supposed to confess and repent. If someone should fail to repent, the church and its leaders must lovingly enact biblical church discipline in hopes of bringing the sinner to repentance and a reconciled relationship with God and his people.

7) The church obeys the Great Commandment to love. The church is supposed to be a Spirit-empowered loving community that devotes itself to fellowship. God's people live together in intentional relational community to seek the well-being of one another in every way—physical, mental, spiritual, material, and emotional. This does not mean that everyone is required to be best friends with everyone else, but it does mean that people take care of each other like extended family. The people who make up the church gather regularly[24] for such things as worship, learning, the sacraments, and encouragement. But even when not gathered, the church is still

---

[24]Acts 20:7; 1 Cor. 5:4; 11:17–20; 14:23–26; Heb. 10:25.

the church. There is a Spirit-bond of belonging and mission that unites the believers wherever they are, in the same way that a family is still a family even when Dad is at work, Mom is at the store, and the kids are at school.

Not only does Scripture command Christians and churches to love, but it also tells us whom we are to love. First, we are to love God.[25] Second, we are to love our family.[26] Third, we are to conduct ourselves in such an honoring and respectful way that our church leaders find it a joy to pastor us, which is a practical way of loving them.[27] Fourth, we are to love fellow Christians.[28] Fifth, we are to love our neighbors even if our neighbor is a difficult person.[29] Sixth, we are to love strangers.[30] Seventh, we are to love even our enemies.[31]

8) The church obeys the Great Commission to evangelize and make disciples. The church is an evangelistic community where the gospel of Jesus is constantly made visible through its proclamation of the gospel, the witness of the members' lives, and its Spirit-empowered life of love. From the first day, "the Lord added to their number day by day those who were being saved"[32] because they took Jesus' command seriously: "You will receive power when the Holy Spirit has come upon you, and you will be my witnesses in Jerusalem and in all Judea and Samaria, and to the end of the earth."[33]

The church is to be an evangelistic people on mission in the world, passionate to see lost people meet Jesus Christ as Savior, God, and Lord. Any church submitting to the Holy Spirit and obedient to Scripture wants fewer divorces, addictions, thefts, and abuses and knows the only way to see that happen is to make more disciples. The church loves people and is continually and painfully aware of the devastation that is wrought in this life and in the life to come for those who are not reconciled to God. Therefore, while

[25]Matt. 6:24; 22:39.
[26]Eph. 5:25; 6:1–4; Titus 2:4.
[27]1 Tim. 5:17; Heb. 13:17.
[28]1 John 3:14.
[29]Matt. 22:39; Luke 10:30–37; Rom. 13:9–10; Gal. 5:14; James 2:8.
[30]Heb. 13:2.
[31]Matt. 5:43–45; Luke 6:32.
[32]Acts 2:47.
[33]Acts 1:8.

not imposing religion on anyone, the church of Jesus Christ is to constantly be proposing reconciliation with God to everyone.[34]

As local churches implement these characteristics of the church, it is vital that the distinction between principle and method be retained. These eight characteristics give us timeless biblical principles that are unchanging regardless of culture. Nevertheless, they also require church leaders to use timely biblical methods that are changing depending upon culture. This is the essence of what it means to be a missional church that contextualizes its ministry. Paul demonstrated this by not changing his doctrine or principles but often changing his methods, depending upon his audience. Paul explains missional contextualization in 1 Corinthians 9:19–23:

> For though I am free from all, I have made myself a servant to all, that I might win more of them. To the Jews I became as a Jew, in order to win Jews. To those under the law I became as one under the law (though not being myself under the law) that I might win those under the law. To those outside the law I became as one outside the law (not being outside the law of God but under the law of Christ) that I might win those outside the law. To the weak I became weak, that I might win the weak. I have become all things to all people, that by all means I might save some. I do it all for the sake of the gospel, that I may share with them in its blessings.

Practically, this means, for example, that it is fine for churches to meet in different kinds of buildings or outside under a tree, have services that take an hour or a whole day, and sing different songs with different instrumentation (if any), as is most fitting for each one's specific cultural context.

We have both given our lives to serving the church. We know the church is imperfect and led by imperfect people like us. But we are thoroughly convinced that the gospel of Jesus Christ through the ministry of the church is the hope of the world. And as these eight characteristics of the church are pursued by grace, we trust that the glory of God the Father

---

[34]Acts 13:43; 17:4, 17; 18:4; 19:4, 26; 26:1–28; 28:23–24; 2 Cor. 5:11, 20; Col. 1:28–29.

will be made visible through lives changed by Jesus Christ through the ministry of the Holy Spirit.

WHAT IS JESUS' RELATIONSHIP TO THE CHURCH?

Jesus' incarnation was in many ways a mission trip led and empowered by God the Holy Spirit.[35] Jesus' cross-cultural transition from heaven was starker than any missionary has ever experienced. Jesus came down from heaven to live in the sinful culture. He participated in it fully by using a language, participating in various holidays, eating food, enjoying drink, attending parties, and befriending people. Jesus identified with its brokenness to bring redemption. Still, Jesus did not condone sin, nor did he himself ever sin. Finally, Jesus sent and sends Christians on the exact same mission. Christians are to be missionaries in culture as he was.

In John's Gospel alone, Jesus told us no less than thirty-nine times that he was a missionary from heaven who came to minister incarnationally in an earthly culture.[36] In his magnificent high priestly prayer,[37] Jesus prayed that we would become neither syncretistic liberals who sin by going too far into culture and act worldly nor separatistic fundamentalists who sin by not going far enough into culture and acting pharisaically. He commands us to live in the world. We must not leave the sick and dying world in order to huddle in a safe subculture of Christian nicety. He also prayed that we would not simply go with the flow of sin and death in the culture but rather swim upstream against it by living countercultural lives like him, guided by the timeless truths of Scripture intended to be lived out by missionaries in every culture. Jesus' commands for us to be missionaries in culture as he was could not be clearer. In John 17:18 Jesus said, "As you sent me into the world, so I have sent them into the world." And in John 20:21 Jesus said, "As the Father has sent me, even so I am sending you."

The Gospels give us the story of the Spirit-empowered ministry of

---

[35]Luke 1:35, 67–79; 2:11, 25–38; 3:22; 4:14; 4:18; cf. Isa. 61:1–2.
[36]John 3:34; 4:34; 5:23, 24, 30, 36, 37, 38; 6:29, 38, 39, 44, 57; 7:16, 28, 29, 33; 8:16, 18, 26, 29, 42; 9:4; 10:36; 11:42; 12:44, 45, 49; 13:20; 14:24; 15:21; 16:5; 17:3, 8, 18, 21, 23, 25; 20:21.
[37]John 17:15–18.

Jesus Christ so we would know who he is. Acts gives us the story of the Spirit-empowered ministry of Jesus' people, the church, who worship Jesus as God and continue his mission. As the church, we follow the example of Jesus by being Spirit-filled and Spirit-led, which defines the mission of the church. This is why Luke is careful to show that the Holy Spirit descended on both Jesus[38] and the church,[39] empowering the church to continue the mission of Jesus in the world.

As we take the gospel to the world, churches, as communities of Jesus followers, will come together. It is essential that we never forget that Jesus and Jesus alone is:

- The head of the church.[40] He is supreme. He is prominent. He is preeminent.
- The apostle who plants a church.[41] There is no church that comes into existence apart from him. Apart from Jesus there is no church. Those who are caught up in the hard work of church planting must always remember that Jesus is the apostle. While we can start an organization, only he can plant a church.
- The leader who builds the church.[42] Many pastors out of foolishness and pride take on the responsibility of building the church. But it is Jesus alone who ultimately builds the church.
- The chief shepherd who rules the church.[43] The Bible is clear that Jesus alone is the senior pastor over the church and that all the other pastors and leaders are supposed to work under his leadership.
- Present with the church.[44] Jesus is the one who says, "I am with you always." In his exaltation, and through the Spirit, he is with us[45] and we are in him.[46]
- The judge of the church.[47] Jesus sometimes shuts churches down when they have become faithless or truthless. Such churches have lost

---

[38]Luke 3:21–22.
[39]Acts 2:1–4.
[40]Eph. 1:22; 4:15; 5:23.
[41]Heb. 3:1.
[42]Matt. 16:18.
[43]1 Pet. 5:4.
[44]Matt. 28:18–20.
[45]Col. 1:27.
[46]John 17:21; Rom. 8:1; 1 Cor. 1:30; 2 Cor. 5:17; Phil. 3:9.
[47]Rev. 2:5.

their love for Jesus and people, refuse to repent, and are shut down because they are doing more harm than good.

Jesus himself said that he is the vine and we are the branches.[48] What Jesus meant is that there is no Christian life for the church apart from him. There are many branches. Assemblies of God, Evangelical Free, Presbyterian, Baptist, Foursquare, and Independent churches are each one of many branches. What keeps every church alive, healthy, growing, and fruitful is an ongoing rootedness in and connectedness to the living Jesus Christ. Some churches, denominations, networks, and the like arrogantly act as if they are the branch and everyone else is a vine. However, when Jesus' teaching is humbly received, we are able to enjoy being fruitful vines and rejoice in the fruit on other branches, since we are all the same proverbial tree.

WHAT IS THE CHURCH'S GOSPEL (ACTS 2)?

The New Testament church was birthed with Peter's preaching of the gospel in Acts 2. This gospel is the means by which God's power is exercised both for and through the church. The gospel pattern of Acts 2, as well as of other Scriptures, breaks down into three aspects: (1) *revelation*, or what God did; (2) *response*, or what we do; and (3) *results*, or what God gives.[49]

Revelation: What God Did

Peter begins by affirming that Jesus fulfills the promises of a divine Messiah, God come among us, with miracles, signs, and wonders (v. 22). Next, Peter declares that Jesus died on the cross according to God's prophetic purpose (v. 23). Then he proceeds to emphasize the reality that God bodily raised Jesus from death in fulfillment of Old Testament prophecy (vv. 24–32). Peter concludes with the final acts of God exalting Jesus to

---

[48]John 15:1–8.
[49]These three organizational points are adapted from Steve Walker, pastor of Redeemer's Fellowship, Roseburg, OR. The same basic outline can be seen in Luke 24:46–47; Acts 10:39–43; 13:26–39; Rom. 4:22–25; and 1 Cor. 15:1–8.

the right hand of the Father and pouring out the Spirit in fulfillment of Old Testament prophecy (vv. 33–35).

Response: What We Do

The first thing we are to do in response to God's revelation is repent (vv. 36–38). Repentance is the Spirit-empowered acknowledgment of sin that results in a change of mind about who and what is lord in our life, what is important, and what is good and bad.[50] This is followed by a change of behavior flowing out of an internal change of values. The second response is to accept the revealed message about Jesus by Spirit-empowered faith (v. 41). Faith means taking God at his word and trusting our life and eternity to the truth of his revelation. All of this is seen in the act of baptism, which is the visible expression of our connection with the death, burial, and resurrection of Jesus through repentance and faith (vv. 38, 41).

Results: What God Gives

Peter immediately announces the gift of forgiveness of our sins, which is the result of the propitiatory death of Jesus (v. 38). This gift flows into justification, or the imputed righteousness of Jesus. Peter goes on to the second gift: the Holy Spirit and the new heart and new life of Christ (v. 38). This regeneration, or the imparted righteousness of Jesus, is for living a new life as a Christian with, like, for, to, and by the living Jesus. The third gift is membership in the body of Christ, the new community of the Spirit called the church. This community is a supernatural community where God's power and generosity are seen from miracles and supernatural signs to the sharing of possessions among the community members and giving to all in need (vv. 41–47). The fourth gift is participation in the mission of the church to join God's mission to rescue the world from sin and condemnation through the gospel (v. 47).

Tragically, many Christians have lost the understanding of the new life of the Spirit. They do not preach or live the regeneration of believers.

---

[50]Acts 26:20.

Rather than living out a joy-filled life flowing from their deepest desire to be like Jesus, they settle for being sinners saved by grace, obligated to do all they can to keep the law of God by duty rather than by delight.

Subsequently, they have not fully enjoyed the double gift of imputed righteousness, which accompanies our justification,[51] and the imparted righteousness of the indwelling Spirit, which accompanies our new heart and regeneration.[52] On the cross God did a work for us by saving us through the death of Jesus in our place for our sins; with his resurrection he conquered death, bringing us the power of his life.[53] We then see at Pentecost that God does a work in us through the Holy Spirit in our hearts for regeneration. Together, both our eternity and every step along the way can be filled with hope, joy, purpose, and passion if we see the relationship between the cross and Pentecost. The regenerating work of the Holy Spirit in the heart is the source of the Christian life and Christian church and the powerful result of the gospel doing its redemptive work.

WHO LEADS A CHURCH?

As we said above, Jesus is the head and senior pastor of the church. Because of this, church leaders must be good sheep who follow their chief shepherd, Jesus, very well before they even think about being undershepherds leading any of his sheep.

The Bible describes three offices believers hold within the church: elders-pastors, deacons, and church members. An office is a position of responsibility and authority, a trust or duty assigned by the church to a person to be performed for the common good. A ministry, on the other hand, is any function that aids the church in accomplishing its God-given marks and fulfilling its God-given purpose. An office has a permanence that extends beyond the tenure of the person holding the office. A person who holds an office has the responsibility and the authority to carry out the specific stewardship associated with that office. A church should

---

[51]Rom. 5:18.
[52]Rom. 5:19.
[53]Eph. 1:19–20; 1 Pet. 1:3.

have the three biblical offices. They are also free to have people holding these offices oversee areas of ministry (worship leader, treasurer, small group leader, usher, etc.) to meet the specific ministry requirements of that local church.

The Bible describes the office of elder-pastor or overseer as the highest office in a local church, a position charged with the responsibility of overseeing the doctrinal soundness and spiritual health of the church. There is no end of confusion over the title *pastor*. It is often used for leaders of the church who get paid for their ministry, or specifically for the preacher. Negatively, this false understanding separates pastors from elders, the biblical term for senior leaders. Worse, it is often associated with a priestly role of one ordained to perform sacraments, creating a wholly unbiblical sacramental office. The Bible uses the noun (*pastor* or *shepherd*) to refer to Jesus[54] or to a spiritual gift,[55] rather than to an office. Usually it is a verb, *to shepherd*.[56] Thus, asking for the biblical definition of the office of pastor gets us nowhere. We suggest that it is best to use the noun as synonymous with the biblical term *elder*, since the Bible uses the two interchangeably, similar to how a man is called both father and dad in reference to his one office.[57]

The duties of elders revolve around two major areas of responsibility: pastoral care[58] (including equipping Christians for ministry[59] and oversight of the church) and guiding and guarding the teaching of the church (including the preaching of God's Word when the church assembles[60]). The elders are the senior leadership team in a church and as such they bear primary responsibility for the well-being of the church's people, resources, and doctrine.

Elders lead not by abusively lording authority over the people but by serving them,[61] not by domineering but by being examples to their fellow

---

[54] John 10:1–30; Heb. 13:20; 1 Pet. 2:25; 5:4.
[55] Eph. 4:11.
[56] John 21:16; Acts 20:28; 1 Cor. 9:7; 1 Pet. 5:2.
[57] Acts 20:28; 1 Pet. 5:1–4.
[58] Acts 20:28, 35; 1 Tim. 3:5; Heb. 13:17.
[59] Eph. 4:11–16.
[60] 1 Tim. 4:14; 5:17; 2 Tim. 1:13–14; 2:2; Titus 1:9.
[61] Matt. 20:25–28.

Christians.[62] The Bible says that only men known for humble and sacrificial success in four areas should even be considered as elders-pastors.[63] First, an elder is to be a godly Christian man whose life is clearly and faithfully devoted to Jesus Christ. Second, an elder is to be a godly husband (if he is married), faithful to and a blessing for his wife. Third, an elder is to be a godly father who lovingly leads his children in the worship of God in all of life. Fourth, an elder is to be a godly man in all other areas of his life. This includes how he works his job, stewards his time, talent, and treasure, respects the other elders as a church member, serves others in ministry, and so on.

We are arguing for the complementarian view of church leadership, whereby only qualified men can occupy the office of elder-pastor (as compared to the egalitarian view, in which women can also serve in the office of elder-pastor). The office of elder and the specific functions that are unique to elders are limited to highly qualified and appointed men. Women should use the spiritual gifts and natural abilities that God has given them to their fullest extent, ministering in every way in which other non-elders do (as compared to the hierarchical view, in which women are allowed to minister only to other women and children).

It is important to note that the Bible always speaks of elders in the plural. This follows the New Testament pattern that ministry is to be done by teams so that everyone is under authority, including those in authority. While there will almost always be one man on the team of elders who is the leader of the elders, a "first among equals" elder, he does not hold a categorically different office from the other elders. This is the kind of deferential humility Peter demonstrated when, though he was the human leader of the apostles and an author of Scripture, he referred to himself as "a fellow elder."[64]

The Greek word for *deacon* simply means "servant," and beyond that title we are given little indication of what a deacon should do. When "dea-

---

[62] 1 Pet. 5:3.
[63] Acts 20:18–35; 1 Tim. 3:1–7; Titus 1:5–9; 1 Pet. 5:1–4.
[64] 1 Pet. 5:1.

con" is used in an official sense, the concept of service is united with the concept of office. Acts 6 speaks of deacons as ones appointed to official positions of leadership in service to benefit others. The motivation of the deacon is humble obedience to God and loving desire to benefit the ones served. The primary list of qualifications for deacons is found in 1 Timothy 3:8–13, and it is nearly identical to that of the elders—minus the teaching and preaching abilities. One significant difference between the two offices is that both 1 Timothy 3:11 and Romans 16:1 point to men and women alike serving as deacons, as assistant leaders under the elders helping them to lead the church.

Paul's order is elder and then deacon.[65] This supports the pattern of Acts 6, where the office of deacon likely originated, suggesting that the deacons functioned alongside the senior leaders but worked under their leadership. Elders and deacons work together like left and right hands, with male elders specializing in leading by their words and male and female deacons specializing in leading by their works.

WHAT IS CHURCH MEMBERSHIP?

Membership is also an office in the church, though many fail to recognize this reality. Church membership is not a voluntary association like membership in a country club or civic organization. Tragically, many churches seem to think membership means simply putting your name on a list that comes with a set of offering envelopes. Church membership is not for selfish people to use the church for their own agendas and felt needs. Church membership is for people who love Jesus, love the church, and want to help the church bring the love of Jesus to the world. The Bible speaks of church membership in relational terms—as members of one body and as members of the household of God—so that God's people live as a gospel community and help one another grow in Christ and reach others for Christ.[66]

Church membership is a commitment made by the member to the church and by the church to the member. It is a public mutual commitment

---

[65]Phil. 1:1; 1 Tim. 3:8, 12.
[66]Rom. 12:4–5; 1 Cor. 12:12–27; Eph. 2:18–19; 3:6; 4:25; 5:29–30.

to participation in a community of ministry and mission. Members invest their passions, service, resources, and relationships for the kingdom. They commit to a holy life characterized by integrity and confession of sin. The commitment to membership means active participation in ministry, in worship, in fellowship, and in service for the mission of the church, along with generous giving and evangelistic living.

The church commits to build, equip, strengthen, encourage, and comfort its members. The church must train and release the members to use their spiritual gifts in various ways so that they too are leading the church, behind the elders and deacons, as the priesthood of believers. Those who function as exemplary church members are then qualified to occupy the church leadership positions of deacon and elder, respectively.

To become a member of the churches we pastor, one must be a baptized believer and take a formal class in order to understand the doctrines, organization, and ministry philosophy of the church. Membership includes signing a written covenant with the elders to do such things as serve in the church, pray for the church, give to the church, read the Bible regularly, love their brothers and sisters in Christ in word and deed, respect the authority of church leaders, including submitting to discipline if necessary, attend church services, and share the gospel with others in word and deed.

At Mars Hill Church, our members also fill out an annual financial pledge, and we send out giving updates to each member. Their pledges help us to set our annual budget based on a credible estimate of what our income will be for that year. Pledges also help our members to have a plan as faithful stewards. Many would see this as an invasion of privacy, believing giving is a purely private matter. But the Bible, and especially Jesus, speaks constantly about money and financial values. We see giving as a key area of spiritual discipleship and also offer free financial coaching and budgeting help to our members.

While only members are allowed to oversee certain areas of ministry, nonmembers, including nonbelievers in many areas, are intentionally encouraged to serve throughout the church as a connecting point for community and for the gospel. This is important so that the church can act missionally by bringing people into active participation in the life of the church with the intent of seeing lost people become Christians and disconnected Christians become vitally connected to the church and also eventually become faithful church members.

WHY IS PREACHING IMPORTANT?

God created the world through preaching. We consider God's speaking to Adam a sermon, as it was the authoritative proclamation of his Word. Then, Satan also preached. He twisted God's Word and declared that God's sermon was a lie. Our first parents, Adam and Eve, believed the Serpent's sermon over God's, and sin, death, and chaos have ensued ever since. The Serpent has continued preaching through false prophets and teachers every day since.

Jesus' ministry included feeding the hungry, healing the sick, loving the outcast, and befriending the sinner, as well as bringing people to repentance and forgiveness. But we must never forget that Jesus' ministry began with and centered on preaching.[67]

When Jesus sent the Twelve on their short-term mission, he told them to preach the message of the kingdom.[68] Peter's sermon was the very first activity of the church after the Spirit came upon them.[69] The rest of Acts records the preaching and teaching ministry of the leaders of the church. Thus, preaching the gospel in its transforming fullness is a priority ministry of the church. God's mission is accompanied by various other ministries that support, supplement, and sustain the preaching of God's Word in truth with passion.

We are to preach the Word of God, the good news of what God has done, not merely good spiritual advice for better living.[70] It has the power to save and bring people to maturity.[71] The power of preaching does not

---

[67]Matt. 4:17, 23; 9:35; 11:1, 5.
[68]Matt. 10:7.
[69]Acts 2:14–36.
[70]1 Thess. 2:13; 1 Pet. 1:12, 23–25; 2 Pet. 1:19–21.
[71]1 Thess. 1:5.

come with clever stories or rhetorical devices but with the power of the Spirit[72] and the answer to prayer.[73] Preaching brings faith for hearers[74] and is spiritual food to nourish people.[75]

Paul warned that times would come when people would not tolerate preaching.[76] Unfortunately, many "progressive" churches want to re-imagine preaching and include no sermon at all. Sadly, even some well-known Christians wrongly claim that preaching is pagan and that preaching has no place in Christian church meetings.[77]

God's people have always viewed preaching as something to be done when the church gathers. Preaching is proclaiming with authority and passion the truth of God's Word. In preaching, the authority of God's Word is upheld and God's people are collectively led and taught according to the Scriptures. The willingness of Christians to sit under preaching is an act of worship, as they are humbly submitting to Scripture and the pastor, who is preaching on behalf of the elder team. Preaching is among the most essential ministries of a church because the authoritative preaching of Scripture informs and leads God's people in the rest of the church's ministries.

The Bible tells us to simply "preach the word" but does not tell us exactly how this is to be done, thereby leaving some creative freedom for preachers.[78] Expository preaching expounds upon the meaning of a particular text or passage of Scripture in the context of the book and the whole Bible. The best expository preaching goes through a book of the Bible verse by verse, bringing the original meaning, intention, or message to the lives of the people.[79] As preachers, we would encourage all

---

[72]1 Cor. 1:17–2:7; 2 Cor. 1:12; 2:17; 4:2; 1 Thess. 2:5.

[73]Eph. 6:18–20; Col. 4:3.

[74]1 Cor. 2:4–5.

[75]1 Pet. 2:2.

[76]2 Tim. 4:3–4.

[77]E.g., see Frank Viola and George Barna, *Pagan Christianity? Exploring the Roots of Our Church Practices* (Carol Stream, IL: Tyndale, 2008).

[78]2 Tim. 4:2.

[79]There are many excellent books on preaching. We recommend John Stott, *Between Two Worlds: The Challenge of Preaching Today* (Grand Rapids, MI: Eerdmans, 1994); Bryan Chapell, *Christ-Centered Preaching: Redeeming the Expository Sermon* (Grand Rapids, MI: Baker, 2006); Haddon W. Robinson, *Biblical Preaching: The Development and Delivery of Expository Messages* (Grand Rapids, MI: Baker, 2001); and Donald R. Sunukjian, *Invitation to Biblical Preaching: Proclaiming Truth with Clarity and Relevance* (Grand Rapids, MI: Kregel, 2007).

preachers to spend most of their time teaching through books of the Bible and interspersing topical sermons and sermon series as needed for variety.

A good church will always have good preaching. The preaching will be (1) biblical, focusing on what Scripture says; (2) theological, teaching what Scripture means; (3) memorable, practically speaking to the lives and culture of people; (4) transformational, leading to repentance, response, and spiritual maturity; (5) missional, explaining why this matters for the mission of God and the salvation of lost people; and (6) Christological, showing how Jesus is the hero-savior.

Faithful gospel proclamation, which began with God in Genesis, is to continue by faithful gospel preachers until the gospel is consummated in the return of Jesus, to whom all biblical preaching points.

WHAT ARE BAPTISM AND COMMUNION?

Baptism and Communion are visible presentations of the gospel performed regularly by the church. Churches in every age and culture perform these special ceremonies to celebrate the transforming reality of the gospel. Christians call them sacraments because they are visible symbols of invisible spiritual realities. We believe in the real presence of Jesus in these services, which are occasions of grace he ordained for his church when the Word is spoken and made visible.

While some faithful Christians would disagree with us, we believe that water baptism is for those Christians who have already received Spirit baptism, making them part of the church.[80] In water baptism, Christians are immersed in water, which identifies them with the death and burial of Jesus in their place for their sins. Coming up out of the water identifies them with the resurrection of Jesus for their salvation and new life empowered by the Holy Spirit. Altogether, baptism identifies a Christian with Jesus, the universal church, and the local church.

When we speak of baptism, we must remember that we are talking about more than a simple rite that people undergo. As a sacrament it is a

---

[80]Rom. 6:1–10; 1 Cor. 12:12–13; 1 Pet. 3:2. See also 1 Cor. 10:1–4; Gal. 3:27; Col. 2:12; Titus 3:5–6.

symbol of something far bigger. It is a visible declaration of the gospel of Jesus Christ. Being baptized in the name of the Father, the Son, and the Holy Spirit expresses the believer's death to sin, burial of the old life, and resurrection to a new kingdom life in Christ Jesus.

Jesus and the apostles commanded that all Christians be baptized as an initial act of discipleship.[81] In the book of Acts and in the early church, baptism is administered upon conversion.[82] Practically speaking, we think it is best that believers be baptized immediately upon credible profession of faith in Jesus.

While virtually every Christian tradition practices baptism, there are deep disagreements on what baptism means, who should be baptized, if you must be baptized to be saved, and how baptism should be administered.[83]

The second sacrament that constitutes the Christian church has several names. When calling it Communion, we emphasize the fellowship we have with God the Father and each other through Jesus. Calling it the Lord's Table emphasizes that we follow the example Jesus set at the Last Supper Passover meal he ate with his disciples. The name *Eucharist* (meaning thanksgiving) emphasizes thanksgiving and the joyful celebration of God's work for us, in us, through us, and in spite of us.

The real issue is not the name but the fourfold meaning of the sacrament itself. It is a dramatic presentation that (1) reminds us in a powerful manner of the death of Jesus Christ in our place for our sins; (2) calls Christians to put our sin to death in light of the fact that Jesus died for our sins and compels us to examine ourselves and repent of sin before partaking; (3) shows the unity of God's people around the person and work of Jesus; and (4) anticipates our participation in the marriage supper of the Lamb when his kingdom comes in its fullness.

Practically speaking, Communion is to be considered as participation in a family meal around a table rather than as a sacrifice upon an altar. Furthermore, it should be an occasion when God's loving grace impacts

---

[81] Matt. 28:19; Acts 2:38.
[82] Acts 2:38–41; 8:12, 36–38; 9:18; 10:47–48; 16:15, 33; 18:8; 19:5.
[83] Those who want to pursue these issues further can reader chapter 5 of our book *Vintage Church*.

us intensely so that the gospel takes deeper and deeper root in our lives. Understood biblically, grace is unmerited favor or God's goodwill,[84] his helpful enablement for life and service,[85] and a transformational power from the Spirit that brings blessing to us.[86] Each of these aspects of God's grace is inextricably connected to the partaking of Communion.

The sacraments are great gifts that help the church stay gospel centered, repentant, and on mission. In preaching, the gospel is spoken. In sacrament, the gospel is seen. And in discipline, the gospel is defended.

WHAT IS CHURCH DISCIPLINE?

Church discipline is one of the most misunderstood and yet most desperately needed ministries within the church. We do not believe that it is an optional ministry of the church but one required of us in Scripture for the glorifying of God, guarding of the gospel, and good of the people.

Sadly, what most people think of when they hear "church discipline" is excommunication, the final stage of the biblical process. Excommunication is what happens when discipline fails to result in repentance and reconciliation.

Biblical discipline is, first and foremost, training. To be a disciple of Jesus means to live a disciplined life and humbly receive discipline as needed. There are two major kinds of biblical discipline: formative and restorative. Formative discipline is primarily positive, instructive, and encouraging. Restorative discipline is primarily corrective.

Every person (except Jesus Christ) is a sinner, both by nature and by choice. Thus, the question is not whether people will sin against one another but rather how they will deal with that sin. Christians who sin should go through the stages of (1) conviction, the work of the Spirit and the church to recognize the sin; (2) confession, telling God and people about and taking responsibility for the sin; (3) repentance, changing one's mind and values

---

[84]John 1:16, 17; Eph. 2:8.
[85]Rom. 12:6; 1 Cor. 15:10; 2 Cor. 9:8.
[86]Rom. 6:1, 14–17; 2 Cor. 6:1ff.; Eph. 1:7; 2:5–8.

about what is really true with a resulting change of behavior; (4) restitution, restoring things to their original state or making good any loss where possible; and (5) reconciliation, the rebuilding of trust and relationship.

Sadly, while everyone sins, not everyone deals with it in this kind of manner, and the result is a need for church discipline. Discipline is the responsibility of the church body, which includes Jesus Christ and the elders, deacons, and members of the church. It cannot be overstated that when rightly done and humbly received, church discipline is good for the sinners, their victim(s), their church, and their witness to the watching world.

Each potential case of discipline is weighed on its own merits and dealt with according to the following scriptural examples:

- When a Christian sins against another Christian and it cannot be overlooked in love.[87]
- When a Christian who professes faith lives in sin without repentance.[88]
- When a Christian continually blasphemes God.[89]
- When someone encourages or promotes false doctrine.[90]
- When a Christian is a habitual doctrine debater.[91]
- When a Christian will heed only false teachers.[92]
- When a Christian is sincere but deceived.[93]
- When a teacher is in moral sin or doctrinal error.[94]
- When an elder is in moral sin or doctrinal error.[95]
- When a Christian appoints himself or herself to leadership.[96]
- When a Christian is divisive.[97]
- When a Christian is an idle busybody.[98]
- When a Christian promotes legalism.[99]
- When a Christian refuses to obey civil laws.[100]

---

[87]Prov. 19:11; Matt. 18:15–22.
[88]1 Cor. 5:1–13; 2 Cor. 2:5–11; Gal. 6:1–5.
[89]1 Tim. 1:18–20.
[90]Acts 20:25–31; Gal. 1:6–9; 1 Tim. 1:4–7; 4:1–8.
[91]2 Tim. 2:14–26.
[92]2 Tim. 4:1–5.
[93]2 Cor. 11:3–4, 13–15.
[94]James 3:1.
[95]1 Tim. 5:19–21.
[96]3 John 9–10.
[97]Titus 3:10–11.
[98]2 Thess. 3:6, 11.
[99]Gal. 5:7–15, Phil. 3:2–3.
[100]Rom. 13:1–7.

- When an alleged offended Christian seeks legal recourse.[101]
- When a Christian has repeatedly rejected counsel by a church elder.[102]
- When a Christian is not consistently in community.[103]
- When a Christian leaves the church to pursue sin or heresy.[104]

When sin has occurred, the Bible gives five steps to be followed by those who have been sinned against. Each of these steps is incredibly important, because if they are not followed the result is division in the church, which is a tragic loss since unity is gained slowly and lost quickly, and during seasons of discipline unity can be most fragile.

Perhaps one of the reasons church discipline is so unpracticed is that it is so untaught. It seems reasonable to expect that if Christians understood how to undertake church discipline practically, they would. To that end, the following five steps are offered.

Step 1: Consider the Crime

Sometimes the offense or sin is also a criminal act. If so, then the police need to be called so that we are obeying the governing authorities and their laws as Scripture states.[105]

Paul also has some things to say regarding the involvement of secular courts in Christian disputes.[106] Ours is an incredibly litigious society. Things were not much different in Paul's day, since Greece, home of the world's first democracy, had a bustling court system. The question Paul seeks to address on this issue is how a Christian should relate to the secular court.

Paul says that trivial cases should be handled within the church by appointed impartial people who love God and his justice.[107] The distinction between trivial and weighty matters in our day is marked by the distinction between civil law and criminal law, which covers such things as treason and

---

[101]1 Cor. 6:1–8.
[102]Heb. 13:17; 1 Thess. 5:12–13; 2 Thess. 3:14–15.
[103]Col. 3:16; Heb. 10:24–25.
[104]1 John 2:19.
[105]Rom. 13:1–7.
[106]1 Cor. 6:1–11.
[107]Rom. 13:1–7.

murder. Christians are welcome to pursue justice on civil matters if they believe they have been wronged and are to do so within the church, if at all possible. Criminal matters must be brought to the attention of the government.[108]

Step 2: Weigh the Offense

Someone who has been sinned against should consider whether to simply forgive the person(s) involved, overlook the sin, and let it go.[109]

It is worth stressing, however, that we cannot simply overlook an offense if doing so is motivated by our cowardice, fear of conflict, and/or lack of concern for others' sanctification. In the end, it is the glory of God, the reputation of Jesus, the well-being of the church, and the holiness of the individual that must outweigh any personal desires for a life of ease that avoids dealing with sin biblically.

Step 3: Admonish

If a sin seems too serious to overlook, we are to go to our brother or sister in private and discover the truth, and if sin is present, appeal to that person with a spirit of reconciliation to repent.[110] In this we trust God the Holy Spirit to be faithful and convict his or her conscience of sin. Furthermore, we desire that he or she would respond with confession, repentance, restitution, and reconciliation as was discussed earlier in this chapter.

In this step, those who have been offended must be careful not to ascribe guilt to others without faithfully seeking the truth about what was done or said. Hearsay and secondhand reports from one person do not qualify as a credible charge.[111]

Step 4: Reprove

If the one who has been confronted will not respond to repeated personal appeals, we are to take one or two other believers to the unrepentant one so

[108]Rom. 13:1–7.
[109]Prov. 19:11.
[110]Matt. 18:15; Rom. 15:14; 2 Cor. 5:18–21; Col. 3:16; 1 Thess. 5:14; 2 Thess. 3:14–15; Titus 3:10.
[111]Deut. 19:15; 1 Tim. 5:19.

that they too can urge the sinner to turn back to God and serve as witnesses that every effort is being made to lovingly bring the sinner to repentance.[112]

If the Christian persists in sin, we may seek the formal involvement of the church, initially by obtaining assistance from the elders, and, if necessary, the elders may inform and invite the prayers and assistance of the entire congregation. Furthermore, specific elders must be appointed to investigate the situation and work for repentance and reconciliation.[113]

Mediation and arbitration may be used at this time to help reconcile two opposing parties. Mediation means bringing another person along to help resolve conflict and explore solutions if the conflict cannot be resolved through private peacemaking.[114] Arbitrators can also be appointed to listen to both sides and render a binding decision about substantive issues.[115] In all of this, it is imperative that both sides of the dispute agree to submit to the findings of the mediator or arbitrator if the process is to be a worthwhile use of time and energy.

Step 5: Separate

If these efforts do not bring a believer to repentance and reconciliation, or if a person refuses to be reconciled, Jesus commands us to treat the person as "a Gentile and a tax collector."[116] This means we no longer have normal, casual fellowship with the believer, but instead use any encounters to bring the gospel of reconciliation to him and lovingly urge him to repent and turn back to obedience to God.[117] Although rejection and disassociation may seem harsh, these responses are simply a means by which the individual in question may come to an acknowledgment of his sin and repent. The idea

---

[112]Matt. 18:15; Eph. 5:11; 1 Tim. 5:20; 2 Tim. 4:2; Titus 1:9; 13; 2:15.
[113]Gal. 6:1.
[114]Matt. 18:16.
[115]1 Cor. 6:1–9.
[116]Matt. 18:17.
[117]In the vernacular of the time of Christ, "Gentile" and "tax collector" referred to those outside the covenant, and hence those outside the fellowship of the gathered assembly. These terms carry a connotation of betrayal rather than of a neutral non-Christian. You don't treat this person merely as a non-Christian but as someone who is collaborating with the enemy.

is not that we stop caring for him, but rather that when he sins and refuses to repent we treat him as if he were an enemy of the gospel.[118]

Church discipline is for all members of the church, including leaders. In fact, teachers are held to a much stricter standard than other Christians.[119] The Bible warns of fierce wolves that will speak twisted things,[120] false apostles,[121] false prophets,[122] and false teachers who bring destructive heresies in their deceptive words.[123] Paul tells the church not to admit a charge against an elder except on the evidence of two or three witnesses. But if the elder persists in the personal sin or if he commits a sin against the office of elder, he must be rebuked publicly[124] or removed from the office,[125] depending upon the severity of the sin.

The goal of these corrective measures is to make every effort for Christians who love their wayward brother or sister to show their overwhelming sorrow and concern in an effort to compel the sinner toward repentance and reconciliation with God and his church. The words of Romans 12:18 are important to remember. They instruct us to be at peace with everybody if we are given the chance. People who know how much they have been forgiven are to be willing to forgive everybody who earnestly repents of anything they have done.[126]

WHY SHOULD CHRISTIANS JOIN A CHURCH?

Some selfish people refuse to join a church because they do not want to learn, obey, serve, or give. Other selfish people join a church primarily to use it for their cause, which can be anything from a political or social agenda to a business endeavor.

Either way, selfish people are more takers than givers, and the more selfish people a church has, the less healthy it will be. Sadly, selfish people

---

[118]1 Cor. 5:1–11; 2 Thess. 3:6, 14; 1 Tim. 1:20; Titus 3:10.
[119]James 3:1.
[120]Acts 20:28–31.
[121]2 Cor. 11:13.
[122]1 John 4:1–4.
[123]2 Pet. 2:1–3.
[124]1 Tim. 5:19–20.
[125]1 Cor. 9:27.
[126]Luke 7:36–50; 17:3–4; Eph. 4:32; Col. 3:13.

also suffer because they fail to mature as generous stewards and humble servants like Jesus Christ.

There are ten primary reasons why a Christian should become a vitally active member of a local church.

1) Salvation means forgiveness *and* new life in the community of the Spirit on mission with Jesus. Salvation is not merely a personal relationship with Jesus that allows us to go to heaven when we die. It is also a communal relationship with the church to live on mission for Jesus' kingdom in this life. And the kingdom begins its reign in the church.

2) Being a Christian means being a Jesus follower, a disciple. His call to "follow me" means come join a group of disciples who together are the people of God. The New Testament uses collective metaphors to describe the church of Christ. They include flock,[127] temple,[128] body,[129] and family[130] or household.[131] Each of the images communicates the same big idea that God's people are to remain together. Sheep die individually but live as a flock, fed and protected by a shepherd; a building falls down if too many bricks are removed; limbs die if removed from the body; a family is destroyed if its members do not live in love together.

3) Real disciples commit to the church because they know they need the help of others to keep following Jesus. They know that fellow members will expect them to attend meetings, and they know they need this kind of incentive and accountability to strengthen their spiritual lives. They know they need to be under the loving protection of other Christians. They are humble and honest enough to know they need the exhortation, strengthening, encouragement, and comfort of other travelers following Jesus. This fact only becomes amplified for those who have the additional responsibility of a spouse, child, or grandchild, or find themselves in a tempting or trying season of life.

---

[127]John 10:11–16; Acts 20:28–29; 1 Pet. 5:2–3.
[128]1 Cor. 3:16–17; Eph. 2:21.
[129]Rom. 12:4–5; 1 Cor. 10:17; 12:12–30; Eph. 4:15–16.
[130]Gal. 6:10; Eph. 2:19; 1 Pet. 4:17.
[131]Eph. 2:19–22; 1 Tim. 3:15; 1 Pet. 2:5.

4) Paul's favorite metaphor for the church that we find in the New Testament is the body. If you are a hand in the body of Christ, then you need an arm and a head to do what the Spirit has gifted you to do. Paul's long exhortation in 1 Corinthians 12 helps us see the value of the complementary diversity of the body that makes everyone effective and fulfilled in the work of Christ. Those who care about living fruitful lives for the advancement of the gospel know that the church with all its gifted people is essential.

5) Disciples know they need to be equipped for ministry. Only in the community of other believers can we be joined together so that every part works properly. Only then will the individuals and the body build itself up in love.[132] Apart from the church, there is no way to be trained adequately to do the ministry of the church or truly live a life of love.

6) If you are wise, you know how easy it is to fall into deception apart from the protective work of wise leaders and the insightful help of other Spirit-led believers.[133] Fools will stand confidently on their own wisdom and eventually find that the power of fine arguments, smooth words, and flattery lead them astray from devotion to Christ.[134] You need elders to watch your soul, to be responsible for you before God.[135] They provide spiritual protection for you and care about your growth in Christ.

7) Jesus followers join churches because they want to be like Jesus and will risk loving others deeply. Don't ever deny the pain of this risk and naively think that truly living in community as the church with sinners is easy. Church squabbles do injure innocent people. Church leaders do disappoint when they don't live up to their calling. Other believers do betray trust and cause disillusionment. Every Christian both suffers these pains and causes others to suffer them. To love is to risk and grow through pain, and those who want to love well choose to suffer pain rather than self-protect by abandoning church.

---

[132]Eph. 4:12–16.
[133]Eph. 4:14.
[134]Acts 20:30–31; Rom. 16:17–18; 2 Cor. 11:3–4; Gal. 1:6–7; 3:1; Col. 2:4–8; 2 Thess. 2:2–5; 2 Tim. 3:6–9; 3:13; 4:3; 2 Pet. 2:1–3; 1 John 2:19–26; 4:1–4.
[135]Heb. 13:17.

8) Disciples know that though the church is imperfect, Christ calls them to strengthen it by their presence rather than criticize it in their absence. The old quip forever rings true: "If you do find the perfect church, don't join it, for then it would no longer be perfect." Spirit-led Jesus followers recognize that they are imperfect Christians working with other imperfect Christians to serve a perfect Christ. When we love and give to one another, then we grow as individuals and as the family of God.[136]

9) Christians join churches because they know it is the right thing to do. From the beginning, God said it is not good to be alone.[137] As God's Trinitarian image bearers, church community is essential and non-negotiable.

10) Jesus' heart for and commitment to the church should compel us to love and serve the church. In Ephesians 5:25 Paul says, "Christ loved the church and gave himself up for her." The context in which Paul speaks is marriage, and without overstating the analogy he is saying that the church is like Jesus' bride, whom he loves and serves despite all her faults and flaws. Those who ignore the church, criticize the church, despise the church, or even harm the church must seriously question whether they truly love Jesus and are his followers, since true Christians love and serve the church because Jesus does.

---

[136]Rom. 12:5–16; 15:5–7, 14.
[137]Gen. 2:18.

CHAPTER 11

WORSHIP: GOD TRANSFORMS

True worshipers will worship the Father in spirit and truth,
for the Father is seeking such people to worship him.

JOHN 4:23

In ancient cultures social life revolved around sanctuaries, temples, and stadiums. There, various gods and goddesses were worshiped as people gave their time, talent, and treasure as sacrifices to the adoration of their deity. Even the buildings themselves were built as acts of worship.

Today, little has changed. The temple of Ra, the sun god, has now been replaced with warm weather resorts and tanning salons where worshipers pay homage to their bronzing god. The temples of Ptah, the god of craftsmen, are today hardware stores and Craftsman tools. The Temples at Nemea, Olympia, Delphi, and Isthmia included stadiums, which have now been replaced with soccer fields, baseball parks, football stadiums, and basketball arenas where pagan fans dress up—like they always have—as birds and animals to cheer for their gods as they score points. The healing cults of Asklepios, with sanctuaries at Epidaurous and Corinth, have now been replaced with holistic health spas.

The Oracular gods often had sanctuaries near fresh water sources that we refer to as beaches, campsites, golf courses, and fishing holes. At the temple of Apollo, prophetic pronouncements about the future were given;

these have now been superseded by speculating newscasts and blogs as a sort of digital divination by which the future can be predicted. The temple of Thoth was where the god of writing and knowledge was worshiped, and he is now housed in local libraries and universities. Monthu, the god of battle, was worshiped at Armant but is now more commonly found at war and veteran monuments along with appearances in violent video games and cage fights.

Min, an early fertility deity, was worshiped at Coptos but today is present at medical fertility clinics. Hathor, the goddess of motherhood, was worshiped at Byblos in ancient days but has relocated to birthing centers. The temple of Neith in the Delta was connected to medical education, which is presently found in medical schools and research centers. The temple of Aphrodite in Corinth where sex was part of worship has now gone global with strip clubs and porn. The small shrines that filled ancient homes and required homage and financial sacrifice have long since been upgraded with home entertainment systems and high-speed Internet connections. Finally, Paul once said that our god is our stomach, and that god is worshiped by the gluttonous and obese at all-you-can-eat buffets.

Indeed, when our culture is considered through the lens of worship and idolatry, primitive ancient paganism seems far less primitive or ancient. This is because everyone everywhere is continually worshiping, and idolatry is, sadly, seen more easily when we examine other cultures rather than our own. This is because we often have too narrow an understanding of worship and do not see that idolatry empowers our sin.

WHAT IS WORSHIP?

Worship, rightly understood, begins with the doctrine of the Trinity and the doctrine of image. In his magnificent book on worship, Harold Best describes the Trinity as the uniquely Continuous Outpourer who continually pours himself out between the persons of the Godhead in unceasing communication, love, friendship, and joy.[1] It follows that humans created

---

[1] See Harold M. Best, *Unceasing Worship: Biblical Perspectives on Worship and the Arts* (Downers Grove, IL: InterVarsity, 2003), 21.

in God's image would also be unceasing worshipers as continuous outpourers. Best says:

> We were created continuously outpouring. Note that I did not say we were created *to be* continuous outpourers. Nor can I dare imply that we were created *to* worship. This would suggest that God is an incomplete person whose need for something outside himself (worship) completes his sense of himself. It might not even be safe to say that we were created *for* worship, because the inference can be drawn that worship is a capacity that can be separated out and eventually relegated to one of several categories of being. I believe it is strategically important, therefore, to say that we were created continuously outpouring—we were created in that condition, at that instant, *imago Dei*.[2]

Indeed, worship is not merely an aspect of our being but the essence of our being as God's image bearers. As a result, all of life is ceaseless worship. Practically, this means that while worship does include corporate church meetings, singing songs, and liturgical forms, it is not limited by these things, defined solely as these things, or expressed only in these things, because worship never stops. Rather, we are continually giving ourselves away or pouring ourselves out for a person, cause, experience, achievement, or status. Sadly, as the doctrine of the fall reveals, much of how we pour ourselves out and what we pour ourselves into in worship is someone or something other than the Trinitarian Creator God.

As the doctrine of image reveals, human beings are unceasing worshipers. We are not created *to worship*, but rather we are created *worshiping*. Everyone worships all the time. Atheists, agnostics, Christians, and everyone in between are unceasing worshipers. Everyone, everywhere, all the time, is always worshiping. While the object and method of worship vary, the act of worship does not.[3]

Best synthesizes his thoughts on worship, saying, "I have worked out a definition for worship that I believe covers every possible human condition.

---

[2]Ibid., 23, emphasis in original.
[3]See ibid., 17–18.

It is this: *Worship is the continuous outpouring of all that I am, all that I do and all that I can ever become in light of a chosen or choosing god.*"[4]

One of the more insightful sections of Scripture on worship is Hebrews 13:15–17, which says:

> Through him then let us continually offer up a sacrifice of praise to God, that is, the fruit of lips that acknowledge his name. Do not neglect to do good and to share what you have, for such sacrifices are pleasing to God. Obey your leaders and submit to them, for they are keeping watch over your souls, as those who will have to give an account. Let them do this with joy and not with groaning, for that would be of no advantage to you.

In this section we see that worship includes (1) praise; (2) proclamation, i.e., lips that confess his name; (3) service, which means doing good as a demonstration of the gospel to the world; (4) participation, which means sharing with others as a demonstration of grace to the world); (5) sacrifice, the giving of time, talent, and treasure; and (6) submission, i.e., respecting godly authority placed over us so that we grow in wisdom and holiness.

In light of this comprehensive overview of worship acts, we can examine our lives to see if our worship is honoring or dishonoring to God:

1) Who or what do you praise most passionately and frequently?
2) How commonly and clearly do you confess Jesus Christ in the words you speak, type, and sing?
3) Are you one who serves others with gladness in response to God's so faithfully serving you? Or are you someone who prefers to be served rather than to serve? Do you serve when it is inconvenient or unnoticed, or when you are unmotivated?
4) Are you an active participant in the life of your church and community? Do you give your time, talent, and treasure to share God's love in tangible ways with others?

---

[4]Ibid., 18, italics in original.

5) For whom or what do you sacrifice your time, health, emotion, money, and energy? What do these acts of worship reveal about what you have chosen to deify in your life?

6) Are you submissive to godly authority or do you tend to ignore or rebel against godly authority (e.g., parent, teacher, pastor, or boss)?

WHAT IS IDOLATRY?

The opposite of worship is idolatry. Every human being—at every moment of their life, today and into eternity—is unceasingly doing either the former or the latter. On this point N. T. Wright says:

> Christians are not defined by skin colour, by gender, by geographical location, or even, shockingly, by their good behaviour. Nor are they defined by the particular type of religious feelings they may have. They are defined in terms of *the god they worship*. That's why we say the Creed at the heart of our regular liturgies: we are defined as the people who believe in this god. All other definitions of the church are open to distortion. We need theology, we need doctrine, because if we don't have it something else will come in to take its place. And any other defining marks of the church will move us in the direction of idolatry.[5]

Worship is a biblically faithful understanding of God combined with a biblically faithful response to him. Conversely, idolatry is an unbiblical, unfaithful understanding of God, and/or an unbiblical, unfaithful response to him. David Powlison goes so far as to say, "Idolatry is by far the most frequently discussed problem in the Scriptures."[6]

Underlying idolatry is the lie. In John 8:44 Jesus describes Satan as "the father of lies." The lie in its various forms says that you are god, you can become a god, you are a part of god, you are worthy of worship as a god, you can be the source of your life's identity and meaning, you can

---

[5]N. T. Wright, *For All God's Worth: True Worship and the Calling of the Church* (Grand Rapids, MI: Eerdmans, 1997), 28.

[6]David Powlison, "Idols of the Heart and 'Vanity Fair,'" *The Journal of Biblical Counseling* vol. 13 (Winter 1995): 35. Also available here: http://www.greentreewebster.org/Articles/Idols%20of%20the%20 Heart%20(Powlison).pdf.

transform yourself, and you can transform the world and its sin problem as a sort of hero/savior. The answer, therefore, is not to look outward to God for identity, meaning, insight, and salvation. Rather, the answer is to look inward to self for identity, meaning, insight, and personal liberation. The answer, the lie says, is to be found in self rather than in a creator God who is separate from me and rules over me. Helpful in this inward process are such things as drugs, trances, yoga, meditation, self-esteem, self-actualization, self-improvement, and self-help, all of which allow a person to go inward for peace, harmony, and enlightenment, it is said, by enabling him or her to experience oneness with the divine consciousness.

This explains why ancient non-Christian spiritual practices are becoming increasingly popular. For example, Wicca and other ancient pagan religious practices, even demonic spirituality, are being promulgated and networked online and are incorporated into the teachings of spiritual gurus such as Deepak Chopra and Oprah and the pagan spiritual leaders she endorses, such as Marianne Williamson and Eckhart Tolle.[7] Sadly, some of this is even finding its way into "Christian" worship practices under the guise of ancient-future worship. Just because a practice is ancient does not mean it is Christian. The Bible warns us against adopting pagan worship practices[8] and commands us to test the spirits.[9] So we examine the source and symbolism of proposed practices. One pagan example is circular prayer labyrinths, where the symbolism is often one walking inward on oneself rather than outward in repentance toward God. This worship is antithetical to the gospel, which commands us to turn to God for our hope and help.

Echoing Jesus, Paul examines worship and idolatry brilliantly in Romans 1:18–32 by contrasting the lie of idolatry with the truth of worship. His thesis statement on all this is Romans 1:25, which speaks of idolaters who "exchanged the truth about God for a lie and worshiped and served the creature rather than the Creator, who is blessed forever! Amen."[10]

---

[7]For one example, my debate with Deepak Chopra on ABC's *Nightline* can be found at http://www.marshillchurch.org/media/in-the-news/nightline-satan-debate.

[8]Lev. 10:1–2; Deut. 12:4; 18:10; 2 Kings 16:3.

[9]Deut. 13:1–11; Matt. 7:15–16; 1 Thess. 5:21; 1 John 4:1–4.

[10]Peter Jones has spent a great deal of his time explaining this issue to me (Mark). Jones is one of the leading experts in the world on paganism, and much of what ensues in this section has been gleaned from time

The truth is what we will call *two-ism*. Two-ism is the biblical doctrine that the Creator and creation are separate and that creation is subject to the Creator. Visually, you can think of this in terms of two circles with one being God the creator and the other containing all of his creation (see Chart 11.1).

CHART 11.1

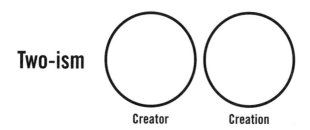

Two-ism

Creator   **Creation**

The lie is what we will call *one-ism*. One-ism is the pagan and idolatrous doctrine that there is no distinction between Creator and creation, and/or a denial that there is a Creator. The popular word for this notion is *monism*. Practically, one-ism is the eradication of boundaries and differences to bring opposites together as one. The materialistic form of one-ism is atheism. Spiritual one-ism is also often called New Age, New Spirituality, or Integrative Spirituality. According to spiritual one-ism, the universe is a living organism with a spiritual force present within everything. Thus, everything is interconnected by the life force or the world soul. This life force manifests as spiritual beings (Christians realize these are demons) that manipulate the course of world events. These spirits can be influenced to serve people by using the ancient magical arts. Humans possess divine power unlimited by any deity. Consciousness can be altered through the practice of rite and ritual. Magic is the manipulation of objects, substances, spirit entities, and minds, including humans and demons, by word (ritual, incantations, curses, spells, etc.) and objects (charms, amu-

---

with him, for which I am very thankful. His thoughts on one-ism can be found at http://www.theresurgence. com/peter_jones_2008-01-08_audio_walking_in_the_land_of_blur and http://www.theresurgence.com/ peter_jones_2008-01-08_video_ walking_in_the_land_of_blur.

lets, crystals, herbs, potions, wands, candles, etc.). Visually, you can think of this in terms of one circle in which everything is contained and interconnected as one (see Chart 11.2).

CHART 11.2

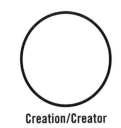

One-ism

Creation/Creator

Often, the circle itself serves as the defining symbol of pagan idolatry. This includes the yantra circle used for Hindu worship, the mandala circle of dharma and Dharmacakra used for Buddhist and Taoist worship, the sun cross used by Wiccans (who also gather in a circle), and Native American medicine wheels, dream catchers, and drum circles. A well-known expression of one-ism is found in the popular song from *The Lion King* that speaks of "the circle of life."

As a worldview, one-ism is antithetical to Christian two-ism because it seeks to place everything in the one circle.

1) There is no distinction between God the creator and creation. This results in pantheism and panentheism, which even some young "Christian" pastors are advocating.[11]

2) There is no distinction between God and mankind. This results in a spirituality that does not look humbly out to God for salvation, but rather arrogantly looks in to self for enlightenment.

3) There is no distinction between good and evil. This results in the claim that all we have are perspectives, opinions, and culturally embedded

---

[11]E.g., see Doug Pagitt, "The Emerging Church and Embodied Theology," in *Listening to the Beliefs of Emerging Churches*, ed. Robert Webber (Grand Rapids, MI: Zondervan, 2007), 142; Doug Pagitt, *A Christianity Worth Believing: Hope-filled, Open-armed, Alive-and-Well Faith for the Left Out, Left Behind, and Let Down in Us All* (San Francisco: Jossey-Bass, 2008), 194–95, 226; and Spencer Burke and Barry Taylor, *A Heretic's Guide to Eternity* (San Francisco: Jossey-Bass, 2006), 195.

"values"; there are no timeless moral truths that apply to all peoples, times, and places because all that is left is situational ethics. Furthermore, there is no distinction between angels and demons because all spirits and spiritualities are considered only good.

4) There is no distinction between mankind and animals. This results in radical animal rights activism, people referring to their pet as their "baby," and, in some cities, a disdain for children but a love for animals expressed as doggie spas, doggie day cares, and legislation to allow animals to eat in restaurants with their owners.

5) There is no distinction between mankind and creation. This results in radical environmentalism that moves beyond stewarding creation to deifying creation as our "Mother Earth" and an opposition to cultivating creation for human life and culture.

6) There is no distinction between men and women; gender is reduced to asexual androgyny. This results in lesbianism, transgenderism, homosexuality, cross-dressing, and the like, which Romans 1 says is the logical conclusion of idolatry.

7) There is no distinction between religions. The result is a vague pagan spirituality that believes the answers to all the world's problems are religious and spiritual in nature and can only be overcome by all religions worshiping together as one. Subsequently, a Christian who makes distinctions (such as between God and man, Jesus and Satan, angels and demons, heaven and hell, man and animals, holiness and sin, the Bible and other texts, male and female, heterosexuality and homosexuality, truth and error, good and evil) is considered a fundamental threat to the utopian world of peace, love, and oneness.

While idolatry is manifested externally, it originates internally. This is first revealed in Ezekiel 14:1–8 as God rebukes the elders of Israel who "have taken their idols into their hearts." Indeed, before people see an idol with their eyes, hold it with their hands, or speak of it with their lips, they have taken it into their heart. What this means is that they have violated the first two of the Ten Commandments, choosing something as a functional god they long for in their heart and then worshiping it by their words and deeds.

Martin Luther's insights on idolatry—that idolatry begins in the heart of the worshiper—are among the most perceptive the world has ever known. Luther says:

> Many a one thinks that he has God and everything in abundance when he has money and, possessions; he trusts in them and boasts of them with such firmness and assurance as to care for no one. Lo, such a man also has a god, Mammon by name, i.e., money and possessions, on which he sets all his heart, and which is also the most common idol on earth. . . . So, too, whoever trusts and boasts that he possesses great skill, prudence, power, favor, friendship, and honor has also a god, but not this true and only God. . . . Therefore I repeat that the chief explanation of this point is that to have a god is to have something in which the heart entirely trusts. . . . Thus it is with all idolatry; for it consists not merely in erecting an image and worshiping it, but rather in the heart. . . . Ask and examine your heart diligently, and you will find whether it cleaves to God alone or not. If you have a heart that can expect of Him nothing but what is good, especially in want and distress, and that, moreover, renounces and forsakes everything that is not God, then you have the only true God. If, on the contrary, it cleaves to anything else, of which it expects more good and help than of God, and does not take refuge in Him, but in adversity flees from Him, then you have an idol, another god.[12]

For those wanting to avoid idolatry, the following insights might be helpful. Be careful of making a good thing, such as marriage, sex, children, health, success, or financial stability, an ultimate thing, or what Jesus called our "treasure." Avoid participating in any religious community where the clear truth-claims of Scripture are ignored while contemplative and mystical practices are favored simply for their spiritual experience. Be careful of any church or ministry wherein acts of mercy and environmental steward-

---

[12]Martin Luther, "The Large Catechism," in *The Book of Concord* (St. Louis: Concordia, 1921), 3.5–28, http://www.bookofconcord.org/lc-3-tencommandments.php.

ship are devoid of a theology of the cross and wind up being little more than the worship of created people and things. And be careful not to worship a good thing as a god thing for that is a bad thing.

HOW DOES IDOLATRY HARM INDIVIDUALS AND SOCIETIES?

We were created to worship God and make culture in which God is worshiped in all of life. Subsequently, when idolatry is committed, all of life is implicated, damaging individuals and societies. This reality negates the popular myth that idolatry is not damaging, or that it is merely a personal matter that does not implicate society at large, as if we were each isolated individuals not affected by or affecting others.

First, idolatry harms the individuals who participate in it. Commenting on Danish philosopher Søren Kierkegaard's 1849 book *The Sickness Unto Death*, Tim Keller says:

> Sin is the despairing refusal to find your deepest identity in your relationship and service to God. Sin is seeking to become oneself, to get an identity apart from him. . . . Most people think of sin primarily as "breaking divine rules," but Kierkegaard knows that the very first of the Ten Commandments is to "have no other gods before me." So, according to the Bible, the primary way to define sin is not just the doing of bad things, but the making of good things into *ultimate* things. It is seeking to establish a sense of self by making something else more central to your significance, purpose, and happiness than your relationship to God.[13]

Whatever we base our identity and value on becomes "deified"; this object of worship then determines what we hold in glory and live for. If that object is anything other than God, we are idolaters worshiping created things. For most people, their proverbial "tell" happens when they introduce themselves: they first say their name and then say something to the effect of "I am a [blank]." How they fill in the blank (e.g., education,

---

[13]Tim Keller, *The Reason for God: Belief in an Age of Skepticism* (New York: Penguin, 2008), 162, emphasis in original.

vocation, number of children, neighborhood they live in) often reveals what they have deified and are building their life on.

The ensuing problem is that our marriage, children, appearance, wealth, success, career, religious performance, political party, cause, loving relationship, possession, hobby, pleasure, status, and power crumble under the weight of being god to us. Regarding the instability of an identity based upon anything other than Jesus Christ's saving work to claim us as his own, Keller says:

> If anything threatens your identity you will not just be anxious but paralyzed with fear. If you lose your identity through the failings of someone else you will not just be resentful, but locked into bitterness. If you lose it through your own failings, you will hate or despise yourself as a failure as long as you live. Only if your identity is built on God and his love, says Kierkegaard, can you have a self that can venture anything, face anything. . . . An identity not based on God also leads inevitably to deep forms of addiction. When we turn good things into ultimate things, we are, as it were, spiritually addicted. If we take our meaning in life from our family, our work, a cause, or some achievement other than God, they enslave us. We have to have them.[14]

As God's image bearers we will have a true, lasting, deep, satisfying, and sufficiently rooted identity only in God's love. Keller says:

> Remember this—if you don't live for Jesus you will live for something else. If you live for career and you don't do well it may punish you all of your life, and you will feel like a failure. If you live for your children and they don't turn out all right you could be absolutely in torment because you feel worthless as a person.
>
> If Jesus is your center and Lord and you fail him, he will forgive you. Your career can't die for your sins. You might say, "If I were a Christian I'd be going around pursued by guilt all the time!" But we *all* are being pursued by guilt because we must have an identity and there must be *some* standard to live up to by which we get that identity.

---

[14]Ibid., 165.

Whatever you base your life on—you have to live up to *that*. Jesus is the one Lord you can live for who died for you—one who breathed his last for you. Does that sound oppressive?[15]

This explains why those whose idol is beauty become frantic to maintain their appearance, even if it should compel them toward eating disorders, abuse of cosmetic surgery, and panic as they age. Similarly, this helps to explain why those who are the richest and most famous among us struggle with substance abuse, depression, and even suicidal longings.

Second, idolatry harms the societies in which it is practiced to the degree it is practiced. In his book *Idols for Destruction*, Herbert Schlossberg surveys the various idols of modern life and thought.[16] According to Schlossberg, the chief errors of our time stem from attempts to deify various aspects of creation: history, nature, humanity, economics, and political power. Only affirmation and application of the Creator-creature distinction can point the way out. The issues, then, are essentially religious and moral; we will not escape our dilemmas by some new form of political organization or a new economic system.

Schlossberg is emphatic to point out that just because a culture turns away from God, it still turns toward something to replace God:

Western society, in turning away from Christian faith, has turned to other things. This process is commonly called secularization, but that conveys only the negative aspect. The word connotes the turning away from the worship of God while ignoring the fact that something is being turned *to* in its place.[17]

One of the great evils of idolatry is that if we idolize, we must also demonize, as Jonathan Edwards rightly taught in *The Nature of True Virtue*. Tim Keller reminds us that if we idolize our race, we must demonize other

---

[15]Ibid., 172, emphases in original.
[16]Herbert Schlossberg, *Idols for Destruction: The Conflict of Christian Faith and American Culture* (Wheaton, IL: Crossway, 1993).
[17]Ibid., 6, emphases in original.

races.[18] If we idolize our gender, we must demonize the other gender. If we idolize our nation, we must demonize other nations. If we idolize our political party, we must demonize other political parties. If we idolize our socioeconomic class, we must demonize other classes. If we idolize our family, we must demonize other families. If we idolize our theological system, we must demonize other theological systems. If we idolize our church, we must demonize other churches. This explains the great polarities and acrimonies that plague every society. If something other than God's loving grace is the source of our identity and value, we must invariably defend our idol by treating everyone and everything who may call our idol into question as an enemy to be demonized so that we can feel superior to other people and safe with our idol.

Some people are aware of this fact and idolize tolerance and diversity, as if they were more righteous because of their open-mindedness. However, even those who idolize tolerance and diversity must demonize those they deem to be intolerant of certain diversities. Simply stated, everyone who idolizes also demonizes and in so doing is a hypocrite contributing to the tearing of a social fabric of love, peace, and kindness they purport to be serving.

WHAT IS REQUIRED IN CORPORATE CHURCH WORSHIP?

We have established that God alone is to be worshiped. We will now examine how the church is supposed to be a countercultural kingdom community that worships God alone and helps people to see and smash their idols.

God's people gather for corporate worship (what Harold Best calls "mutual indwelling") in a way that is somewhat akin to the Trinity. Best describes what this corporate worship looks like:

> Mutual indwelling demands company. Continuous outpouring demands fellowship. The corporate assembly is where love and mutual indwelling congregate; it is where believers have each other within eye- and earshot, within kindly embrace. If there were no such things as church

---

[18]Keller, *The Reason for God*, 168–69.

buildings and regularly scheduled services, Christians would, out of necessity, seek each other out for the sheer pleasure of finding Christ in each other, hearing different stories about his work in them, enjoying the ordinary and the exceptional, and perhaps only then gathering around what we call a liturgy. In such a gathering there would be little need at some point to say, "Now let us worship," because no one would be able to locate the dividing line between "now" and "always."[19]

The mutual indwelling that God's people enjoy in corporate worship is essential to our growth personally, joy collectively, and witness culturally. God's people gather because, in the depths of their regenerated nature, the Holy Spirit gives them deep desires to worship God with his people. We want to see God's people, we want to hear of God's work in their lives, we want to know of ways we can lovingly serve them, and we want to be part of something bigger than ourselves that reaches beyond the mundane details of life and connects us all together despite our differences in age, race, gender, and income to seek and celebrate evidences of God's grace.

Regarding how God is to be worshiped, God must be worshiped as he wishes, not as we wish. The Bible is clear that God is to be worshiped in ways and forms that he deems acceptable. This explains why God judges those who seek to worship him with either sinful forms externally[20] or sinful hearts internally.[21] This is incredibly important. Some churches care more about what is in people's hearts than about what they do in their lives, whereas others are more concerned about doing things the "right" way and care little about the motivations behind those actions. When it comes to worship, which is all of life, the God of the Bible cares about both what we do and why we do it. We first see this, for example, in Genesis 4 where Cain and Abel bring their worship offerings to God and while what is in their hands is acceptable, Cain's offering is rejected because what is in his heart is unacceptable to God—he was jealous of his brother.[22]

[19]Best, *Unceasing Worship*, 62.
[20]Lev. 10:1–2; Isa. 1:11–17; Jer. 7:9–10; Ezekiel 8–9.
[21]Genesis 4; Isa. 1:11–17; Jer. 7:9–10; Mic. 6:6–8.
[22]1 John 3:12.

A biblically informed Christian definition of worship includes both adoration and action. John Frame says:

> In Scripture, there are two groups of Hebrew and Greek terms that are translated "worship." The first group refers to "labor" or "service." . . . The second group of terms means literally "bowing" or "bending the knee," hence "paying homage, honoring the worth of someone else." The English term *worship*, from *worth*, has the same connotation.
>
> From the first group of terms we may conclude that worship is *active*. It is something we *do*, a *verb*. . . . From the second group of terms, we learn that worship is honoring someone superior to ourselves.[23]

Our worship also includes what we do as Christians when we scatter for action[24] and gather for adoration.[25] D. A. Carson has said, "We cannot imagine that the church gathers for worship on Sunday morning if by this we mean that we then engage in something that we have not been engaging in the rest of the week. New-covenant worship terminology prescribes *constant* 'worship.'"[26]

The New Testament is clear that God's people are to regularly gather for corporate worship. This is apparent by the frequent use of the Greek word *ekklesia*, which simply means "gathered assembly of God's people." Likewise, Hebrews 10:24–25 commands, "Let us consider how to stir up one another to love and good works, not neglecting to meet together, as is the habit of some, but encouraging one another." When God's people gather for corporate worship, church leaders must ensure that the methods they employ align with six biblical principles for worship.

1) Corporate worship is to be God-centered.[27] Simply, worship is not an occasion for us to hear sermons about us, sing songs about us, or focus on how to make ourselves feel happily inspired. Since we are prone

---

[23]John M. Frame, *Worship in Spirit and Truth: A Refreshing Study of the Principles and Practice of Biblical Worship* (Phillipsburg, NJ: P&R, 1996), 1–2, emphases in original.
[24]1 Cor. 10:31.
[25]Heb. 10:24–25.
[26]D. A. Carson, "Worship under the Word," in *Worship by the Book*, ed. D. A. Carson (Grand Rapids, MI: Zondervan, 2002), 24, emphasis in original.
[27]Matt. 4:8–10.

to worship ourselves as idols, corporate worship is an important occasion to redirect our worship back to God.

2) Corporate worship is to be intelligible.[28] This means that not only is the service conducted in the known language of the hearers but also that technical doctrinal terms are explained so that everyone understands what is being said and sung. This also means that the pastor should not seek to impress the congregation with his vast knowledge of Greek and Hebrew terms but, as John Calvin and other Reformers argued, love his people by speaking to them plainly; the pastor should want the people to be impressed with Jesus Christ rather than with himself.

3) Corporate worship is to be seeker sensible.[29] Because there are non-Christians present in corporate worship meetings, people leading those meetings need to be hospitable to non-Christians. This includes the preacher presenting the gospel to the non-Christians, someone explaining why the church meetings have certain elements such as Communion or singing, and explaining Christian terms in a way that allows the non-Christian to understand what the Bible says. This does not mean that the entire service is to be seeker sensitive and designed mainly as an evangelistic rally but that a sincere effort is made to help non-Christians understand and experience the gospel.

4) Corporate worship is to be unselfish.[30] If people want to express their personal response to God in a way that draws undue attention to them and distracts others from responding to God, then they should do that kind of thing at home in private, because the meeting is for corporate response to God, not just individual response. In worship, God gives to his people truth, love, hope, and the like, and those who distract others from receiving what God has for them and from focusing on God need to be rebuked so that they may mature and learn to consider others more highly than themselves, as Scripture says.

5) Corporate worship is to be orderly.[31] While the Bible does not pre-

---

[28] 1 Cor. 14:1–12.
[29] 1 Cor. 14:20–25.
[30] 1 Cor. 14:26.
[31] 1 Cor. 14:40.

scribe or describe any church service order, it is important that such meetings actually function with enough administrative foresight to be useful and not frustrating and distracting for the worshipers. While no church is perfect, nor is the goal of corporate worship meetings an impressive performance, musicians who cannot keep time, singers who cannot sing, audio speakers with continual feedback, long awkward pauses because no one knows what is happening next, and people speaking in tongues or prophesying out of turn in a way that the Bible forbids all distract people from being able to focus on God and, furthermore, falsely portray God as chaotic.

6) Corporate worship is to be missional.[32] Human beings are, as God's image bearers, culture makers, receivers, and interpreters. Subsequently, it is nonsensical for Christians to ignore culture or assume that Christianity is in itself a culture that exists completely separated from the cultures in which the church exists. To be missional, a church meeting has to fit the culture it is in rather than being a subculture imported from another time or place. This does not mean that older traditions (e.g., hymns, creeds) are not used, but that they are used because they contribute to informing faithful worship of God rather than perpetuating a dated form that is no longer best for ministry. Such methodology is actually *methodolatry.* Still, this must be done with great theological reflection so as not to turn artistic expression and music into idols.

If someone is alive, they are cultural. Furthermore, culture, in general, and creativity and the arts, in particular, are expressions of our worship and do not lead us into worship. When such things as the arts and music are used to lead God's people into worship, the understanding that we are continually worshiping has been lost and we have supplanted the leading of the Holy Spirit with music and the arts. Such a move is pagan because music becomes mediatorial in a way that only Jesus Christ is supposed to be.[33] This kind of pagan thinking is commonly articulated following corporate worship services when people say things like, "The music really led me into God's presence," or "I could not worship well because of the music."

---

[32] 1 Cor. 9:19–23.
[33] 1 Tim. 2:15.

When God's people gather, the church leaders are also required to ensure that what the Bible commands for worship is actually done. There are certain elements that Scripture prescribes for corporate worship services of the church. Many theologians refer to these as the elements of corporate worship, and they include the following:

1) Preaching[34]
2) Sacraments of baptism and the Lord's Table[35]
3) Prayer[36]
4) Reading Scripture[37]
5) Financial giving[38]
6) Singing and music[39]

God in his great wisdom has given clear principles and practices to guide the corporate worship of his people. However, he has not given his people clear methods or an order of service. There is no clear prescription of an entire worship service anywhere in Scripture, and there is no record of any early church worship service.[40]

Therefore, while God is very clear on the principles and practices to govern corporate worship, he has left it up to church leaders led by the Holy Spirit to determine the methods and service order used to implement them. This means that, for example, what kind of music is sung, in what order the elements are arranged, how Communion is administered, and the like, can and should vary from culture to culture and church to church because God provides just such tethered freedom for his people.

However, this freedom does not include the freedom to sin and do what God forbids in the name of worship. An Old Testament example is found in Deuteronomy 12:4, where God points to how other religions worship their demon gods and commands, "You shall not worship the LORD your

---

[34]2 Tim. 4:2.
[35]Matt. 28:19; 1 Cor. 11:17–34.
[36]1 Tim. 2:1.
[37]1 Tim. 4:13.
[38]2 Corinthians 8–9.
[39]Col. 3:16.
[40]See Carson, "Worship under the Word," 21–22, and Frame, *Worship in Spirit and Truth*, 67.

God in that way." Another Old Testament example is found in the second commandment,[41] which forbids idolatry—that is, the worship of any created thing, or seeking to reduce God to something that is made.

A timely New Testament example is found in 1 Corinthians 10:14–22, where God through Paul forbids Christians from worshiping with members of other religions, because to do so is to entertain demons. In our day, this means that while Christians should have evangelistic interfaith friendships with members of other religions, we must never do such things as pray or sing with members of other religions because they worship different and false gods.

HOW DO WE BECOME LIKE WHAT WE WORSHIP?

In his book *We Become What We Worship*, G. K. Beale states, "What people revere, they resemble, either for ruin or restoration."[42] Because we are created in the image of God, everyone is always, without exception, reflecting either God or a god. If we do not reflect our Creator to our restoration then we will reflect creation to our ruin.

This explains why one of the recurrent themes in the Bible is that idols are deaf, mute, and blind, and so are idol worshipers who do not hear from God, speak to God, or spiritually see God. Perhaps the most legendary account of idolatry in all of Scripture is the worship of the golden calf in Exodus 32. There, Israel is portrayed mockingly as rebellious cattle because they worshiped a calf and thus became like it. Just like a stubborn cow that refuses to go in the right direction, idolatrous Israel is "stiffnecked."[43]

Idolatry began with our first father, Adam. Because Adam was committed to something over God, namely himself, he was guilty of idolatry. Therefore, Adam set in motion a course of history in which the most common created thing we worship in idolatry is ourselves; we live for ourselves and our perceived glory, which is actually our shame, in priority over God.

---

[41]Ex. 20:4–6.
[42]G. K. Beale, *We Become What We Worship: A Biblical Theology of Idolatry* (Downers Grove, IL: IVP Academic, 2008), 16.
[43]Ex. 32:9; 33:3, 5; 34:9; Deut. 9:6, 13; 10:16; 31:27.

In the New Testament Gospels, the idol revered by the Jews and renounced by Jesus is religion. Even though there are not many explicit references to Jewish idol worship in the Gospels, Beale argues that it is clear that the generation of Jews at the time of Christ were at least as sinful as their spiritual forefathers: "The Jewish nation took pride in the fact that they were not like the nations who bowed down to stone and wooden images. Yet what is also clear is that the majority of the Israelite nation were at least as sinful as their forbearers, especially because they crucified the Son of God (Matt. 23:29–38)."[44] Israel worshiped their dead tradition rather than the living God according to his living Word.

Moving on to the book of Acts, Luke presents the fact that the temple actually became an idol for theocratic Israel. Jesus exposed this idolatry when he said he would destroy the temple. Rather than letting Jesus destroy the temple, the religious leaders chose instead to destroy Jesus. They preferred the temple as their place of meeting with God and presence of God over God himself in their midst. Subsequently, God had the temple destroyed in AD 70.

Similarly, in our own day religious people continue in various idolatries when they elevate their denomination, church building, liturgical order, Bible translation, worship music style, pastor, theological system, favorite author, or ministry program to where it is a replacement mediator for Jesus, one in which their faith rests to keep them close to God. This also explains why any change to the tradition of a religious person is met with such hostility—people tend to cling to their idols, including their church buildings, which are worshiped as sacred, just as the temple was.

Like the Jews in Jesus' day, Christians must be continually aware of their religious idols. Religious idols include truth, gifts, and morality.[45] These are things people trust in addition to Jesus Christ for their salvation,

---

[44]Beale, *We Become What We Worship*, 162.
[45]These categories are taken from Tim Keller's session, "The Grand Demythologizer: The Gospel and Idolatry (Acts 19:21–41)," at the Gospel Coalition 2009 National Conference, April 21, 2009. The audio and video of his session are available here: http://www.thegospelcoalition.org/resources/a/The-Grand-Demythologizer-The-Gospel-and-Idolatry.

not unlike the Judaizers who added circumcision to the gospel and were rebuked by Paul in Galatians as heretics preaching a false gospel.

Truth idolatry is perhaps most common among those who are most committed to sound doctrine and biblical study. These people are prone to think that they are saved because of the rightness of their belief rather than the simple fact that Jesus died for them. Religious people who idolize truth are often guilty of the rankest sense of superiority. They continually enjoy sarcastically making fun of their opponents and find great pleasure on the Internet, where to be famous generally means you have to be a truth idolater who feeds the idolatry of religious mockers for whom their ideology has become their idolatry.

Gift idolatry is perhaps most common among those most gifted and capable in ministry service who mistake spiritual gifts for spiritual maturity and spiritual fruit. These people commonly think that they are saved because of the great gifts they possess and that any ministry they have accomplished—and subsequently their faith—rests more on the fact that God is using them than that Jesus died for them. Sadly, this is common among Bible preachers who have made their pulpit into an idol where they go for identity and joy. They seek the approval of their hearers who cheer them on, and eventually the pastor whose idol is preaching becomes the idol of his listening flock, whose devotion to him is nearly god-like, and he becomes virtually sinless in their eyes.

Morality idolatry is perhaps most common among the most well-behaved and decent religious people. Often these people think that they are saved because they have lived a decently moral and good life of devotion and obedience rather than seeing themselves as sinners by nature whose sin is serious enough to require Jesus' atoning death. Such people are much like the older brother in the story of the prodigal son—they are offended when grace is given to repentant sinners because it is undeserved. Their attitude in such moments reveals their idol of self-performance; their ultimate trust resides in their performance and not in Jesus.

One of the lengthiest treatments of idolatry in all the New Testament is found in 1 Corinthians 10, where Paul describes idolatry as participation with demons that leads to all kinds of evil, including gluttony, drunkenness, sexual sin, and grumbling. Indeed, the more we commit ourselves to our idol, the more we become one with it and increasingly like it, to our destruction. Furthermore, as 1 Corinthians 10 makes clear, our idolatry also strains our relationships with fellow Christians, gives a false witness to non-Christians, and causes others to be tempted to join us in idolatrous sin. Subsequently, idolatry damages every category of relationship we have and is a deadly cancer in a church body and in society as a whole.

Beale concludes his biblical survey of idolatry in the book of Revelation, noting how those who worship idols are referred to as "earth dwellers."[46] According to Beale:

> [The] earth dwellers [in Revelation] cannot look beyond this earth for their security, which means that they trust in some part of the creation instead of the Creator for their ultimate welfare. Thus people are called "earth dwellers" because this expresses the object of their trust and perhaps of their very being, in that they have become part of the earthly system in which they find security—they have become like it. Because they commit themselves to some aspect of the earth, they become earthy and come to be known as "earth dwellers."[47]

Lastly, Christians must never forget that they too are prone to the same kinds of idolatry as the "earth dwellers." Religious idolatry is often the most pernicious of all. Religious idolatry uses God for health, wealth, success, and the like. In this grotesque inversion of the gospel, God is used for our glory; not only do we worship ourselves but we try to make God a worshiper of us. This kind of false gospel preaching is evident whenever Jesus is presented as the means by which idolaters can obtain their idol. Examples include promises that Jesus will make you rich, happy, healed, joyfully married, parentally successful, and the like, as if Jesus exists to aid our worship of idols.

---

[46]Rev. 8:13; 13:8, 14; 14:6–9; 17:2, 8.
[47]Beale, *We Become What We Worship*, 255.

HOW ARE REGENERATION AND WORSHIP RELATED?

Because sin is not merely doing bad things but an even deeper problem of building our identity on someone or something other than God alone, the solution to idolatry is not to change our behavior but to have a complete reorientation of our nature at the deepest level of our being, or what Jesus called being born again.

In the third chapter of John's Gospel, a man named Nicodemus came to meet with Jesus. Nicodemus was a devoutly religious man. As a Pharisee he would have committed large sections of the Hebrew Old Testament to memory and been revered as morally upright, intelligent, and among the holiest of men. In John 3:3, Jesus said to him, "Truly, truly, I say to you, unless one is born again he cannot see the kingdom of God." This confused Nicodemus, so Jesus explained that there are two births. The first birth is our physical birth that occurs when our mother's water breaks and we are brought into this world. By virtue of our first birth we are physically alive but spiritually dead. The second birth is our spiritual birth whereby God the Holy Spirit causes us to be born again so that we are both physically and spiritually alive.

Nicodemus considered himself spiritually alive by virtue of his religion, spirituality, theology, and morality. But he was likely astounded when Jesus told him plainly, "You must be born again."[48]

In this way he was much like those today who know some theological truth, have been baptized, attend religious meetings, live a moral life, believe in God, devote time to serving others, and even give some of their income to spiritual causes and organizations as members, leaders, and pastors, but who need to be born again. Why? Because they are living out of their old nature solely by their will and effort rather than out of a new nature by the power of God the Holy Spirit. John Piper says:

> What Nicodemus needs, and what you and I need, is not religion but life. The point of referring to new birth is that birth brings a new life into the world. In one sense, of course, Nicodemus is alive. He is

---

[48]John 3:7.

breathing, thinking, feeling, acting. He is a human created in God's image. But evidently, Jesus thinks he's dead. There is no spiritual life in Nicodemus. Spiritually, he is unborn. He needs life, not more religious activities or more religious zeal. He has plenty of that.[49]

Being born again is theologically summarized as the *doctrine of regeneration,* which is the biblical teaching that salvation includes both God's work for us at the cross of Jesus and in us by the Holy Spirit. To say it another way, regeneration is not a separate work of the Holy Spirit added to the saving work of Jesus; rather, it is the subjective actualization of Jesus' work.

While the word *regeneration* appears only twice in the Bible,[50] it is described in both the Old and New Testaments by a constellation of images. It is important to note that each signifies a permanent, unalterable change in someone at his or her deepest level.

The Old Testament frequently speaks of regeneration in terms of deep work in the heart, our total inner self, so that a new life flows from a new heart empowered by the Holy Spirit, just as Jesus explained to Nicodemus.[51]

Like the Old Testament, the New Testament speaks on many occasions of being born again.[52] The New Testament uses many other images to explain regeneration. These include "partakers of the divine nature,"[53] "new creation,"[54] "new man,"[55] "alive together with Christ,"[56] and "created in Christ Jesus."[57]

Three very important truths help to illuminate regeneration in the New Testament. First, regeneration is done to ill-deserving, not just undeserving, sinners.[58] Therefore, regeneration is a gift of grace, as

---

[49]John Piper, *Finally Alive: What Happens When We Are Born Again* (Fearn, Scotland: Christian Focus, 2009), 29.
[50]Matt. 19:28; Titus 3:5.
[51]Deut. 30:6; Jer. 24:7; 31:31–33; 32:39–40; Ezek. 11:19–20; 36:26–27.
[52]John 1:13; 1 Pet. 1:3, 23; 1 John 5:1.
[53]2 Pet. 1:4.
[54]2 Cor. 5:17.
[55]Eph. 2:15; 4:24.
[56]Eph. 2:5; Col. 2:13.
[57]Eph. 2:10.
[58]Eph. 2:1–5.

Titus 3:5 says: "He saved us, not because of works done by us in righteousness, but according to his own mercy, by the washing of regeneration and renewal of the Holy Spirit." Second, regeneration is something God the Holy Spirit does for us.[59] Therefore, unless God accomplishes regeneration in people, it is impossible for them to live as worshipers of God. Third, without regeneration there is no possibility of eternal life in God's kingdom.[60] Therefore, regeneration is required for someone to be a true worshiper of God.

Accompanying the new birth are ten soul-transforming, life-changing, and eternity-altering occurrences.[61]

1) Regenerated people have the Trinitarian creator God of the Bible as their new Lord, thereby displacing all other false and functional lords who had previously ruled over them.[62]

2) Regenerated people are new creations so that they are transformed at the deepest levels of their existence to begin living a new life. People being renamed upon conversion, so that Saul becomes Paul and Cephas becomes Peter, illustrates that we are new people in Christ.[63]

3) Regenerated people have a new identity from which to live their new life because their old identity no longer defines them.[64]

4) Regenerated people have a new mind that enables them to enjoy Scripture and thus to begin to think God's truthful thoughts after him.[65]

5) Regenerated people have new emotions so that they love God, fellow Christians, strangers, and even their enemies.[66]

6) Regenerated people have new desires for holiness, and no longer is their deepest appetite for sin and folly.[67]

7) Regenerated people enjoy a new community and fellowship with other Christians as members of the church.[68]

---

[59]John 3:5–8.
[60]John 3:3, 5; cf. 1 Cor. 2:6–16.
[61]For further reading, see Question 4 in our book *Religion Saves: And Nine Other Misconceptions* (Wheaton, IL: Crossway, 2009).
[62]1 John 5:18.
[63]2 Cor. 5:17; Gal. 6:15.
[64]Eph. 4:22–24.
[65]Rom. 7:22; 1 Cor. 2:14–16; 1 Pet. 2:2.
[66]1 John 4:7.
[67]Ps. 37:4; Rom. 7:4-6; Gal. 5:16–17.
[68]1 John 1:3.

8) Regenerated people live by a new power to follow God by the Holy Spirit's enabling.[69]

9) Regenerated people enjoy a new freedom to no longer tolerate, manage, excuse, or accept their sin but rather to put it to death and live free from habitually besetting sin.[70]

10) The culmination of the effects of regeneration is a new life of worship that is markedly different from how life would otherwise be.[71]

In some ways our new birth is like our physical birth. At birth babies cry, move, hunger, trust their father to protect and provide for them, enjoy human comfort, and begin to grow. Similarly, newly born-again people cry out to God in prayer, move out in new life, hunger for the Scriptures, trust God as Father, enjoy God's family the church, and begin to grow spiritually, maturing in their imaging of God. Beale explains regeneration in terms of how Christians become restored into the image of God:

> It is in Christ that people, formerly conformed to the world's image (Rom. 1:18–32), begin to be transformed into God's image (Rom. 8:28–30; 12:2; 2 Cor. 3:18; 4:4). . . . This process of transformation into the divine image will be completed at the end of history, when Christians will be resurrected and fully reflect God's image in Christ (1 Cor. 15:45–54; Phil. 3:20–21). They will be resurrected by the Spirit-imparting power of the risen Christ. Since it was the Spirit who raised Jesus from the dead (Rom. 1:4), so the Spirit of Christ will raise Christians from the dead at the end of the age. . . . The Spirit's work in people will enable them to be restored and revere the Lord and resemble his image, so that God will be glorified in and through them. [72]

Therefore, it is only through the regenerating and ongoing empowering ministry of the Holy Spirit that we can worship, until one day in our glorified resurrected state we will image God perfectly as unceasing worshipers. This is exactly what Jesus meant when he said in John 4:24, "God

---

[69]Rom. 8:4–13.
[70]Rom. 6:6; 7:6.
[71]Gal. 5:19–23.
[72]Beale, *We Become What We Worship*, 282.

is spirit, and those who worship him must worship in spirit and truth." Commenting on this verse, Andreas Köstenberger says:

> The terms "spirit" and "truth" are joined later in the expression "Spirit of truth," referring to the Holy Spirit (see 14:17; 15:26; 16:13; cf. 1 John 4:6; 5:6; see also 2 Thess. 2:13) . . . the present reference therefore seems to point John's readers ultimately to worship in the Holy Spirit. Thus, true worship is not a matter of geographical location (worship in a church building), physical posture (kneeling or standing), or following a particular liturgy or external rituals (cf. Matt. 6:5–13); it is a matter of the heart and of the Spirit (Talbert 1992: 115). As Stibbe (1993: 64) puts it, "True worship is paternal in focus (the Father), personal in origin (the Son), and pneumatic in character (the Spirit)."[73]

Because of our new hearts, worshiping God by imaging him well through the empowerment of the Holy Spirit is exactly what we want to do in our innermost depths. Speaking of the Spirit-empowered regenerated desires of the heart, Psalm 37:4 says, "Delight yourself in the LORD, and he will give you the desires of your heart." Practically, this means that as we enjoy and delight in who God is, what he has done, and what he will do for us, our regenerated hearts share in the same desires of God. Subsequently, unlike religion, which is based on fear that forces people to do what they do not want to do, regeneration is based on love and on God inviting new people to live new lives of worship, which is exactly what their new hearts want to do at the deepest level. The result is ever-growing, never-ending, ever-worshiping, passionate joy!

HOW DOES WORSHIP TRANSFORM US?

Because we worship our way into sin, ultimately we need to worship our way out.[74] As we have studied, when Christians commit sin, they do not

---

[73] Andreas J. Köstenberger, *John: Baker Exegetical Commentary on the New Testament* (Grand Rapids, MI: Baker Academic, 2004), 157.

[74] Much of what ensues in this chapter was shaped and informed by a collection of biblical counseling resources from the Christian Counseling and Educational Foundation (CCEF) at www.ccef.org, including the *Journal of Biblical Counseling*. CCEF is directly affiliated with Westminster Theological Seminary, and the contributors to the *Journal* promote biblical counseling from a distinctly Reformed, gospel-centered theological paradigm.

cease worshiping. Rather, their worship is directed away from the Creator and toward created things. Repentance is the act of turning from sin and returning to God by trusting in Jesus Christ, who alone is the perfect worshiper. This fact helps idolaters be transformed into worshipers. John had just this in mind when he summarized his entire epistle with the closing line, "Keep yourselves from idols."[75] The following examples are intended to be of some practical help in uncovering our idols so that we can smash them in repentance and worship God alone.

Following a sermon on dating, a young woman, who claimed to be a Christian but was dating, sleeping with, and living with a non-Christian, came forward for prayer. She asked me (Mark) to pray that God would save her boyfriend so they could marry and be a Christian family. I then quoted Romans 11:36–12:1 to her: "To him be glory forever. Amen. I appeal to you therefore, brothers, by the mercies of God, to present your bodies as a living sacrifice, holy and acceptable to God, which is your spiritual worship." I explained to the woman that their bed was a pagan altar and that when she lay down on it with her boyfriend, she was presenting her body as a living sacrifice to the guy as her real god and that their fornication was her idolatrous worship of a created thing, namely, her boyfriend. Thus, she was choosing the guy over Jesus as the most important person in her life, the basis of her identity, the source of her joy and love, and her hope for affection.

A young man had suffered from panic attacks for some months and the various medications he had taken were of no help. He was a newer Christian, and his family was avowedly anti-Christian and very angry that he had converted to Christianity and that he was greatly enjoying such things as church attendance, fellowship, and Bible reading. His immediate and extended family were very close, but they had been shunning him and mocking him in an effort to get him to stop practicing his faith. When that did not work, his parents cut off his college funding, which required him to start working long hours to pay his way through school. The situa-

---

[75] 1 John 5:21.

tion escalated when his parents found out he had met a Christian woman he loved and was considering pursuing marriage with her. The couple was considering attending seminary and preparing for a life of ministry together. His parents sat him down in front of the rest of the family, and he was belittled and berated for hours. It was obvious that he loved Jesus and his family and that his understandable anxiety was caused by being forced to choose between them.

I explained to him that his anxiety and subsequent panic attacks were the result of being conflicted between the fear of the Lord and the fear of man. Proverbs 29:25 says, "The fear of man lays a snare, but whoever trusts in the LORD is safe." Indeed, this man's family had set the snare he was in, as they sought to control him through the fear of man. Biblical counselor Ed Welch says:

> Fear in the biblical sense . . . includes being afraid of someone, but it extends to holding someone in awe, being controlled or mastered by people, worshipping other people, putting your trust in people, or needing people. . . . The fear of man can be summarized this way: We replace God with people. Instead of a biblically guided fear of the Lord, we fear others. . . . When we are in our teens, it is called "peer pressure." When we are older, it is called "people-pleasing." Recently, it has been called "codependency."[76]

The only way out of his panic was to fear God, as Proverbs 1:7 says: "The fear of the LORD is the beginning of knowledge." While he should not stop loving his family, praying for his family, and honoring his parents while guarding his heart from bitterness, he needs to obey God, even if that should mean disobeying his family. If he were to obey his parents, he would turn them into an idol, placing them above God as the true Lord of his life. Conversely, if he were to obey God, he would no longer be controlled by the idol of his family. Since he had been using them for everything from financial support to identity and approval over the years, releasing them as

---

[76]Edward T. Welch, *When People Are Big and God Is Small: Overcoming Peer Pressure, Codependency, and the Fear of Man* (Phillipsburg, NJ: P&R, 1997), 14.

an idol would allow him to actually stop using them and start loving them by doing and saying what was truthful and best for them without regard for their judgment of him.

A woman revealed that she had had a few abortions before becoming a Christian, marrying a godly man, and birthing their own healthy children. She explained that she had been tormented by her sin and did not how to get out of the pit of despair she was living in. With tears streaming down her face, she explained how she had confessed to God her sin of murdering her unborn children and did believe that Jesus Christ's death had paid her penalty and secured her forgiveness. I explained to her that although her sin was grievous, I did not understand why she was not enjoying forgiveness. She said it was because even though God had forgiven her, she could not forgive herself. So I explained to her that she had become her own idol, the lord and functional god of her life. In saying that Jesus had forgiven her but she could not forgive herself, she was in effect saying that she was a god above Jesus, and although her lesser God, Jesus, was forgiving, her highest god, herself, was not.

In a pastoral counseling session, a man confessed to being sexually addicted to pornography and masturbation and was guilty of committing adultery on his wife and even engaging in homosexual sex. He had been meeting with a counselor who was not a Christian and was merely trying to modify his behavior rather than smash his idol. His questions to me were all about behavior modification; he was trying to figure out how to avoid television and Internet access.

To be fair, he knew that sin leads to death and that his sin was killing him and his wife and their marriage. He meant well, but he had been pointed in the wrong direction in pursuit of a solution. I explained that while we must not tempt our flesh and that the changes he had made were likely good, they were not nearly enough, because his real issue was not the Internet but rather idolatry. What he needed was not behavior modification but worship transformation.

In his condemnation of idolatry, Paul predicted the same lifestyle that this man was living.[77] Those who fail to worship God their creator worship that which is created. This can be any created person or thing but is often the worship of the self and sex. Why? Because, of all the things God made, the human body is the apex of God's creative work.[78] This fact makes its passions and pleasures the most likely candidate for idolatrous worship. In our age, this includes an addiction to beauty, pornography, sexual sin, drunkenness, drug abuse, people-pleasing fear of man, and gluttony, as Paul said, since for some people their god is their stomach.

For this man, the real issue was that he was worshiping the created body rather than the creator God. He was therefore breaking both the first and second commandments, which led to his breaking the seventh.

Lastly, upon entering the home of an understandably tired young mother, I (Mark) heard her lament the fact that her house was not tidy. She also described how she had prayed to Jesus for the kids to be more organized and clean but that Jesus was of no help at all. As I looked around the house, it actually seemed quite clean and tidy for being occupied by young children. There were a few toys out on the floor, but that was about it. Later in our visit, she actually said, "Everything is perfect until the kids wreck it."

Her home had become her idol. Whenever her children left a toy out or spilled their juice, they were not merely sinning or making a mistake. To her, they were ruining her life and vandalizing her perfect, heavenly home. Or, to say it another way, they were not worshiping her idol. So she prayed to Jesus, asking him to turn her children into idol worshipers who never left anything out or made a mess. Her frustration with Jesus was that he did not respect her dominion in her home/kingdom and was refusing to submit to her rule and serve her idol.

Furthermore, she was making her children miserable, with the exception of one daughter who labored to keep the house clean like her mom and berated her siblings; she was turning into a second-generation, self-righteous idol worshiper. Making matters worse, when Dad got home from work he would grab a beer, sit in his chair, watch his television, and tune

---

[77]Rom. 1:25–28.
[78]Gen. 1:31.

out his wife and children, ignoring what was going on in the home. His idol was comfort, and his beer, chair, and flat-screen television were his functional saviors that he preferred worshiping over Jesus, who wanted him to apply the gospel to himself, his wife, and their children so that they could each smash their idols and live as worshipers of God alone and wait for the day when they get to enjoy the perfect home Jesus is preparing for us.

The examples are endless because, as John Calvin rightly said, the human heart is an idol factory. Thankfully, as we seek and smash our idols by the grace of God, our lives are transformed into acts of worship to God's glory, our joy, and others' good as we enjoy and steward created things without deifying them and love people rather than use them.

CHAPTER 12

STEWARDSHIP: GOD GIVES

As each has received a gift, use it to serve one another,
as good stewards of God's varied grace.

1 PETER 4:10

God came into history as the man Jesus Christ. He left the riches and glory of his heavenly kingdom for poverty and humility.

His life was perfectly stewarded. Vocationally, he spent most of his life working an honest job as a carpenter. Financially, even though he was poor, Jesus paid his taxes and generously gave to those in need. Jesus' public ministry included, as he said, doing the works the Father had given him to do. His time and effort were so perfectly stewarded that he was able to pray, in John 17:4, "I glorified you on earth, having accomplished the work that you gave me to do."

On the cross, Jesus became the most generous giver that the world has ever known. There, he took our sin and gave us his righteousness. He took our condemnation and gave us his salvation. He took our death and gave us his life. Following his resurrection, Jesus has continued to be generous; he gave us the Holy Spirit and spiritual gifts for ministry service and is preparing for us a kingdom in which we will enjoy his generosity together with him forever.

The early church was marked by generous stewardship because they followed the example of Jesus. Randy Alcorn reminds us of "the Jerusalem converts who eagerly sold their possessions to give to the needy (Acts 2:45; 4:32–35). And the Ephesian occultists, who proved their conversion was authentic when they burned their magic books, worth today what would be millions of dollars (Acts 19:19)."[1]

Christians and non-Christians alike celebrate Jesus' birth every year by giving gifts in the tradition of the Magi, who brought gifts to Jesus as a young boy. Moreover, Christians should desire to live their lives as good and godly stewards like Jesus, investing their time, talent, and treasure for God's purposes.

WHAT IS A STEWARD?

Generally speaking, there are two ways to see our life and possessions. One is through the perspective of ownership, whereby I and my life and possessions belong to me alone. The other is through the perspective of stewardship, whereby I and my life and possessions belong to God and are to be invested for his purposes.

In Titus 1:7 Paul speaks of pastors serving as "God's steward" of the church. Similarly, 1 Peter 4:10 commands every Christian to be "good stewards of God's varied grace." Randy Alcorn describes his own learning about being a steward:

> If God was the owner, I was the manager. I needed to adopt a steward's mentality toward the assets. He had *entrusted*—not *given*— to me.
>
> A steward manages assets for the owner's benefit. The steward carries no sense of entitlement to the assets he manages. It's his job to find out what the owner wants done with his assets, then carry out his will.[2]

Three facts distinguish a steward:

---

[1] Randy Alcorn, *The Treasure Principle: Discovering the Secret of Joyful Giving* (Sisters, OR: Multnomah, 2001), 10.
[2] Ibid., 25.

1) A steward gladly acknowledges that he or she belongs to the Lord. This is exactly what Paul says in Romans 1:6 when he reminds Christians that they "belong to Jesus Christ." Subsequently, stewards understand that everything they have and are logically belongs to the Lord. Paul teaches that this should result in deep humility: "For who sees anything different in you? What do you have that you did not receive? If then you received it, why do you boast as if you did not receive it?"[3]

2) A steward recognizes that everything ultimately belongs to the Lord. The Bible recognizes private property ownership, which explains why it forbids stealing. Above all, though, the Bible repeatedly teaches that God alone is the ultimate owner of everything, because it comes from him and is ruled over by him. God's ownership includes all wealth: "The silver is mine, and the gold is mine, declares the LORD of hosts."[4] God's ownership extends to the natural resources we cultivate for wealth, as God says in Psalm 50:10: "For every beast of the forest is mine, the cattle on a thousand hills." Even the abilities we use to earn a living are gifted to us by God and are to be humbly used, as Deuteronomy 8:17–18 says: "Beware lest you say in your heart, 'My power and the might of my hand have gotten me this wealth.' You shall remember the LORD your God, for it is he who gives you power to get wealth." And just in case anything has been overlooked, Jesus' brother reminds us, "Do not be deceived, my beloved brothers. Every good gift and every perfect gift is from above, coming down from the Father of lights with whom there is no variation or shadow due to change."[5]

Simply put, stewards know they deserve hell. Everything that they enjoy belongs to God and is gifted to them for enjoyment and service. Practically, this means the air we breathe, the food we eat, and everything else is a gracious gift from our loving God.

3) Stewards seek to faithfully oversee all that God has entrusted to their oversight. Because they see that they and all that has been entrusted to their care belong to God alone, they aspire to manage everything in their

---

[3] 1 Cor. 4:7.
[4] Hag. 2:8.
[5] James 1:16–17.

life in a God-glorifying way. Additionally, they do not want to be guilty of robbing God by failing to manage his resources according to his wishes. Malachi 3:8 rebukes such unfaithful stewards, saying, "Will man rob God? Yet you are robbing me."

Practically, stewards have a very distinct mentality. Rather than wondering how they should spend their time, talent, and treasure, they ask how they should invest God's time, talent, and treasure. This means, as an example, that rather than asking why they should give their money to God, or wondering how much of their money they should give to God, they instead prayerfully consider how much of God's money he wants them to keep as well as what he wants done with that portion not used for bills and such.

HOW IS STEWARDSHIP ACTUALLY WORSHIP?

Jesus devoted roughly 25 percent of his words in the Gospels to the resources God has entrusted to our stewardship. This includes some twenty-eight passages in the Gospels. In the Old and New Testaments combined there are over eight hundred verses on the subject, addressing topics ranging from planning and budgeting, to saving and investing, to debt and tithing. Furthermore, money and wealth and possessions are among the greatest idols in our culture, and there is simply no way to be a disciple of Jesus apart from learning to worship God with stewardship.

Jesus stressed that we either worship our wealth or worship with our wealth. In Matthew 6:24 he said, "No one can serve two masters, for either he will hate the one and love the other, or he will be devoted to the one and despise the other. You cannot serve God and money."

Money is either a tool or an idol. When wealth is an idol, it is worshiped in pursuit of other perceived blessings, such as comfort, security, status, and power. But the Bible warns that money-idolatry, called "the love of money," is a trap:

> Those who desire to be rich fall into temptation, into a snare, into many senseless and harmful desires that plunge people into ruin and destruc-

tion. For the love of money is a root of all kinds of evils. It is through this craving that some have wandered away from the faith and pierced themselves with many pangs.[6]

The Bible speaks of many financial sins that accompany money idolatry. These include being continually torn between whether to obey God at financial loss or disobey God in order to retain wealth (as with the rich young ruler),[7] giving from pride so that others will be impressed with your generosity and praise you,[8] getting into the slavery of debt,[9] enviously coveting the success and possessions of others rather than rejoicing with them,[10] a diminished fear of the Lord,[11] laziness,[12] not providing for one's family,[13] poor financial planning leading to poverty,[14] not leaving a generous financial legacy to your children and grandchildren,[15] becoming a heretic because it is profitable,[16] becoming selfish and therefore a bad friend,[17] and robbing God by not giving to the cause of his ministry.[18]

Simply put, if we love money, we use God and people. However, if we love God, we are free to use money to love God and people. Our money is inextricably linked to our worship, both corporately and individually. As gathered Christians, we worship corporately by financially contributing to our local church as well as other ministries. We respond to God's gifts and kindness by giving in return, so that the gospel can continue to reach other people, just as someone paid for it to reach us.

As scattered individuals, we worship by loving our family and loving others with our money by being considerate and generous. This may take the form of sharing our home and a meal with friends, loaning our truck

---

[6]1 Tim. 6:9–10.
[7]Luke 18:18–30.
[8]Matt. 6:1–4.
[9]Prov. 22:7.
[10]Eccles. 4:4.
[11]Prov. 15:16.
[12]Prov. 13:4.
[13]1 Tim. 5:8.
[14]Prov. 15:21–22; 21:5.
[15]Prov. 13:22; 19:14.
[16]1 Tim. 6:3–10.
[17]James 4:1–4.
[18]Mal. 3:8–10.

to a neighbor, giving or lending money at no interest to someone who is in need, paying some bills for a single mother, or buying a Bible for our unbelieving coworker. Our whole lives are to be marked by worship, and how we use our money plays a role in this every day. Worship does happen on Sundays, but it does not end there. Every day with every dollar we are committing either worship or idolatry.

Paul speaks of worshiping with our money. In Philippians 4:18 he speaks of generous financial giving as a worship sacrifice, saying, "I have received full payment, and more. I am well supplied, having received from Epaphroditus the gifts you sent, a fragrant offering, a sacrifice acceptable and pleasing to God."

To help you grow as a worshiper with wealth rather than as a worshiper of wealth, five principles are helpful.

1) Jesus is your treasure. As Christians, we cannot too often or too deeply consider that God has given himself to us as a gift to receive and enjoy. As we see and savor Jesus as our treasure, our hearts are guarded against the idolatrous pursuit of lesser created things, and we are satisfied in the wonder of God's loving generosity.

2) More stuff won't make you happier. Ecclesiastes 5:10 says, "He who loves money will not be satisfied with money, nor he who loves wealth with his income; this also is vanity." Despite all the advertising and marketing to the contrary, true, deep enduring joy does not come from what we possess. Why? Because our idols fail us by falling apart, becoming outdated, underperforming, and ultimately revealing themselves as liars.

3) Jesus said, "It is more blessed to give than to receive."[19] Indeed, if you reflect on the most joy you have had from your wealth, you will surely realize that your best memories are connected to your generous giving to others rather than to your receiving of generous gifts. This explains why generous people are more joyful than greedy, stingy people and also why God, who is the most generous, is also the happiest.

---

[19]Acts 20:35.

4) We should aspire to grow in our financial giving to our church, as well as to other ministries, as part of our spiritual maturation. Second Corinthians 8:7 says, "But as you excel in everything—in faith, in speech, in knowledge, in all earnestness, and in our love for you—see that you excel in this act of grace also." Too often the church is guilty of encouraging growth in all the spiritual disciplines and gifts other than giving. Of course, some churches emphasize giving at the expense of being Christ-centered, but it is vital nonetheless that Christians be exhorted and instructed in everything from biblical preaching to budgeting and investment training on how to seek to increase their giving every year and grow as godly financial stewards.

5) Generous stewards are storing up treasures in heaven. In Matthew 6:19–21, Jesus says:

> Do not lay up for yourselves treasures on earth, where moth and rust destroy and where thieves break in and steal, but lay up for yourselves treasures in heaven, where neither moth nor rust destroys and where thieves do not break in and steal. For where your treasure is, there your heart will be also.

Commenting on storing up treasures on earth, Randy Alcorn says, "Why not? Because earthly treasures are bad? No. *Because they won't last.*"[20] He continues:

> As a Christian, you have inside knowledge of an eventual worldwide upheaval caused by Christ's return. This is the ultimate insider trading tip: Earth's currency will become worthless when Christ returns—or when you die, whichever comes first. (And either event could happen at any time).
>
> Investment experts known as market timers read signs that the stock market is about to take a downward turn, then recommend switching funds immediately into more dependable vehicles such as money markets, treasury bills, or certificates of deposit.

---

[20]Alcorn, *The Treasure Principle*, 13, emphasis in original.

Jesus functions here as the foremost market timer. He tells us to once and for all switch investment vehicles. He instructs us to transfer our funds from earth (which is volatile and ready to take a permanent dive) to heaven (which is totally dependable, insured by God Himself, and is coming soon to forever replace earth's economy).[21]

By inviting us to store up treasures in heaven, Jesus is not encouraging us to be selfish, because treasures in heaven don't come at the expense of anyone else's well-being. Rather, he is inviting us to be wise stewards who invest the wealth he has entrusted to our oversight for a good return. Jesus promises nothing short of a 10,000 percent return on investment for treasures stored in heaven.[22] As Randy Alcorn has said, "You can't take it with you—but you *can* send it on ahead."[23]

Indeed, Jesus was correct to say that where our treasure is, our heart ultimately is. Therefore, those who struggle to be generously wise stewards would be well served to simply start being obedient with their finances. As they are, their heart will follow their treasure. Such people will soon find not only their money going to their church but also their time, prayer, and service. They will stop treating their church like a hotel and start treating it like their home.

Lastly, those who are righteous stewards and generous givers should not be surprised to see God entrust to them increasing treasure to steward. Jesus taught just this in Luke 16:10: "One who is faithful in a very little is also faithful in much, and one who is dishonest in a very little is also dishonest in much." For those who experience this grace of God, Randy Alcorn gives wise counsel, saying, "When God provides more money, we often think, *This is a blessing*. Well, yes, but it would be just as scriptural to think, *This is a test*."[24] He also says, "God prospers me not to raise my standard of living, but to raise my standard of giving."[25]

---

[21]Ibid., 14–15.
[22]Matt. 19:29.
[23]Alcorn, *The Treasure Principle*, 18, emphasis in original.
[24]Ibid., 75.
[25]Ibid.

WHAT DOES IT MEAN TO STEWARD OUR TIME?

The Bible teaches that God has meaningful and purposeful things for his people to accomplish during their life on the earth.[26] To accomplish this we must always seek out God's priorities for our life and remain devoted to them and balance our work and Sabbath so that we can steward our time well. Regarding the stewardship of our time, R. C. Sproul says:

> Time is the great leveler. It is one resource that is allocated in absolute egalitarian terms. Every living person has the same number of hours to use in every day. Busy people are not given a special bonus added on to the hours of the day. The clock plays no favorites.[27]

The opening pages of the Bible reveal that for six days God worked, and on the seventh day God rested from his work. The Ten Commandments establish a rhythm for us patterned after God's, with a seven-day week marked by six days of work and one day of Sabbath.[28]

Work

Work is laboring well as an act of worship that glorifies God. Subsequently, the father who goes to the office, the mother who stays home to care for her young children like the woman in Proverbs 31, and the student who heads off to school are each called by God to labor in their work. Each has sacred tasks that God has appointed for them to capture as opportunities to worship him. Furthermore, work includes formal and informal ministry, such as having an official volunteer role serving in the church, and being a dependable volunteer meeting community needs outside of the church as an act of worship to Jesus Christ.

Jesus' life exemplifies both the informal and formal aspects of ministry work. Until roughly thirty years of age, Jesus worked a common laborer's job as a carpenter. For the remaining roughly three years of his life, Jesus

---

[26]Eph. 2:10.
[27]R. C. Sproul, "Time Well Spent: Right Now Counts Forever," *Tabletalk* (September 1997): 4. The article is excerpted here: http://www.sovereigngraceministries.org/Blog/post/Time-Redeemed.aspx.
[28]Ex. 20:11.

said he was about his Father's work.[29] Jesus' ministry work included exhausting preaching, teaching, demon-confronting, feeding, healing, traveling by foot, and more.

Both the Old and New Testaments have much to say about work, including: God made us to work,[30] work hard,[31] find some satisfaction in our work,[32] provide sustenance by our work,[33] and work by the grace that God gives us.[34] Colossians 3:23–24 summarizes a good steward's work, saying, "Whatever you do, work heartily, as for the Lord and not for men, knowing that from the Lord you will receive the inheritance as your reward. You are serving the Lord Christ."

The Scriptures are clear that God made us to work and that despite the curse, which makes our work all the more difficult, it is good and honorable for us to labor as unto the Lord Jesus. Then, as we will examine, we can enjoy a restful Sabbath as God intends. Sadly, however, this sort of balanced lifestyle is sorely lacking in our culture. For some, work has become an idol, which prevents them from being good stewards of their Sabbath time.

The advent of electricity has distanced us from the creation rhythms of day and night. Electricity brought about a twenty-four-hour lifestyle that includes constant interruption by technology, even on our Sabbath days. The result is that people are overworked: the number of hours worked by the average employee has gone up considerably in almost every modernized nation in the past generation. Furthermore, the proliferation of temporary jobs that lack security means that people are less likely to take a day off or a vacation. Success causes even more stress and a workload that pressures people not to take their Sabbath days or vacations. Even those who do take vacations bring their work with them.

I will never forget the day I was in a pool while on vacation, playing with my five children, when we were inundated with other children want-

---

[29]John 4:34; 5:17, 36.
[30]Gen. 2:15.
[31]Prov. 18:9; 21:25.
[32]Eccles. 3:22.
[33]2 Thess. 3:10.
[34]1 Cor. 15:10.

ing to play catch and also be thrown up into the air so they could splash in the pool. As I looked around, the chairs encircling the pool were occupied with fathers talking on their phones and working on their laptops rather than enjoying their children.

Indeed, God in his loving wisdom instructs us to work and sabbath equally well. If we fail to do so, we must ask ourselves what our god truly is and where our faith truly lies.

Sabbath

To sabbath is to rest from one's labor. The first Sabbath day was a Saturday and was enjoyed by God.[35] The first recorded command for humans to sabbath is in Exodus 16:23, and honoring the Sabbath is listed as the fourth commandment.[36]

Regarding the purpose of the Sabbath, it does indeed have benefits for all people. Workers and animals are permitted to rest as an act of justice and compassion to ensure the dignity of God's creation. Both rich and poor are invited to stand in equality for one day as they rest from their labors, knowing that our sovereign God is on our side and is able to hold the universe and our lives together even when we rest and sleep. For those who fail to sabbath, a sabbath is eventually imposed on them by illness or some other means.

In regards to the particular day of the Sabbath, some have maintained that it should be celebrated on Saturday like the Hebrews did, the final day of their week. However, the early church abruptly changed the day of worship to Sunday to commemorate the resurrection of Jesus from death[37] on that first day of the new week.[38] Sunday remained a workday in the early church until Emperor Constantine instituted it as an official day of rest in AD 321. In America, there was a debate as to whether the Jewish Sabbath of Saturday or the Christian Sabbath of Sunday should

---

[35]Gen. 2:2.
[36]Ex. 20:8–11.
[37]Matt. 28:1; Mark 16:1–2; Luke 24:1; John 20:1.
[38]Acts 20:7; 1 Cor. 16:2.

be recognized, and the compromise was to keep both, which is why we have two-day weekends.

Sadly, for some the Sabbath has become a religious idol. Subsequently, legalistic attempts have been made to rob the Sabbath of its worship and joy by carefully mandating what can and cannot be done. However, Jesus seemed to have intentionally lived in public view in order to serve as a model of the Sabbath contrary to that given by legalistic teachers. For example, Jesus healed on the Sabbath,[39] taught on the Sabbath,[40] and promoted evangelism on the Sabbath.[41] Jesus demonstrated that the Sabbath is not to be enforced legalistically but that it exists for worshipful fun and rest. Furthermore, our true Sabbath is not found in a day but ultimately in a saving relationship with Jesus, where we can rest from trying to earn our salvation and find rest in his finished work.[42] Therefore, the Sabbath is not a law for believers to obey but instead a grace to enjoy.

Some people have also turned the concept of sabbath into an idol by not working hard. Such people do not steward their time well and they are prone toward laziness like the sluggard, whom Proverbs frequently rebukes.

Still others are not good stewards of their Sabbath time. Rather than using it to worship God, enjoy fellowship, rest, read the Bible, and have some sanctified fun, they waste their life watching inane television shows, surfing the Internet, and playing video games. These people are not investing their Sabbath as much as they are squandering it. Worse still, some people are on the phone or their handheld Internet device so much on their day off or during their vacation that they do not even get to enjoy the people in their life. For such people, technology has become their functional lord that demands the sacrifice of their health, joy, friendships, and family in order to be appeased.

Even the modern goal of retirement is an idolatry of the Sabbath. It is

---

[39]Matt. 12:1–14; John 9:1–17.
[40]Mark 6:1–2.
[41]John 7:21–24.
[42]Matt. 11:28–30; Rom. 4:5; Col. 2:16–17.

not sinful for those who have worked hard their entire life to cease working at a paid job to serve their grandkids and volunteer time to their church and other worthwhile ministries. However, the biblical idea of sabbath is not embodied by meeting one's life goal of spending as many years as possible golfing, playing shuffleboard, and doing much of nothing. Tragically, the gospel has an army of older saints with much life experience who, rather than investing it in lost people, young people, and new converts, are right now preoccupied with playing the slots at the casino. Such people need to retire from retirement and steward their final days better.

In his book *Don't Waste Your Life*, John Piper tells the story of two missionaries in their eighties, Ruby Eliason and Laura Edwards.[43] One day while driving through the mountains of Cameroon, West Africa, where they had been serving for some time, their brakes gave out and they died tragically when the car went over a cliff. Then Piper tells another story from *Reader's Digest* of an American couple who retires early to the Florida coast. They spend their time relaxing on their yacht, playing softball, and collecting seashells. To an outside observer, they have everything they could possibly want. Piper brings the story to a halt with this penetrating question: who has truly wasted their life? Think of the missionaries who spent their lives in service to God, even unto their unfortunate deaths. Think of the rich couple in Florida who spends their days collecting seashells. Then Piper asks us to imagine this couple standing before the God of heaven and earth to give an account. What will they say? "Look, Lord. See my shells."[44]

How many of us have spent our life pursuing wealth and comfort at the cost of our lives? How long have we been collecting seashells when we ought to be about our Father's work? The American dream of collecting seashells at age fifty is motivated by at least three things: (1) comfort, or avoiding trials and suffering; (2) achieving immediate joy; and (3) not postponing our glory. According to Piper (and James), this American dream is a tragedy: "People today are spending billions of dollars to persuade you to

[43]John Piper, *Don't Waste Your Life* (Wheaton, IL: Crossway, 2007), 45–46.
[44]Ibid., 46.

embrace that tragic dream. Over against that, I put my protest: Don't buy it. Don't waste your life."[45]

Sadly, young people are no better. Young people are generally high on conviction and low on action. They will rant passionately about what the church needs to do, particularly online from the safe confines of their parents' home, but there is far more smoke than fire. The studies confirm that the most unlikely tithers and servers in churches are people under the age of twenty-five, single adults who have never been married, and theological liberals. Hypocrites!

WHAT DOES IT MEAN TO STEWARD OUR TALENTS?

During his life on earth, Jesus was empowered by the Holy Spirit to do ministry. Jesus said that one day Christians would do even greater ministry than he did.[46] While this does not mean that Christians are greater than Jesus, it does mean that Christians who are gifted and empowered by the Holy Spirit can minister to more people than Jesus could, because there are a few billion professing Christians today spread across the earth. Therefore, our personal ministry is the continuation of Jesus' ministry. Or, to summarize, the talents of God are dispensed through the Spirit of God so that the church of God can minister like the Son of God.

We do this, individually as Christians and corporately as the church, by utilizing both our natural abilities and spiritual gifts, which together we will refer to as talents. Our talents are God-given opportunities to do good as an act of worship. While non-Christians enjoy only their natural abilities, Christians enjoy both Spirit empowerment of their abilities and additional gifts from the Spirit.

Our natural talents come from God's common grace to his image bearers. They are possessed from birth, serve the common good of mankind on the natural level, must be cultivated to be fully utilized, and serve to make our fallen world a more livable home. Natural talents include, among other things, relational skills, communication skills (e.g., writing, conversing,

---

[45]Ibid.
[46]John 14:12.

public speaking, teaching, poetry, advertising, song writing, playwriting), performing ability (e.g., acting, singing, playing an instrument, giving presentations, teaching), artistic ability (e.g., painting, architecture, interior design, culinary arts, graphic design, video production), organizational ability (e.g., planning and managing), physical ability (e.g., athletic skill), problem-solving skills, computer skills, researching capabilities, intuition, and many more.

Our spiritual gifts are a special grace of the Holy Spirit given to us at our new birth. They may be enhancements of our natural talents or wholly supernatural endowments. In either case they benefit the forward progress of the gospel and allow the Christian to live a passionate life of humble service as an act of meaningful worship. Wayne Grudem captures this well when he defines spiritual gifts as "any ability that is empowered by the Holy Spirit and used in any ministry of the church."[47]

The New Testament has many lists of spiritual gifts. First Corinthians 12:8–10 lists wisdom, knowledge, faith, healing, miracles, prophecy, discerning of spirits, tongues, and the interpretation of tongues. First Corinthians 12:28–30 lists serving as an apostle, prophesying, teaching, performing miracles, healing, helping, administrating, speaking in tongues, and interpreting tongues. Romans 12:6–8 lists prophesying, serving, teaching, exhorting, giving, leading, and showing mercy. Ephesians 4:11 lists serving as an apostle, prophesying, evangelizing, pastoring, and teaching. And 1 Peter 4:11 distinguishes between speaking and serving gifts, as some people minister primarily with their words while others do so with their works.

Since no complete list of spiritual gifts exists in the New Testament, we are not to regard these lists as exhaustive. In fact, the point of the New Testament seems to be to use whatever talent (natural ability or spiritual gift) one has as is wise for the cause of the gospel.

There has been no shortage of controversy regarding some of the spiritual gifts—especially tongues, miracles, and prophecy—and whether

---

[47]Wayne Grudem, *Systematic Theology: An Introduction to Biblical Doctrine* (Grand Rapids, MI: Zondervan, 1994), 1016.

they are to be practiced by the church today. Chart 12.1 outlines the basic positions without getting into great detail, which would require another book to be written on the subject. We will simply say here that we hold the continuationist position, and I (Mark) also hold the charismatic position.

CHART 12.1

Cessationist	Continuationist	Charismatic	Charismaniac
Supernatural gifts (e.g., tongues, miracles, and prophecy) functioned only in the early church and are not to be practiced today. God speaks today but only in Scripture.	Supernatural gifts are given to every generation and should be practiced today but always tested according to the guidelines of Scripture.	Supernatural gifts are given to every generation. Contemporary revelations are valued but always secondary to Scripture. Supernatural manifestations are sought, but must show the fruit of the Spirit.	Supernatural gifts are given to every generation. Contemporary revelations are, in effect, more valued than Scripture. Dramatic supernatural manifestations evidence God's presence.

Since many in the church at Corinth were poorly informed about spiritual gifts, Paul wrote 1 Corinthians 12 to 14 to speak at length about the source and function of them. We can learn at least seven things about stewarding our talents from his teaching.

1) God determines which gift(s) we do and do not receive; we do not. Therefore, rather than lamenting what we are not gifted to do, we should rejoice in what God, in his wise love, has gifted us to do without trying to be someone we are not or do things we cannot do well.

2) Different people are given different portions of their natural abilities and spiritual gifts. Subsequently, some people, for example, with the gift of teaching excel in one-on-one discipling while others function better in a class or group, and still others are most effective teaching large crowds.

3) Ability and maturity are two different things. Paul opens his letter to the Corinthians by noting how gifted they were, but then spends the remainder of the book rebuking them for being immature, selfish, and worldly. It is a great mistake to correlate ability and maturity, because it allows gifted but immature people to occupy leadership positions, or,

conversely, encourages mature but not competent people to lead. Ministry leaders must have both ability and maturity equal to the task.

4) We are to steward our talents so that the entire church benefits. This means that we are to humbly serve and not be devoted only to our cause, ministry area, faction of the church, or even our own desires and longings, but primarily to the good of the whole church.

5) In addition to our talents, God also gives us passions to help motivate and compel us toward ministry service. This means, for example, that someone with the gift of encouragement may also have a passion for junior high students, single mothers, young men, or people dying of cancer, and that specific spiritual gift combined with that specific passion work together for a ministry to flourish.

6) Every talent must be cultivated if it is to be effectively stewarded. Paul urged Timothy to fan into flame the gift of God in him.[48] Just like athletes or musicians must practice to improve their skill, so too servants must steward their abilities in order to serve God and people as effectively as possible.

7) We must be willing to serve outside our area of talent if there is a pressing need. This kind of humble service is to be undertaken as a fill-in measure until someone gifted and passionate is found to fill the need.

Practically, most Christians know what they are good at and what they enjoy doing. Seek the Spirit's empowerment to use it for Jesus. Beyond that, Christians should examine themselves both for sin that will hinder their stewardship and also for gifting they may not be aware of. Part of this includes seeking and submitting to the wise counsel of others as they help evaluate believers' talents. Christians must humbly accept who God made them to be and cultivate their talents. They also need to combine their talents with their passions as an indicator of what ministry God may be calling them to serve in. Then they need to find a church where that need exists and either serve in an existing ministry to meet that need or humbly help to start one. This kind of mentality is antithetical to our consumer culture in

---

[48] 2 Tim. 1:6.

which people seek out a church that serves them well. We are to follow the example of Jesus, who came to serve rather than to be served.

The result of stewarding one's talents is nothing short of amazing. Because it is worship, it glorifies God if done humbly. Because it is love, it cares for people and improves their lives if done graciously. Because it is right, it results in deep and profound joy for those who are graced by God to serve him with their talents and passions.

God invites us to steward our talents and serve in ministry not because he needs us to accomplish his will, but because he wants us to share in his joy. Similarly, when I (Mark) was a little boy of perhaps three or four, I remember my construction-worker father taking me to work with him. Like my dad, I wore steel-toed boots, jeans, a T-shirt, and a hard hat, and I carried a lunch box and thermos. My dad let me see him work and gave me some small tasks to do, like piling up scrap wood and pounding a few nails. My dad did not take me to work because he needed me and was using me as free labor. Instead, my dad took me to work because he wanted to spend time with his son. He wanted his son to learn about him by seeing him at work. He wanted his son to enjoy good, honest work like his dad did. When the Bible says that God is our Father, this is the kind of thing it is speaking about, which explains why the children of God who go to work in paid or unpaid ministry with their dad know him best and love him most.

WHAT DOES IT MEAN TO STEWARD OUR TREASURE?

Everything we have—including our finances, jobs, houses, products of our land, real estate, investments, credit, equity, cash, businesses, automobiles, and personal items—is given to us by God and is part of our treasure, or wealth. Good stewards make every effort to manage their treasure as an act of worship.

Sadly, much of the teaching about stewarding one's treasure is prone to either poverty or prosperity theology. *Poverty theology* considers those who are poor to be more righteous than those who are rich; it honors those who choose to live in poverty as particularly devoted to God. Conversely, *prosperity theology* considers those who are rich to be more righteous than those who are poor; it honors those who are affluent as being rewarded by God because of their faith. In fact, both poverty and prosperity theology are half-truths because the Bible speaks of four ways in which treasure can be stewarded:

1) Righteous rich stewards
2) Unrighteous rich stewards
3) Righteous poor stewards
4) Unrighteous poor stewards

Righteous rich stewards are those who gain their treasure by righteous means, such as working hard and investing wisely. Righteous rich stewards also manage their treasure righteously by living within a reasonable budget, paying their taxes and bills, and giving generously. Righteous rich stewards take particular delight in giving to the righteous poor so that the single mother can buy groceries, the hardworking, first-generation immigrant father who hurt himself on the job can pay his medical bills, the child from the impoverished family who was gifted by God with a bright mind can afford to attend college, and the church planter can launch a church. These are examples of God's financial grace through God's stewards. Biblical examples of righteous rich stewards include Abraham, Isaac, Jacob, Joseph, Job (both before and after his life tragedy and season of poverty), Joseph of Arimathea (who gave Jesus his personal tomb), Lydia (who funded much of Paul's ministry), and Dorcas (who often helped the poor).

Unrighteous rich stewards gain their treasure through sinful means, such as stealing and dishonest business practices, because their idolatry of money drives them toward greed. Unrighteous rich stewards poorly manage their treasure because they do not budget prudently, spend reasonably, invest cautiously, or give generously. In fact, one thorough study reported, "Earning higher incomes does not make American Christians more generous with their money. It actually appears to make them more stingy, protective, and distrustful."[49] It also said, "Higher income earning American Christians—like Americans generally—give *little to no more money* as a percentage of household income than lower income earning Christians."[50] That study also reported:

> Generally, between 1959 and 2000, while the financial giving by American Christians was *declining*, the personal consumption expenditures of Americans *increased* for eating out in restaurants, toys, sports supplies, live entertainments, foreign and domestic travel by U.S. residents, lottery tickets, casino gambling, photography, sports and recreation camps, and other entertainment expenses.[51]

Biblical examples of unrighteous rich stewards include Laban, Esau, Nabal, Haman, the rich young ruler, and Judas Iscariot.

Righteous poor stewards work hard, act honestly in business dealings, live within their means, stay out of debt, and live in contentment with the treasure God has appointed for them to manage. There are apparently many righteous poor stewards, since the poorest Christians give more than all but the wealthiest Christians.[52] Biblical examples of righteous poor stewards include Ruth and Naomi, Jesus Christ, the widow who gave her mite, the Macedonian church, and Paul, who often knew want and hunger.

Unrighteous poor stewards, like unrighteous rich stewards, seek to gain their treasure through sinful means, such as freeloading and stealing, but fail to succeed. Unrighteous poor stewards do not invest their treasure wisely, are prone to foolish spending (such as eating and drinking too much), gambling, chasing get-rich schemes hoping to obtain wealth without wisdom or effort, and/or are lazy and do as little as possible. Biblical examples of unrighteous poor stewards include the sluggard and the fool, who are repeatedly renounced throughout the book of Proverbs.

---

[49]Christian Smith and Michael O. Emerson, with Patricia Snell, *Passing the Plate: Why American Christians Don't Give Away More Money* (Oxford: Oxford University Press, 2008), 171.
[50]Ibid., 43, emphasis in original.
[51]Ibid., 63.
[52]Rob Moll, "Scrooge Lives!" *Christianity Today*, December 5, 2008.

The Scriptures give us a far richer understanding of stewarding our treasure than the errors of poverty and prosperity theology. In Scripture, the issue is not primarily whether people are rich or poor, but whether they are righteous or unrighteous stewards in how they obtain and manage their treasure.

There are four treasure truths that undergird righteous stewardship.

The first treasure truth is that this world is not our home.[53] When we understand that this world is a journey on the way to our true home, we live differently. We do not settle in with all of our hopes tethered here but rather see this life and the treasures we steward in it as opportunities in which to be sanctified and serve.

The second treasure truth is that wisdom is more valuable than wealth. Indeed, if people obtain wealth without wisdom, they will see it vanish.[54] In Proverbs 8:17–21, Lady Wisdom says:

> I love those who love me,
>> and those who seek me diligently find me.
> Riches and honor are with me,
>> enduring wealth and righteousness.
> My fruit is better than gold, even fine gold,
>> and my yield than choice silver.
> I walk in the way of righteousness,
>> in the paths of justice,
> granting an inheritance to those who love me,
>> and filling their treasuries.

Righteous stewards pursue wisdom with at least as much tenacity as they pursue wealth.[55]

The third treasure truth is that righteous stewards budget prudently and live within their means. Proverbs 21:5 says, "The plans of the diligent lead surely to abundance, but everyone who is hasty comes only to

---

[53]Heb. 11:13; 1 Pet. 1:1.
[54]Prov. 23:4–5.
[55]To grow in financial wisdom, visit http://www.crown.org and http://www.daveramsey.com.

poverty." Included in a budget are paying taxes,[56] giving first and best to God,[57] avoiding debt slavery,[58] having money in savings and having good insurance,[59] being generous instead of stingy,[60] and investing cautiously and patiently.[61]

The fourth treasure truth is that righteous stewards leave a legacy. This begins with men working hard to be the provider for their family, as 1 Timothy 5:8 extols, saying, "If anyone does not provide for his relatives, and especially for members of his household, he has denied the faith and is worse than an unbeliever." Righteous stewards are also a blessing to multiple generations of their family. Proverbs 13:22 says, "A good man leaves an inheritance to his children's children." This legacy would include, for example, college funds, homes or down payments on the first home purchase, and funding for ministry, such as missions work and church planting, for children and grandchildren. Conversely, unrighteous stewards do not leave a legacy but instead put inane bumper stickers on their cars that brag, "We're spending our children's inheritance."

One stark illustration of the difference between the ability to make money and the wisdom to steward it comes from history.[62] In 1928, some of the planet's most wealthy people met at the Edgewater Beach Hotel in Chicago. Those in attendance included the president of the largest utility company, the greatest wheat speculator, the president of the New York Stock Exchange, a member of the president's cabinet, the greatest "bear" in Wall Street, the president of the Bank of International Settlements, and the head of the world's greatest monopoly. Altogether, they enjoyed more wealth than was held in the U.S. Treasury. These people were regularly highlighted in media coverage as examples for others to follow. A short twenty-five years later, these were their fates:

---

[56]Rom. 13:7.
[57]Prov. 3:9–10.
[58]Prov. 22:7.
[59]Prov. 30:25.
[60]Prov. 11:24–25; 23:6–7.
[61]Prov. 13:11.
[62]This illustration comes from the NET Bible, "Sermon Illustrations on the Love of Money," http://net.bible.org/illustration.php?topic=1762.

- Charles Schwab, who had been president of the largest steel company, lived on borrowed money the last five years of his life and died broke.
- Arthur Cutten went from the greatest wheat speculator to dying broke.
- Richard Whitney, who had been president of the New York Stock Exchange, served a term in Sing Sing Prison.
- Albert Fall, who had served as a member on the president's cabinet, was imprisoned for fraud and corruption.
- Jesse Livermore, who had been Wall Street's greatest "bear," committed suicide.
- Leon Fraser, who had served as the president of the Bank of International Settlements, committed suicide.
- Ivar Drueger, who had been head of the world's greatest monopoly, committed suicide.

All these men had learned how to make money, but not one of them had learned how to live with it as godly stewards.

SHOULD CHRISTIANS TITHE?

Tithe literally means "tenth." In the Old Testament, the tithe referred to God's people giving the first 10 percent of their gross income (also called "firstfruits") to God to fund the Levite priests' ministry.[63] In addition to that there were other tithes and offerings required of God's people, including 10 percent paid for festivals to build community and for celebration,[64] 3.3 percent given to help the poor,[65] crop gleanings collected for the poor and aliens,[66] and other occasional additional tithes above and beyond regular giving.[67] Therefore, the total "mandatory" Old Testament tithe resulted in over 25 percent of a family's gross income going to God and ministry.

In the New Testament, financial giving among God's people focuses on grace, generosity, and the heart, and not actual percentages of one's income. The word *tithe* is rarely used in the New Testament,

---

[63]Num. 18:21–29; 27:30.
[64]Deut. 12:10–11, 17–18; 14:22–27.
[65]Deut. 14:28–29.
[66]Lev. 19:9–10.
[67]Neh. 10:32–33.

and when it is, it is usually mentioned negatively in rebuking religious types such as the Pharisees who gave their money to God but not their hearts and lives.

It cannot be overstated that when we give to God, we are not deciding how much of our wealth to give. Rather, we are determining how much of God's wealth we are keeping for our own uses. In 1 Chronicles 29:14 David articulates precisely this fact, saying, "But who am I, and what is my people, that we should be able thus to offer willingly? For all things come from you, and of your own have we given you."

Perhaps the most thorough teaching in all the New Testament on giving is found in 2 Corinthians 8–9, where we discover eight principles regarding generous giving.[68]

1) Generous giving is sacrificial.[69] For example, Paul says that the Macedonian Christians were experiencing severe affliction and extreme poverty but responded with abundant joy and overflowing generosity.

2) Generous giving is something that only some people are spiritually gifted for.[70] For those who have the spiritual gift of giving, righteous stewardship and generous giving seem like obvious aspects of Christian life, but since the majority of people do not have the gift of giving, they must be taught biblical stewardship and discipline themselves to live obediently and labor to live out of the Bible's teaching on stewardship. Therefore, those with the gift of giving and church leaders must not cowardly avoid the subject of stewardship but rather teach and model it with love as with all other aspects of Christian discipleship.

3) Generous giving is a gospel issue.[71] Just as Jesus left the riches and glory of heaven for the poverty and humility of earth, so too Christians are to enjoy being generous givers because doing so is a response to and reflection of Jesus' gift of salvation to them.

4) Generous giving encourages churches to share with other churches

---

[68]These points are adapted from John Stott's book *The Living Church: Convictions of a Lifelong Pastor* (Downers Grove, IL: InterVarsity, 2007).
[69]2 Cor. 8:1–6, 10–12.
[70]2 Cor. 8:7.
[71]2 Cor. 8:8–9.

and ministries in need.[72] Practically, this means that all but the most destitute churches should both live within their means and help support righteous poor churches, such as those in impoverished nations, new church plants, and churches filled with new converts and college students.

5) Generous giving is motivated by friendly competition.[73] Paul challenged the wealthier Corinthian church, for example, to match the financial giving of the impoverished Macedonian church. Likewise, churches need to be aware of what other churches in their area are receiving so as to know how their people are doing and to help encourage them to be more generous.

6) Generous giving is about sowing and reaping.[74] Unlike prosperity theology, which encourages people to give to God so that they might get more money, generosity theology aims to sow, or invest, in ministries that will reap a gospel reward of converts to Jesus and mature disciples. Therefore, the sowing and reaping that the Bible speaks of is not necessarily personal as much as it is missional. Those who love the gospel know that while many of the spending and investing decisions they make do not reap a fruitful reward, monies given to faithful ministries always have a wonderfully satisfying return on investment, because lives are changed by Jesus.

7) Generous giving is one of many evidences that someone is truly a Christian.[75] Paul's point is that if someone has truly received the generous grace of the gospel of Jesus Christ, he or she will be generous. Conversely, if someone is not generous, it may be because he or she does not understand grace and has not received the gospel of our generous Lord Jesus Christ.

8) Generous giving promotes the worship of Jesus as God. This is among the ultimate goals of generous giving—seeing as many people as possible enjoy the generosity of God's grace and respond in worshipful joy. Paul says this repeatedly at the close of his lengthy teaching on generous giving:

[72]2 Cor. 8:13–15.
[73]2 Cor. 9:1–5.
[74]2 Cor. 9:6–12.
[75]2 Cor. 9:13–14.

- You will be enriched in every way to be generous in every way, which through us will produce thanksgiving to God.[76]
- For the ministry of this service is not only supplying the needs of the saints but is also overflowing in many thanksgivings to God.[77]
- By their approval of this service, they will glorify God because of your submission flowing from your confession of the gospel of Christ, and the generosity of your contribution for them and for all others.[78]
- Thanks be to God for his inexpressible gift![79]

Therefore, God's people today are not required to tithe. But, like everything else in the new covenant, our grace giving is to exceed Old Testament requirements of the law. Therefore, for God's people, 10 percent should be a floor, not a ceiling, and a place to begin, not a place to end.

HOW WELL ARE CHRISTIANS WORSHIPING WITH THEIR WEALTH?

Practically speaking, it is a good rule of thumb that Christians give generously to their local church and above and beyond that sacrificially to other ministries. Sadly, "the vast majority of the money that American Christians do give to religion is spent in and for their own local communities of faith—little is spent on missions, development, and poverty relief outside of local congregations, particularly outside the United States, in ways that benefit people other than the givers themselves."[80] The statistics reveal that most professing Christians are simply not generous givers:

- More than one in four American Protestants give away $0.[81]
- From 1968 to 2005, giving to Protestant churches declined from 3.1 percent of income to 2.6 percent of income.[82]

---

[76]2 Cor. 9:11.
[77]2 Cor. 9:12.
[78]2 Cor. 9:13.
[79]2 Cor. 9:15.
[80]Smith, et al., *Passing the Plate*, 51.
[81]Moll, "Scrooge Lives!"
[82]Ronald E. Keener, *Church Executive*, July 2008, http://www.churchexecutive.com/articleprint. asp?print= 1&IndexID=1052 (accessed May 31, 2009).

- The average regular churchgoer, compared to those who say they are Christians but rarely attend church, gives 6 percent of their after-tax income.[83]
- The median annual giving for a Christian is $200—just over half a percent of after-tax income.[84]
- Mormons give more than seven times the amount of money as a percentage of income than do Catholics.[85]
- About 27 percent of evangelicals give away 10 percent or more of their income.[86]
- About 5 percent of Christians provide 60 percent of the money to churches and religious groups.[87]
- Twenty percent of all Christians account for 86 percent of all giving.[88]
- Among Protestants, 10 percent of evangelicals, 28 percent of mainline folk, 33 percent of fundamentalists, and 40 percent of liberal Protestants give nothing.[89]

Christian Smith, sociologist and expert on American Christianity,[90] says in his authoritative book on Christian giving called *Passing the Plate* that every year American Christians earn "more than the total Gross Domestic Products of every nation in the world except, at most, the six wealthiest—United States, Japan, Germany, China, the United Kingdom, and France."[91]

Smith conservatively estimates what would happen if only those professing Christians who attend church a few times a month or more, the "committed Christians," gave 10 percent of their after-tax income:

We estimate that if committed Christians in the United States gave 10 percent of their after-tax income—fully but no more than 10 percent—

---

[83]Moll, "Scrooge Lives!"

[84]Ibid.

[85]Smith, et al., *Passing the Plate*, 5.

[86]Moll, "Scrooge Lives!"

[87]Ibid.

[88]Ron Sider, "A Lot of Lattés," *Books and Culture*, October 30, 2008 (http://www.christianitytoday.com/bc/2008/ novdec/5.11.html).

[89]Ron Sider, "A Lot of Lattés."

[90]Christian Smith is the William R. Kenan Jr. professor of sociology and director of the Center for the Study of Religion and Society at the University of Notre Dame. He received his MA and PhD from Harvard University in 1990. Smith was a professor of sociology at the University of North Carolina at Chapel Hill for twelve years before his move to Notre Dame and is arguably the leading researcher of American Christianity.

[91]Smith, et al., *Passing the Plate*, 12.

that would provide an *extra* $46 billion per year of resources with which to fund needs and priorities. That represents nearly an additional 25 percent of what *all Americans*—Christians or otherwise—currently give in *all* types of private philanthropy.[92]

Just some of the things this money could fund, according to Smith, include:[93]

- 150,000 new indigenous missionaries and pastors in nations most closed to foreign religious workers.
- Triple the resources being spent by all Christians on Bible translating, printing, and distribution to provide Bibles in the native languages of the 2,737 remaining people groups currently without Bible translations.
- Finance the organizational infrastructure of a major Christian research and advocacy organization fighting against contemporary economic and sexual slavery worldwide.
- Quadruple the total resources being spent by all Christians globally on missions to evangelize the unevangelized world.
- 5,000,000 grass-roots, micro-enterprise economic development projects per year in poor countries worldwide.
- Eradicate polio worldwide.
- 1,000,000 new clean water, well-drilling projects per year in the poorest nations (25 percent of the world's population drinks unsafe water).
- Prevent and treat malaria worldwide.
- Provide food, clothing, and shelter to all 6,500,000 current refugees in all of Africa, Asia, and the Middle East.
- Quadruple the budget of Habitat for Humanity.
- Double the budget of World Vision, which serves 100 million people in 96 nations.
- Sponsor 20 million needy children worldwide, providing them food, education, and healthcare.
- Quadruple global Christian medical missions work.
- Provide financial and debt management training to 200,000 U.S. Christians per year who are deeply in debt.

---

[92]Ibid., 13, emphases in original.
[93]See ibid., 13–18.

Jesus' words from Luke 12:47–48 seem a fitting and sobering closing reminder:

> That servant who knew his master's will but did not get ready or act according to his will, will receive a severe beating. But the one who did not know, and did what deserved a beating, will receive a light beating. Everyone to whom much was given, of him much will be required, and from him to whom they entrusted much, they will demand the more.

WHAT SHOULD GENEROUS STEWARDS LOOK FOR IN A MINISTRY?

When Paul received financial support for his ministry work, he was careful to explain how the money was accounted for, handled, and spent by trustworthy church leaders.[94] Paul even explained that he did not handle the money himself, but rather entrusted that accounting to Titus and other gifted godly leaders.

Paul's point is that not only are Christians to be righteous stewards, but so are Christian churches and ministries. To that end, the following are features that wise stewards should expect of any church or ministry they support.

The chain of custody for all monies should have multiple witnesses who are paid and unpaid church members to ensure that the ministry is above reproach and not open to fraud or theft. Practically, this means that different people fill the following roles: taking offering, counting money, double checking offering counting, depositing money, verifying deposit receipts, signing checks, and reconciling account statements. In addition, there should be an annual independent financial review by a licensed CPA who is a Christian but does not attend the church and who will give a written summary report of how well he believes the church is handling its resources. Some people will bristle at the thought of a church running like a business, but in many regards a church should steward its resources better than a business, out of love for God and his reputation.

---

[94] 2 Cor. 8:16–23.

Because spiritual leaders are supposed to be exemplary,[95] they should be good stewards of their own household and generous givers.[96] An example of this is found in 1 Chronicles 29:6–9 where the people knew their leaders were generous:

> Then the leaders of fathers' houses made their freewill offerings, as did also the leaders of the tribes, the commanders of thousands and of hundreds, and the officers over the king's work. They gave for the service of the house of God 5,000 talents and 10,000 darics of gold, 10,000 talents of silver, 18,000 talents of bronze and 100,000 talents of iron. And whoever had precious stones gave them to the treasury of the house of the LORD, in the care of Jehiel the Gershonite. Then the people rejoiced because they had given willingly, for with a whole heart they had offered freely to the LORD. David the king also rejoiced greatly.

Any church or ministry that is serious about stewardship must track the giving of its leaders to ensure they are modeling generosity. If the senior leaders in a ministry are not giving significantly more than the average church attendee, then there is likely a serious spiritual problem in the leadership.

Any church serious about stewardship also has to set an example by giving generously to outside works. For example, at Mars Hill Church we have always given 10 percent of our income to church planting, and we now have the great joy of seeing many churches planted through the Acts 29 Church Planting Network[97] as other generous churches are likewise giving.

To help people mature as stewards, churches should also provide financial coaching and training for its members. This will help train people in biblical principles and give them the opportunity to get their budget organized, live within their means, pay off their debt, and give generously.

A church or ministry that wants to aid people in being generous givers should provide as many ways to give as possible. This includes collecting offerings during church services, receiving checks via mail at the office

---

[95]Heb. 13:7.
[96]1 Tim. 3:3–5.
[97]See http://www.Acts29Network.org.

during the week, having secure online giving options, providing a means for automated giving, and supporting a process for receiving stocks, property, and other donations.

One of the most controversial parts of a church budget is staffing costs. On this issue, five things must be considered.

1) There should not be too many people on staff or else the Christians in the church will not be required to serve; there should not be too few people on staff or else they will burn out. Most churches have one staff person for every fifty adults attending the church on an average Sunday, and a staff of good leaders should be able to train and mobilize enough volunteers to enable roughly one staff member for every seventy-five to one hundred or more people.

2) Those on paid staff deserve to be paid at least the median level of the church members who do similar work in the marketplace. Numbers 18:24 reveals that the Old Testament practice of funding the ministry of the priests was actually giving to the Lord: "For the tithe of the people of Israel, which they present as a contribution to the LORD, I have given to the Levites." Also, Galatians 6:6 says, "One who is taught the word must share all good things with the one who teaches." Those for whom ministry is their paid vocation should be paid enough to care for their family, if they are the head of a home,[98] which would include a reasonable benefits package containing such things as medical coverage and a retirement account.

3) Salary compensation should vary by responsibility and performance. Paid ministry leaders, and even unpaid ministry leaders, need clear job descriptions and performance reviews to evaluate how hard they are working and how fruitful they are. Those who are excelling should be given a salary commensurate with their workload. On this point 1 Timothy 5:17–18 says, "Let the elders who rule well be considered worthy of double honor, especially those who labor in preaching and teaching. For the Scripture says, 'You shall not muzzle an ox when it treads out the grain,'

---

[98] 1 Tim. 5:8.

and, 'The laborer deserves his wages.'" Indeed, one of the major ways a church honors its senior leaders is to pay them decently so that they can also live generously by taking care of their family, practicing hospitality, giving generously back to the church, and helping those in need. If ministry leaders are godly stewards, the truth is that much of what they are paid will be put right back into the ministry anyway.

4) Ministry salaries should be comparable to other ministries of the same size and budget. Therefore, churches wanting to know what a reasonable compensation range is must do homework; they can review the national surveys of the budgets for churches their size, confidentially ask to know the pay scale in sister churches of similar size, and track what similar churches are advertising as compensation packages for new hires, all to get a good idea of what a fair wage is. Pastors who are paid too little often force their wives to work and function as the breadwinning head of the household, which offers a horrible example to the congregation. In contrast, pastors who are paid too much are in threat of violating 1 Peter 5:2, which commands them not to be motivated by "shameful gain."

5) Sometimes a ministry leader needs to temporarily forego a deserved salary for the sake of the gospel. Paul explains a situation in which, although he deserved a salary, he chose not to receive one while in Corinth. In the lengthy section of 1 Corinthians 9:3–19, Paul is clear that his rejection of salary was unusual. He did so because in Corinth there was a wealthy class of patrons accustomed to paying orators to work for them. It was expected that the orator would speak well of the patrons as a sort of marketing agent and not criticize the patrons in any way. Paul knew that he could not preach the gospel and call the rich patrons to repentance if he took their money, thereby essentially agreeing to be their obedient employee. So he chose not to take their money but instead to preach the gospel freely, calling them to repent of their sin. Similarly, a church planter with no funding, a pastor with a struggling church, and other ministry leaders may for a variety of reasons choose to forego a salary for a gospel reason as an exception to the biblical principle of being worthy of a decent wage.

HOW HAS CONSUMERISM SUPPLANTED CHRIST?

Some will wonder why we have devoted an entire chapter in a book about Christian doctrine to stewardship. The answer is simple: consumerism has supplanted Christ.

Consuming is the quintessential American activity. It has even caused the church to be perceived of as less of a worshiping people on mission and more of a business that dispenses religious goods and services to consumers who are "church shopping." Life without credit cards, constant advertising, big-box wholesalers, mail-order catalogs, temple-esque shopping malls, and Internet shopping is almost unthinkable because it is as pervasive as the air we breathe. Edward Song writes, "A wider range of goods are being bought and sold and market-talk is being applied to areas where it had previously been foreign. Virtually anything can become a commodity now, and nothing is unaffected by the market's logic and categories of thought."[99]

Consumerism is driven by the idols of pride and status. Consumerism is nothing short of a religion that defines our identity by such things as the car we drive. This idea was most notably articulated by the sociologist Thorstein Veblen, through whom the phrase "conspicuous consumption" gained prominence. Veblen argued that the chief way we obtain social prestige and power is through conspicuous displays of leisure and consumption. Social prestige is connected to wealth, and we demonstrate our wealth by flaunting it.[100]

Consumerism isn't just a behavior, but it is an outlook, an ideology, and a religion. It isn't just that people happen to shop more than they used to. Rather, they shop more than they used to precisely because they are in the grip of the ideology of consumerism that is transmitted to them through the chief cultural institutions (e.g., television, media, magazines).[101] Sadly, the most respected sociologists have concluded that to be consumers,

---

[99]Edward Song, "Commodification and Consumer Society: A Bibliographic Review," *The Hedgehog Review* 5:2 (2003): 109.
[100]Ibid., 111.
[101]Ibid., 116–19. His section on shopping and advertising discusses the transmission of consumerism as an ideology.

people have to work longer and harder and are subsequently less happy and less healthy.[102]

It is important to note that products are not simply valued for their usefulness but have meanings and play central roles in the cultivation and maintenance of our identities.[103] This is a powerful explanation for why consumer goods are so much more than objects that we use or wear. The point is that in today's consumer culture, goods are carriers of meanings that we use to define ourselves, to send social signals to others, and to construct our identities apart from God, worshiping the idols of created things rather than the creator God.

Instead of consumerism, there is Christ. In consumerism you are defined by whose name is on your underwear and what kind of car you own. You are driven to buy stuff you don't need with money you don't have to impress people you don't like. Our homeless, generous God, Jesus Christ, nailed stewardship, saying, "No one can serve two masters, for either he will hate the one and love the other, or he will be devoted to the one and despise the other. You cannot serve God and money."[104]

---

[102]See Juliet Schor, "The New Politics of Consumption," *Boston Review*, Summer 1999, http://bostonreview.net/BR24.3/schor.html; Song, "Commodification and Consumer Society," 121.
[103]Song, "Commodification and Consumer Society," 111.
[104]Matt. 6:24.

CHAPTER 13

KINGDOM: GOD REIGNS

Your kingdom come, your will be done,
on earth as it is in heaven.

MATTHEW 6:10

You will die.

Too many people naively try to convince themselves that if they simply don't think about death then things will be fine. They are living both foolishly and dangerously.

Our world does not know what to do with death. When people begin to die, we put them in retirement homes, care centers, and hospitals. We tuck them away out of sight, fill them with medications, and try to make death seem not so deadly. When someone does die, we put them in a box so that we do not have to stare death in the face, and if the box is open, we see the deceased with makeup and nice clothes so they appear not so dead. When the deceased is finally buried, it is usually in a memorial garden replete with flowers and fountains to maintain the illusion that death is not really an enemy, as Paul says.[1] Not knowing what to say, the living who remain assert things they really don't have any evidence for, such as "They are in a better place now," which may not be true, or "I'm just glad their suffering has ended," as if they may not be suffering at that very moment for a life of unrepentant sin.

---

[1] 1 Cor. 15:26.

You will die.

That unavoidable and inevitable fact will occur, perhaps even while reading these words.

Do you know what will happen to you after you die?

Are you ready for the day of your death and the days that follow it?

Whom will you trust to help prepare you for death and beyond?

Will you believe the naturalists, who say that you are only a body without a soul and that once you die there is nothing more? If so, you will need to squeeze as much joy as possible out of this life, and if it is filled with pain and regret, then you are simply a loser. Not surprisingly, even the most hardened naturalists find it psychologically devastating to accept the logical conclusion of their own beliefs. Subsequently, they try to live on forever through the memory of others, their offspring, or their efforts to change the world in some way that their mark on it remains after their death.

Will you believe the universalists, who say that in the end everyone goes to heaven no matter what they have done in this life? Does it seem fair to you that rapists, pedophiles, murderers, thieves, and the worst human beings could live their entire life harming others without ever changing and be rewarded eternally? Because we are God's image bearers and have a conscience with a longing for justice, the universalists' cheery claim that sociopaths who rape women and molest children, along with Hitler and a lengthy line of other sadistic dictators from Genghis Khan to Stalin who devoted their lives to evil and cruelty, get to live forever with their victims sounds like anything but a win-win scenario.

Will you believe the Catholics' claim that purgatory is a place or state in which those who died in the grace of God expiate their unforgiven sins by being punished before being admitted to heaven? God said he made us "alive together with him [Jesus], having forgiven us all our trespasses, by canceling the record of debt that stood against us with its legal demands. This he set aside, nailing it to the cross."[2] Do you really think he would

---

[2]Col. 2:13–14.

go back on his word and make us burn in the fires of hell for thousands of years so we could be with him?

Will you believe the reincarnationists' claim that after you die you will come back repeatedly until you have paid off your karmic debt? If so, you are trapped in a cycle of rebirth where the only hope is that after millions of attempts, you finally get it right and escape into the eternal oneness, often called *Nirvana*, which is the end of all personhood. A lot of Americans follow their personally devised versions of neo-paganism, Tibetan Buddhism, Kabala, and gnosticism. They reject most of the disciplines and beliefs of the original religions in favor of some sort of naive dream that they are doing it right and that in their next life they will be ascended masters of the universe. Reincarnation cannot solve the sin problem for the simple reason that even if you could live multiple lives, you would not be paying off your old sin as fast as you would be adding on new sin, and you would thus return as a lower life form every time, which means when you die you have nothing to look forward to forever.

WHAT HAPPENS WHEN WE DIE?

God created humans as thinking, feeling, moral persons made up of spirit and body tightly joined together.[3] Death is not normal or natural, but an enemy, the consequence of sin.[4] Death is the tearing apart of these two intertwined parts, the end of relationship with loved ones, and the cessation of life on this earth. The body goes to the grave and the spirit goes into an afterlife[5] to face judgment.[6] The Bible is clear that there will one day be a bodily resurrection for everyone to either eternal life with God or eternal condemnation apart from him in hell.[7]

Christianity differs from all religions in that Christians believe our eternal status depends on our relationship with Jesus. We really believe that "God so loved the world, that he gave his only Son, that whoever believes

---

[3]Gen. 2:7.
[4]Gen. 2:17; Rom. 5:12.
[5]Pss. 104:29; 146:4; Eccles. 3:20–21; 12:7; James 2:26.
[6]Heb. 9:27.
[7]Dan. 12:2; Matt. 25:46.

in him should not perish but have eternal life."[8] It may not be politically correct, but our lives are shaped by the reality that "whoever believes in the Son has eternal life; whoever does not obey the Son shall not see life, but the wrath of God remains on him."[9]

Upon death, a believer's spirit immediately goes to heaven to be with Jesus.[10] Some cannot see how a soul can exist without a body. They mistakenly believe that the soul sleeps unconsciously between the death of the body and its resurrection on judgment day. Others believe the soul exists in God's memory until it is "re-membered" at the end of the age. Such existence in the divine database doesn't fit with John's vision of the souls of the martyrs crying out with a loud voice, "How long before you will judge and avenge our blood on those who dwell on the earth?"[11] Paul's confidence that death will be "far better" than fruitful work here on earth can hardly mean only a long nap with Jesus.[12]

Jesus gives us a picture in Luke 16:19–31 of existence after death. Lazarus, the godly beggar, goes to be with Abraham, while the self-indulgent rich man is in a place of torment. His deeds show that he does not love God.[13] The rich man, self-absorbed to the end, expects Abraham to be his servant and bring him some water. In this place, there is neither repentance for his sin nor the expectation that he can get out of torment now that he is dead.

Jesus, who has come back from death and is thus the expert on what awaits us on the other side, was emphatically clear that a day of judgment is coming when everyone will rise from their graves and stand before him for eternal sentencing to either worship in his kingdom or suffer in his hell.[14] At the final judgment, all—even you—will stand before Jesus. Jesus followers whose names are written in the Book of Life will be with him forever. The Bible could not be clearer: "If any-

---

[8]John 3:16.
[9]John 3:36.
[10]2 Cor. 5:1–10; Phil. 1:23.
[11]Rev. 6:10.
[12]Phil. 1:23.
[13]1 John 3:10; 4:8–21.
[14]John 5:21–30.

one's name was not found written in the book of life, he was thrown into the lake of fire."[15]

WHAT IS THE KINGDOM OF GOD?

At its simplest, the kingdom of God is the result of God's mission to rescue and renew his sin-marred creation. The kingdom of God is about Jesus our king establishing his rule and reign over all creation, defeating the human and angelic evil powers, bringing order to all, enacting justice, and being worshiped as Lord.

Tragically, there are many erroneous views of the kingdom that misrepresent the glories of God's eternal kingdom. The kingdom is not like the cartoonish inanity that shows heaven as a white cloud upon which we will sit wearing diapers and playing harps with wings far too small to carry us anywhere fun. The kingdom is not the naïve dream of liberalism, that with more education and time sin and its effects will be so eradicated from the earth that utopia will dawn. The kingdom is not the deceptive dream of Christless spirituality where all learn to nurture the spark of divinity within themselves and live out their true good self in harmony. The kingdom is not the political dream that if we simply get the right leaders in office and defeat all the bad guys good will rule the earth.

The kingdom is both a journey and a destination, both a rescue operation in this broken world and a perfect outcome in the new earth to come, both already started and not yet finished. This distinction is incredibly important. When the already-ness of the kingdom is overly stressed, the result is an over-realized eschatology. In this case, the presence and power of sin are not fully accounted for, and there is a naive belief that life should be enjoyed with health and wealth, as if the kingdom has already been fully unveiled, and a sort of simplistic optimism sets in. Conversely, when the not-yet-ness of the kingdom is overly stressed, the result is an under-realized eschatology. In this case, sin seems to be at least as powerful as the gospel and there is little hope or enthusiasm for evangelism, church

---

[15]Rev. 20:15.

planting, or opposing injustice in the world, and a sort of hopeless fatalism sets in.

God does not want us to be naïve, as if the kingdom is fully here. And God does not want us to be hopeless, as if the kingdom has not yet begun. The kingdom has come and is coming. God will work his rescue not by obliterating the physical earth but by recreating it. He will use humans, who are part of the problem as well as part of the solution, to bless, redeem, and restore. In all this we are not observers of a divine drama but participants helping with the redemption, each playing the role God has assigned for us to play in making the invisible kingdom visible.

God created the heavens and the earth, making space-time and mass-energy, material and immaterial, very good. He created man, male and female, to rule God's good creation as image bearers of the triune God, reflecting his character in their dominion.[16] He planted a garden to be a place where God could live together with people.[17]

But Eve, followed by Adam, listened to the enemy, and they decided to make their own choices against God's loving command. Sin and shame brought spiritual death and they hid from the Lord. Physical death destroyed the unity of the living person. The ground was devastated and cursed because of human sin. Relationship was ruined. Everything and everyone that God made good was infected, polluted, and corrupted.

Still, God did not leave us on our own or reject us. Rather, he came and called Adam and Eve as they hid in their shame.[18] In the middle of cursing the Serpent, God promised an offspring who would crush the Serpent's head, the first promise of the coming Messiah.[19] God made skins to cover their nakedness, a picture of what the Messiah would do in covering our sin and shame.[20]

God inaugurated his kingdom rescue mission by calling Abraham,

---

[16]Gen. 1:26–28.
[17]Gen. 2:8.
[18]Gen. 3:8–9.
[19]Gen. 3:15.
[20]Gen. 3:21.

blessing him, and making him the father of an offspring and a nation through whom all the sin-ruined families would be blessed.[21] Again, God works through a man, Abraham, who is part of the problem as well as part of the solution. God promised that Abraham would also enjoy a plot of land that had previously been the garden of Eden as a place from which the nations would be blessed.

But things did not go well. Abraham, and then his son Isaac and his grandson Jacob, increasingly failed to be faithful to the covenant call. The kingdom family found themselves exiled in the kingdom of Egypt. In an ironic twist, the rescuers needed to be rescued. So God in his faithfulness brought them back to ensure the continuation of his kingdom mission. As a response, Exodus 15 sings the triumph of God over the pagan power of the defeated king, the gods of Egypt, and the dark forces behind the kingdom.[22]

At Mount Sinai, God's people were once again reminded of their kingdom role among the nations. God called them his "treasured possession among all peoples, for all the earth is mine; and you shall be to me a kingdom of priests and a holy nation."[23] As such, they existed to bring his glory to the whole earth. But despite God's gift of a beautiful land,[24] they longed to return to Egypt;[25] they preferred slavery to freedom and a pagan earthly kingdom to his perfect heavenly kingdom. Despite God's command,[26] the people turned back to the defeated gods and continually preferred a kingdom of darkness.[27]

The glory of God's kingdom comes briefly in the rule of David and in the promise of the Messiah's coming as the kingdom king.[28] Nonetheless, David's very serious sin ruins the glorious reign,[29] and conflict rules through the rest of his time on the throne. In the following years, the twin

---

[21]Gen. 12:1–3.
[22]Ex. 12:12; Num. 33:4; Zeph. 2:11.
[23]Ex. 19:5–6.
[24]Ex. 3:8–9; Numbers 13.
[25]Num. 14:3–10.
[26]Ex. 20:3; 23:13–33.
[27]Exodus 32.
[28]2 Sam. 7:1–17; Psalm 89.
[29]2 Samuel 11–12.

sins of idolatry and injustice dominate in the land. The whole nation goes into exile in Babylon until God rescues them.

Upon their rescue from Babylon, God tells Israel they will see the return of the Lord to Zion. This is not just a vision for redeemed Jerusalem but for all nations because "all the ends of the earth shall see the salvation of our God."[30] Instead of seeing a king in splendid robes of glory, though, they will see the battered and mangled body of a servant who bears pain and torture, who is wounded for our transgressions, who takes the chastisement for our sins, and who died for our sins only to rise again and make the many righteous.[31]

The kingdom hope is revealed repeatedly in the Old Testament as a universal hope through Israel and the Messiah. The psalmist paints a mysterious vision of a coming king who will break the nations with a rod of iron and make them the Lord's heritage.[32] The psalmist promises that the king will cry, "My God, my God, why have you forsaken me?" as they pierce his hands and feet. Because of this messiah king, not only Israel but all the nations were promised inclusion in worshiping God alone, for the Lord rules over the nations as the King of kings.[33] He will shatter kings on the day of his wrath.[34] He is to be feared and praised above all gods.[35]

The Old Testament kingdom hope is that God will work his rescue mission in and through Israel to all nations. God's Messiah will bring righteousness where there is injustice, beauty where there is devastation, peace where there is conflict, unity where there is division, forgiveness where there is sin, healing where there is sickness, and worship where there is idolatry. He will defeat the evil powers, reverse the curse of the fall, give fullness of life in place of death, and restore harmony to all creation. Tragically, many of the Jews had lost sight of this universal hope. They were expecting God to send a king who would lead a military uprising to free them from Roman rule. They wrongly believed that they would then

---

[30]Isa. 52:8–10.
[31]Isa. 52:14–53:12.
[32]Ps. 2:8–9.
[33]Psalm 22.
[34]Psalm 110.
[35]Pss. 95:3; 96:4–5; 97:7–9; 135:5; 136:2; 138:1.

be vindicated so they could enjoy the exclusive blessings of being God's people.

When Jesus came, he repeated the prophets' calls for repentance of sin and turning back to God. For the selfish and proudly religious looking to be blessed and affirmed, Jesus' message of humble repentance was not enticing. In Jesus' first coming, the seeds of the kingdom were scattered, but the soil in the hearts of many was not good, and they did not respond to Jesus in faith.[36] Likewise, when Jesus told his disciples that he would be killed, they refused to believe it,[37] preferring a messiah who would conquer their enemies so they could sit on thrones beside him.[38]

Jesus' kingdom message is not a new teaching but a reiteration of the same themes God has continually revealed to his people throughout the Old Testament. Jesus' kingdom message is not that he was merely a good moral example for us to follow; rather, we are utterly unable to follow his sinless life apart from new life in him. Jesus' kingdom message is not primarily about how to go to heaven when we die. And Jesus' kingdom message is not primarily about how to have a personal relationship with Jesus in which we enjoy him privately, as if the rule of his kingdom was intended to be over only our hearts and not all of creation.

The kingdom message is that Jesus is Immanuel, God with us.[39] Spiritual death, the ruptured relationship with God, can be healed through his atoning death alone.[40] The internal destruction sin has brought to our hearts can be renewed through the power of his resurrected life.[41] The real enemy conquered by his victory is not political but sin and the god of this world, Satan himself, along with the spiritual forces of darkness.[42] Jesus formed a new movement, the church, a redeemed people from every nationality and ethnicity, who will come into the unity of the Spirit to participate in God's rescue mission to the whole world.[43]

---

[36]Matthew 13.
[37]Matt. 16:21–23; 17:22–23.
[38]Matt. 20:17–28.
[39]Matt. 1:23; 28:20; John 1:14–18.
[40]2 Cor. 5:14–15; Eph. 2:1, 4–6; Col. 2:13.
[41]John 1:13; 3:5-8; 2 Cor. 5:17; Titus 3:5.
[42]John 12:31–32; 16:11; Col. 2:15; Heb. 2:14.
[43]Matt. 28:16–20; Acts 1:5–8.

Jesus' resurrection prefigures our resurrection.[44] In Jesus' death and resurrection not only is the price of our sin paid, and our life after death secured, but the eternal life of God has truly come to this cursed earth; with the coming of the King, God's kingdom has come into this world.[45] Because of King Jesus there will be physical life again after a period of physical death.[46] After the intermediate state, a time when believers' spirits are with Jesus in heaven while their bodies lie in the grave, there will be a new heaven and a new earth.[47]

The reality of the full unveiling of Jesus' kingdom is both history altering and mind-bending. Jesus' people will enjoy full life in body and spirit, delighting in an Edenic world where there is no sin, no curse, no death, and subsequently no tears. Life will be as it was when God last said all was "very good." We will see the face of Jesus and rule with him in a perfect city on the new earth. This is God's coming kingdom, and by faith its citizens, Christians, long for it.

No one can ignore the reality of wars, disease, tyranny, violence, abuse, poverty, death, injustice, and famine. Evil persists despite all the efforts of all leaders of all nations from all history. We can't solve the problem, because we are the problem. Our hope isn't in self, nation, culture, people, leaders, or politics. It is in God and his love, the only possible source for true and unending justice, kindness, love, unity, compassion, and health. His kingdom is our only hope.

Believers join Jesus and his people in the hopeful quest of the kingdom. We commit to our King's rescue mission seeking to bring redemption and renewal to everyone. We form churches that are outposts of the coming kingdom, shining forth as kingdom light in cultural darkness. We long for and trust in the day when, as Romans 8:21–23 says:

> Creation itself will be set free from its bondage to corruption and obtain the freedom of the glory of the children of God. For we know that the

---

[44]1 Cor. 15:12–57.
[45]John 3:16; 5:24; 6:40; 2 Cor. 4:10–11.
[46]1 Cor. 15:44–46; 2 Cor. 5:1–8.
[47]Isa. 65:17–66:27; 2 Pet. 3:10–13; Rev. 21:1.

whole creation has been groaning together in the pains of childbirth until now. And not only the creation, but we ourselves, who have the firstfruits of the Spirit, groan inwardly as we wait eagerly for adoption as sons, the redemption of our bodies.

Indeed, creation comes from God, belongs to God, and will be restored by God in his kingdom. In that restored Edenic state, the cry for justice, the yearning for beauty, the eagerness for true fellowship, and the longing for true spiritual life with God will be fulfilled. In this way, the Bible is a story told in beginning-middle-beginning format. The opening book of the Bible, Genesis, begins with two chapters of creation, followed by a chapter of judgment for sin. Likewise, the closing book of the Bible, Revelation, ends with two chapters of new creation preceded by final judgment for sin.

WHO IS THE KING?

As we examine the kingdom, we must establish who the king is, because a kingdom is the extent of the rule of a king. It was prophesied in Genesis 49:10 that Jesus would rule with a king's scepter. In John 12:14–15 we read of the humble King Jesus riding a donkey.[48] When his enemies pressed a crown of thorns into his head, they were in fact revealing the truth. Additionally, Pilate's mocking notice hung above Jesus as he was crucified; it read, "Jesus of Nazareth, the King of the Jews."[49]

Following his resurrection and ascension to heaven, Jesus is revealed throughout Revelation to be seated upon a throne, ruling and reigning as sovereign Lord over all creation, including all peoples, times, and places. The revelation of Jesus seated upon his throne appears no less than forty-five times in Revelation. Truth and judgment come from this throne while worship, praise, glory, and adoration will go to his throne. By placing the throne of Jesus Christ at the center of creation and history, John is radically displacing humanity from the position it normally occupies; the goal

---

[48]Cf. Zech. 9:9.
[49]Matt. 27:37; Mark 15:26; Luke 23:38; John 19:19.

of redemption and kingdom is to orient all worship toward God, creator and redeemer.

In Revelation 17:14 we read of Jesus crushing all enemies and other kings and kingdoms, saying, "They will make war on the Lamb, and the Lamb will conquer them, for he is Lord of lords and King of kings, and those with him are called and chosen and faithful."

One day King Jesus will wear white and mount his white horse.[50] He will lead his army to wage war against evildoers. Revelation 19:15 says, "From his mouth comes a sharp sword with which to strike down the nations, and he will rule them with a rod of iron. He will tread the wine-press of the fury of the wrath of God the Almighty."

This Jesus is a warrior. He inspires those who follow him to defend and protect the widow, orphan, elderly, and vulnerable from the bullies, mur-derers, thieves, pimps, rapists, and sadists. Those who love King Jesus hate all that dishonors him and are motivated to see all evil come to an end. They are hoping for a front-row seat to the second feast of Revelation 19, where evildoers will have their flesh feasted upon by flocks of carrion birds.

Until the end, God's people are to wait patiently and serve diligently. In this life we are to suffer courageously and serve humbly like Jesus did during his incarnation, trusting that all will be made right in due time.

WHAT JUDGMENT AWAITS CHRISTIANS AT THE END OF THIS LIFE?

Christians will not be judged at the end of this life in the same way that non-Christians will be. The Bible teaches this truth clearly and repeatedly. In John 5:24, Jesus said, "Truly, truly, I say to you, whoever hears my word and believes him who sent me has eternal life. He does not come into judgment, but has passed from death to life." In Romans 8:1, Paul also says, "There is therefore now no condemnation for those who are in Christ Jesus." Simply stated, in Christ all sin is forgiven.[51] Subsequently, Christians are members of the family of God now and forever.

Nonetheless, Christians will be judged at the end of this life in a way

---

[50]Rev. 19:11.
[51]Col. 2:13; 1 John 2:12.

that is different from the judgment of non-Christians. This life, and what we do and do not do with it, matters greatly. The Holy Spirit has given every Christian time, talent, and treasure that they are to steward well for the kingdom. The Christian's judgment is a day of assessment when "we must all appear before the judgment seat of Christ, so that each one may receive what is due for what he has done in the body, whether good or evil."[52] This theme of accountability and reward runs all through Scripture as a continual reminder not to waste our life but rather steward it in light of eternity.[53]

To illustrate this concept, Jesus tells a kingdom story in which he gives believers ten minas, a large amount of money, and commands them to do business with it.[54] This pictures the ministry resources believers have from God and their service for Jesus. The servant who brings ten more minas receives authority over ten cities in the kingdom, while the servant who brings five minas receives authority over five. The last servant, who hides his mina from fear of the master, typifies someone who does not have a grace relationship with Jesus. The point of Jesus' story is that if we are truly Christians and know the love of our Master, we should faithfully invest our lives in the service of his kingdom. The quality of work we do will be revealed and tested in the end, and only work that survives Jesus' evaluation will be worthy of a reward. Positively, our day of testing can be a day of great rejoicing when we hear Jesus declare, "Well done," if we are faithful stewards in this life.

Negatively, some Christians will be grieved by the lack of reward given to them for the life they lived. In 1 Corinthians 3:15 Paul says, "If anyone's work is burned up, he will suffer loss, though he himself will be saved, but only as through fire." The Bible is clear that there are eternal consequences for believers doing both good and evil.[55] The idea of different levels of rewards upsets many. They feel offended that Jesus doesn't give everyone a gold star,

---

[52]2 Cor. 5:10.
[53]Matt. 24:45–47; 25:14–30; Luke 12:42–48; 16:1–13; 17:7–10; 19:12–27; Rom. 2:16; 14:10; 1 Cor. 3:8–15; 4:5; 9:17–27; Col. 3:23–25; 1 Tim. 2:3–6; 2 Tim. 4:8; 1 Pet. 1:7; 5:4; Rev. 4:4, 10; 22:12.
[54]Luke 19:12–27.
[55]2 Cor. 5:10.

as if everyone should automatically get an "A" on their report card, but to do so would be unjust and would encourage Christians to waste their lives.

This doctrine is not salvation by works or some sort of legalism. Those who love Jesus will strive to be like him. Because we are God's workmanship, created for good works, we should do them.[56] We should "make every effort" to be faithful to our calling, as the Bible often exhorts.[57]

We are children of God with the full right of inheritance. Participation in the kingdom is already ours, not because of the good we have done, but because of God's gracious inclusion of us in his kingdom. However, having been so lavishly graced, we should respond by being trustworthy. Part of the reason God sanctifies us throughout life after we are born again is to help prepare us for the kingdom we are to live in forever. Bit by bit, we learn and grow in faithfulness with the small kingdom works he has entrusted to us. We know that God is a Father whose love for and devotion to his children is purely by grace and will never change. Still, as a good Father he also gives chores and responsibilities to each of his children to help them mature and grow so that he can entrust to them increasingly important things; he rewards the children who are faithful in ways that he does not reward the children who are unfaithful.

What do these rewards look like and what do they involve? Because the biblical descriptions of rewards (e.g., money, crowns) are likely figurative, it is hard to be sure what is meant. Most importantly, rewards are greater opportunity and responsibility in the kingdom.[58] We will be able to fulfill our original purpose to rule God's creation in partnership with him.[59] Paul hints that a reward will be seeing the full impact we have had on other people. Perhaps our deepened relations with them will be a reward.[60] For all believers, a rich reward will be our capacity to know and experience God himself, to see Jesus face-to-face.[61] Whatever the reward, the important idea is that life matters and God is watching.

---

[56]Eph. 2:10.
[57]Luke 13:24; Rom. 14:19; Eph. 4:3; Heb. 4:11; 12:14; 2 Pet. 1:5–10; 3:14.
[58]Luke 16:10–12; 19:17–19.
[59]Gen. 1:26–28.
[60]2 Cor. 1:14; 1 Thess. 2:19–20.
[61]1 Cor. 13:12; 1 John 3:2.

WHAT JUDGMENT AWAITS NON-CHRISTIANS AT THE END OF THIS LIFE?

God's rescue mission to sinful creation is to transform the entire cosmos into a glorious community where all beings fulfill God's Edenic purpose and enjoy relationship with him, worship him, and serve him in ways completely consistent with who he is.[62] In the kingdom, the twin sins of idolatry and injustice will be transformed into obedience of Jesus' twin commands to love God and neighbor.[63]

Judgment is God assessing the response to his call to reconciliation to himself through Jesus Christ. The issue is simple: have people accepted or rejected his invitation, his command to join him? The new creation can be new only if everyone in it loves God and obeys him. There can be no sin or sinners. They must be separated out.

A day is coming when God will judge the living and the dead[64] through the Son.[65] When the Son of Man comes to sit on his throne, all will stand before him for judgment.[66] From the beginning of creation[67] to the end,[68] the Bible makes it clear that the basis of God's judgment is our deeds.[69]

Jesus made this very clear, saying in John 3:36, "Whoever believes in the Son has eternal life; whoever does not obey the Son shall not see life, but the wrath of God remains on him." Jesus' death propitiated God's wrath against sin.[70] Those who refuse this gift have the double penalty of wrath for their sins and for rejecting God's Son. Jesus himself taught this in John 3:18, saying, "Whoever believes in him is not condemned, but whoever does not believe is condemned already, because he has not believed in the name of the only Son of God." Unlike Jesus' words to the sheep, to the

---

[62]Gen. 1:26–28. The Westminster Catechism summarizes this in its answer to question 1: "Man's chief and highest end is to glorify God, and to enjoy him forever."

[63]Deut. 6:5; 10:12; 30:6; Lev. 19:18; Matt. 22:37–40; Mark 12:30–31; Luke 10:27; Rom. 13:9–10; 15:2; Gal. 5:14; 6:10; James 2:8.

[64]Acts 10:42; 2 Tim. 4:1; 1 Pet. 4:5.

[65]Ps. 2:12; Mark 14:62; John 5:22; Acts 17:31.

[66]Matt. 25:31–46; Rev. 20:11–15.

[67]Gen. 2:15–17.

[68]Rev. 20:12–13.

[69]Jer. 17:10; 32:19; Matt. 16:27; Rom. 2:6; Gal. 6:7–8; Rev. 2:23; 22:12.

[70]Rom. 3:25; Heb. 2:17; 1 John 2:2; 4:10.

goats on his left he will say, "Depart from me, you cursed, into the eternal fire prepared for the devil and his angels."[71]

However, this does not mean that the relatively nice sinner suffers equally with Satan or his most committed human servants. There are degrees of punishment in hell like there are degrees of reward in heaven. Jesus told the people of Capernaum that it would be worse for them in the judgment than for Sodom.[72] The one who sins knowingly and willfully will receive a more severe beating than the one who did not know.[73] Both in life and in hell some sins receive more severe punishment, because that is just.[74] This fits the scriptural teaching that some sins are qualitatively worse than others in that the depth of their evil and the damage that ensues is greater. Jesus illustrated this when he told Pilate, "He who delivered me over to you has the greater sin."[75]

WHAT DOES SCRIPTURE TEACH ABOUT HEAVEN?

Heaven is *not* where believers spend eternity. Contrary to the popular misconception, we do not spend eternity off in space somewhere separated from our body and the rest of God's physical creation.

When Christians die, their spirit goes to heaven to be with Jesus.[76] Thankfully, we will always be with him.[77] Subsequently, when he returns to earth, we will come with him.

God creates the heavens in Genesis 1:1 and the new heavens in Revelation 21:1.[78] These heavens are the place where the sun, the moon, and the stars are;[79] they are also the place where the birds fly.[80] These created heavens are not the dwelling place of God.

There is another heaven that is the divine throne room;[81] this is the

---

[71]Matt. 25:41.
[72]Matt. 11:21–24.
[73]Luke 12:47–48.
[74]Num. 15:22–30; Lev. 4:1–35; 5:15–19; Matt. 18:6; 1 Tim. 5:8; James 3:1; 1 John 5:16–18.
[75]John 19:11.
[76]Luke 23:43; Acts 7:59; 2 Cor. 5:8; Phil. 1:23; Rev. 6:9–11.
[77]John 14:3; 17:24; 1 Thess. 4:14, 17.
[78]Isa. 65:17–25; 66:22; Rom. 8:19–22; 2 Pet. 3:10–13.
[79]Gen. 1:14–16; 26:4; Pss. 33:6; 19:1.
[80]Gen. 1:20–22.
[81]Pss. 2:4; 11:4; 103:19; 110:1–2; Dan. 7:9.

place where Jesus currently dwells at the right hand of God[82] with God and the angels.[83] This is also called the third heaven.[84] To show the multiple meanings of the word *heaven*, it is helpful to remember that Jesus will come *from* heaven[85] and will appear *in* heaven when he returns.[86]

Most people use the word *heaven* to refer to a condition or place of great happiness, delight, or pleasure where people go when they die. For this reason, heaven is described in funeral eulogies as the place where the dearly departed will enjoy to a fuller extent the same pleasures they knew during their earthly life. It is described as the place where the golfer never slices a drive and the fisherman never misses a cast.

According to the Bible, our eternal home will be on the new earth, a time-space place, where we will live forever. The heavenly city of Jerusalem will come down out of heaven and God will dwell with his people. We will always live as human persons, with our spirits combined with resurrected physical bodies perfectly suited for this perfect place. This is the Edenic project come to completion.

There are lots of questions about heaven that the Bible doesn't answer: Will we know each other? What age will we appear to be? Will there be gender in heaven? Will there be animals? Will we know of loved ones in hell? We can imagine what heaven will be like, but we must not presume too much. And don't listen to someone who claims to have been there. Stephen and Paul saw the throne room of God and could say nothing more than what the Bible says.[87] More to the point, they did not see our eternal dwelling place on the new earth.

Heaven is all about getting to be with Jesus and all the people who love him and, like us, want to be like him. It is totally light, full of brightness and color, and completely real. We want to be there because Jesus is there. We get to dwell in the personal presence of the One who is infinitely greater than we will ever be. To anyone but a lover of Jesus,

---

[82]Acts 2:34; 3:21; 7:56; Heb. 8:1; 9:24; 1 Pet. 3:22.
[83]Revelation 4–5.
[84]2 Cor. 12:2.
[85]1 Thess. 1:10; 4:16; 2 Thess. 1:7.
[86]Matt. 24:29–31; 26:64; Acts 1:11.
[87]Acts 7:55–56; 2 Cor. 12:1–4.

this existence would be hell itself! For those who love him, there could be no greater pleasure.[88]

WHAT DOES SCRIPTURE TEACH ABOUT HELL?

Jesus talks about hell more than does anyone else in all of Scripture. Jesus' words come in the context of the rest of Scripture, which says that God "desires all people to be saved and to come to the knowledge of the truth."[89] Furthermore, he "is patient toward you, not wishing that any should perish, but that all should reach repentance."[90]

Despite God's love for and patience with sinners, it is a horrid mistake to dismiss the Bible's clear teachings on hell. Richard Niebuhr characterized the ongoing attempt of liberal Christians to deny hell as "a God without wrath brought men without sin into a kingdom without judgment through the ministrations of a Christ without a cross."[91] Jesus said more about hell than about any other topic. Amazingly, 13 percent of his sayings are about hell and judgment; more than half of his parables relate to the eternal judgment of sinners.[92]

The Bible does not give us a detailed exposition of hell, but there are many descriptions of the fate of its inhabitants in that place of eternal punishment. They include (1) fire;[93] (2) darkness;[94] (3) punishment;[95] (4) exclusion from God's presence;[96] (5) restlessness;[97] (6) second death;[98] and (7) weeping and gnashing of teeth.[99]

Admittedly, there is a long discussion among Christians regarding how literally to take these descriptions. Evangelicals usually follow John

---

[88]The best book available on this topic is Randy Alcorn, *Heaven* (Carol Stream, IL: Tyndale, 2004).
[89]1 Tim. 2:4.
[90]2 Pet. 3:9.
[91]H. Richard Niebuhr, *The Kingdom of God in America* (New York: Harper & Row, 1937), 193. For a contemporary attempt to explain away hell, see Brian D. McLaren, *The Last Word and the Word after That* (San Francisco: Jossey-Bass, 2008).
[92]John Blanchard, *Whatever Happened to Hell?* (Durham, England: Evangelical Press, 1993), 128.
[93]Matt. 13:42, 50; 18:8, 9; Rev. 19:20; 20:14–15.
[94]Matt. 25:30; Jude 13.
[95]Rev. 14:10–11.
[96]Matt. 7:23; 25:41; Luke 16:19ff.; 2 Thess. 1:9.
[97]Rev. 14:11.
[98]Rev. 2:11; 20:6, 14; 21:8.
[99]Matt. 13:42, 50; 22:12–13; 24:51; 25:30; Luke 13:28.

Calvin in seeing them as metaphorical figures trying to describe the inde-scribable.[100] These evangelicals don't decrease the severity but only the specificity of the descriptions.

The Bible's portrait of hell is nothing like the mocking cartoon cari-catures drawn by Matt Groening or Gary Larson. Likewise, hell is not a fun place where sinners get to live out their sinful pleasures, as if Satan rules over hell and sin can be pursued without inhibition. This erroneous view of Satan ruling in hell comes not from Scripture but from Puritan John Milton's *Paradise Lost*, which has the Devil arrogantly declaring, "Better to reign in Hell, then serve in Heav'n."[101] But Satan will *not* reign there. Hell is a place of punishment that God prepared for the Devil and his angels.[102] It is where the beast and the false prophet and those who worship them

> will drink the wine of God's wrath, poured full strength into the cup of his anger, and he will be tormented with fire and sulfur in the presence of the holy angels and in the presence of the Lamb. And the smoke of their torment goes up forever and ever, and they have no rest, day or night.[103]

At the end of the age, the Devil will be "thrown into the lake of fire and sulfur where the beast and the false prophet were, and they will be tor-mented day and night forever and ever."[104] Hell will be ruled by Jesus, and human and demon alike, including Satan, will be tormented there continually.

Hell is real and terrible. It is eternal. There is no possibility of amnesty or reprieve. Daniel says that some of the dead will be resurrected "to shame and everlasting contempt."[105] Jesus says, "Depart from me, you cursed,

---

[100]See John Calvin, *Institutes of the Christian Religion*, 2 vols., ed. John T. McNeill, trans. Ford Lewis Battles (Philadelphia: Westminster, 1960), 2:1007; (3.25.12). Others who agree that the figures are meta-phorical include Billy Graham, Leon Morris, J. I. Packer, Millard Erickson, and D. A. Carson, according to William Crockett, *Four Views on Hell* (Grand Rapids, MI: Zondervan, 1997), 44–45n6.
[101]John Milton, *Paradise Lost*, bk. 1, ln. 263.
[102]Matt. 25:41.
[103]Rev. 14:10–11.
[104]Rev. 20:10.
[105]Dan. 12:2.

into the eternal fire prepared for the devil and his angels. . . . And these will go away into eternal punishment."[106] Paul tells us:

> God considers it just to repay with affliction those who afflict you, and to grant relief to you who are afflicted as well as to us, when the Lord Jesus is revealed from heaven with his mighty angels in flaming fire, inflicting vengeance on those who do not know God and on those who do not obey the gospel of our Lord Jesus. They will suffer the punishment of eternal destruction, away from the presence of the Lord and from the glory of his might.[107]

Perhaps the clearest and most gripping depiction of hell in all of Scripture is the frequent mention of hell as "Gehenna." The name refers to an area outside of the city of Jerusalem where idolatry and horrendous sin, including child sacrifice, were practiced.[108] Gehenna was a place so despised and cursed by God's people that they turned it into the city dump where feces, refuse, and the dead bodies of criminals were stacked. Jesus spoke of Gehenna as the hellish final home of the wicked.[109] Since Gehenna is described as a fiery abyss,[110] clearly it is also the lake of fire[111] to which all the godless will ultimately be eternally sentenced,[112] together with Satan, demons, and unrepentant sinners.[113] So when the Bible speaks of hell as a place where the fire is not quenched and the worm does not die, the original hearers would easily have remembered Gehenna, where this reality was ever present outside of their city.[114]

Our attitude toward hell should be the same as the Father's, who takes no pleasure in the death of the wicked but begs them to turn from their evil ways.[115] Jesus joins the Father's compassionate yearning as he weeps over

---

[106]Matt. 25:41, 46.
[107]2 Thess. 1:6–9.
[108]2 Kings 16:3; 21:6; 2 Chron. 28:3; 33:6; Jer. 19:56; 32:35.
[109]Matt. 5:22; 10:28; 18:9.
[110]Mark 9:43.
[111]Matt. 13:42, 50.
[112]Matt. 23:15, 33.
[113]Matt. 25:41; Rev. 19:20; 20:10, 14, 15.
[114]Isa. 66:24; Mark 9:47–48.
[115]Ezek. 18:23; 33:11; 1 Tim. 2:4; 2 Pet. 3:9.

Jerusalem.[116] Paul also has "great sorrow and unceasing anguish in my heart. For I could wish that I myself were accursed and cut off from Christ for the sake of my brothers, my kinsmen according to the flesh."[117] Furthermore, he "did not cease night or day to admonish everyone with tears."[118]

Feeling as he ought about hell, Charles Spurgeon rightly began his sermon on the eternal conscious torment of the wicked in hell this way: "Beloved, these are such weighty things that while I dwell upon them I feel far more inclined to sit down and weep than to stand up and speak to you."[119]

WHAT ARE SOME OF THE MAJOR OBJECTIONS TO THE DOCTRINE OF HELL?

A loving God would not send billions of people to a horrible hell. In a very important sense God doesn't send anyone to hell. The only ones there are those who have rejected his revelation, choosing to suppress the truth he made plain to them.[120] God made people in his image, after his likeness, with the power to say no and to reject the universal revelation of himself. Subsequently, sinners have no one to blame but themselves if they are damned.

To get to hell someone must reject the God who shows them his goodness[121] and out of love for all "gives to all mankind life and breath and everything";[122] reject the Spirit who "convicts the world concerning sin and righteousness and judgment";[123] and reject the crucified Son who said, "I, when I am lifted up from the earth, will draw all people to myself."[124] Obviously, God has been exceedingly gracious to sinners.

The Lausanne Covenant (1974),[125] an evangelical manifesto that is one of the most influential documents in Christendom, puts it this way:

[116]Jer. 31:20; Hos. 11:8; Matt. 23:37–38; Luke 19:41–44.
[117]Rom. 9:2–3.
[118]Acts 20:31; cf. Acts 20:19–20; Phil. 3:18.
[119]Charles Haddon Spurgeon, "The Final Separation," sermon no. 1234, preached in 1875, *The Charles H. Spurgeon Library Version 1* (AGES Digital Library, CD-ROM), 353.
[120]Rom. 1:21, 24–25.
[121]Acts 14:17.
[122]Acts 17:25.
[123]John 16:8.
[124]John 12:32.
[125]In July 1974, 2,700 evangelical leaders from 150 countries convened the Lausanne Congress, made

All men and women are perishing because of sin, but God loves every-one, not wishing that any should perish but that all should repent. Yet those who reject Christ repudiate the joy of salvation and condemn them-selves to eternal separation from God. To proclaim Jesus as "the Saviour of the world" is not to affirm that all people are either automatically or ultimately saved, still less to affirm that all religions offer salvation in Christ. Rather it is to proclaim God's love for a world of sinners and to invite everyone to respond to him as Saviour and Lord in the whole-hearted personal commitment of repentance and faith. Jesus Christ has been exalted above every other name; we long for the day when every knee shall bow to him and every tongue shall confess him Lord.[126]

People who reject Jesus in this life will not rejoice in him after this life. Revelation tells us that all sinners flee from the vision of Jesus pre-cisely because they do not desire him.[127] Unrepentant sinners hide from him, even preferring death to seeing the face of Jesus.[128] Even when faced with the unmistakable reality of Jesus, they "did not repent of the works of their hands nor give up worshiping demons and idols of gold and silver and bronze and stone and wood, which cannot see or hear or walk, nor did they repent of their murders or their sorceries or their sexual immorality or their thefts."[129]

Hell is only for those who persistently reject the real God in favor of false gods. So in the end, people get to be with the god they love. To para-phrase C. S. Lewis, either people will say to God, "Thy will be done," or God will say to them, "Thy will be done."[130] Not only is God loving, but he is also just. Heaven and hell are the result of his love and justice.

A loving God would be more tolerant. People who judge God need

up of an unprecedented diversity of nationalities, ethnicities, ages, occupations, and denominational affiliations. *Time* magazine described it as "possibly the widest-ranging meeting of Christians ever held" ("A Challenge from Evangelicals," *Time*, August 5, 1974, http://www.time.com/time/magazine/article/0,9171,879423,00.html). They composed the Lausanne Covenant. In faithfulness to Jesus, it was a direct challenge to the widely held philosophy that Christians do not have the right—let alone the duty—to disturb the honest faith of a Buddhist, a Hindu, or a Jew by evangelizing them.
[126]The Lausanne Movement, "The Uniqueness and Universality of Christ" (par. 3) in *The Lausanne Covenant*, http://www.lausanne.org/covenant/.
[127]Rev. 20:11.
[128]Rev. 6:15–17.
[129]Rev. 9:20–21.
[130]C. S. Lewis, *The Great Divorce* (New York: HarperCollins, 2001), 75.

to really consider if they would be more pleased if God were tolerant of everyone, including rapists, pimps, pedophiles, and even those who have sinned against them most heinously. The idea is completely absurd and unjust. Not everyone in hell is a rapist, of course, but everyone there chose sin over God throughout his or her entire life.[131]

God is not tolerant of people who don't like the way of Jesus. He is completely committed to a new earth where no one will have to be on guard against idolatry and injustice. The new earth will include a redeemed community that reflects the character of God, who is "merciful and gracious, slow to anger, and abounding in steadfast love and faithfulness, keeping steadfast love for thousands, forgiving iniquity and transgression and sin, but who will by no means clear the guilty."[132] So it will be a place where community will be characterized by "compassionate hearts, kindness, humility, meekness, and patience . . . [and] love, which binds everything together in perfect harmony."[133]

A loving God protects his children from sin and evil by separating them. In this way, God is a father who is tolerant of all who obey him and are safe for his children. But he is intolerant of those who sin against him and do evil to his children. Subsequently, God is intolerant in a way that is like our own cultural intolerances of those who drink and drive, steal, rape, and murder; we, too, demonstrate our intolerance by separating such people from society. To call such actions on God's part intolerant is shameful, because tolerance would denote both approval and support of evil.[134]

Hell is mean. In one sense, that is exactly right. Hell is for people who don't like the love of God. So it is a place for people who are mean. To understand what love is, look at what Jesus did at the cross.[135] He suffered and died for the ungodly, for sinners, for his enemies.[136] Or, to say it another way, Jesus suffered and died for mean people. A God who will

---

[131]Rom. 1:18–31; 2:4–11.
[132]Ex. 34:6–7.
[133]Col. 3:12–14.
[134]C. S. Lewis wrote a brilliant essay refuting the liberal approach to dealing with sin and crime, entitled "The Humanitarian Theory of Punishment," that can be found on the Internet or in *God in the Dock: Essays on Theology and Ethics* (Grand Rapids, MI: Eerdmans, 1970), 287–300.
[135]John 3:16.
[136]Rom. 5:6–11.

suffer and die for mean people is not mean. In fact, such a God alone is altogether loving; to be condemned by a God of perfect love shows how damnable our sin truly is.

Eternal torment in hell is an unjust punishment for people who sin for a few decades. Some argue that the punishment of sinners is annihilation. This means that after someone dies apart from faith, they suffer for a fitting period of time and then simply cease to exist so that hell is not eternal in duration. In question is the nature and length of the punishment.

Despite having proponents who are otherwise fine Bible teachers (such as John Stott),[137] annihilationism is simply not what the Bible teaches. Daniel 12:2 says, "Many of those who sleep in the dust of the earth shall awake, some to everlasting life, and some to shame and everlasting contempt." Jesus teaches the same thing and speaks of those who "will go away into eternal punishment, but the righteous into eternal life."[138] Grammatically, there is no difference here between the length of time mentioned for life and that for punishment; rather, there is simply eternal life and eternal death.

The Bible tells us that "the smoke of their torment goes up forever and ever, and they have no rest, day or night, these worshipers of the beast and its image"[139] and "they will be tormented day and night forever and ever."[140] The word *forever* (Greek *aion*) means unending. This word is used to describe the blessedness of God,[141] Jesus after his resurrection,[142] the presence of God,[143] and God himself.[144] As uncomfortable as some may be with it, it also describes eternal, conscious punishment.

The key arguments for annihilationism are (1) the nature of fire (which consumes), (2) the use of the word *destroy*, which means "the extinction of being," (3) the concept of justice, whereby God punishes "according to

---

[137]Evangelical proponents of annihilationism include John Stott, John Wenham, Clark Pinnock, and Edward Fudge. J. I. Packer's excellent article addressing this topic, "Evangelical Annihilationism in Review," *Reformation & Revival*, vol. 6 (Spring 1997), is available at http://www.the-highway.com/annihilationism_Packer.html.
[138]Matt. 25:46.
[139]Rev. 14:11.
[140]Rev. 20:10.
[141]Rom. 1:25.
[142]Rev. 1:18.
[143]1 Pet. 1:25.
[144]Rev. 4:9; 20:10.

what they had done,"[145] and (4) the passages that speak of God triumphing over evil, so that God is all in all and reconciles all things to himself.[146] We'll address each point in turn.

First, fire does consume but only things that are inherently destructible. For example, if you put metal in a fire it burns forever, but it does not cease to exist.[147] Humans, like angels, are created for unending existence; hence their contempt and punishment is forever and ever. Thus, the result of the unpardonable sin is eternal punishment.[148] Hebrews 6:2 establishes eternal judgment as a fundamental doctrine.

Second, the English words *destroy* and *destruction* do seem to indicate the end of existence. If so, passages such as Matthew 10:28 and Philippians 3:19 that describe the destiny of the wicked with these words would mean that these people would cease to exist. However, the Greek words (noun *olethros*; verb *apollumi*) never mean the end of existence. In the three parables in Luke 15, the coin, the sheep, and the son are "lost." Likewise, destroyed wineskins do not cease to exist but become useless.[149] Jesus says, "For whoever would save his life will lose it, but whoever loses his life for my sake will save it."[150] The lost life continues. The people upon whom "sudden destruction will come" at the end of the age still appear before the judgment seat.[151] The temptations of riches that "plunge people into ruin and destruction" ruin them but do not end their existence.[152] Paul explains the meaning of "the punishment of eternal destruction" as being "away from the presence of the Lord."[153] This rules out the idea that *destruction* means "extinction." Only those who exist can be excluded from God's presence.

The point of the destruction of the wicked is that they are wrecked, ruined, and useless. Thus, destruction is a sudden loss of all that gives worth and meaning to existence. Those who are destroyed are like the

---

[145]Rev. 20:12.
[146]E.g., 1 Cor. 15:28; Col. 1:20.
[147]Zech. 13:9; Mal. 3:3; Rev. 3:18.
[148]Mark 3:29.
[149]Matt. 9:17.
[150]Luke 9:24.
[151]1 Thess. 5:3.
[152]1 Tim. 6:9.
[153]2 Thess. 1:9.

prodigal son: far from home and father. They continue to exist but are broken in spirit, miserable, and without hope in that state.

This is why the Bible speaks of hell as conscious, eternal punishment. One summary of the Bible's teaching on the pain of hell says:

> Those in hell suffer intense and excruciating pain. This pain is likely both emotional/spiritual and physical (John 5:28–29). Hell is a fate worse than being drowned in the sea (Mark 9:42). It is worse than any earthly suffering—even being maimed (Matt. 5:29–30; Mark 9:43). The suffering never ends (Matt. 25:41; Mark 9:48). The wicked will be "burned with unquenchable fire" (Matt. 3:12). Those in hell will be thrown into the fiery furnace and will experience unimaginable sorrow, regret, remorse, and pain. The fire produces the pain described as "weeping and gnashing of teeth" (Matt. 8:12; 13:42, 50; 22:13; 24:51; 25:30). The intensity of the suffering seems to be according to the wickedness of the person's behavior (Rom. 2:5–8). Hell is utterly fearful and dreadful (Heb. 10:27–31). This punishment is depicted as "coming misery," "eating flesh with fire," and the "day of slaughter" (James 5:1–5).
>
> Those in hell will feel the full force of God's fury and wrath (Rev. 14:10). They will be "tormented" with fire (14:10–11). This suffering is best understood as endless since the "smoke of their torment rises forever and ever" (14:11). This suffering is constant because it is said that those in hell "will have no rest day or night" (14:11) and "will be tormented day and night forever and ever" (20:10).[154]

Third, we have already supported the points that humans are created to live forever, and their rebellion and rejection of God continues as long as they themselves do. Thus, continued exclusion from God's fellowship is fully appropriate and just.

Fourth, there are passages teaching that Christ will "reconcile to himself all things, whether on earth or in heaven, making peace by the blood of his cross."[155] If this were the only passage in Scripture speaking to the

---

[154]Christopher W. Morgan, "Biblical Theology: Three Pictures of Hell" in *Hell Under Fire*, ed. Christopher W. Morgan and Robert A. Peterson (Grand Rapids, MI: Zondervan, 2004), 144.
[155]Col. 1:20.

issue, we would have to believe in some sort of universal saving reconciliation with God. But the eternal punishment passages require us to adopt the understanding that the peace spoken of is not a peace of salvation for all sinners but, rather, peace that comes by God triumphing over all sinners. The enemies will be conquered and their destructive agenda destroyed. The new earth will be a place of only peace and godliness because the enemies have been crushed and removed forever.

In summary, annihilationism is not biblical. For this reason, it was condemned by the Second Council of Constantinople (AD 553) and the Fifth Lateran Council (1513).

Today, though, it is becoming popular to hope that sinners will eventually repent and everyone will end up in heaven. This is universal reconciliation, the ancient view of Origen. However, there is not a shred of evidence for post-mortem repentance. The continual teaching of the Bible is that we die once and are then judged, without any second chance at salvation. As one clear example, Hebrews 9:27 says, "It is appointed for man to die once, and after that comes judgment."

At the end of the discussion we must admit the total irrationality of those who resist and refuse the grace of Jesus Christ. Any attempt to make sense of their rebellion will have to remain a mystery. But we never stop trying to persuade them to receive forgiveness and new life through the crucified and resurrected Lord Jesus because, among other reasons, the conscious eternal torments of hell await the unrepentant.

DO PEOPLE WHO HAVE NEVER HEARD ABOUT JESUS GO TO HELL?

Jesus said, "No one comes to the Father except through me."[156] Peter preached, "There is salvation in no one else, for there is no other name under heaven given among men by which we must be saved."[157] The conclusion is simple: there is only one way to the Father and that is through Jesus Christ. All other religious roads lead to false gods and a real hell.

But there are many ways to Jesus. While the norm is responding to

---

[156]John 14:6.
[157]Acts 4:12.

the preached Word of God,[158] there are biblical examples as well as life experiences where God gives special revelation of the Messiah to unsaved people in other forms, including direct speech, dreams, and visions. God called Abraham directly.[159] He gave Pharaoh dreams.[160] He spoke to the treacherous prophet Balaam in a vision so that he prophesied about the Messiah.[161] He appeared to Cornelius in a vision,[162] which resulted in his being saved.

I (Gerry) once talked with a Chinese man who was a brilliant university student and a rising member of the Communist party. One night as he slept, a shining person appeared in a vision, saying in Chinese, "I am who you are looking for. My name is 'Gospel,'" with the last word in English. The young man had never heard the word *gospel* before but soon found it in his dictionary. He is now a Christian pastor with a very effective ministry.

There are many such stories. The reality is that anyone who is searching and willing to respond to the goodness of God as Cornelius did will receive special revelation. God is perfectly able to bypass the "normal" channels to accomplish his purposes.

No one who comes to the Lord will be cast out.[163] As Paul says:

> The Scripture says, "Everyone who believes in him will not be put to shame." For there is no distinction between Jew and Greek; for the same Lord is Lord of all, bestowing his riches on all who call on him. For "everyone who calls on the name of the Lord will be saved."[164]

Therefore, while there is no salvation apart from faith in Jesus Christ, there is also no reason to overlook the creativity of God to get the gospel out. His creativity includes using us to preach the gospel to the ends of the earth as pioneering missionaries to unreached people groups and generous givers to ministries that translate the Bible into new languages.

---

[158]Rom. 10:13–15.
[159]Gen. 12:1–3.
[160]Genesis 40–41.
[161]Num. 24:4, 16–19.
[162]Acts 10:3–6.
[163]John 6:37.
[164]Rom. 10:11–13.

DO UNBORN BABIES AND YOUNG CHILDREN GO TO HEAVEN?

This is one of the questions the Bible does not answer for us. The best biblical response is this: "Shall not the Judge of all the earth do what is just?"[165] We can trust the God who died so that his enemies could be saved to do what is right in the case of infants who die.

Some appeal to David's statement after his son died: "I shall go to him, but he will not return to me."[166] The argument is that David knew he was going to heaven, so the baby must be there. However, the point of David's statement is that the baby is in the grave. David will visit the grave, but the baby will not come back to life no matter how much he agonizes in fasting and prayer.

Many agree with Millard Erickson that the universal atonement pays the penalty for all Adamic guilt and condemnation, so babies who do not commit personal sin will be in heaven by application of the atonement.[167] Others argue that death in infancy is a sign of special election. Some believe that children spend eternity with their parents. But none of these theories have clear biblical warrant.

Grace and I (Mark) enjoy five children. We would have enjoyed six but, like many couples, we suffered a miscarriage. Because we love children, it was very difficult for us, and I often tear up when I talk about that loss. Our children and friends have asked me what I think happened to the baby and whether or not I believe the baby is in heaven. My simple answer is that I do not have a clear biblical answer as much as I have God who is a loving and gracious Father whom I trust. The fact that John the Baptizer was known and named by God in the womb and filled with the Holy Spirit before his birth gives me much comfort.[168]

AM I GOING TO HELL?

The closing verses of the Bible say, "Come!" as an invitation for all who desire to receive God's saving grace as a gift. The gospel says that Jesus

---

[165]Gen. 18:25.
[166]2 Sam. 12:23.
[167]Millard J. Erickson, *Christian Theology*, 2nd ed. (Grand Rapids, MI: Baker, 1998), 654–66.
[168]Luke 1:5–25, 39–45.

is Immanuel, God with us. Jesus died and rose and is exalted in heaven. If you repent of sin, change your mind about who or what is Lord of your life, and believe, trusting that you can stake your life and eternity on the truth of what God says, then you will receive full forgiveness of all sin, new life in and by the Holy Spirit, membership in the church of Jesus Christ, a meaningful part in his rescue mission in the world, and citizenship in his kingdom. You will be with Jesus and his people now and forever.

We want this for you, and we would be unloving if we finished this book without seeking to ensure that you are a Christian.

Have you confessed your sins to Jesus Christ, seeking forgiveness and salvation?

What changes need to happen in your life to enjoy Jesus more thoroughly, worship him more passionately, follow him more closely, serve him more diligently, trust him more fully, and proclaim him more boldly?

Small Group Resources

By Pastor Brad House, Community Groups Pastor, Mars Hill Church

The purpose of this book is not to simply inform you of the basic doctrines of the Christian faith. The goal behind it is to do more by challenging you to live out your faith in life and practice. Belief without action is no belief at all, as we see in James 2:14–26. The goal of this section is to guide you and your group through a discussion of what you have learned and how it should apply to your life. For each chapter you will find:

- *Introduction*: A reminder of the main idea in the chapter.
- *Discussion*: A general question meant to spark conversation during a group's pre-discussion dinner or mingling time.
- *Examination*: A list of questions to encourage your group to engage the biblical text related to the topic for group examination.
- *Application*: A list of questions designed to apply the doctrine examined to your personal life and experience.

This study format is not meant to be a rigid formula, but we hope that it provides a means for intentional study, discussion, and life application. Although it is designed for a group discussion, we hope it is also helpful for personal study.

CHAPTER 1: TRINITY: GOD IS

Introduction

We begin our study of essential doctrines of the Christian faith with the question, who is God? It is paramount that we distinguish and clarify whom we worship when our culture defines God in so many different ways.

Thankfully God has revealed himself to us through Scripture so that we may know him and glorify him.

Discussion

If asked, how would you distinguish God from the countless false gods promoted and worshiped in our world?

Examination

- How is the Trinitarian nature of God revealed in the Old and New Testaments?
- What are the three biblical truths that are brought together with the doctrine of the Trinity?
- Find three places in Scripture to support each of these truths.
- How is the statement in John 3:15 a reflection of the Trinity?
- What does the Trinitarian nature of God reveal about him?

Application

- How do you personally resonate with the human longings (e.g., community, relationship, humility, peace) rooted in the Trinitarian nature of God?
- Why is a right understanding of the Trinity essential to our faith?
- How does the doctrine of the Trinity affect your worship of God?
- Which of the doctrinal errors or false views of God are you most familiar with or wrestle with personally?
- How does your life reflect the Trinity?
- Which of the practical implications listed in this chapter is most significant to you and why?

CHAPTER 2: REVELATION: GOD SPEAKS

Introduction

God has revealed himself to us so that we might know him and worship him. Our understanding of his revelation and our view of Scripture will dramatically affect our understanding of all other doctrines.

Discussion

How does your view of the Bible affect all other doctrinal beliefs?

Examination

- What is the fundamental purpose of God's revelation through Scripture?
- What is the difference between general and special revelation?
- How does Jesus view the Bible?
- Who wrote the Bible, and why is it important to distinguish between the different views on inspiration?
- What is inerrancy, and why can we trust the Bible?

Application

- How do your views of Scripture align with what the Bible testifies about itself?
- What does it mean that the Bible is authoritative? How does it relate to other authorities?
- How is the Bible personally sufficient for your life?
- What have you learned in this chapter about interpreting Scripture?
- How is your view of Scripture evident in your life?

CHAPTER 3: CREATION: GOD MAKES

Introduction

The way we view our world begins with our understanding of our origins. How did we get here and why? This chapter examines these origins as revealed in Scripture. There is plenty of room for debate over some aspects of creation, but the fundamental truths of creation are essential for clear doctrine.

Discussion

How does understanding your origin affect your worldview?

Examination

- What are the debatable or open-handed views of creation?
- What are the essential or closed-handed views of creation?
- What does the creation indicate about the character of God?
- Which Christian view of creation best describes your understanding of creation? What are the biblical strengths and weaknesses of your view?
- What effect can a wrong view of creation have on your understanding of life and theology?

Application

- How does your understanding of creation affect your view of God?
- How does the purpose of creation affect your view of your life and world?
- Why is it important to have a clear understanding of open-handed issues related to creation?
- Which non-Christian views of creation have had the most effect on your understanding of creation? How has Scripture clarified those views?

CHAPTER 4: IMAGE: GOD LOVES

Introduction

Our purpose in life is rooted in the fact that we are created in the image of God. In this chapter we explore what it means to be created in God's image and how that should affect the way we view God and ourselves.

Discussion

What does it mean to be human?

Examination

- How does Genesis 1 distinguish humankind from the rest of creation?
- In your own words, what does it mean to be created in the image of God?
- In what way does the doctrine of image speak into modern-day gender issues?
- How has the idea of *imago Dei* changed the way you look at yourself and humankind in general?

• In what ways did Jesus image God in his humanity?

Application

- • What are the dominant worldviews regarding the nature of humanity in your culture?
- • How are they in opposition to the doctrine of *imago Dei* found in Scripture?
- • How does a nonbeliever image God? How does that change the way you view the unregenerate?
- • In what ways does your life image God well, and in what ways does your life reflect a false image of God? What does repentance look like in these areas?

CHAPTER 5: FALL: GOD JUDGES

Introduction

In order to understand the condition of our world, and ultimately the plan for redemptive history, we must know the origin and nature of sin. This chapter deals with both of these topics biblically.

Discussion

What evidence do you see in nature and culture that reveals truth behind the idea that something is broken?

Examination

- • What is sin?
- • How were Adam and Eve tempted to rebel against God? How were their sins the same and how were they different?
- • How have we been affected by original sin? How has this affected our relationship with God?
- • What is the difference between total depravity and utter (or absolute) depravity?
- • How does God view and respond to sin?

Application

- In what ways has your view of sin been challenged by this chapter?
- In what ways are you tempted as Adam and Eve were tempted?
- How does sin affect your ability to abide in Jesus?
- How do you respond to sin in your life? How do you respond to sin in others' lives?
- Where in your life is God calling you to specific repentance in regard to your view of sin and your response to it?

CHAPTER 6: COVENANT: GOD PURSUES

Introduction

In the last chapter we explored the origin of sin. Next, we turn our attention to God's plan for redeeming his creation and restoring it to its original glory.

Discussion

How do you respond to people who hurt, betray, and/or disregard you?

Examination

- What is a covenant?
- Why is it necessary for us that God covenanted with us?
- What are the five features of God's covenants with his people?
- As we look at the Old Testament covenants, how is Jesus foreshadowed in each?
- How is Jesus the fulfillment of each of these covenants?
- What is the new covenant and what makes it superior to the others?
- How would you use the doctrine of covenant to explain the gospel?

Application

- How is God's response to being sinned against different from your response?
- In what ways is a covenant different from a contract?
- What does the doctrine of covenant teach you about the character of God?

- What covenants have you made, and how are they reflected in the gospel?
- How does your life reflect the heart of God to covenant with his people and where do you need to grow?

CHAPTER 7: INCARNATION: GOD COMES

Introduction

The pinnacle of God's pursuit of worshipers is manifested in the incarnation. In Jesus, God enters into human history so that his perfect grace and justice can be satisfied in the only possible way.

Discussion

What do you find most amazing about the Creator of the universe entering into human history as a man?

Examination

- What does *incarnation* mean?
- Why is the incarnation necessary for the redemption of humanity?
- Why is the role of prophecy important to the incarnation, and what does it teach us about the character of God?
- What support do we find in Scripture that Jesus was fully God and fully human? Why are these two points significant?
- What do we learn about the character of God in Philippians 2:5–11?
- Why is the incarnation a pivotal doctrine of Christianity?

Application

- How does the incarnation affect your view of God?
- How is the incarnation a source of comfort for you personally?
- Do you relate more to the deity of Jesus or to the humanity of Jesus, and why? What are the pitfalls of overemphasizing one to the detriment of the other?
- How does your life reflect the incarnational image of God?

CHAPTER 8: CROSS: GOD DIES

Introduction

God's ultimate act of love culminates with his pouring out his wrath on himself so that those who believe may be saved. "For the word of the cross is folly to those who are perishing, but to us who are being saved it is the power of God" (1 Cor. 1:18).

Discussion

Whom would you be willing to die for?

Examination

- Why is it imperative for the redemption of mankind that Christ literally died?
- Explain the following terms in your own words with regard to redemption:
  - Atonement
  - Propitiation
  - Justification
  - Ransom
  - Expiation
- How is God's wrath poured out on Jesus an act of love?

Application

- What implications does *Christus Victor* have on the way you approach sin and freedoms in your life?
- In what practical ways do you look at the life of Jesus as an example for how to live yours?
- What have you personally learned about God in this chapter, and how does it change the way you worship him?
- How should you live your life differently in light of and in response to the atonement?

CHAPTER 9: RESURRECTION: GOD SAVES

Introduction

No doctrine is more critical to the Christian faith than the resurrection. Paul says in 1 Corinthians 15:17, "If Christ has not been raised, your faith is futile and you are still in your sins." It is clear from Paul that we cannot take this doctrine lightly. It defines our faith, and our salvation itself rests on its truth.

Discussion

Why would our faith be futile if Christ had not risen from the dead? (1 Cor. 15:17).

Examination

- What does it mean that Jesus was resurrected?
- Why is the resurrection central to the gospel?
- What is the most compelling evidence of the resurrection for you personally?
- Why do you think there are so many attempts to explain away the resurrection?
- What are the consequences of denying the resurrection? How would this affect other areas of theology?
- How does the resurrection speak to our eternal life in Christ?

Application

- Which views of death and the state of being after death have shaped your view of afterlife?
- Are there any areas of the resurrection that you have had trouble with?
- What does it mean to you that you are united into Christ in his death and resurrection? (Rom. 6:1–14).
- In what ways does the resurrection give you hope and change the way you live?

CHAPTER 10: CHURCH: GOD SENDS

Introduction

The church is not a building or a stoic institution; it is the living, breathing vessel through which God preaches the gospel and draws worshipers to himself. The correct understanding of the church should excite and motivate us to participate in the work of the gospel.

Discussion

What ideas contribute to a view of the church as being an institution rather than a people?

Examination

- What is the church and what is its purpose?
- Why is the leadership structure of the church important?
- What are sacraments, and what is their role in the church?
- What is church discipline? Why is it vital to a healthy church?
- Why is it important to become a covenanting member of a church?

Application

- What views of the church have you had that were challenged by this chapter?
- How do you see the church fulfilling its role to make disciples for God's glory? Where do you participate in that role?
- What is your role in the church? How are you being faithful to this role and how are you not?
- If you are not a member of a church, what is keeping you from becoming one?

CHAPTER 11: WORSHIP: GOD TRANSFORMS

Introduction

Our lives testify to the fact that we were created to worship. The question is what or whom we worship. Sin is the result of worshiping created things rather then the Creator, God. God built us to worship him, and when we do, we are most satisfied and filled with joy.

Discussion

Where do you see worship as a common practice inside and outside the church today?

Examination

- How is worship related to the doctrines of image and Trinity?
- In what ways does worship express our doctrinal beliefs?
- What is idolatry, and how is it related to worship?
- How do we break free from idolatry and begin to worship God in spirit and truth?
- How does understanding sin as a worship problem change your approach to addressing it?
- What should true worship do in and through our lives?

Application

- How has your understanding of worship been changed or enriched by this chapter?
- When do you find it natural to worship, and when is it a struggle?
- How has idolatry affected your life and the lives of those around you?
- What does worshiping Jesus look like for you as a lifestyle?
- How has worship led to transformation in your life?

For Additional Study

1) Who or what are your external idols?
   - Who or what is the lord that rules over your life, determining how you live?
   - Who or what is your judge? Whose approval are you living to earn?
   - Where do you give the firstfruits of your wealth?
   - Where do you give the firstfruits of your time?
   - What people and things take the majority of your life?

- What do you plan and pray for?

2) Who or what are your internal idols?

- What false beliefs do you hold about God?
- Which parts of Scripture do you deeply doubt or even disbelieve?
- Deep down in your heart, whom or what do you love, cherish, treasure, and long for the most?
- Deep down in your heart, whom or what do you despise and hate the most?
- Who or what makes you happiest? Why?
- Who or what makes you saddest? Why?

3) Who or what is the mediator between you and God?

- Whom or what, other than Jesus, do you use to get closer to God?
- Who or what, if taken from your life, would cause you to not walk as faithfully with God?
- How do you define yourself, especially when introducing yourself to others?

4) Where is your functional heaven?

- When daydreaming about escaping this life, what does your functional heaven look like, and how is it different from the real heaven?
- On earth, where do you run for your safety or comfort (e.g., the fridge, alcohol, the television, a person, a place, a hobby)?

5) Who or what is your functional savior?

- What is your picture of hell in this life (e.g., being single, not having children, being poor)?
- Who or what do you use to save you from what you fear (e.g., a relationship, children, money, shopping, sex)?

6) What good thing has become a god thing?

- Which idols are in your life that, when appreciated and/or stewarded correctly, are means of worship but instead have become objects of worship (e.g., work, family, health, friendship, pleasure, leisure, hobby)?
- If you could obtain or change one thing or person in your life, what would that be?
- Which idols are you selling to others?

To Read:

> Best, Harold M. *Unceasing Worship: Biblical Perspectives on Worship and the Arts.* Downers Grove, IL: InterVarsity Press, 2003.

> Lane, Timothy S., and Paul David Tripp. *How People Change.* Greensboro, NC: New Growth Press, 2006.

CHAPTER 12: STEWARDSHIP: GOD GIVES

Introduction

How we view and act regarding money and possessions tells a lot about our heart and theology. Scripture talks about money frequently because of its propensity to become an object of our worship. A proper understanding of money, however, allows us to use it to advance the gospel and bring glory to Jesus.

Discussion

How is God's view of money different from the view of money in our culture?

Examination

- What is stewardship, and how is it related to the character of God?
- How is stewardship a response of worship?
- How is the stewardship of our time, talent, and treasure related to the character and glory of God?
- What is the ultimate purpose of the spiritual gifts and treasure that God has given you?
- What is the difference between the Old Testament tithe and stewardship?

Application

- How does the way you view and use money reflect the condition of your heart?
- How has your view of money been challenged by this chapter?
- What does your stewardship reveal about who or what you worship?

• How are you using your time, talent, and treasure to glorify God?
• In what areas of time, talent, and treasure do you need to repent and grow?

CHAPTER 13: KINGDOM: GOD REIGNS

Introduction

God's redemptive plan for history will culminate in the return of Jesus and his kingdom. His return will be glory for those who believe and judgment for those who don't, displaying his perfect grace and justice to his glory.

Discussion

What do you think eternity will be like? What informs your picture of heaven?

Examination

• What is the kingdom of God?
• How will we participate in this kingdom?
• What is Jesus' role in the kingdom of God?
• How will Christians be judged at the end of their life? What awaits nonbelievers?
• Why is it important not to dismiss the doctrine of hell?

Application

• How has your view of death and the afterlife been challenged by this chapter?
• What have you learned about God's character through this study of his kingdom?
• What about eternity and the reign of Jesus are you most excited about?
• What informs the common objections to the doctrine of hell?
• What gives you confidence that you are going to heaven?
• How has God changed and challenged you through this study on doctrine?

GENERAL INDEX

Holy Spirit: as God, 15; and Jesus, 232–34, 314–15. *See also* inspiration
Homer, 283, 284, 285
Homo sapiens, 97
homoousios (Greek: of one substance), 25
Howe, Thomas, 59n108
Hoyle, Fred, 99
Hugo of St. Cher, 42
humanism, 162
"Humanitarian Theory of Punishment, The" (Lewis), 429n134
humility, 34, 59, 131, 166, 241
Huxley, Aldous, 235
hypostasis (Greek: person), 230

idolatry, 149, 151, 227, 341–47, 356–57, 358–59; how to avoid idolatry, 346–47; how idolatry hurts individuals and societies, 347–50; New Testament definition of, 133. *See also* idolatry, religious; one-ism
idolatry, religious, 357–58, 359; gift idolatry, 358; money idolatry, 374–75; morality idolatry, 358; Sabbath idolatry, 382–83; truth idolatry, 358
Idols for Destruction (Schlossberg), 349
Ignatius, 221
image of God (Latin: *imago Dei*), 134; common Christian errors regarding, 130–34; how we can best image God, 138–40; human beings' creation in the image and likeness of God, 114–17; and human dignity, 131; and humility, 131; Jesus as the image of God, 137–38; renewal of, 139; restoration through regeneration, 363; retention of after the fall, 156; what it means to be the image of God, 118–22; what a life that images God looks like, 140–42
incarnation, the, 41, 209–10, 218–20; the difference the incarnation makes in one's life, 240–42; false teachings about, 234–36; how God became man, 230–34; misconceptions regarding, 218–20; Old Testament prophecy regarding, 214–18; what *incarnation* means, 210–14; why the incarnation is of such great comfort, 240
Incarnation of God, The (Neusner), 217–18
inerrancy, 58–59
inspiration, 48; plenary inspiration, 48, 49; verbal inspiration, 48, 48–49
Integrative Spirituality. *See* one-ism
Invitation to Biblical Preaching (Sunukjian), 324n79
Irenaeus, 116
Isaac, comparison of to Jesus, 191–92
Islam, 295, 298, 300

James, William, 112
Jehovah's Witnesses, 30–31, 32, 221; New World Translation of Scripture, 72
Jesus: baptism of, 22–23; as the central message of Scripture, 43–47; as *Christus Exemplar,* 274–75; as *Christus Victor,* 270–72; comparison of to Isaac, 191–92; comparison of to Joseph, 167; comparison of to Moses, 196; conception of, 22; as David's final heir, 201–4; as "the firstborn of all creation," 20; as fully God, 221–28; as fully human, 228–34; as God, 14–15; and the Holy Spirit, 232–34, 314–15; how Jesus is like us (as our priest), 236–38; how Jesus is unlike us, 238–40; as the image of God, 137–38; as the King of the kingdom of God, 417–18; as the Logos, 212–14; the meaning of the name Jesus, 215; as Messiah, 415; as a missionary, 240–42, 314; as one person with two natures (hypostatic union), 26; relationship to the church, 314–18, 335; as Son of God, 224; as Son of Man, 224. *See also* crucifixion, the; incarnation, the; resurrection, the
Jesus Storybook Bible, The (S. Lloyd-Jones), 179
Jones, Peter, 342–43n10
Joseph (Old Testament), 167, 187, 193; comparison of to Jesus, 167
Josephus, 226, 247, 296–97
joy, 35
Judaism, 295
judgment, at the end of life, 410; of Christians, 418–20; of non-Christians, 421–22

justification, 198, 260–62, 317

Kaiser, Walter C., Jr., 197n69
Kamsler, Harold M., 179
kanon (Greek: a rule, a measuring rod), 51
kardia (Greek: heart), 127
Keller, Timothy, 35, 347, 348–49, 349–50, 357n45
Kierkegaard, Søren, 347, 348
kingdom of God, 411–17; as already/not yet, 411–12; erroneous views of, 411; Jesus as the King of, 417–18
Kinnaman, David, 306
Köstenberger, Andreas, 364
Kuyper, Abraham, 232–33

Lactantius, 116
Ladd, George Eldon, 213
Lane, William L., 55
Langman, Jan, 134n86
Langton, Stephen, 42
Language of God, The (Collins), 103n55
Latourette, Kenneth Scott, 292–93
latreia (Greek: worship, service), 310
Lausanne Covenant (1974), 427–28, 427–28n125
Law of Moses, 197–99; ceremonial laws, 198; civil laws, 198; moral laws, 198–99; and new-covenant Christians, 198–99. *See also* Ten Commandments
leb (Hebrew: heart), 126
Leibniz, Gottfried, 165
leitourgeo (Greek: to worship, to serve), 310
Lewis, C. S., 158, 301, 428, 429n134
Lewontin, Richard, 102
liberalism, 79
Living Church, The (Stott), 394n68
Lloyd-Jones, D. Martyn, 219–20, 232
Lloyd-Jones, Sally, 179
logos (Greek: word), 211–12
"lost gospels," 55–57
love, 34; the church's obedience to the Great Commandment to love, 311–12; God as, 16
Lubeck, Ray, 72n179
Lucian of Samasota, 293–94
Luther, Martin, 69, 76, 83, 83n18, 138–39, 262, 346

Machen, J. Gresham, 221
macro-evolution, 98–103; and spontaneous generation, 98
Manetho, 60
Manichaeism, 153
marriage, 123; and creation order (complementarianism), 123–24; and sin, 124–25
Marx, Karl, 114
Maslow, Abraham, 112–13
materialism, 162
McLaren, Brian D., 424n91
Messiah: Jesus as, 415; Old Testament expectations of, 414–15
Metzger, Bruce M., 286, 286–87n32
Michaels, J. Ramsey, 55
Milton, John, 425
mind, in the New Testament, 127
mission, 180, 317; what an incarnational missional life is like, 241–42
modernism, 79, 132
monism. *See* one-ism
monogenes (Greek: only begotten), 27
Moo, Douglas J., 197n69
Moore, Keith L., 134n86
Morgan, Christopher, 432
Mormonism, 31, 33, 73, 218–19, 219
Morris, Leon, 211, 425n100
mortification, 161
Moses, 193–97, 265; comparison of to Jesus, 196
Moule, C. F. D., 296
Müller, Fabiola, 134n86

Nagel, Thomas, 103
naturalism, 79, 80, 97, 408. *See also* macro-evolution
Nature of True Virtue, The (Edwards), 349

SCRIPTURE INDEX

 # RE:LIT

Resurgence Literature (Re:Lit) is a ministry of the
Resurgence. At www.theResurgence.com you
will find free theological resources in blog, audio,
video, and print forms, along with information
on forthcoming conferences, to help Christians
contend for and contextualize Jesus' gospel. At
www.ReLit.org you will also find the full lineup
of Resurgence books for sale. The elders of Mars
Hill Church have generously agreed to support
Resurgence and the Acts 29 Church Planting
Network in an effort to serve the entire church.

FOR MORE RESOURCES

Re:Lit – www.relit.org
Resurgence – www.theResurgence.com
Re:Sound – www.resound.org
Mars Hill Church – www.marshillchurch.org
Acts 29 – www.acts29network.org